OLD LOUISIANA PLANTATION HOMES AND FAMILY TREES

By
Herman de Bachelle Seebold, M.D.

In Two Volumes
Volume One

PELICAN PUBLISHING COMPANY
Gretna 1971

PELICAN PUBLISHING COMPANY
630 Burmaster Street
Gretna, Louisiana 70053

Affectionately Dedicated

To

MY WIFE

who has greatly aided me in the collecting of

the material for this work.

ACKOWLEDGMENT

THE author takes this opportunity of thanking the many families he has come in contact with for the numerous courtesies shown him while collecting material for this work. Their generosity in opening their homes with the same gracious hospitality associated with old plantation days has been greatly appreciated.

These ante-bellum homes have intrigued me time and time again when visiting them. Their before-the-war quaintness spurred me to write of them and their owners. And I am glad that I have undertaken the task of recording their past greatness, as so many interesting old places have disappeared since this work was started five years ago.

The author would like to offer a special word of thanks to those who so generously gave of their time, and put at disposal their treasured family books, family records frail with age, their family miniatures, ancestral portraits and old letters and documents. Others offered able assistance so that this work may be authentic and of service to future students interested in the lore of an age that is gone forever, even the memories of which are rapidly vanishing.

Many of these plantation families have been lifetime friends of our family, and it has made the task easier than it would have been had I been a stranger in their midst; still I have considered it a great privilege to be permitted to choose such material as was found best suited for my purpose.

I wish to thank The Louisiana Historical Society for permission to reproduce portraits of members of distinguished old Louisiana Families in their portrait Collection and for the privilege of reproducing extracts from the "Historical Quarterly." I have also consulted freely "New Orleans As It Was" by Henry C. Castellanos; "'New Orleans the Place and the People" by Grace King; Gayarre's "History of Louisiana"; Fortier's "History of Louisiana"; and the New Orleans Times-Picayune; the New Orleans Daily States; and the New Orleans Item-Tribune.

I am indebted to Mrs. Thomas Sloo for permission to use her Family Book to obtain data on the Bringier, Kenner, Brent, Minor, Du Bourg, de Luzon, Trist and other branches of her family, for use of Miniatures, daguerreotypes, photographs, ancestral portraits, memoirs and other private papers of historical interest, for my record of the Bringier Dynasty in Louisiana; to Mr. Trist Wood for his great assistance in correcting data and arranging branches of these families and of the many families to whom he is related; also for the use of many of the reproductions of miniatures, ancestral portraits, and other paintings in his extensive collection of family data, family crests and coats-of-arms, etc.; also for data on the Trist, Taylor, Stauffer, Wood, and other branches of his family; to Miss Tristy Bringier of Tezcuco Plantation for data on Bringier, Trudeau, Tureaud, and other branches of the family and history of her old plantation home at Burnside, La.; to Mrs. Sylvester P. Walmsley, Sr., and Sylvester P. Walmsley, Jr., for data on the Semmes, Knox, and Walmsley families and photos, ancestral portraits, pictures of Knox Hall and Knox Crest and coat-of-arms; to Mrs. Fernan Claiborne for permission to reproduce the de Villere crest and coat-of-arms; to Mrs. A. Sidney Ranlett, Sr., for data on the Ranlett family and family photographs; to Miss Ethel Hutson, Secretary to the President of the Delgado Art Museum of Art, for permission to use her article on Ante-Bellum Artists, (Warrington Messenger, Sept. 1938); also for data on the Artist Association of New Orleans, La.; to Mrs. David Pipes, Sr., for data on the Pipes Plantation, the Pipes family, the Fort, Stewart, and Randolph families, for photographs, miniatures, daguerreotypes, etc., to be used in my article on the above families; to Dr. Rudolph Matas for use of his article on the late Dr. John Smyth; to Miss Nellie Farwell for data on the Milliken and Farwell families, and pictures of her ancestral portrait collection, miniatures, and daguerreotypes, and Farwell coat-of-arms; to Messrs. Charles A. and F. Evans Farwell for data and pictures of their families and homes; to Mrs. Henry Landry de Freneuse for data on the de Freneuse, de la Vergne, de St. Paul, Seghers, Schmidt, and Hinks families, also for the use of miniatures, ancestral portraits, photographs, and the various crests and coats-of-arms of the various branches of the family and homes; to Professor Walter Prichard of the Louisiana State University, Baton Rouge for use of extracts from his article on J. W. Dorr, in the "Louisiana Quarterly"; to Miss Marguerite Renshaw of the Howard Library, New Orleans, for assistance in research work; to Mr. and Mrs. Robert Dugue (de Livaudais) and Mrs. J. N. Roussel for data on the Dugue de Livaudais, the Forstall, De Dreux families, data on Home Place (Forstall) plantation, also for permission to reproduce letters written by Louis Philippe King of France to members of the de Marigny, and de Livaudais families; to the late Mr. Leak of St. Francisville, La., for data on the Union Officer buried in the Cemetery of St. Francisville, La.; to Miss Eva Scott of the Shades Plantation for data on the Scott family and plantation; to Mrs. Gardner Voorhees (Ninette Chretien) for data and photographs of the Chretien family; for data on the Chretien plantation home at Chretien Point; to members of the Chretien family formally at that place; to Mrs. Joseph Louis Le Bourgeois for data on the Le Bourgeois and Lassasier families, and histories with pictures of Belmont and Mount Airy Plantations; to Weeks Hall for data on "The Shadows" New Iberia; to Dr. A. B. Fossier, Miss Clelie Labatut, Mrs. John Tobin and other members of the family for data on the Labatut Plantation and family pictures; to the D'Estrehan family for family data and pictures; to the late Robert S. Landry for data on the Mizaine plantation; to Mrs. Augustus H. Denis for data and crest and coat-of-arms of the de Marigny family; to Mrs. Robert Ruffin Barrow, Jr., for data and pictures of the Barrow, Perez, and other branches of the family; to Mrs. Mary Barrow Collins for permission to reproduce the portraits of her grandparents painted by Thomas Sully; to the Sparks, Daspit, and Barrow families of Baton Rouge and the Felicianas, also to Mrs. Livina Barrow Mays (Mrs. J. R. Mays) of Rosedale, La., for data that aided me with the various histories of the different Barrow mansions and plantations and article on the BARROW DYNASTY in Louisiana; to Mr. Emile Ducros, Louisiana Historian, for Authentic Notes on the de la Ronde, Plantation mansion, Avenue of Oak trees, the de la Ronde, Almonaster, de Pontalba, family and plantations in the St. Bernard Area, also the de la Ronde Crest and coat-of-arms; to Miss Louise Butler (Louisiana Historian), the family of Judge Thomas Butler, near St. Francisville, Mrs. Edward Butler, Sr., Misses Sarah and Mamie Butler of the Cedars plantation, for their united assistance in furnishing data for the various homes and families and permission to use and reproduce family portraits, memoires, miniatures, etc., and aiding in compiling THE BUTLER DY-NASTY in Louisiana; to Mr. and Mrs. Walter Charles Parlange of Parlange Plantation Home, Point Coupee for data on their old plantation home, the use of old family documents, records, of the Parlange, de Lassus, de Luziere, Reynaud de Cuzot, de Vezin, Van Vrandenburg, de Grand Pre, D'Herbigny (Derbigny) families and a record of "River Lake" plantation, ancestral plantation home of Mr. Parlange's grandparents the Denis family; to the Thomas Hewes family for data on the Pleasant View plantation and Hewes and Grymes families; to Mrs. Breaux for data on Austerlitz Plantation; to Col. Henry Rougon for data on plantation and pictures of home and garden; to Dr. and Mrs. L. R. de Buys and other members of the family for data on the de Macarty, Forstall families and plantations, the de Buys, Rathbone, Duggan and Hicky families, pictures of many of the portraits painted by the late Miss Edith Duggan, also for crests and coats-of-arms of the de Buys, Rathbone, Forstall, Lopez families, and to repro-duce part of the portrait collection of the late Mrs. Rathbone de Buys; drawing of the old plantation home of Col. Hicky (Hope Estate); to Mrs. P. L. Howell, Curator of the Louisiana Histor-ical Assn., Confederate Memorial Hall, New Orleans; to Dr. E. D. Fenner for data on the old Payne Plantation home, and Payne Fenner home and families; to Senator Edward J. Gay for data on the St. Louis Plantation and the Gay family and family pic-tures; to Dr. W. J. Owen for data on Nottaway Plantation; to the Misses Smith for data on Asphodel Plantation and permission to photo home; to the Le Jeune family for data on the old planta-tion home of the family in New Roads, La.; to Mr. J. Hereford Percy and the family for data on Beechwood Plantation, the Percy Family and kodaks of graves in Beechwood Cemetery; to Mrs. John Smyth for data on the Sully and Smyth families, data on Wavertree manor and plantation, Rosedown plantation with histories of these places and pictures also for family portraits and crests and coats-of-arms; to Miss Julia Sully of Richmond, Va., for history of the Pocahontas picture, etc.; to Mrs. Mabel Richardson for data and pictures of her grandparents plantation and home, "Hickory Hill," and family civil war record; to Miss Lucy Matthews of "Oakley Plantation" for data on Oakley, history of the fine collection of ancestral portraits by noted artists, data on the Pirrie, Alston, Bowman and Matthew families, etc.; to

Mrs. Edwin Xavia de Verges for her great assistance in compiling the record of the de Verges family and its branches, data on the family plantations, family miniatures, daguerreotypes and other portraits, pictures of Chateau Senlis and of the other ones of the Almonaster and de Pontalba families, coats-of-arms of the de Macarty, de Lino de Chalmette, de Cruzat, de Poupart, and others of her family. The description of the de Verges Crest and coat-of-arms; to Miss Marguerite Fortier of the Louisiana State Museum for photographs of the Edmond Fortier plantation "Concession" known as the Keller Place, also for data on the Fortier family; to Miss Laure Beauregard Larendon for data on the Beauregard Reggio, and de Villere families and family photographs; to the Stauffer family for data on their old plantation Home in Metairie Lane; to Mrs. Helen Pitkin Schertz for data on her old plantation home (Old Spanish Customhouse) record of the Pitkin family in America, for photos of her home, garden and portrait by Allen St. John; to Mrs. John F. Coleman for data on the Rouyer de Villere, Lanaux, Rareshide, Baker, Poujaud de Jouvisy families and crests and coats-of-arms of these families, and family photographs, also for copy of painting of Conseil plantation owned by Mrs. W. O. Humphries; to the Walter Parker family for data on their old plantation home and family with photographs, crest, etc.; to Mr. and Mrs. Gustaf Westfeldt, Jr., for data on their old plantation home (The Old Dugue de Livaudais Plantation), the Westfeldt, Dugan and Monroe families and family and house pictures; to Miss Edith Kernaghan for data on the D'Arensbourg family and permission to use an ancestral portrait of the D'Arensbourg family; to Mrs. Wilson Williams and Miss Doris Walker for data on Kenilworth Plantation and Wilson family with photographs, etc.; to Miss Louise Crawford for data on Kenilworth Manor and the Bienvenu, and Crawford families; to the von Phul, Cade, Soniat, du Fossat and Allain families pictures, records, etc., of family and home; to Deleon "Belles, Beaux and Brains of the Sixties"; the Frotscher and Koch families for data on the Frotscher Plantation, the Koch home, and both families and photographs; to Mrs. Grady Price (Miss Edith Dart) for data on the Plauché family; to Mrs. William MacCormac Younge for poem on "Molinary's Grave"; to Mrs. Logan Perkins (Miss Elizabeth Kell) for data on her family's old plantation home "Point Clear," Madison Parish, La., and data on the family, also portrait; to Mrs.

Eugene Ellis for data on the Ellis family and Magnolia Plantation; to Mrs. T. L. Raymond for memoirs of her grandfather's plantation and home "Evergreen," Rapides Parish, La.; to her sister Mrs. P. L. Girault, now of Chicago, Ill., for data on the family and family pictures; to Mrs. Felix Larue for data on General J. B. Levert; to Mrs. Andrew Stewart for data on the family also of Oak Alley (Beau Sejour) plantation and home; to the various branches of the Prudhomme family for data on the family, the old plantation and home, family pictures and miniatures, etc.; to Mrs. Cammie Henry for permission to visit her old plantation garden and lower floor, the studios, and for picture of home "Melrose Manor"; to Baron Albert deBeaulieu de Marconnay of Manitou Springs, Colorado, for data on the various branches of his family and pictures of the family and chateau; to Charles Konzelman for data and pictures of his family; to Miss Vera Morel for permission to use her drawing of Kenilworth Plantation Manor; to Rev. Father Eck for history of St. Catherine's Chapel, False River; to Mr. Allan Wurtele for pictures of Ramsey Plantation home; to B. R. Foster of the Louisiana State Museum for use of portraits for illustrations; to Mrs. O. LeBlanc and Mrs. H. Lorio for aid in obtaining data; to Mrs. Flo Field for article on Molinary; to Mrs. Adel Lebourgeois Chapin for extracts on "Their Fruitless Ways" (Henry Holt & Co., N. Y.); and to many others —some of whom are mentioned in this work—for information and assistance in compiling this data.

Naturally in a work of this kind, in spite of great care and thorough checking a few errors will creep in. Because of the thousands of details, names, dates, etc., it is impossible to avoid a few mistakes, also the spelling of names varies—even when spelt by different members of the same family.

I therefore ask the reader's indulgence for such errors or failings as this work contains. I will endeavor to correct such mistakes in future editions.

Herman de Bachellé Seebold, M.D.

CONTENTS

The Old Antoine Bienvenu Plantation
Bienvenu - Crawford Families
The Wilson Williams Family
Concord
(The old Plantation of the de la Vergne family)

River Lake Plantation—built for Isaac Gaillard
*(Later Arthur Denis Plantation—now the Major
Plantation)*

Live Oak Plantation
(J. R. Mays home, Rosedale)
Shady Grove Manor
(On Bayou Grosse Tete)
Belmont Plantation
(The old Wyley Barrow Plantation)

St. Louis Plantation—West Bank of the Mississippi
(Originally called Home Plantation)

Chretien Plantation
Chretien family
Williams family
Grand Coteau
Jesuit Seminary
Fusilier de la Claire Plantation

(Near Washington, La.)
Jacob Upsher Payne
Captain Charles Fenner
Fenner family

Marco Plantation Home

Magnolia Plantation (Herzog family)
Yucca Plantation
*(Now known as Melrose Plantation—home of
Mrs. Cammie Henry)*
BERMUDA (La Cote Joyeuse)
(Plantation and home of the Prudhomme family)
Town of Natchitoches
Grand Encore

CORRECTIONS

Under "Acknowledgment"—"Smyth" should be spelled without the "e".

Page 8. First line of quoted matter read "homes" instead of "home".

Page 72. Old Delord Sarpy Plantation Home—in second paragraph, third sentence, two lines have been transposed. The sentence should read: "This old house was a handsome place in its day, with rows of medium-sized solid brick columns heavily stuccoed that surrounded the place originally, resting on tall heavily built square ones."

In List of Illustrations (opposite page 96)—"Darensbourg" should be "D'Arensbourg".

Opposite Page 288. (Under cut)—read Miss Clelie Ranson instead of Clelie Labatut.

LIST OF ILLUSTRATIONS

Pages

CHAPTER HEADINGS AND OTHER LINE DRAWINGS

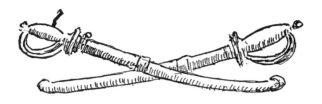

INTRODUCTION

A T the time that the colonists were rebelling against the English, a large number of loyal British subjects sold their lands and improvements, converting as much property as they could into gold coin which they put into their strong-boxes, and departing from Maryland, Virginia and Carolina, headed for the English possessions in the South. (The Feliciana Parishes and the vicinity of the present city of Baton Rouge, La.) On this trek South, most of these planter families took with them their movable property, forming caravans which included ancestral portraits, crested silver, household articles, their numerous slaves, cattle and animals, travelling part of the way by water on flat-boats and part of the way overland in covered wagons. It must be remembered that the records of that day show that many°of these families were English aristocrats who had fled England at the time of the execution of Charles I.

In the army of slaves that each of the wealthy planters took with him were many skilled mechanics, costing several thousands of dollars each, who soon were to show their ability in the new country. At that time little thought was given to the possibility that the Union Jack would soon cease to float over this beautiful land. In this way the section that was soon to become the state of Louisiana, gained a large number of aristocratic families with immense wealth who had large plantations of thousands of acres and who had erected palatial mansions, magnificently furnished, and surrounded with beautiful gardens. These citizens of good birth, culture and wealth added to an earlier crowd of patrician settlers from France and Spain, at once gave Louisiana a class of people who formed an aristocratic element.

From the first they proceeded to establish themselves on their estates, and, secure in their social position, conducted their business and social affairs with as much formality as their ancestors had done in Europe. They made their plantations centers of distinctly genteel gathering. One then can see readily that it was not as is so often stated by writers unfamiliar with the aristocratic class of Louisiana, "that it was the great plantations and sale of large crops of sugar and cotton during the Golden Era that made the Louisiana planter an aristocrat," but it was the plantations that proved a means of permitting the born aristocrats to live as their families before them had lived in their former homes in Europe.

The settling of the earliest Louisiana colony was somewhat different from the English ones of Maryland, Virginia and Carolina, as that in the far south was the outcome of a plan of the King of France to scheme that country out of debt. King Louis XIV by many costly wars, and the erection of the fabulously extravagant palace of Versailles—a strategic move to break up the power of the wealthy and powerful nobles by concentrating the Court and all its social functions, as well as official residences in the immediate vicinity of the palace as a center with the King of France supreme. The unbridled extravagances continued when the country was on the verge of bankruptcy, and generation after generation ground down the middle classes and peasantry by unbearable taxes and finally brought on the French Revolution.

When the King of France, represented by the Regent, with the aid of the Scotch wizard, John Law, (see "The Mississippi Bubble") organized the Mississippi Land Scheme, France and all Europe rushed to purchase stock. He pictured in the most extravagant terms the vast territory of Louisiana as being a veritable el dorado of gold and silver mines with an ideal spring climate and a luxuriant growth of tropical eatable fruits—all to be had for the picking. All this appealed strongly to the unsuspecting French aristocracy, and the population in general who were anxious to get away from the awful taxes. The result of all this advertising was the selling of vast estates to French patricians. They and others who came to Louisiana and later with the aid of slave labor found that many of these plantations were veritable gold mines.

In 1793 during the French Revolution any number of French aristocrats sought refuge in Louisiana. Having fled France, taking part of their wealth with them, they settled here and became planters on a large scale. Again during the uprising of the slaves in San Domingo and the other neighboring islands hundreds of other French patricians came to Louisiana and bought plantations.

Even though there were undesirables in the colony, with so many aristocratic families, it was not long before a strong class demarcation was in evidence, especially since from the earliest days of the settlement the passengers on the various ships were registered on their arrival in the colony—their names, sex, color, occupation and class. All of the details were carefully recorded as they had been in Canada in earliest days. Thus it was a difficult matter for one to pass as an aristocrat unless his claim could be verified, for the colony was in close touch with Europe. In the West Indies a similar check had been kept on the families. So when one made claims to be a member of the aristocracy, like Bienville, the founder of New Orleans, the son of an ambitious father who had his children christened with the titles of noble families attached to their names to aid them socially, he had to prove his claim. It was not long before it was known that the names that Bienville's father had given his sons were not hereditary ones, and they were so registered as such. Despite the fact that he was Governor of the colony, historians make no attempt to misrepresent his true origin. Miss King gives a detailed account of the naming of Bienville and his brothers.* So particular were those in authority in the earliest days on these matters, that it became a routine thing for families to bring to French America with them their family record. Today in hundreds of Louisiana families these old family records, telling of their good birth, are among the family's most cherished possessions. I have been shown any number of them in my studies of old families, some of these documents falling to pieces with age, but still bearing the signatures of French and Spanish royalty.

In contrast to the better born planter families, were the small farmers and planters, who purchased their parcels of land bit by bit, and who made but little attempt to attain social recognition from the prominent families. Between the two a friendly acquaintance existed, but all attempts at familiarity on the part of those of lesser birth were frowned on, for democracy as yet did

* (New Orleans the Place and the People" by Grace King).

not play much part in the plantation life of those days. According to the late Charles Gayarre, noted Louisiana historian, it only really appeared after the sixties.

When the refugees from the West Indies arrived in Louisiana, many of them purchased the plantations of the small planters, and throwing a number together, formed extensive holdings which soon became notable places of their kind.

FURNISHING OF AN ANTE-BELLUM PLANTER'S HOME

Pen pictures do scant justice to many of these old Southern Homes in the midst of their endless estates. Old prints, drawings and detailed descriptions which ante-date the Civil War, tell in a measure the beauty and glory of it all—faint reminders of how they appeared in the hey-day of their glory. It is not the grandeur of palace with pomp and stately dignity of castle hall, but rather the charm of perfect taste that was displayed in their homes and furnishings.

One gets a good idea of how the finer of these old Greek Revival mansions looked on the inside, especially the homes of those who had come from what had been the English colonies. They have an air somewhat like but less staid than that found in the various rooms of the American Wing of the Metropolitan Museum, where such charming furnishings are shown, most of them showing the English influence. In the old plantation homes of the French and Spanish families—the representative Creoles— a blending of the two styles developed to be supplanted later in most instances by examples of furniture from the New Orleans ateliers of Signorette and Prudence Mallard. These styles replaced the earlier quite simple furnishings of the first homes of the early Louisiana plantation settlers. However, previous to the founding of the two famous French furniture establishments, fine furniture from France had been brought to Louisiana, and when the immense rooms began to appear both in city as well as in plantation homes, these French designs were reproduced on a much larger scale and in original designs of the most magnificent sort. With the rebuilding of the area destroyed by the great fire in New Orleans in the year 1788, and a new type of home was developed, the houses being built of brick, many of them three storied in height having immense rooms with very high ceilings, some eighteen feet in height. The long warm summers caused the owners to plan their houses along the lines of those in Cuba. To suit these large-room houses, at first furniture of a larger size was ordered from Europe. This furniture in many instances replaced the slave-fashioned articles that were made in the early days of the settlement. One rarely finds any of this kind of furniture today except in the small homes of poorer planters in the interior parts of the state. These large splendidly built brick homes erected after 1788 reflected the Spanish influence in many instances, but as a whole, it is a development of a mixture of French and Spanish which gives the "Vieux Carre" an individuality that is generally termed the Creole type.

These homes for the most part were the town houses of the richer planters. While the Spanish Crown ruled Louisiana from 1762 until 1800, on the whole Louisiana was influenced but little by the Dons. After the transfer of Louisiana to the United States, and Americans began to pour into the newly annexed territory, great activity was noted throughout the section. With the start of the "Golden Era" of the South, there began the trips to Europe by plantation families who, selected more costly furnishings for the new palatial mansions that were replacing their first plantation homes. Costly furniture, art objects and the finest of lace curtains, linen, satins, brocades, and draperies of all kinds were imported. Magnificent mirrors, pier glasses and cornices, beautifully carved in Louis XIV, Louis XV and Louis XVI designs gilded with real gold leaf; the finest of oriental rugs and carpets, paintings, crystal, silverware in fact, everything to embellish a wealthy home were ordered. Louisiana was long considered by the French as their best customers, and the French porcelains and crystal ware rivaled the German and Venetian.

Finally the volume of fine furniture that was being made for Louisiana in France became so great that a Frenchman named Francois Signorette saw an opportunity and came to Louisiana. He located in New Orleans and erected a large brick building at what is now 520 Royal Street. On the ground floor was his factory or atelier where the making of the finest of furniture was done by skilled artisans from Paris, France. In this building he also had stored vast quantities of the finest of rare wines, special vintages that he disposed to his wealthy customers.

With the planters erecting such immense plantation homes

Monsieur Signorette soon found that he was unable to supply the demand for this fine large furniture. Soon another Frenchman started a similar atelier, and he was followed by a man named Charley Lee.

By this time England was clamoring for millions of pounds of cotton, the sugar industry was at the height of its success, and the lands of Louisiana filling up with great plantations on both sides of the Mississippi River and every one of its larger bayous. The "Golden Era" was in full bloom. As a result a hundred other fine furniture establishments filled the old city and overflowed into the newer section on the uptown side of Canal Street, New Orleans. The furniture of Siebright, Signorette and Mallard was of the finest. It was magnificently carved and brought immense prices. As the house servants were slaves, each house had large quantities of money, jewelry, and silverware as well as other valuables, it was the rule when ordering furniture to have made into some pieces secret drawers. These secret places were hidden behind mouldings, in the bases, behind columns and in secret panels. Some of the beds were ten feet in height with columns ten inches in diameter. So unusual and beautiful were these plantation homes that visitors from other parts marveled at it all.

One finds in many of the old city homes as well as in those on old plantations, little mahogany and rosewood ladder-like steps that are used to get into these high old beds—quite quaint in this day and age.

LIFE ON A GREAT PLANTATION IN ANTE-BELLUM DAYS

Plantation families in olden days as a rule were large, and a house full of growing children led to a variety of amusements, depending on the ages of the youngsters. Private tutors became the rule in many of the wealthy homes, the young folks later going to college or convent and in many instances to colleges or finishing schools abroad. It was when the sons and daughters of the household returned at holiday season and during vacation that dances, balls, parties, etc., usually took place. The older members habitually entertained with a series of dinners, balls and similar festivities, especially if there were grown daughters to bring out in society. Life on a great plantation in those days permitted leisure for the pursuit of the arts, good music, books, and the gathering of a congenial company by the planter and his friends.

As time went on with increasing wealth coming to the South, this ample leisure brought about a brilliant social life at home and abroad, many of the families having homes both in America and in Europe. This was especially true of the wealthy Creoles. Up until the present war, many Louisianians visited their relatives abroad yearly.

Unlike the rustic squires of England who remained on their estates the year round, the majority of these great plantation owners also had town houses to which they came in the Winter season to hear good music and drama and to enjoy the city's social life. Many of the richest Creole planter families had opera boxes, both in New Orleans as well as in the French Capitol. In many instances, in fact as a general rule among the richest planter families, the lives of the men were so arranged that financial matters were attended to by capable and trustworthy overseers, who kept the family from coming in contact with "business", and who prevented any scheming individual from getting the best of any of its members. This also permitted luxury and ease, with time for fox hunting and other out-door sports. The smaller planter, of course, attended to his own business affairs, which accounts for so many of them eventually becoming quite wealthy.

The continuous round of costly entertainments, the elaborate carriages, coaches with handsome harness trappings often held together with silver and gold plated buckles; their fine strings of blooded horses and their stables; the appearance and training of their numerous servants (slaves); the beautiful and costly clothing, gowns and wearing apparel of the family; their bearing, dignity, culture and luxuriant ease all seemed to enjoy, made life in old Louisiana idyllic for those fortunate people. It is little wonder then that visitors to the South in days antedating the War Between the States, carried away with them the memories they did of the stately elegance of the aristocrats and their families, as well as the grand manner in which they were housed and entertained.

In the earliest days in Louisiana, compared with the English colonies, the number of very rich planters were not nearly as great, or the larger mansions nearly so numerous or handsome as those of the British. However, with the arrival in the colony of the Marquis and his Marquise deVaudreuil, the new governor, who had brought a ship load of fine furniture and handsome equipment for the court he intended to establish in New Orleans as the capital of the colony, a new era began. Planned as were the courts at the smaller continental capitals of Europe, deVaudreuil had brought with him imposing chairs, draperies, pictures, etc., and at the court balls, he insisted that all present come de rigeur, or in military uniform. Thus the year 1737, with the arrival of this French nobleman, the Marquis de Vaudreuil, began the first real social life in Louisiana. Besides the court balls and levees, the first attempt to establish a theatre was made.

After the "Golden Era" had set in, it was soon noted that an opulence in the style and manner of living existed and great attention was paid to the details of high bred courtesy which we find lacking at times in the highest circles of wealthy present-day patricians. Throughout the plantation area good living with the polish of continental etiquette based on tradition, backed by well stacked pantries and cellars, could extend to the assemblies gathered about the mahogany, the choicest delicacies and rare wines of the world.

The planters of the wealthier class took advantage of their leisure to study law, politics and the sciences generally. Naturally they became very proficient in the administration of governmental affairs when elected to office, being graduates of the best colleges of Europe and America.

It is little wonder then that stories dealing with old plantation days in the South possess a glamorous fascination peculiarly their own. Miss Louise Butler (Louisiana Historian) describes* life as it existed on old plantations, her own old plantation home in which generations of her family were born, being one of the most interesting old places in West Feliciana parish.

> Centers of gracious hospitality were most of these homes in days gone by. Let us recall a (shall we say happily?) lost custom and 'spend the day' as one of the guests who arrived in the family coach which (the coach, not the family) was usually upholstered in soft grey broadcloth, as the owners had too much pride to be ostentatious, and was provided with embroidered strap by which to hang, for roads were rough and the vehicle swung high on prodigious springs, so the lurching was frightful and the occupants usually reached their

---

* In the Louisiana Historical Quarterly, Jan. 1924.

The old Milne Sugar Plantation, now Belle Chasse Plantation. The Sugar and Cotton Plantations did not make the Louisiana Aristocrat, but gave the born aristocrat an opportunity to live in America as his ancestors had done in Europe. See page 2. (From an old print.)

CUTTING SUGAR-CANE BY HAND
(From an old print.)

destination suffering from mal de mer, slight or violent, according to their powers of endurance. The ladies were taken to the company room to remove their bonnets and pelisses, which careful maids laid on the white counterpane of the silk-hung old four-poster bed of ample dimensions. After surveying their charms in the Psyche, adding a dab of pomatum to smooth their disarranged curls, they adjourned to the parlour, which was usually furnished in rosewood, intricately carved above the satin brocade of medallion backs. Then, according to invariable custom, cordial, Maraschino, or Curocoa, was served with fruit cake in winter or orange flower or raspberry syrup with a lighter cake in summer, different members of the family taking turns in entertaining while others, in private, were superintending the elaborate menu or beating the egg whites for the floating islands with peach switches or showing Delphy, the perspiring cook, how to sear the spanish cream with a red hot salamander. Meanwhile the men of the party were inspecting the crops, or passing judgment on the stock, but returned to the parlour just before the door of the dining-room opened to give passage to Nathan or Preston or Jeems bearing a silver salver laden with crystal goblets surrounding the julep bowl that rose from the center like a bouquet, being filled with crushed ice in which was stuck sweetpea blossoms, or any flower in season, and mint to flavor the contents. After this was partaken of dinner was announced, and the guests entered the large dining-room that was furnished in massive mahogany, the sideboard alone long enough to fill one wall of a modern apartment and broad enough to support the splendid silver and cut glass and a punch bowl, as mammy often said, 'big ernuff to swim de baby, effen he tuck his baff in hit.' At the dinner was served claret, as per usual, sherry with the soup, Roman punch with the meats and, on gala occasions champagne, then with the coffee came in a silver dish with lumps of loaf sugar blazing with spirits to be put in the tiny cups, often of old Chelsa or Sevres. You may credit my statement that the gentlemen, especially departed with eyes considerably brighter than when they arrived.. Dear, generous, lavish, warmheartedly hospitable old giver of pleasure! Many a one of you literally entertained himself out of his home and into the poor-house.

GARDEN AND PLANTATION TOURS
FASHIONABLE DIVERSIONS

Plantation gardens have always been noted for their quaint beauty and romantic charm, and now that garden tours are the present rage, the country homes and plantation mansions too are in many instances shrines to which pilgrimages are made regularly. No longer are these old mansions closed most of the year. All of the fine old things that escaped when Sherman spread his fiery torch throughout the Southland, that were formally permitted to be seen by a selected few, now are viewed by a world of eager appreciative sightseers, who for the first time are getting glimpses into old plantation homes of which they have been reading about. These old estates were in many ways like the feudal estates of Europe. Especially so previous to 1914 in Russia was a great similarity noted. They were conducted with this difference however. The Southern planter realizing that his slaves were valuable property and was governed as they were by "slave laws", which held the owner strictly accountable for any neglect or abuse of them. Almost without exception every large plantation had its own church, hospital, and place of amusement, private slave cabins, poultry and pig-pens, as well as vegetable and cotton patches. These latter gave the slaves an opportunity to make a little extra money for themselves and perhaps little luxuries for his family. Today visitors to the old plantations of Louisiana like those of Virginia, Maryland, Carolina, Georgia and Tennessee find them open throughout the year.

In making these tours of the old plantations one comes across old places completely run down. In many instances these places show what happened after everything but the old house and a little of the once vast acreage had been swept away as a result of the Civil War and reconstruction days. The men all killed off and with no help to work the land, all went to seed—nothing remained but a once great name. An occasional relic from the past tells of its once glorious furnishings. Visits to neighboring cemeteries, often will reveal from the crumbling old marble of the once magnificent tomb and lengthy wording on the old time-stained slabs, how prominent and prosperous these old families were. The destruction of the plantation areas was so complete that one wonders that so many of the old places survived at all. Leaving these wrecks, the pilgrimage takes a more delightful turn when it reaches the old plantation homes still preserved with open, spacious hallways and great spiral stairways winding upward, finally reaching observatories on the roof from which the planter could survey his endless acres and know that all was going well. Here in these immense mansions one finds gorgeous drawing-rooms, banquet-rooms, libraries, reception and bed-rooms galore, all furnished in the period of a century ago. They take on new life and as of yore azaleas, gardenias and japonicas mingle with sweet olive, making of the spacious rooms delightful, alluring retreats. They are filled with beautiful costumed hostesses, negro mammies, and old black Jo's, for the darkies delight in dressing as their folks did before the war and taking their part in the pageant. One sees century-old crystal chandeliers of (Warterford) sparkling and scintilating, their lighted tapers reflected again and again in immense mantel and console-mirrors, in gilded frames with rich ornamentation; epergnes and tall alabaster urns, numberless rare ornaments and signed bronzes, with finest of furniture; ancient spinets, old square pianos with pearl keys, zithers, and century old music boxes. Or perhaps one hears a mechanical singing bird in gilt cage, their plaintive thrills filling the air as of yore, while the strains of Ben Bolt, Flow Gently Sweet Afton, and old army songs come from the music boxes. All this creates an ante-bellum setting for the beautiful girls and stately ladies in hoop-skirts, in creations of Worth, Madame Olympe, and other noted modistes of that era. Old wedding gowns, and ball dresses that have been laid away in lavender and rosemary for over half a century, are unwrapped, brought forth again, once more to be worn by grand-daughters in these candle-lit rooms. Dozens of ladies, young, middle-aged, and elderly, all costumed in period of the long ago, and looking as if they had just emerged from the pages of a "Godey's Lady's Book". We find them resting on little mahogany and rosewood 1840 sofas, and love-seats with gowns wide-spread fan fashion, or strolling about in little groups wearing lace mantillas, or quaint dolmons giving them a sedate appearance. Many Scarlett O'Haras, and Melanies in these crowds, for crowds they are.

Many hundreds of these aristocratic planters of the South when compared to any standard were immensely wealthy. They were reared in the culture of the manner born as was but natural, which included education at the best schools of Europe and America and yearly trips to Europe. The Grand Tour meant the taking of the entire family, their valets and maids, with especially built carriages strongly made so as to make tours about the continent and to visit the continental capitals. It was on these trips that so many unusual articles, and art objects were purchased, which at that day as well as this made these plantation homes outstanding places of interest to visitors. One finds in a number of these homes immense dinner sets of finest Havaland china, decorated by the naturalist James J. Audubon while he resided in the Feliciana area, with hundreds of pieces each bearing the birds of America beautifully painted on them. Other dinner sets costing thousands of dollars were painted by noted French artists, with the family crest and coat-of-arms on each piece. Visitors marvel at the vast quantities of costly ornaments to be found in these homes. Records now carefully preserved in historical museums, show wills, diaries and bills of sale and ship inventories, which prove that to Virginia and the Carolinas in early days came boat load after boat load of household articles of every description. Besides the most beautiful and costly furnishings, there were imported elaborate costumes of cut velvet, gold brocade and other priceless fabrics. These were made to order by the leading fashionable tailors and modistes of the day in Europe. Rarest of hand made lace for every use, costly brocatelles with applique of gold and silver, gorgeous table services of sterling silver, all crested and monogrammed; in fact everything that was newest and best was shipped to these great planters who desired to live in America as their families had done abroad.

Much of this has found its way to Louisiana, brought to this state by the aristocratic families from the English settlements at the time that the colonies rebelled against the English tyranny. Many of these articles tourists now see when visiting these old plantation homes, especially in the Feliciana areas and in the vicinity of Bayou Lafourche where so many fine people of English extraction settled. Some of the things have become faded and worn in the three quarters of a century since the cessation of hostilities between the North and South. However, the galleries of old family portraits by celebrated artists, fine old furnishings, miniatures, daguerreotypes, silhouettes and the hundred and one articles that are to be found in these places having been cherished all these years as mementos of the glorious days when life in the South on a great plantation was to some a continuous holiday.

With the passing of three quarters of a century, during which time almost all of our fathers who were engaged in the conflict of the Sixties have passed on, one feels safe in reviewing the true story of the old plantations of Louisiana without fear of being accused of opening old wounds. The true story of the happenings on these places could have been told by eye witnesses to the events, but they modified and toned down their writings so as not to antagonize Northern magazines and newspapers who bought the stories for publication. The impoverished South was not in position to publish or give to the world in books information or the truth of which it was already too painfully conscious, and the publishers of the North did not want stories which truthfully told of the horrors of it all. Reconstruction saw some of the worst happenings when the whites were put under the black yoke. Under the circumstances much that would serve as valuable historical data has had to be left unwritten, and with the deaths of able writers who could have told, it must now remain a closed book. One feels safe now in reviewing incidents of days long past, filled with pleasure, pain and joy and sorrow, and tragic horror of the worst sort.

A NEW SOCIAL ORDER

The Mississippi River was filled with thousands of crafts from St. Louis to the gulf during the "Golden Era". The rapidly growing wealth meant keeping the South a land of slave labor, and slave labor had the effect of keeping the South for most part free from so much of the undesirable element that poured into America. The immigrants that flooded the country were mostly peasants dissatisfied with their curtailed freedom in their homeland. Within a few years these newcomers became naturalized and lost no time in getting into politics. When the aristocracy of North, East and Middle West came to a realization of what a powerful group this new immigrant element formed, and that politics were being taken out of the hands—not partially but completely— of the better element, who had controlled the welfare of the country since colonial days, they saw how helpless they were to prevent it. The better element in the cities felt that family prestige at least could be preservd with exclusiveness, if they for most part withdrew from civic gatherings. (Democracy as we know it today had as yet not arrived.) Even before the Civil War exclusive sets were formed which was necessary, if they were to maintain any social standard at all. While these sets, taken as a whole, were smaller in number than those of the South, the former were just as jealous of their exclusiveness as were the Southerners.

However, the great wealth that flowed into New York City,

Philadelphia, Boston, Chicago and other of the larger Northern cities, made itself felt by enriching a new element. In spite of all the protests of the "Old Guard" who at first with thumbs down, flatly refused to have anything to do with the newcomers, or to accept their hospitalities. But gradually they had to give in and accept the changing times. However, it was apparent that they feared what would happen to the politics of the country, knowing what had occurred in the past—of the awful graft and political steals that had taken place in the cities and towns of the North, over which the better element no longer had control. The West and Middle West long had endured and graciously submitted to the snubs and insinuations of the North and East, and listened to the taunts of "beef barons" and "woolly West." But with the passing of the "Old Guard" in the North and East and its counterpart in other sections above the Mason-Dixon line, replaced by the estimated standard of society throughout the country.

After the days of Reconstruction had ended, the entire South was too impoverished and sad to have any heart for society, the newcomers to the South for most part doing the entertaining. The South's bitterness towards the North (the Union) persisted for many years. It felt, not so much the outcome of the war and its effects, but the great injustice that had been done them by Sherman, in his determination to completely ruin the Southern Country for generations, and later the attempt by those in charge of reconstruction to exterminate the Southerners. The efforts of carpetbaggers and politicians to Africanize the South, while the North looked on indifferently at the defeated country being crucified, horrified the rest of the world. For the first time in the world's history the victors of a defeated nation placed it under and at the mercy of semi-civilized negroes. The Southerners, noting this indifference, held aloof when it was all over, and established a social class where money played but a small part in their scheme of things, thus preserving for many years their old social standards. Sad to say since the great "World's War" this too has in a great measure given way to the age of jazz and the modern trend.

It is no longer the brilliant South of Ante-bellum days, so changed and desolate looking has the plantation country become. The splendid manors were numbered by the thousands, while the smaller ones were almost numberless, many still being in existence. Most of the golden empire of the South was wiped out in a spirit of vengeance, little of its once great glory remaining. Ancient maps show how numerous were these old places and their magnitude. For hundreds of miles along Southern water-ways, fringing both banks—plantation touching plantation with hardly half dozen acres frontage not under cultivation; they are fully named and designated in detail, so valuable was land at that date. It is not unusual to see the remnant of some famous plantation mansion with tall crumbling columns surrounded by a park of ancient oaks, and great trees a half century old growing within the foundation walls of what was a spacious drawing-room where a future king of France once danced. Tourists visiting these old places marvel at the sight of palatial mansions with exquisitely carved woodwork and marble mantels, abandoned and gradually falling to pieces, housing tramps during the winter who come South to escape the severe weather. It takes a fair-sized fortune to maintain these great houses, so long ago many owners have had to mortgage them for what they could get, and the present owners live in the hope that oil will be found on their land.

A lover of the beautiful in architecture, a writer of ability, and who probably does not know much of plantation history, states that America anxiously awaits an architectural development by which all who build will desire homes of a dignified type solidly built and beautiful. If Americans would cease their reckless waste of money expended on speed and noise and devote it to a more sane manner of living they could look forward to an improvement on what we have known in the past, and a new era of beauty would be the result.

In the South up until the time they were destroyed by the Union forces in the Sixties, there existed on a magnificent scale, in sumptuous settings modelled after the finest of European country homes of the gentry, in endless numbers in each of the Southern states all that the poet heart of this able writer now wishes for. Today as one wanders through areas again claimed by nature as woodland, one comes across ruined palatial mansions with massive walls heavily coated with stucco, enclosed by twelve-foot verandas from which rise on each facade eight or ten massive columns crumbling like the entire structure, long since abandoned to the elements after the family fortunes were swept away by the war.

Alas! In a spirit of vengeance when the power was placed in his hands to do so, a celebrated General with flaming torch wiped from the Southlands a wealth of architectural treasure which can never be replaced. These magnificent homes filled the needs of an aristocracy that still cherished the cultured home life of the best that was in Europe, and which replanted it in the New World. Estates designed and laid out by the finest landscape artists of Europe added to the magnificence of the finer of these splendid mansions.

A story is told in the deep South by distant relatives of the young lady whose families are mentioned in this book, and who lived in the locality where he visited, about the celebrated general mentioned above. While teaching in Baton Rouge, Louisiana, a position obtained for him by the fathers of some of his classmates while a cadet at West Point, he fell in love. The father of the young lady he was in love with refused to permit him to attempt to gain her affections so that he might marry her. This young lady, the daughter of one of the most aristocratic families in America, was from Virginia and was then visiting in Mississippi. When refused the hand of this aristocrat's daughter, the officer became embittered and swore that should it ever be in his power "he would burn every damnable aristocrat's home in the South." This he came pretty close to doing when the power was placed in his hands. The daughter of this proud family who knew the future general then but slightly, and who frowned at his presumption afterwards stated that, "she would have married the devil himself rather than have the South suffer what it did". From the tales of his own men who witnessed many of the mansions burning when this general was present, to quote them, "never did a pyromaniac gloat in greater glee, than did this general from whom the world would have expected a more sane warfare". Thus glorious mansions were put to the torch, against the wishes of officers and soldiers in his command, who were forced to make helpless old people and children, often sick and crippled, get out of their homes with only the clothing on their backs, so that the homes could be stripped of their contents before being fired.

Thus was wiped from the South a wealth of magnificent homes unequalled in its day anywhere for architectural beauty, leaving only the grandeur of the conception of a type of country home that has never been improved upon for beauty or comfort.

An early method of separating the seed from the cotton.
(From an ante-bellum print.)

During the "Golden Era" Steamboats loaded with thousands of bales of cotton
reached the port of New Orleans weekly to be shipped to England.
(From an old print.)

A Plantation Garden on the east bank of the Mississippi.

GOVERNOR VILLERE
First Creole Governor of Louisi-
ana. (See page 65). Courtesy of
Mrs. E. X. de Verges.

The mansions that remain are now selected by the United States Government as examples for posterity to be guided by. They are being carefully photographed and copied by architects in the United States employ, who are taking careful measurements, noting details and structural materials, all of which are being carefully preserved in the archives of the Library of Congress at Washington, D. C.

Paintings and drawings of the most important of what is left of these old places being carefully treasured together with what data obtainable about their history.

The plantation mansion of the southern planter was a type of country house unique in America, and it was indigenous to the South. As a rule it was spacious, and its type, mostly Greek Revival, gave it stateliness. With much fine building materials on his land, and in an age when distinguished architects were planning some of their most attractive as well as practical designs for country homes, the southern planter builded well. Stately columned verandas, a general classic air, guest houses and kitchens all carefully planned so as to avoid noises and odors, the combination of buildings was designed generally so as to form a harmonious whole and give magnificence to the ensemble.

COTTON IS KING

One is interested to know what it was that sustained the great wealth of the Southern planters and permitted culture to develop as it did in a newly settled country.

English inventors were experimenting with weaving machines as early as 1725. Spinners and weavers had grown weary of the inefficient methods then in use when Paul Wyatt developed the method of "roller spinning" as it was then termed. Later a method which permitted the spinning of a great number of threads on one machine was called the Hargreve Jenny. It had a rotating carding machine engine. One invention after another improved upon the previous ones as the years passed until the Arkwright machine was able to produce a great number of threads of various thickness and hardness was invented. Then Cartwright's power loom was finally combined with the Wyeth steam engine and this brought on a ravenous demand for more spinning material.

The fact that cotton was hard to remove from the seed made the supply of this material in large quantities a difficult matter.

In 1795 Eli Whitney, a New Englander, patented the cotton gin that he had invented, and the export of cotton to Europe from the Southern part of the United States rose from nothing in 1790, when as yet no cotton from America was exported, to five million pounds in 1795 when that quantity was shipped to England. Just before the South was practically wiped out by the North, that section was supplying England alone with two thousand million pounds of cotton annually.

Such cotton crops yielded princely fortunes to the South and these enabled Southern planters to live in the ways of the aristocracy of Europe—that of a country gentleman and his famliy. As the climate and soil of the South were peculiarly fitted for the cultivation of cotton, it was not long before thousands of plantations had their entire acreage planted in cotton. Realizing that this staple was a crop that produced a greater return than any other grown in the South, planters from all parts of the United States flocked to Louisiana, Mississippi, Georgia, Tennessee and Alabama to help make the "Golden Era".

The great mansions to be detailed in the following chapters sprang up like mushrooms, along all the waterways of the state, as wealth poured into the Southland. In the far South where the French influence is noted, one finds pigeonnaires, mostly in pairs, flanking the mansions. They are as a rule delightfully planned—octagonal, round or square buildings with turreted tops crowned with attractive finials. When well located these little buildings enhance the grounds, and lend an air of the old chateaux country of France, full of charm and reminiscent of old feudal days. With the burning of these plantation homes, and after the war, reconstruction following in its wake, there was wiped out a culture that never has been replaced. With it went much of the social life and the high standard of that day uniquely Southern in America. Union Histories in their comments on the state of Southern society at that time, the era of the great fratracidal strife of the sixties, devote much space to this subject. See "The Civil War in America" by John W. Draper, published by Harpers Brothers, 1868.

The plantations in Louisiana in ante-bellum days were numerous, and as a rule the great land owners were not only wealthy, but well born, cultured and well educated, despite the fact that many uninformed writers lead one to believe differently. A goodly number of them, under the circumstances possessed a natural pulchritude inherited from a long line of distinguished ancestors. Coming from homes that were adorned with the portraits of their forebears, it was but natural that they like their parents should likewise hang their walls with family portraits, and we find in the homes of many of these old families splendidly painted portraits of themselves, as well as of past generations all beautifully portrayed by notable artists. This vast number of fine old portraits give us a fair idea of what the members of these old families looked like. For while artists like Rembrant Peale, Sir Thomas Sully, Arman, Healy, Gilbert Stuart, and many others equally as famous may have flattered their subjects, there is no doubt that many of these ancient portraits bear a resemblance to those that they are supposed to represent.

Like most important European families, the more important old Louisiana families had veritable portrait galleries in their spacious homes, both on their plantations as well as in their city homes. The result was that Louisiana is very rich in magnificent ancestral portraits, painted by the greatest artists of the day as well as older ones by the greatest painters of Europe.

In a study of old family records one finds that previous to the Civil War most of the patrician families married into their own class, and after hostilities despite the resultant impoverishment, for most part they refused to better their financial status by an alliance outside their own circle. Where we find marriages with others than Southerners it was invariably with patricians, and not with upstart new-comers.

CHAPTER I

EARLY LOUISIANA ARTISTS.

A S so many of the notable families of Louisiana in early days when their homes and plantations had been established, began to improve the furnishings of their homes. Family portraits, miniatures, daguerreotypes (later) and silhouettes began to appear in the colony along with other articles of luxury, being brought to America with the owners when they came or brought later when the families made trips abroad.

As Miss Ethel Hutson has written a splendid article on this subject covering the ground thoroughly, and for fear of omitting important parts, as so many of the families appearing in this book on the old plantations loaned family portraits, etc., to the various exhibitions she mentions. I therefore have obtained her permission to reproduce in full her article on the Isaac Delgado Museum of Art appearing in the September number of the Warrington Messenger, 1938.

ISAAC DELGADO MUSEUM OF ART.
By ETHEL HUTSON

Though New Orleans has long had a reputation as a center toward which artists tend to gravitate, and though it has a tradition dating back to the early days of its first prosperity,—when sugar and cotton and steamboat brought wealth and encouraged luxury, of art patronage and connoisseurship, yet few of us today know much about the art which laid the foundations for this reputation and this tradition. Old families still retain handsome old portraits of their ancestors, cherish exquisite miniatures, bronze, fans, and jewelry, and recall the stories in connection with these heirlooms handed down from great-grandparents. But few recall the names of the artists who executed these works of art;

and of the dozen or so names of 19th century artists, such as Jarvis, Jouett, Sully, Bernard, Amans, Vaudechamps, Healey, Moise, Clague, Poincy, Perelli, Molinary, Wikstrom, and Buck, which are known to the general public, hardly any biographical details are available in print.

This lack the Isaac Delgado Museum of Art has undertaken to supply, with the assistance of the research workers supplied by the Works Progress Administration, who for two years and a half have been compiling lists of artists who have worked here, and securing biographical and critical data about them. Over 700 names have been listed from the earliest days—the latter part of the 18th century—down to the present time. Of these, many are so far only names, from old city directories or newspaper advertisements; but examples of the work of a good many have been found in private homes and public institutions, and this summer it was decided to try to gather together a loan collection of work done by artists working in New Orleans prior to the present century, and, with the consent of the Board of Administrators of the Delgado Museum, to display them in three upper galleries.

Beginning in July, therefore, the Delgado Art Museum Project, W. P. A., assembled some 30 examples of work done here before 1830, in one of the smaller rooms. Portraits in oil, sculpture in wood, and miniatures on ivory were arranged so that they present a picture of changes in style and costume, from the closing years of the Colonial period (1785), with scarlet-faced coats, frilled shirts, and elaborate hair-dressing, down to the simple "Directoire" modes, with white stocks, short hair, and short-waisted gowns, that came in after the turn of the century. F. Godefroid, Louis Godefroy, Louis Collas, French artists who worked here; F. Salazar, a Spanish painter; and the Americans, Wheeler, Jarvis, Jouett, Audubon, Sully, William West, are among the painters who are represented in this early group; quaint carvings in native woods by Pierre Landry lend interest by their "primitive" naivete; and miniatures by Collas, J. F. de la Vallee, Ambrose Duval, Mr. (or Mrs?) Antoine Meucci, and Mrs. J. Reynes, give a picture of the art of New Orleans in the time of our great-grandparents, more than 100 years ago.

Traditions that certain artists had painted here have been verified with care before the work was admitted to this exhibition, thus, there was doubt whether Thomas Sully was eligible, though it was known that he had a sister and a brother living in New Orleans, and that many portraits of New Orleans people bore his signature, with dates before 1830. Yet he had not been found in any directory or newspaper of the period. But Mrs. John Smyth, whose father, Thomas Sully, has lent four of the five "Sully" items in the exhibition, produced a photograph of a sketch by her famous great-grand-uncle, of "General Andrew Jackson," with the notation in the artist's handwriting "taken immediately after the battle of New Orleans,"—which is held to prove that he must have been here in 1815.

A portrait of Etienne de Bore, first Mayor of New Orleans, and "father of the sugar industry in Louisiana," lent by Miss Nina King, is of special interest, not only for its subject, but for the excellence of its executions. The artist is unknown, but it is regarded as certain that it was painted here.

August saw the opening of the long gallery with more than 40 additional examples of the work of artists who were here between 1830 and 1860—the time of New Orleans' great "boom" when money and trade and population were pouring into Louisiana and it was no uncommon thing for portraits to be ordered at prices ranging from $500 to $1000—a large sum of money in those days!

From France came such accomplished painters as Jean Joseph Vaudechamp (1770-1866), who worked here from 1820 to 1834, with a studio at 147 Royal Street; A. D. Lansot, introducer of the daguerreotype, the earliest form of photography, in this city in 1837, just seven years after its invention by Daguerre in Paris; Francisco Bernard, an exhibitor in the Salon who came at the invitation of a group of sugar planters to do their family portraits; and Alfred Boisseau, (1823-1848) who sent his Louisiana scenes of Indians and Creoles to the Salon in 1842; Ernest Ciceri, decorator of the French Opera House; Philippe Gabrielle, sculptor; Jules Lion, lithographer (1810-1866), Gaston de Pontalba, and many more.

From Italy came Dominique Canova, (1800-1868), also decorator of the French Opera House, and of the Saint Louis Hotel, who is also believed to have painted the altar-piece in the Saint Louis Cathedral; and Peter Cardelli, whose bust of "Pierre Soule" is from the collection of the Louisiana State Museum.

From Belgium came Jacques Amans (1801-1888), a most

conscientious and capable painter; whose portraits are full of personality,—especially when he painted himself, and his brother artist, Alexander Charles Jaume (1813-1858), a youth almost as handsome as Raphael!

From Germany came Peter Schmidt, (1822-1867), and François Fleischbein, of the school of Munich, who had a studio in Paris under Girodet but painted in New Orleans from 1830 to 1866. German in style, but Italian in name, was L. Lotta, a sculptor who worked here in 1842, with a studio at 67 St. Peter Street, but who also painted portraits of Mrs. Leonard Wiltz and others.

A. D. Rink was another artist, and exhibited in the Salon, but worked here from 1841 to 1856, and did a number of admirable portraits and miniatures.

Artists who came here from other parts of America during this period were many. John Vanderlyn of New York, Chester Harding of Massachusetts (1792-1866), Henry Byrd, James Henry Beard (1814-1867), of Buffalo, N. Y., Stephen Williams Shaw of Vermont (1817-1900), G. P. A. Healy of Boston (1813-1894), Benjamin Franklin Reinhart, N. A., of Pennsylvania (1829-1885), and many more.

Theodore Sydney Moise (1806-1883), was born in Charleston, S. C., and came here in 1836, to paint many noted men, women and horses! For he was noted for his ability to make spirited likeness of a favorite racer or war-horse. With Amans, he made a likeness of General Jackson and his charger in the City Hall which won a $1000 prize in 1844.

But New Orleans had her own artists at this time, too. Foremost among these was Richard Clague, who was born here in 1821, and died about 1874. Landscapes showing the typical live-oaks, the bayous, cattle and horses and hogs and other farm surroundings were done by Clague with artistic insight and skill, and that he was also a portrait painter of distinction is shown by his own self-portrait, dedicated "A Ma Chère Grand Mère" and signed "R. Clague, 1850", which is one of the many unique items lent by the Louisiana State Museum. In addition, the Delgado Museum possesses Clague's own "Sketch-Book", in which he recorded sights in Morocco, Algiers and other foreign places visited when he went abroad to study under Ernest Herbert and in the Ecole des Beaux Arts, and also, on the reverse pages, scenes on the Gulf Coast done after his return. This was given to the Museum some years ago by the late S. A. Trufant, a member of the Board of Administrators.

Another New Orleans-born painter was William H. Baker, (1825-1875), who studied here, became associated with E. Wood Perry, and became a successful portrait painter. He went to New York in 1855, helped organize the free Schools of Design of Brooklyn Art Association, and in 1872 was appointed head of those schools. Jules Hudson, an octoroon, and a "free man of color", was another native New Orleans artist of this period. His self-portrait shows pronounced Jewish as well as negroid characters. He was a pupil of Abel de Pujol in Paris, and on his return to New Orleans in 1821, taught art as well as painting portraits and miniatures, George D. Coulon being one of his pupils!

THE ART ASSOCIATION OF NEW ORLEANS

By ETHEL HUTSON
Secretary to President of Artist Association. New Orleans, La.

The Art Association of New Orleans was formed by the merger of two organizations in 1904. The Artists' Association of New Orleans, which held its First Annual Exhibition at Nos. 51 and 55 Camp Street in the State National Bank Building, (presumably in 1887, as the Eleventh Annual Exhibition, the first one which had a date on its catalogue, as far as we have been able to find out, was held in March, 1897) was the oldest of these. The second was the Arts and Exhibitions Club founded in 1901, with Judge William Wirt Howe as President. He served for two years, and on his death in 1903 was succeeded by Mr. Gustaf R. Westfeldt, who was serving as President when the merger took place between the Artists' Association and the Arts and Exhibitions Club, and when the name of "The Art Association of New Orleans" was thus formally adopted. He was thus the first president of the new organization.

Records of the Artists' Association so far found do not show who the early presidents were: in 1897, William Woodward is given as president, but the date of the foundation of that body is given in some records as 1885, and it is likely that both Andres Molinary and B. A. Wikstrom served in that capacity previously.

THE GANGLIONICS AND ART ASSOCIATION.

By KATE MONROE WESTFELDT

It was early in the 90's that a group of cultured people, men and women, organized a club known as the Ganglionics among whose members were Miss Grace and Nan King, Prof. and Mrs. John Ficklen, (co-author with Miss Grace King of a History of Louisiana). Dr. and Mrs. Sharp, afterwards President of Tulane University, Mr. and Mrs. Clarence Low, Dr. and Mrs. Benjamin Smith, (noted mathematician), Dr. and Mrs. Ellsworth Woodward, Prof. Orr, Mr. and Mrs. Gustaf Westfeldt I, Major Harrod, Mr. and Mrs. Patrick Westfeldt; Mrs. Gertrude Robert Smith, Miss Mary G. Sherer (Newcomb Crowd) and several others, for the discussion of things Literary and Artistic.

Out of this group in conjunction with the leading artists of the city and those deeply interested in the future of art, emanated the nucleus of the New Orleans Artist Association which surplanted the original group that had organized the Art Union the first association of Artists and those interested in Art to form as a body in the state of Louisiana. Mr. Gustaf Westfeldt I became the first president of the new Artist Association which replaced the old Art Union which dissolved during an era of great depression in Louisiana.

Mr. Alfred Penn became the treasurer, succeeded by Major Harrod, Ellsworth Woodward, Hunt Henderson, etc.

Mr. Samuel Delgado, a bachelor, and his brother Mr. Isaac Delgado were wealthy sugar merchants and having no heirs were anxious to leave some lasting contribution to this city. (Andres Molinary, artist who had painted some portraits for the Delgado family, learning that Mr. Delgado contemplated leaving money for an Art Museum for this city, having been broached on the subject by Mr. Gustaf Westfeldt I, was worried what to do with the contents (art objects) in his beautiful home. Mr. Molinary told him to build the museum during his lifetime, so he would know that his wishes were carried out as he wished them to be.

After a conference with Mr. Westfeldt and other members of the group that had urged him to leave money for the Art Gallery he decided to have it built while he still lived. Mr. P. A.

Lelong who was then a prominent member of the Directors of the City Park was greatly instrumental in getting the Art Gallery for its present location instead of its being placed in Audubon Park, as well as one who urged the gift to the city by the Delgados.

ART IN NEW ORLEANS
Andres Molinary
1872 - 1915

Although removed by death from Art Circles in New Orleans for the past twenty-four years, the strong vibrant figure and cheerful personality of Andrés Molinary, still stands undimmed in his home by adoption.

Born in Gibraltar, November 2nd, 1847, of an Italian father and a Spanish mother, his parents had distinctly other views for his future than that of the palette.

His father and older brothers were in command of the department supplying the Military with uniforms, and it was hoped that, after graduating from the Academy in Gibraltar, he would enter the School of Engineering there, and prepare for a Military career.

He, however, had been ambitious to be an artist from early boyhood, even at school, being often censured for making drawings of his class-mates on the margins of his books instead of studying what was in them.

Finally, after many heated family sessions, pro and con, ending always, in his determination to learn to paint—and particularly, after winning a competitive scholarship to the San Lucas Academy in Rome.

Then, it was decided to let him have his way. He studied there under Vallas and Alvery, later, at the Academy of Seville. Fortuny was among the students and they became fast friends. With Escault, Reginald and Delageau, happy days were spent sketching scenes filled with brilliant sunlight, going into East Africa and Morocco and thereabouts.

After a while, Gibraltar called him back. While there, a letter came from America—from his mother's brother, Mr. John Brunasso, of the Spanish importing firm of Brunasso & Fatjo, conducting business in New Orleans.

Mr. Brunasso, having heard from his sister of affairs at

home, thought perhaps to help matters by inviting the young man to visit him in America, hoping to interest him in business with the firm. This was about 1872.

Molinary accepted—and landing at New York, spent sometime there—finally came to New Orleans.

Office work did not make a great appeal, but it was agreed that it be tried out—though he was often missing from his desk, and when sought for, would be found far up in the storage warehouse, where he had rigged up his easel among the boxes and barrels, painting away, unconscious of the lapse of time or the entries and bills below.

Finally, to his great delight—he was dismissed. His uncle, thinking that Art was all he was fit for anyway. Then he opened a small studio on Camp street. Later, he took a larger one, left vacant by the death of Julio. Young and gay, he soon drew an artistic circle about him. Here, they came for talk and criticism. The first Art Club was formed—"The Cup and Saucer Club", gaining its title from the necessity of each member bringing a cup and saucer—when the membership grew beyond bounds.

Here came the Bakers, Page and Marion, Mary Ashley Townsend, Catherine Cole, George Cable. Cora Townsend, Livingston and many others not remembered, who came regularly or just dropped in. Molinary made the tea and it was good tea, flavored with reminiscences of many lands.

After this he was called to Mexico and Central America to paint some portraits, and remained there almost a year, doing both oil painting and crayon, finding everything very agreeable because of his Spanish affiliations. The Art Spirit had spent itself by the time he returned so he started afresh, and in a few months the Art Union began to be talked about. This was followed by the Art Association which still lives, and thrives mightily under the care of a large membership, with exhibitions in the Delgado Museum. It was his greatest pleasure to spend each Sunday morning looking over the various paintings and chatting with friends. He had almost a paternal feeling for the Museum, for it was while painting the portraits of the Delgados, uncle and nephew, for the Delgado Memorial Hospital, that the subject was broached, of what would ultimately become of all the many objects of Art contained in the Mansion on Philip street? Endow a Museum and reserve a large space for your beautiful things, was the answer—and the thought grew.

Many portraits were painted at this time, some for organizations, some as memorials—Judges for the Court Building—Sugar planters for their meeting hall—Mayors for the City Hall—Doctors for Hospitals—Governors for the Cabildo—donors of Memorial buildings. Art was in the ascendency.

Molinary was his own model on two occasions, with the aid of a looking-glass. As he said to his wife, "It is great, when the painter is ready to paint, the model is always in the mood to pose."

He also made a wonderful thing of his portrait of Perelli, the Sculptor and painter of game and fish. The Perelli hangs in the museum, as does his own portrait; the latter, a gift to the Museum from his wife, who was first his student, then assistant, and towards the end, as his health failed, finished many commissions and painted outright many others, and still goes on. A prized possession, is a portrait of Mrs. Molinary in an old fashioned Gown, painted many years ago by her husband as an exhibition piece, while she was still Marie Seebold.

One of the outstanding examples is the portrait of Mayor Mims, of Atlanta. Other portraits that gave great pleasure in the doing were of the Hill family of Port Allen. Two were painted for the Hill Memorial Library in Baton Rouge, three others were also painted and are in the homes of the family, on the plantation at Port Allen. Mrs. Thos. J. Semmes, widow of the Jurist, ordered six portraits of her husband to give as memorials to various institutions. Everywhere one finds examples of his brush.

Following is a list of prominent Louisianians painted by Andres Molinary:

Gov. W. C. C. Claiborne, Gov. Jacques Villere, Gov. O'Reilly, Gov. Veudreuil, Gov. Antonio de Ulloa, Gov. Estavan Miro, Gov. Barnado de Galvez, in State Museum, N. O.; Judge Nicholas Henry Rightor, Judge Pierre Adolph Rost, Judge Robert Hardin Marr, Judge Albert Vories, Judge Alexander McKensie Buchannon, Judge Felix Pierre Poche, Judge Thomas J. Semmes, Chief Justice Thomas Merrick, McC. Hyman, Clerk of Supreme Court of Louisiana; Wm. J. Behan, John Fitzpatrick, Mayors of New Orleans; Dr. Albert B. Miles, Dr. Picard, Alexander Hutchison, Dr. Stanford Chaille, in Charity Hospital; John Hill of Port Allen, La., (full

A CREOLE BELLE — A portrait by Francisco
Bernard, 4x5 feet. From the Seebold Collection,
now in the Art Collection of the Rice Institute,
Houston, Texas—Donated by the Seebolds.

MRS. ANDRES MOLINARY neé MARIE MADELINE SEEBOLD.
(Painted by Andres Molinary.)

A Sketching Party at Mandeville, in the early days of the Artist Association of New Orleans. Standing—Viva Saxon, Edward Shields, Marie Seebold (Mrs. A. Molinary), Mr. Lewis, Mrs. Edward Shields, Charles W. Boyle, Andrew Saxton. Sitting—Walter L. Saxon, Mrs. W. L. Saxon, Margaret Coles, Andres Molinary.

Andres Molinary in his studio; portrait of his mother on the easel, large portrait of the late Mrs. Henry P. Dart behind the artist.

"I Came from a Rock, Place a Rock
on My Grave."

length) ; John Hill, Jr., Port Allen, La., Memorial Library, Louisiana State University, Baton Rouge, La. Dr. B. M. Palmer, Peter Helwege, W. O. Hart, J. M. Quintero, J. B. Sinnott, C. E. Chapman, C. V. Moore, E. J. Gay, S. O. Thomas, W. E. Seebold, Lawrence Fabacher, Mr. and Mrs. John Hill, Sr., Mr. John Hill, in possession of family, Port Allen, La.; Mrs. H. P. Dart, Mrs. Lamar Quintero, Mrs. Durant Da Ponte, Mrs. W. O. Hart, Mrs. W. E. Seebold, Miss Alice Bloomfield, Miss Cora Townsend, Miss Marie Seebold, Mrs. Geromina Molinary, the artist's mother.

THE GRAVE OF MOLINARY

By LILITA LEVER YOUNGE

"Let a staunch rock be hewn from the mountains, to lie
At my head", quote the Artist, and sighed,
For the splendor of mountain-tops, piercing the sky,
Was the vision he glimpsed ere he died,
Who had loved the high places where God seems to walk
And commune with His likeness in clay,
And the angels and archangels silently stalk,
In the primeval hush of the day.

So they fetched him the boulder to lie at his head,
From the mountains he loved; and they came
To the place where he bides, in the House of the Dead,
And they carved on a tablet his name.
And they left Molinary to sleep, 'neath the stone,
That slumber unbroken, profound,
In his bed in the earth, with green ivy o'ergrown,
And the symbols of death all around.

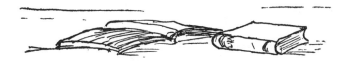

Chapter II

HONORABLE THOMAS J. SEMMES.

A born aristocrat of the old school, as he grew older and noted the vast changes that had taken place during his lifetime, he often talked of ante-bellum days, of the life he knew and loved so well. To quote a few remarks of this loved advisor and jurist, who had reached the pinnacle of his profession as President of the American Bar Association: "No life could be like the life of those old days. The South had an element in its society—a landed gentry —which afforded ample opportunity for extraordinary culture, elevated the standard of scholarship in the section and emancipated social intercourse, while it established schools of individual refinement. We had a vast agricultural country, and the pursuit of agriculture in the South had its fixed features."

Having in his home the old negro mammy that had nursed his wife when she was a little child, and in turn nursed his own children as they arrived, notwithstanding several other servants sought that privilege, Judge Semmes, like all true southerners accustomed to slaves in their households, was bound by a strong tie to this faithful old servant, a reminder of the vanished glory of another time. Firmly believing that no life was like that of the life of a cultured wealthy planter's family and no one but the southern child that had experienced the kind and thoughtful care of an old negro mammy could appreciate the bond of sympathy which then often united the races, he said: "The thought of wounding the feelings of that faithful devoted old woman was appalling, even to outsiders much less a member or employee of this household."

In early days before the days of automobiles, even though all households of pretentions maintained their own carriages, street cars were used generally. It was no uncommon thing to see Mrs. Semmes, or other Southern ladies of her class give their old negro mammies their seats in the car if crowded, and stand, letting the faithful old black women make themselves comfortable with the bundles on their laps. In those days the faithful old negro women followed their mistresses closely when shopping—a sight one no longer witnesses in the South, the faithful old souls having all passed away. At Mammy's death the Semmes boys acted as pall bearers for the faithful old woman, and genuine sadness cast a gloom over the household for a long period. Her portrait hung in Judge Semmes' library and he always proudly pointed to it, never forgetting to extol her virtues.

"The people of the north could not understand all this, the landed gentry of the south had pursuits, their love of field sports: they were a prodigal aristocracy that dispensed their stores in constant rounds of hospitality, and gayety. The south had a rich population then, and dispensed baronial hospitality. No traveler was ever allowed to go to a tavern after he had been the guest of one of these old families, but was handed over from family to family through entire states. The holidays were celebrated by masters and slaves with feasting and music, great balls and banquets given in the old spacious mansions, while the sugar houses and cotton gins provided large areas for the banquet boards of the slaves groaning under the weight of Christmas foods in ample quantities and variety, and allowances of wines and liquor."

Dancing too followed for the slaves, from which many of our modern cabaret novelties get their origin, especially the crooning blues stepping, and questionable gyrations, which find their fountain head in the wilds of Africa among the voodoo cults.

Among the true aristocrats of the old school "There was an unwritten code of honor, but that code was so beautiful, (states Judge Semmes) that no one who called himself a gentleman would have dared to break it." The south of those days yielded to none in her love for the union, but state's rights were the most marked peculiarity of her politics, and it was this doctrine, Judge Semmes always maintained, that gave to the Union its moral dignity. Judge Semmes was a member of the convention, and was proud of the fact that he was one of the committee that drafted the secession ordinance. His wife had him bring her the pen that he used on that occasion and it has always been carefully preserved as a historical relic in the family.

The family also have a letter from Mr. Knox, father of Mrs. Semmes, who made the first loan to the Confederacy through the bank of which he was president, as testified by Mr. Memminger in a letter to the Confederate Congress, after Judge Semmes had been called in 1861 by Jefferson Davis to Montgomery to consult with him as Attorney General of the state about the suspension of specie payment by banks. In his letter Mr. Memminger, knowing that Mr. Knox also had contributed an immense sum from his plantation fund, justly praises the devotion of this patriotic gentleman.

When brides began in the presence of Judge Semmes to dilate on the magnificence of their trousseaus, in a teasing manner Judge Semmes, beaming on his lovely wife, would tell of the "beautiful outfit that Mr. Knox had given his daughter, Mrs. Semmes, when her husband was elected as a member of the Confederate Congress at Richmond, and took his seat with his colleague from Louisiana, General Edward H. Sparrow." So delighted was this ardent Confederate that a son-in-law of his should have this high honor conferred upon him, he stated that his daughter should have a trousseau befitting the wife of "a Confederate Senator."

The Semmeses occupied the Cruikshank home in Richmond, a beautiful mansion quite like that occupied by President and Mrs. Jefferson Davis (The White House of the Confederacy) and directly opposite it. In fact it was a facsimile of the one occupied by the Davis family, and Mrs. Semmes said she preferred it to its counterpart. Both were among the finest and stateliest mansions in Richmond.

The social life of the Semmes home at that time was somewhat that of the life of a European court, for until reverses began to be felt to maintain the establishment records show that the yearly expenses amounted to about one hundred thousand dollars. With ample room to house his friends, it was not long before Alexander H. Stephens of Georgia, vice-president of the Confederacy, who was a bachelor, and a close friend of the Semmeses, Mr. Garland who was later a member of President Cleveland's cabinet, and General Sparrow, colleague of Judge Semmes and close friend of the family, teased both Judge and Mrs. Semmes until they finally said they could become "their boarders". By boarders Judge Semmes meant that fine old Southern hospitality that gave all and asked nothing in return.

In speaking of running the place at the rate of one hundred

THE WHITE HOUSE OF THE CONFEDERACY

MRS. THOMAS J. SEMMES, neé MYRA
EULALIE KNOX of Knox Hall, Montgomery, Alabama. A painting by G. P.
A. Healy, noted American portrait painter. (Courtesy of Mrs. Sylvester P. Walmsley.)

thousand dollars a year, Judge Semmes used to say, "we used Confederate money, and Mrs. Semmes used to state that she sent a whole basketful of money to market in exchange for provisions. Our boarders knowing that I was not a rich man insisted in paying something which amounted to about one hundred dollars a month each. However, my father-in-law who was one of the wealthy men of the South insisted in supplying us freely with money".

In telling of old times Judge Semmes told about the wonderful supplies of provisions of all kinds that used to come to them for their Richmond table, and how they never could understand how they got through so safely for everything at that time was contraband.

He also told how bountifully their table was supplied, of their continuous series of dinner parties attended by less fortunate senators from the border states. These states were divided and fared very badly. Their people lived on the simplest of rough food, as their food supply was cut off. They had a very hard time of it, but stood it all courageously until the end.

His memory was as clear as a bell about the many happenings of those Richmond days. He recalled how the air was filled with shells and shot, filling all with terror, and despite this in order to keep up the spirits of the people, how the ladies went ahead with their entertainments to raise funds for supplies for the soldiers. He related that parties were given every night so that the boys passing through the town might have some diversion to keep up their jaded spirits. "Of how groups of handsome officers would dance the hours away at the Semmes mansion, and go forth to fight on the morrow and be buried in the evening shadow on the blood soaked battle field". There was General J. E. B. Stuart, the Rupert of the Confederacy, the dashing cavalry officer, who played charades at the home of Judge Semmes' sister, wife of an officer on President Jefferson Davis' staff, and that night left the smiling throng with a flower some pretty Richmond girl had just pinned in the lapel of his coat. The next day the news came that he had been mortally wounded at Yellow Tavern. Mr. Semmes was very fond of General Stuart and often recalled the night he saw him last, dancing and making merry with the most beautiful girls in Richmond. It was a gala night, and there were present at Mrs. Ives charade party, Mr. Jefferson

Davis, Mr. Stevens, Mr. Mallory, Judah P. Benjamin, in fact all of the cabinet officers and their wives, the representatives in Congress, justices of the Supreme Court, and so on, and General Stuart—laughing, dashing General Stuart—was the observed of all observers. He was so brilliant, so handsome and used to dash around Richmond on his noble charger with his black plumes flying in the breeze, and all the town on tip toe—to catch a sight of him. The body was brought to Richmond the following day for burial; and every eye was dimmed with tears as the military funeral of their dead General wound its way through the streets of the Confederate capitol, while the strains of "Maryland my Maryland" were his funeral dirge. "Only a few hours before," said Judge Semmes, "the stalwart soldier had been singing 'Old Joe Hooker, Will You Come Out of the Wilderness'? And now he was dead, and the world would never look upon his like again."

Judge Semmes was a close friend of Stonewall Jackson, and in speaking of this great soldier said, "his death cast a shadow on the fortunes of the Confederacy that reached to the catastrophe of the war." "Richmond refused to believe the news of his death, and could not bring itself to the realization that 'the noblest Roman of them all' had passed from life. Mrs. Semmes would not believe it, and went out to hear for herself that the terrible news was only too true. As she approached the capitol she met some soldiers carrying a covered corpse, marching with bowed heads to the notes of the muffled drum. 'Who are you carrying?' she asked with whitened lips, and the simple answer came back: 'Stonewall Jackson'." Continuing he would tell of the great General's funeral where thousands consecrated his grave with their tears.

General Robert E. Lee was a close friend of the Semmes household, and visited the family frequently. He was the ideal of Southern chivalry and truth, and his visits when in Richmond, meant a gathering of special notables. All of the great men of the day were friends of this distinguished family—Slidell, Mason, Breckenridge, Yancy and Beauregard, not forgetting Johnston. Judge Semmes often recalled the day that a special messenger from President Davis arrived announcing the death of his honored friend, General Albert Sidney Johnston, and how the eyes of strong men glistened with tears as with a sob-choked voice Jeff. Davis announced the sad news.

Warrenton Virginia, the old home of the Semmeses during these hectic days, was the scene of death and suffering. The Semmes family rendered undying service to the Confederate cause, even to turning the family homes into hospitals, and lodging and feeding the Confederate soldiers. The siege of Richmond caused the Confederate Congress to abandon their seats to shoulder guns and mount guard around Richmond. Often when seated at a banquet table and glancing round the heavily laden mahogany, Judge Semmes would tell of the siege. "For days," he said, "these volunteer soldier-senators had nothing to eat," and he would declare that the heartiest meal that he ever enjoyed was a piece of dry bread and a raw onion that he asked of an old market woman who passed the spot where he was keeping guard.

At last the surrender came, and then the greatness of his character came forth in its true light, when stripped of all his worldly possessions as was his own family and the family of his wife—everything confiscated because the entire family had been such loyal Confederates.

Being in the bad graces of the victors for his devotion to the Confederate cause, Judge Semmes was in danger of arrest. In order to obtain a pardon he left Montgomery, Alabama, where he had gone, and went with his wife to Washington, and after a five-minute interview with President Johnson a pardon was granted him. During that interview, as related by Judge Semmes the President asked him what he had done, and he replied: "All that a man could possibly do by deeds or words to promote the Confederate Cause; but the Cause having been defeated I desire to practice in peace the practise of my profession in order to support my family." The President smiling said, "Well, go to work."

Returning to New Orleans with Mrs. Semmes, he resumed practice with his old law partner, Mr. Robert Mott, the firm continuing until 1875. In 1873 he was appointed to the chair of Professor of Civil Law at the University of Louisiana, holding it until 1875, when owing to the pressure of other duties he resigned. From the time of his return to New Orleans his law practice grew by leaps and bounds. He became the head of the bar in Louisiana and his name appeared as counsel in many leading cases in Louisiana court annals. Judge Semmes' death was sudden and his funeral was one of the largest seen in the city in years. Representatives from all of the professions where brilliancy made their friendship acceptable to the friend who was leaving them forever attended. He was given full military honors due a great Confederate who had used to the full his brilliant mind in behalf of "The Cause." A guard of honor watched by the Confederate flag-draped casket as thousands marched by to get a last look at their friend, embowered in a wealth of floral tributes, all realizing that a great and good man was being taken from them. As the burial service ended, the last notes of taps sounded and proclaimed the passing of a soldier.

CHAPTER III.

NOTES OF A JOURNALIST

MR. WALTER PRICHARD, in the Louisiana Historical Quarterly of October 1938, Vol. 21, has quoted a series of articles written in 1860 by J. W. Dorr, who was connected with the New Orleans Crescent. Mr. Dorr made a trip over the state with a horse-and-buggy and reported on the condition of the state in general.

His reports are reliable, as he carried with him letters of introduction and all the necessary credentials to obtain accurate information on the subjects of which he has written. His pen pictures convey a true picture of the plantation country of the era, for as yet the ruin that was soon to destroy most of this magnificence had not disturbed its beauty or tranquility. Believing that his simple descriptions are far more convincing than any report of its former beauty written after hostilities, I have quoted at length from Mr. Prichard's article.

NUMBER 1. UP THE COAST.

There are many in New Orleans who have lived there many more years than your correspondent, who have a very poor idea as to what the "coast" is. They fancy they have seen it from the deck of steamers plying on the river, but they are mistaken. They have only glimpses of the country and dissolving views of the tops of houses behind the high levee as they dashed past. To see and appreciate this Acadian land they should be behind a good horse and rattle along the levee road, which is now as smooth as the New Canal Shell Road. A constant succession of wealthy estates keep the interest alive, for there are few of them that will not repay pausing to admire. Splendid old homesteads dot the road at the distance of a quarter of a mile apart, the out buildings, negro quarters, etc., forming at each a considerable village, so that the road up the coast is almost like a street of a vast, thinly built city.

The plantations having a narrow front on the river and running far back, the homes are thus brought close together and render the levee road a suburban avenue unequalled in the world, bordered on one side, as it is, by the unequalled river of the world, the clustering steamers and other crafts on which give an animated variety to the changeful scenery.

It is no sort of use for me to attempt to describe any of the splendid residences of the princely planters, for during yesterday's journey I passed dozens, each worthy of more than a passing notice. All that tasteful architecture, ornamental shrubbery and magnificent moss-hung trees can do towards the beautifying of the sugar planter's residences in Jefferson and St. Charles Parishes as far as I have been, is effected. The farther I go from the city, the more costly, elaborate and extensive the planter's houses seem to be. Seven or eight miles above the city the estates begin to show the more striking evidences of wealth and refined occupancy, though there are a few fine places in the lower part of Jefferson Parish.

Along the pathway of the wide river, a constant current of cool air pours above its rolling tide below, and thus the temperature is kept comfortable in the warmest season. A continual draft is created by the cool air of the river rushing across the banks to supply the heated interior.

There are a large number of fine estates in St. John the Baptist parish as "Belle Point", place of A. Deslonde, "Mount Airy", owned by Joseph LeBourgeois, "Esperance", place of Dr. Loughborough, and others not inferior, if not dignified with names. The planters, constituting a staple population of the parish, are almost to a man, of the old Creole type gentleman, hospitable, chivalrous and high spirited. The Anglo-Americans are few.

NUMBER 2. PARISH OF ST. JAMES.

But let them travel inside the levee, and through this paradisacal climax of luxurious plantation rurality, and if they do not admire the aspects of the scenery—the splendid villa-like or castle-like mansions of the planters, the cheerful and comfortable villages of negro houses, the magnificent old trees with their wavy glory of moss, the beautiful gardens filled with rarest shrubs and plants, the affluent vegetation of the broad fields, the abundant greenery with which lavish nature coats every inch of this prolific soil.

In this manner throughout his entire trip about the state he describes the glory and magnificence of it all—the immense wealth, the endless acres under cultivation—now nearly all gone.

Many hundreds of these handsome old mansions and splendid sugar-houses and cotton gins fringed the banks of rivers and bayous, and made easy targets for the gun-boats of the Federal fleet after the fall of New Orleans.

A book printed many years ago, and recently reprinted, "Forty Years of American Life 1821 - 1861", tells about the plantation country of Louisiana in minute detail. The writer tells of how, after a fifteen-day trip, their steamer at last came to the plantation country of Louisiana. He tells what a pleasant surprise it was to him to find himself in a land, to use his own words "with enchanting scenes" which he cannot find words to adequately describe. He tells how for miles lining both banks could be seen the magnificent plantation homes with their splendid gardens, and beyond and between the manor houses and the cane fields the slave quarters. He compares the waving sugar cane to a vast green ocean, bright as an emerald. He tells how when the steamer stopped for wood he got out and saw at close range the glorious plantation gardens where flowers and fruit of every description were within reach of all who chose to pluck them. With its mild climate the whole country was a veritable garden of Eden.

From his rhapsody brought on by so much beauty he roused himself to note that he was in a Creole land where little but French was heard, and where even the negro slaves driving the cane carts joked and laughed as they worked. Here he found the fire wood brought down as driftwood by the great river which seemed to lay it at the planter's door. He seemed delighted with everything that he saw—the planter that appeared as if created especially for his work of being a kind and careful master, and the darkies, as if made to drive the mules, and as for the mules they too seemed designed by nature to be handled by their dusky drivers. He came from the North, but disagreed with the people of his land. He believed that any change that might be made would be a grave mistake. Seeing their comfortable little cabin homes, their gardens, poultry pens, and realizing that all responsibility was assumed by the planters, he thought it an ideal existence.

CHAPTER IV

THE ST. GEME PLANTATION.

The St. Geme plantation, an ancient one in Louisiana, occupied the site of the present Edgewood Park on Gentilly Avenue in New Orleans, and the family a wealthy as well as aristocratic one, who owned it had a large "early type" plantation residence and which was a most important social center in old plantation days.

The first one of the name of St. Geme to come to Louisiana was Chevalier Baron Henry de St. Geme who traced his family back to the year 1500. At New Orleans he married Madame (widow) Jeane Francois Dreux, nee Delmas, of the patrician families of Dreux and Delmas. A son, named for his father and who later made his home in the family chateau de Barbazin in France, married Melle. Eugenie de Puech, daughter of Louis de Puech and Althee D'Aquin of New Orleans.

The de Puech family were prominent Huguenots who had come to America and located in Boston, Mass., after the Revocation of the Edict of Nantes. The family later became planters in San Domingo, where they owned immense plantations. However, it was not long before the negro uprisings in the Islands caused the family to flee from that place. Going to Philadelphia Louis de Puech and his wife and their children were registered at the French Consulate as subjects of France, where the children were later sent to be educated. In 1878 the revolution in France which overthrew the Republican Government and substituted in its place Louis Philippe as Citizen King, at which time Ernest de Puech, a student at the Ecole de St. Cyr, returned to New Orleans and later became one of the leading citizens of the city. Always alert to matters pertaining to the growth of the community, and prominent in social activities, he became the organizer and was made President of the New Orleans Cotton Exchange. At that time New Orleans was becoming the greatest cotton port in the world. In the long list of prominent citizens of this state few have exceeded him in ability as an executive. All his actions brought honor, and credit to his state. He was among the first to enlist at the outbreak of the Civil War, and as a Major in the Garde D'Orleans, was in the thickest of the fighting. In later years

MRS. SYLVESTER P. WALMSLEY, Sr., neé MISS MYRA E.
SEMMES, daughter of Mr. and Mrs. Thomas J. Semmes, in
her wedding dress.

Knox Hall, Montgomery, Alabama. Ancestral home of the Knox, Semmes, Walmsley and Raslett families.

he was a strong friend of the soldiers of the "Lost Cause". At his death he was sincerely mourned by the city for which he had done so much, and given the funeral of an honored soldier and citizen. The floral tributes were magnificent and his casket laid in state draped with a Confederate flag. His funeral was immense, with a large number of Confederate soldiers and a guard of honor. As taps were sounded all realized that a man of unusual ability had been taken from their midst.

CHAPTER V.

THE OLD HURST PLANTATION HOME—NOW THE STAUFFER FAMILY HOME, METAIRIE LANE.

A visit to a new suburban section of New Orleans, a fashionable development among magnificent oak trees named Metairie Lane, brings one to a splendid old plantation home of unusual beauty.

The home attracts by the charm of its setting, and the purity of its architectural lines and detail, all of which have the appearance of being quite old but carefully cared for. The house was originally built in Hurstville, an early Louisiana settlement above what was then the city of New Orleans, for the Hurst Family. The old plantation house was transplanted to its new site, and so carefully and perfectly has the work been done, that the mellow time stained brickwork of the foundations and chimneys lead one to believe that the old place has stood in its present location a century. The owner, Mrs. I. H. Stauffer wished for the plantation type of country home befitting the beautiful oak grove she owned. This lady had often driven past the old Hurst house long for sale and wished that it could be moved to a spot among her beautiful oaks.

The old Hurst house was finally purchased and when the required photographs, drawings, measurements, notations and all necessary data taken, the house was dismantled and moved piece by piece. The architects (Koch and Armstrong) in rebuilding achieved splendid results. For the house outside and inside in its charming new setting has the appearance of having been originally built on this site in 1830, the date it was constructed in Hurstville. The Patina of time has truly been preserved, and nature coming to the aid of the architects has in the shady damp places of the basement deposited a rich velvety green mould which truly completes the illusion of great age. As one strolls about the walks close to the house, on all sides are evidences that would readily mislead the observer were he not aware that it is an old house that has been rebuilt. Old brick walks, curbing, drains and a hundred little points insignificant in themselves, as a whole create in this instance a work of perfection.

The original owner for whom the house was built, having accumulated an immense fortune at the very beginning of the boom days of the plantation era of Louisiana, had this beautiful home built, and for reasons that the writer has been unable to learn lost his fortune a few years later. The plantation as it is shown on maps of that era joined Rickerville which lay to the South of Hurstville, its Northern boundary being Bloomingdale. Foucher, and Greenville following in succession as one drove South on the River Road. As the city grew the Hurst plantation, which had passed into other hands, as was usually the case at that date, was cut up into city blocks. With the rapidly growing city spreading out in all directions the vast sugar plantation became a thing of the past. However, the splendid old home which fronted the river some distance back from the river-road was kept intact, with it the rest of the land which formed the city block. The house became the home of a family who wanted a large home in the new residential area with a vineyard and garden.

Many years ago Casper Wild, the noted grape culturist who also had a fine vineyard corner of Bellcastle and Magazine Sts., New Orleans, had charge of the old Hurst vineyard. He specialized in fine white wine made from grapes grown in his own and on the old Hurst place. Joseph Jefferson, the famous actor and a close friend of my father's, frequently visited Casper Wild and sampled his vintages. The artist actor also painted a portrait of the old vine culturist.

As the years passed the neighborhood declined, the old house became a tenement house and was beginning to fall into ruin when purchased by Mrs. Stauffer.

At the time that the Hurst plantation was cut up into city blocks, one of the streets was called Hurst, after the planter, another named Arabella, and still another Eleanor, for the planter's daughters.

When the house was built in 1832 the Greek Revival type of architecture was at its height and had already gained a strong foothold in the South, and the greatest of care was displayed in the perfection of the details of the mansions being built. Such was the case quite evidently with the Hurst plantation home. As one notes the beauty of the ornamentation, mouldings, and interior woodwork they afford an architectural charm that is unique. The house is unusual in many particulars, deviating just sufficiently to make it an example of unusually good architecture of that type of plantation home. The body of the house was constructed of brick with heavy walls painted white on the outside. All of the woodwork above the columned cap line including the gables was painted white to match. On the cornice beautifully executed by the wood carver, is a pedimented frieze with tryglyphs, above the white columns also of choice cypress of the Greek fluted design.

The house is the raised basement type, having a typical stairway with broad easy treads easy of ascent, leading up to the wide gallery surrounding the house. The facade shows a central hall entrance doorway quite wide with side lights and panels below. The heavy knocker is attached a little below the upper second panel, a low fan light surmounting all. A heavy pure Greek cornice with dentils recessed over the door opening, supported by fluted Doric columns on either side of side lights, completes a most inviting appearing entrance. A paneled casement frames the door showing the thickness of the brick work. Latticed blinds are fitted to all of the long windows, dormers also where we find the central dormers above the entrance doorway, and each of the others above a column, showing careful spacing so that the view from the windows below is not blocked by the column shafts.

In the large arched windows of the gables a somewhat similar arrangement of columns and entablature is noted as is found about the main entrance. Here we find recessed spaces on the cornice above the two side lights, as well as above the central larger window. In this place also are found Ionic pilasters on the outside of the side lights and Ionic columns on the inner side, and bars instead of fan ribs over all. Within, one is greeted with the kind of rooms and finish one might anticipate from such an inviting exterior. Here we find doors with handsome paneled casements, the frames with facings of a fluted design, having beautifully carved corner blocks, center ornaments and acanthus-leaf swirls which twine the fluting. All of this is carved with skill in a delicate manner and forms a most charming finish, not over-elaborate, as one might suppose, but quite elegant and distinctive. Below some of the shorter side windows cabinets with paneled doors have been fitted, and high baseboarding with a design of fluted mouldings completes a most satisfactory woodwork planning. An arched doorway quite wide with Ionic pilasters divides the hallway from the spacious drawing-room which overlooks the beautiful garden in the rear. At the east end of this spacious room is a splendid black marble mantel surmounted by a handsome antique mirror having a gilt frame which reflects many of the choice family heirlooms to be found here. The long French windows open onto the wide rear porch with an inviting vista in every direction, for on all sides are masses of fragrant blooming plants and attractive lawns of the immense garden.

This large drawing-room like the other leading rooms of the house has the beautifully carved acanthus scrolls twining the fluting of door and window frames.

It is altogether a charming salon, restful and interesting. Handsome pieces of choice antique furniture, ancestral portraits painted by celebrated artists, rare pieces of bronze and beautiful bric-a-brac, with attractive window drapes and rugs create an ante-bellum setting of great allure. The effect of spaciousness prevails, for the large dining-room almost the same size owing to the interior plan, connects with this drawing-room, both of them being quite light and sunny. This dining-room, the scene of many notable banquets, is equally as handsome in its appointments, having the same attractive wood-work. The dining-room furniture is of mahogany of the Adam period, and the mirror-like waxened surface tops of buffet and dining table reflects the choice examples of rare old family silver. More portraits by celebrated artists, antique crystal and chinaware, complete an unusually charming ensemble. Tucked away in an alcove is a winding stairway which leads to the rooms above. A living-room on the left of the wide hallway as you enter the main door-way contains much of interest, showing a discriminating taste and rare judgment in the selection of its furnishings which are for most part heirlooms. The bed-rooms too are all of great interest with typical plantation pieces from the ateliers of Mallard and Signorette.

The original old Stauffer mansion, which stood on the present site of the Orpheum Theatre, was a splendid spacious three-storied brick structure with a high raised basement. In this part of the Stauffer home at Metairie Lane all of the brickwork is of the same heavy construction as was found in the original structure, having a solid brick wall in the front of the basement with lunettes fitted with iron grilles. The doors are found on the sides of its walls.

On the original site the basement plan contained dungeons to imprison unruly slaves. Iron barred openings permitted air and light, and deeply imbedded in the brickwork was found remnants of chained manacles and other instruments of punishment to be used when vicious slaves planned murder, mutiny or unusual trouble on the plantation. These gruesome finds many years ago gave this old plantation house the reputation of being haunted, and another old plantation manor not far away, the old de la Chaise home, bore the same reputation. Here, too, it was due to a discovery of the same sort in the basement. The newspapers of that era stated that these dungeons were a necessity at the date these plantation homes were erected. They were built in order to keep the negroes of the plantation cowered as well as for punishment. Plantation history is replete with the plottings and crimes of unruly slaves.

The murder of a neighboring planter by a petted slave, and the massacre of the whites during the San Domingo slave uprisings were still fresh in the memories of the Louisiana planters when the Hurst plantation home was originally built. In the new plan of the Metairie Lane house, the dungeons were eliminated, culinary and service departments being established in this part of the building. Originally, as in most plantation houses, the kitchen and service rooms were in a separate building. This out-building was omitted in the new plan and the space added to the garden grounds.

To return to the old Stauffer home in what was then known as Dryades Street, New Orleans, now called University Place. This old mansion was the scene of some of the most noted social events of New Orleans of its era, and the neighborhood contained the homes of distinguished families. It remained a fine residential section until some thirty -five years ago, when along with the first block on the South side of Rampart it became a business area.

The garden plan of the Metairie Lane house of the Stauffer family, planned so as to be typical of similar plantation places has many of the details that go to complete such a setting. Hedges of Louis Philippe roses, jasmine, camellias and the usual plantation shrubbery to be found in plantation gardens are found here. The beautiful grounds with the century old oaks gave the opportunity to accomplish such delightful results. The splendid collection of artistic treasures, paintings, antique furniture and furnishings from the old Stauffer home in town now fill these rooms. It is as of old one of the most important social centers in New Orleans.

Richard Taylor, son of President Zachary Taylor, married Myrthe, youngest daughter of Aglaé and Michel Douradou Bringier of the wealthy aristocratic plantation family of St. James Parish, Louisiana. Richard Taylor during the Civil War was known as the dashing Dick Taylor. "Following the battle of Baton Rouge during the Civil War, he was appointed commander of the District of Louisiana having already served with distinction in Virginia. His campaign in Upper Louisiana and on Red River was one of the brilliant military episodes of the Confederate War."

After the close of the war he returned to New Orleans and lived in the old Bringier home in Melpomene Street. He had three daughters; one of them Bettie, married Walter R. Stauffer; her sister, Myrthe, married Isaac H. Stauffer—sons of the prominent and wealthy merchant and philanthropist Isaac Stauffer, of New Orleans. The children of both sisters still proudly maintain the prestige of their blood and name in New Orleans. Louisette, the eldest daughter, died unmarried.

CHAPTER VI.
BAYOU ST. JOHN AREA.
THE DUCAYET PLANTATION HOME

Originally built for a planter of that name who with his family occupied the place for many years, the Ducayet house shows its century of age in a pleasing manner. It is in good condition, and the colors of the old house have been toned down to blend with the foliage which shade its spacious front and rear grounds.

Several tall palms also add a tropical touch to its West Indian type of architecture, as also does the outside stairway on the up-town side of the house that leads to the broad encircling gallery above. Its architectural details are perhaps not as pretentious as some of the other similar places along the Bayou, but there is much room in its pretty garden, and the grounds enhance the charm of the place. Therefore its rivals do not diminish its attractiveness by comparison.

During the occupancy by the original owner it was a social center, and a show place, as the family owned many beautiful things in the way of antiques and art objects. Later the family of the distinguished Louisiana Judge John L. Tissot, purchased the place. The banquets given by this family to important members of the bar and their friends formed noted gatherings and were among the social events of each season.

Like the Ducayets the Tissots were great collectors of beautiful things. So much so was this the case with Judge Tissot, that in many a private collection in this state today the owners point with pride to a number of old articles in their collection as having come from the Tissot collection.

The rooms, divided by spacious hallways, lead to a rear porch. The ground floor rooms have been converted into living quarters —forming living-room, dining-room and library, all of which have been fitted with black marble mantels. Upstairs, the original

The Old Hurst Plantation Home—now the Stauffer family home, Metairie Lane, New Orleans.—Rebuilt by Koch & Armstrong.

The old plantation home of the Ducayet family, Bayou St. John, New Orleans.

Old plantation home of the Blanc family, Bayou St. John.

The old Spanish Customhouse, Bayou St. John.
Plantation home of Mrs. Helen Pitkin Schertz.

living rooms were converted into sleeping quarters, and have white marble mantels and interesting plaster work.

The gallery plan of the house shows brick-paved lower galleries and an encircling wide gallery resting on circular solid brick plaster-covered Doric columns with colonette above the gallery line supporting the roof.

An old photograph of the place shows it as it appeard before the present high brick wall in front enclosed the place. A light wood and metal fence permitted a view of the lower front of the house and garden, and the original wooden balustrade surrounds the gallery. The place now belongs to the Catholic Church that owns the adjoining villa, the fence screen that closes off the view of the yard having been put up lately.

THE OLD BLANC PLANTATION HOME

This splendid old residence is of a more imposing type of the same style of architecture, and is a delightful example of the plantation houses of this period. Its front enclosure, part heavy masonry, half wood paling fence, is at once distinctive, and makes of its large grounds an arresting vista when viewed from across the bayou. The history of the place is that of the distinguished family whose descendants reside in New Orleans proper, for the property was willed by a member of the family to a religious order, on condition that at no time should the architecture be changed, thus assuring to posterity the charming view we have today.

THE SCHERTZ VILLA, 1300 MOSS STREET, BAYOU ST. JOHN.

SAID TO BE THE ANCIENT SPANISH CUSTOMHOUSE

The old plantation house which later became a customhouse, where the inspection of goods coming to New Orleans by way of Lake Pontchartrain took place, laid empty for many years and gradually fell into partial ruin. Its distinctive architecture finally attracted the attention of the present owner. The date of its construction was somewhere between 1721 and 1734 (according to the Department of the Interior, Washington, D. C.), making it the oldest house on Bayou St. John. It still maintains its dignity and offers shelter as in old plantation days when it was the property of a Creole family by the name of Roux.

Originally, according to the owner, the ground floor was laid with slabs of pink marble, and the exposed beams are the original hand-adzed cypress ones placed there 150 years ago. Slave-made brick was used mostly in the construction, the walls being two feet thick; the lower floor finished with stucco while as was commonly done at that time weather-boards were used over the brick (the red brick being soft and easily eroded) as a protection. The pink marble slabs were found when the house was being restored, some of them still below the wooden floor that had been placed above them at a later date.

The free-growing fiscus repens vine fairly blankets the structure which is set in a formal garden of the old plantation type. Here one finds magnolia fuscata, hollyhocks, dahlias, iris, a large variety of roses, geraniums, hydrangeas, sweet olive, day lilies, myrtles, and in autumn, a riot of chrysanthemums of many hues. There are two fountains—gold-fish pools with flowering lilies and lotus blooms, cypress plants and the delicate bloom of 'arrow heads".

The hardware was all original and hand-made by slave labor at the date of erection of the house. It comprises 'H' hinges, great bolts on batten doors and windows. Oval brass knobs were imported from France and attached to the hand-made iron work. "Jalousies" or quaint mullioned transoms supply the interior with daylight. Wisteria and a mass of honeysuckle vines give shade on loggias. One of the traditions of the house is that Jean Lafitte made there his proffer of aid to the American army just before the Battle of New Orleans (Jan. 8th, 1815), submitting to a grilling interview with General Andrew Jackson and the territorial governor, Claiborne, who distrusted the sincerity of the buccaneer. Governor Miro, under the Spanish domination, used the house as a duana or customhouse, as Bayou St. John was the main artery for traffic into the city. Contrabandistas were incarcerated in a small cell with a brick floor and with a slit a few inches wide in the outer wall protected by a bar of heavy iron. A story is also told that Lafitte secreted a treasure behind a heavy mantel-piece made of mahogany wood in an upper room, and this matches exactly an old marble one there now stained by time, probably of later date.

The music room is 31 feet in length and rises above the main house roof. Its base is pinkish flagstones and a mezzanine floor is outlined by design in old iron. There is a wall fountain on the main floor, souvenir of a winter spent in North Africa. A huge brazier designed by Benvenuto Cellini is heavily silvered on copper, also a silver basin for coals and large silver spoon of size to stir them.

A portrait of the grandmother of the owner of the house, hangs on an inner wall, the work of Sir Thomas Sully painted at the time he was doing Queen Victoria in her coronation robes. Another portrait by Julio, over the mantel, is the mother Mrs. Schertz in the lace and rose of the gay 70's. A third portrait is that of the hostess done life size in a standing posture by Allen St. John, picturing this gracious lady in Empire gown and mantle. There are also "Il Pognomara", the piper by Julio, a pastoral by Richard Clague, "The expulsion of the Jews" unsigned from the Burnside collection, and "The Spanish Dancer" by Edouard Antonin Vysekel. A splendid study of roses painted by the mother of Allen St. John, is also an important item of this collection which is a veritable art-gallery. The furniture here too, is most attractive, all being museum pieces. In the dining-room all sorts of delightful surprises await one: beautiful carved antique Flemish pieces of dark oak, rare crystal and quantities of quaint old family silver. A wealth of fine old china at every turn, and many objects reminiscent of plantation days make the room a charming one indeed. In the drawing-room are many lovely things in the way of rare antiques: pieces of Buhl and other inlaid furniture, quantities of bric-a-brac, much of it the gifts of notable people, autographs of celebrities, the handsome harp of the owner who is an able harpist. Miniatures and many heirlooms too go to complete the collection in this interesting home.

Upstairs in the main bedroom is an immense four-poster bed with heavy cornices, and many other pieces of crouch mahogany to match—all from the magazine of Prudence Mallard, period furniture like that of Signorette that will never become out-moded. The furnishings of this old plantation home are typical of the early period of the house and the culture of old Louisiana. The study, workshop and library are all in one in the adjoining room, for Mrs. Schertz is not only an able harpist but a writer of distinction. She has ability as an organizer too, and has had much to do with the early success of the Little Theatre. She was likewise the main spirit in the organization of the New Orleans Spring Fiesta and its tours.

Among the prominent latter-day visitors to this charming old home may be named the Prince and Princess de Ligne, Maurice Maeterlink, Edward A. Southern, Julia Marlowe, Gertrude Franklin Atherton, Minnie Maddern Fisk, General and Mrs. Smeedley Butler, Sir Bertrand Russell, Ella Wheeler Wilcox, Dr. Arnold Genthe and many eminent divines, architects, actors, musicians and singers.

CASA SOLARIEGA "THE SHADY HOUSE"

The original land grant of Casa Solariega was made to the Almonaster family, and later sold to Mr. Louis Blanc, Feb. 8th, 1789, on which he shortly afterwards had this old plantation home built.

At present the home of the Walter Parker family, this house has been restored to its original beautiful condition. While the rear buildings that had fallen into a ruined state have been rebuilt, the main house has only been restored to its pristine charm. In this manner is preserved its ancient atmosphere.

This old plantation house is one of the spacious ones of the vicinity, and like the others in later years underwent changes in its basement planning, the lower or basement floor in all of these houses in this section being converted into living rooms. This arrangement gives a great deal more room for family use than the house had when first planned. Originally this basement space was used for the carriage, garden implements, etc., as in French and Spanish places in Europe today. At present in the Parker home this ground floor space is occupied by the living room, hallway and dining-room, all well planned and comfortably spaced.

The front of the house presents an unusually attractive appearance with a thick growth of wisteria and other blooming vines and tropical shrubbery beyond the handsome ornamental iron fence. A wide brick-paved loggia front and rear is bordered by a luxuriant growth of tropical plants, fragrant with perfume. The beautiful bayou in front, a vista of open spaces, and similar villas nearby add to its charm.

The main hallway is entered through a wide doorway, transom lighted with side lights as well, the same fan light and door arrangement repeated in the rear. Towards the back of the hall the space widens to receive the spiral stair-way specially well-designed, being of a graceful swirling curve twining to the floor above and terminating in the wide hall. The entrance doors front and rear are repeated on the second floor, and these when open furnish attractive vistas with the garden in the distance. The greater part of the garden is in the rear, and the long line of brick arcaded rear buildings form a charming back ground to the immense patio court-yard. All here is very interesting as the brick is unpainted and old looking and great masses of tall trees, wide spreading shrubbery and climbing vines create a tropical effect. Garden furniture and urns flower beds, and innumerable other attractive conceits make this patio one of the most attractive spots in New Orleans.

Downstairs the rooms are spacious. Antiques, good paintings, ancient rugs and carpets, fine old draperies, choice books, beautiful old silver of antique design, crystal and china, handsome antique oak furniture lend interest to the lower apartment. Upstairs the rooms are also large and furnished with heavy mahogany furniture of proper period with all of the accessories in keeping. As a whole the house and contents harmonize well. It is a natural and livable home, not having the appearance of a place arranged for sightseers.

One may be sure such an old house and such an old garden must have witnessed many a pleasant gathering when belle in wide spreading gown and powdered hair danced with her ardent swain caparisoned in knee pants, silk hose, buckled shoes and ribboned queus at a time when these old plantation homes were summer retreats for the elite of Bienville's city. It is doubtful, however, whether even in the hey day of its glory when loggias, house and garden were crowded, did as great and select a gathering ever fill the old place as does it now, when Mr. and Mrs. Walter Parker and her sister, Miss Hester Hernandez entertain. On these occasions a background similar to the courtyards of Italian villas in the long ago is reproduced with fine effect.

In the court-yard a raised stage is set against tropical greenery and tall cypresses forming a truly delightful vision with the electrical lighting cleverly hidden in the foliage. When the improvised stage is enlivened by gaily costumed characters in bright silk, satin and velvets appearing as the occasion demands, the remembrances of these evenings recall the Fetes Champetre, Italian Pastorals and woodland comedies of Shakespeare.

CHAPTER VII.

FAUBOURG DE MARIGNY

THE DE MARIGNY PLANTATION

The old de Marigny plantation, located a little below the present Esplanade avenue, fronting on the river and extending almost to the woods, is today but a memory.

The plantation house was of the early Louisiana type with a high basement below and a series of square brick pillars on which rested the wide gallery that encircled the house, the over-hanging roof line supported on collonettes. A wide stairway led up from the garden to the gallery entrance, the veranda bright at all times with a quantity of blooming plants in flower pots.

The residence was about the size of two ordinary early plantation homes, containing a number of large rooms, the ceilings made of cypress boards so carefully matched that after being painted they looked as if they had been plastered. The wooden mantels had columns and the door frames and window casements were substantial but simple in design. All of the windows were of the French type, that is a double-glazed door arrangement, which opened inward while heavy solid batten shutters opened on the outside. A large central hall room and sitting room in one and the rear gallery served as dining-room in warm weather when guests were numerous. George W. Cable has a good illustration of the old house in his "Creoles of Louisiana", showing the old house after it had been fenced in when the plantation had been cut up into city blocks.

It was handsomely furnished with European furniture. As the family was an immensely wealthy one, yearly visits were made

to Europe and gradually the house became a vertitable treasure
house of fine furniture and objects of art. Fine ancestral portraits painted by noted French artists adorned the walls of all of
the rooms. Many of these portraits now are in the possession of
descendants or in the Cabildo collection as is much of the fine
bric-a-brac from this home. A quantity of the finest carved rosewood now in the homes of relatives, is part of the rare, museum-
piece furniture which replaced the early slave-made furniture that
had been in their earliest home. It was in this second home that
the Duke of Orleans and his two brothers, who were exiles in
Louisiana after fleeing France at the time of the Revolution, were
housed and lavishly entertained by the Marquis and Marquise de
Marigny de Mandeville, who at the time of the visit of the royal
visitors to Louisiana, were the richest couple in the colony. Later
when these royal exiles returned to France and Louis Philippe
became King of France, they sent their host and hostess, and numerous others who had befriended them, costly presents which
today are priceless heirlooms treasured by the descendants of the
families to whom they were sent. The King of France also had
the son of Philippe Enguerrand Marquis de Marigny educated
and given a commission in the Royal Troops, but the princely
fortune loaned to Louis Philippe at the time he departed from
New Orleans was never returned.

BERNARD DE MARIGNY, THE GREAT SPENDER OF HIS ERA WHO SET A PACE FOR ELEGANCE

Born of wealthy parents who gratified his every wish, later on
as one might expect from the spoiled son raised like a prince,
Bernard de Marigny became a wastrel, squandering the vast fortune placed at his disposal. On his return to New Orleans to
live, after his life abroad where his contact was with royalty and
all of the extravagances attached to it, he set a pace for extravagant entertainment and a general mode of living that caused many
wealthy Creole families to emulate the ways and extravagances
of the French Court itself. Whatever may have been his faults,
he was always a gentleman and one feels that he spent his money
on beautiful surroundings, fine clothes, horses, etc., wherein lay
his extravagances, and the joy of entertaining on a regal scale
and not in immorality. He loved gaming, but it was an age in
which gentlemen played for high stakes.

He surrounded himself and his family with the finest of furniture, bric-a-brac, costly articles of all kinds, a taste that was partly natural and partly acquired from the French Court where he had been educated. He never caused his old home to be modernized or changed in any way, but he made of it a veritable jewel case, each of its many rooms being compartments which he filled to overflowing with priceless articles of every description. He never considered the cost of an article, provided it was fine and what he wanted. He was generous to a fault, and many households in this state contain priceless gifts from him. When the Civil War had swept the fortunes of the South away, it was not long before the curio shops were flooded with treasures such as only the capitals of Europe had at that day. These articles had been purchased by friends and relatives of Bernard de Marigny who tried to emulate his standard of living. The Marquis de Vaudrieul in all his glory, did not at any time live as extravagantly as did this son of the old nobleman. De Marigny's manners were polished, and his education made him a scholar as well as a gentleman. He spent much time duelling at which he was an adept. In his old age having but a small remnant of his collossal fortune of eight million dollars, he spent his time paying social calls on old friends. He used to walk to and fro from their homes to his own, and on the 4th of February, 1868, on his way homeward he slipped and fell, striking his head and died shortly afterwards.

Bernard de Marigny was buried on a cold wet day. Somehow it seems that Heaven weeps when a favorite dies. In spite of the weather his funeral was a large one and was attended by many of the most important people of the city. In fact the whole town felt it had lost one whose memory will linger.   ˙

Towards the end of his life, he was very much like another prominent French nobleman who died a few years ago in Paris. This nobleman too was a lover of beautiful things and fine living, but Bernard de Marigny always remained the gentleman, while the other Duke proved to be otherwise.

In 1910 Prosper de Marigny, the last of the de Marigny name, died and the name became extinct, two hundred years and over having passed since the first one bearing it had come to the colony. To Bernard de Marigny in 1830 King Louis Philippe "After a faithful correspondence sent him a magnificent dinner

Garden Party during the Spring Fiesta in grounds of the Old Spanish Custom-house, Bayou St. John.

The old Casa Solariega, Bayou St. John.   Walter Parker home.

Carved wooden mantel (above).   Spiral stairway (below), Casa Solariega.

service of solid silver, each piece bearing a portrait of the royal family. The King also insisting on Bernard, and his young son paying him a visit. It was then that Bernard and his young son Mandeville, then 19 years of age, accepted the invitation, both were received at the palace where they remained six months enjoying the hospitality of the French Court."

(From Miss Marie Crusat de Verges' letter to the New Orleans Picayune).

CHAPTER VIII.

PLANTATIONS OF ST. BERNARD

THREE OAKS PLANTATION

The plantation having been cut up to make a canal, the old Three Oaks Plantation mansion now stands in the shadow of an immense sugar refinery and is all that remains. The plantation house is an ancient place, for during the Battle of New Orleans one of its massive solid brick columns heavily coated with cement was demolished by a cannon ball.

Mr. Edgar Dahlgren, nephew of General Dahlgren, occupied the home and maintained the plantation as a going concern for many years previous to the Civil War. (Mrs. Frank Dahlgren is the authority for this statement). General Dahlgren of Natchez, Miss., rebuilt "Dunleith" at Natchez after the first beautiful home that had been given his wife by her father, Job. Routh, had burned to the ground. The Natchez mansion was struck by lightning in 1857 while General Dahlgren and his wife were away visiting a spa in the North. The Dahlgren's plantation home was handsomely furnished, but nothing was saved from the flames, the house and contents being a total loss. After Mr. Edgar Dahlgren and his family moved from Three Oaks Plantation, the Cenas family became owners, and lived there many years during which time it was noted for its beautiful garden. The interior with ante-bellum furnishings was also very lovely. It is still a spot that is much visited by tourists, and one of the fine old plantation houses of the state. It is typical of the true Louisiana home of the more pretentious type.

The only reason that this old mansion escaped being burned by Sherman's orders, was because it was like several others in the vicinity needed by the Federal officers after the fall of New Orleans. No sooner had this occurred than the family then residing there were ordered out and they were not permitted to take any of their belongings. When the house was finally returned to the family it had been swept clean of all that had been in it.

BUENO RITERO (The Old Beauregard Place)

In St. Bernard Parish a short distance from the Three Oaks Plantation, almost hidden from view by the moss hung oaks that surround it, lies Bueno Ritero plantation home, built in 1840 from a design by James Gallier, Sr., noted architect of that day, for his friend the Marquis de Trava. It was a beautiful old place, and it lies almost in the shadow of the Chalmette Monument, being a stone's throw from that historical edifice. Entrance to the old plantation house, which is open to visitors to view, is through the wire enclosure, by way of the pathway leading to the river road through the monument grounds gateway.

The house is in a dilapidated condition, especially the ground floor. It has been vacant for a number of years, and is now the property of a railroad company.

Birthplace of Gen. G. T. Beauregard.
Old Beauregard Plantation home, St. Bernard Parish, La. Birthplace of General Beauregard as it looked after a century of neglect.

The house is of the typical early type of large solid brick cement-coated columned plantation home. It is of brick construction with heavy walls cement-covered on the outside and plastered over hand-made laths within. The cement coating on the exterior is in reality a combination of burnt oyster shell lime combined with sharp sand—very durable and used as a means of preserving the soft brick used. The soil in Louisiana and Mississippi afforded only this material, as the brick as a rule were slave-made and not imported as some writers contend.

The long heavy Doric columns that support the front and rear galleries give great dignity to the place. The simple entablature supports a nicely pitched roof pierced by two dormer windows front and back and one at either end. The attic is immense and high and one can see much of the fitted and pegged wood structural work as it is unfinished. A lightning rod of good design is placed on the roof ridge to the right side. A chimney juts from the center of the roof and in the attic we can see the construction design used at this date, generally used, as I have noted it in many places, with specially heavy brick work as at the old Andrews place, Belle Grove, on the west bank of the Mississippi. It is a method of connecting the chimneys of either side of the house which supply a means of heating by fireplace the six rooms comprised in the main house—three on each floor excluding the hallways on the right side as we face the place. In this hall we find a simple winding stairway now quite dilapidated. It has a nicely finished unpolished mahogany rail, and with a sweep winds to the floor above—repeating this again to the attic. The facade presents a simple dignified appearance the diamond arrangement of the wooden balustrade relieving the severeness of its classic lines. The wide balcony downstairs, laid in brick on the same level with the floor of the house, is but slightly above the ground. The floor which has badly rotted with age and neglect shows that the area below was slightly excavated—not sufficient for a cellar, but in order to ventilate the floor beams, and flooring. The rear downstairs veranda which is also very wide, was bricked as is the front one.

The two columned sections, being almost identical in construction with the exception the upstairs wide rear porch, is enclosed in a carefully detailed manner with wood panelling as high as the balustrade rail, and glazed upright panels reaching to long transom lights above—enclosing the entire rear upstairs balcony. This makes an immense solarium and keeps the house free from the northern exposure. All the woodwork of this enclosure is

Home of the Marquis de Marigny, Faubourg de Marigny. (From
an old Print—Courtesy of Mrs. Edwin X. de Verges.)

Loggia opening on to Courtyard—Walter Parker Home.

Three Oaks Plantation Home—St. Bernard Parish.

Rear view of "Bueno Ritero". Built for the Marquis de Trava in 1840 by Jas. Gallier, Sr. Later belonging to the Renée Beauregard family.

Magnificent oak avenue of the de la Ronde Plantation—
miscalled "The Packenham Oaks".

Ruin of the old de la Ronde Plantation Mansion as it appeared before the
storm of Sept. 29th, 1915.

Crest and Coat-of-Arms of the Rouyer de
Villere family. (Courtesy of Mrs. John F.
Coleman.)

done in a way to enhance the charm of the old house, as no doubt the place, in a great measure, was used as an out-door reception room. Below it is all fitted with a cross moulding forming a base to the casement which encloses the ends of the balcony also.

Within on the ground floor the space is divided into the stair—hallway and three fairly large rooms, one room in depth with French door having batten shutters opening to the wide galleries. These rooms which have high ceilings are connected by a wide classic door casement with dog ear mouldings; the second and third room by a smaller doorway and similar casement.

The floors have rotted away in this part of the house and the front doors are at present nailed up.

A Pickaninny

On the second floor we find the plan much like the floor below, the rooms connected by regulation-sized doors. The rooms being square and high—the one towards the left as you face the house is very long with windows at the end as in the room below.

It must have been a very comfortable place, delightfully cool in summer, with the river breezes sweeping through the rooms. We are told that the Marquis de Trava was a Spaniard of the old school, a Spanish Grandee with very strong adherence to the Castillian etiquette even in small matters of social affairs, and rigid about the pomp of stately functions.

He is pictured as a proud grandee and his Marquise equally as exacting.

Their receptions (as there were still in the state many old Dons and their families at that date) reflected much the air of a minor European Court. A bid to their gatherings was considered a special mark of honor. Many a pompous grand dame vied with her neighbor in the magnificence of her toilette, and the habiliments of her slaves that accompanied her to the entrance of the mansion, for all knew the circle in which the Marquis and his family moved was considered the haughtiest in the state. Garden parties at that period found a special way of entertaining, and one can visualize the grounds as they must have appeared in those far-off days.

The house has the simple lines one finds in old Spanish homes. It became the plantation home many years later of Judge Rene Beauregard (who married Alice Cenas), the Judge being a son of the famous Confederate General. It also was a social center while occupied by that aristocratic old family during which time it contained many family heirlooms and mementos of both the Cenas and Beauregard families.

Its garden was a delightful spot, Louis Philippe roses edging the walk leading from the river to the house. Traces of the ancient garden and old walks still can be found in the rear of the house where the oak trees are thickest forming great spots of shade. One hears that a movement is on foot to restore the old structure and convert it into a Confederate Museum. Let us hope so—anything to preserve an old plantation house so close to the city.

VERSAILLES

PLANTATION HOME OF MAJOR GENERAL PIERRE DENIS DE LA RONDE

This is an historical place situated about one and one-half miles below the Plains of Chalmette. At the end of a magnificent avenue, a double row of Centenary Oaks extending from near the river front, for quite a distance, at the extremity of which are the charred remains of the once palatial home of Major General Pierre Denis de la Ronde.

Among the priceless objects of historical interest on exhibition in the amoral section of the Louisiana State Museum, otherwise known as the Cabildo two pictures arrest attention of the visitors. They are excellent specimens of the photographer's skill. One represents a bright cheery edifice, an old plantation house possessing to perfection all those picturesque characteristics for which that particular type of architecture was so remarkable throughout the South in pre-Civil War days; the other an old vine-clad ruin amid picturesque surroundings, leading to which, from its river side, is one of the most beautiful oak avenues in all the world.—J. E. D.

* The mansion had two stories of cement-covered brick, containing a total of sixteen rooms. On its four sides were spacious galleries supported by a beautiful collonade, the whole covered by a sloping roof with vertical windows projecting.

Numerous stories have been written about this old house, its origin, its history and the circumstances attending its destruction, all absurdly incorrect, the merest fiction. Few houses in the country have suffered as this old de la Ronde mansion has in this respect and genius of fabrication, invention or hallucination, or whatever it is, is still alive. The only justifiable reason for its being called the "Packenham House" might be to the fact that when Major General Sir Edward Michael Packenham, the hero of Salamanca and Bajadoz, commander-in-chief of the British Army of invasion, was mortally wounded on the Chalmette battle field, January 8th, 1815, and died under one of the four gnarled and venerable live oaks (which are still standing, their site at the time of the battle was the Bienvenue Plantation, subsequently Mercier's Place now known as the Colomb Place).

The shells of the enemy made a hole in the roof of Versailles Mansion, but beyond this little physical damage was done the property. The English, however, emptied the well-stocked wine cellars of the mansion, the product of which, they frankly admitted, was of choicest vintage. The family was at the time, which was during the social season, spending the winter in New Orleans, their city abode being 35 Conde Street, now Chartres Street, new number 1021, near Ursuline Street.

Finally, this lovely mansion became the property of a Mr. Luaga, a dairy-man, who stalled his animals on the first floor of the mansion and in other ways desecrated the premises. It was during his ownership, subsequent to 1876, that the house caught fire and was destroyed, a rather ignoble end of one of the proudest edifices at that day in the land. The walls were still standing. however, until the storm of September 29th, 1915, when sections of them were blown down, leaving the ruin as it is today.

In one of the rooms of the de la Ronde mansion lay gallant Major General Samuel Gibbs (of the second brigade) second in command; in another room was Major General Kean who was

---

* This description of Versailles Plantation was written by Emile Ducros and is used with his permission.

seriously wounded, and many of the British officers mortally wounded on the field here breathed their last. From the de la Ronde family Versailles Plantation passed to Norman Story, a brother of Benjamin Saxon Story. Subsequently the property, including the Versailles Plantation, its manor and wonderful collection of art objects and furnishings was acquired by Armand Heine, at one time a citizen of New Orleans, but then a resident and banker of Paris, France, who was familiar with the Louisiana Versailles and its wealth of beautiful things. The decorations and objects of art and much of its interior embellishments and appointments were utilized by him in the rehabilitation and redecorating of his Parisian residence. This gives an idea of the interior grandeur of the old mansion whose pathetic ruin has become a sort of shrine in Louisiana.

The mansion called Versailles (at times "the Palace") was known for many years of its existence, although incorrectly designated by many writers not familiar with its history, nor that of the family who occupied it. It was constructed in 1805, just two years subsequent to the memorable event which made Louisiana a part of the United States. Ante-dating all homes of its type, the old fashioned plantation house, it was nevertheless not only comfortable, but interiorly was magnificently embellished and most substantially constructed. It was said architecture was at its best in the house. Its owner and builder (Pierre Denis de la Ronde) was perhaps the wealthiest planter of his time in this part of Louisiana. Versailles plantation, twelve arpents front and extending in depth to the prairie, containing twelve hundred and forty-six arpents bounded originally on the upper side by land of Francisco Maria de Reggio, and on the lower side by land of Chauvin Delery, (Confirmation in 1812 appears in third volume American State papers) and was cultivated with scientific skill, and with success quite remarkable in those days.

The famous plantations and property owners of St. Bernard Parish in 1815 in order of the distance from the city to Bayou Terre Aux Boefs were, Montreuil, Macarty, Lavau, Duplessis, Butler, Dupre, Solomon, Prevost, Piernas, Dezilet, Delere, (acres) Sigur, Languile, Macarty, Chalmette (owned by Ignace Martin de Lino de Chalmet). Antoine Bienvenu, (1425 acres), Versailles (owned by Casmir Lacost, son-in-law of Pierre Denis de la Ronde), and subsequently acquired by Drauzin and Ereville Villere).

Overseers House, Conseil Plantation—home of the de Villeré family. (Original painting owned by Mrs. W. O. Humphries, New Orleans.)

Kenilworth Plantation Manor. (Drawing by Miss Vera Morel.)

Mrs. Wilson Williams, neé Rebecca Wilkinson Carradine of Kenilworth Plantation and her daughter Miss Doris Walker.   Above them is the portrait of Mrs. Williams' paternal grandmother, Rebecca Chew Carradine of Natchez, Miss.

Conseil (owned by Jacques Villere and his son Rene Philip Gabriel Villeré, Major of Third Regiment First Battalion of Louisiana Militia, and son-in-law of Pierre Denis de la Ronde). Joumoville, later acquired by M. Cuculli, and subsequently by A. W. Walker, a Parisian of English descent, who had cut a wide swath in olden days of the parish. The next place was that of Rodolph Joseph Ducros, Jr. It subsequently passed to Captain Henry Clement Story, finally to his brother Captain Benjamin Saxon Story who acquired his holdings. The next was the Celestin Lachapelle (Chiapelle grant of 1896 acres), patented May 19th, 1832, later acquired by Capt. Henry Clement Story, finally his brother, Captain Benjamin Story acquired his holdings. The next was the Celestia Lachepelle and Magloire Guichard grant (1445) acres, a part of this property was covered by probably the oldest French grant (dated July 6th, 1723), in the parish. The next was that of Magloire Guichard (531) acres, this property was acquired by Dr. Knapp, the dentist, and finally to its present owners. Magloire Guichard was Speaker of the House of Representatives of Louisiana, 1812-1815, and gave much concern to General Jackson, belonging to the opposition political party, and suspected of English sympathies. The next tracts in their order were, the old Antoine Philippon claim (5270) acres, later known as Merrit plantation, widow Michel Louis Toutant Beauregard (born Victoire Marie Ducros, grandmother of Pierre Gustave Toutant Beauregard), claim 1625 acres, Rodolph Joseph Ducros (a pioneer settler in St. Bernard parish), claim 1645 acres, eight arpents front by a league and a half in depth, confirmed prior to 1832. It was inherited by Marcel Joseph Ducros, Attorney, State Senator and planter, who figured largely in legal matters of St. Bernard. Laise (2252 acres), acquired by B. Morgan and known as Magnolia Plantation, and subsequently passed to Jourdan Brothers, John Davidson, Poydras planting Company, (called Poydras Plantation), and finally to Russel and son. A portion of the Poydras plantation is in Plaquemine Parish, Louisiana.

CONSEIL PLANTATION

In another early type cottage plantation house quite similar to the one in which he was born, Jacques Philippe Villere and his bride started their married life at Conseil. Surrounded by large trees as was customary, and with garden shrubbery the house with wide porches and overhanging roof made a comfortable home on their sugar plantation. Located as it was among the estates of the de la Ronde's, Bienvenu and Chalmette families all owning fine homes and large plantations, land that was later to go down in history as the famous battlefield on which General Packenham, leader of the English army was to be killed and the English army defeated by the Americans under command of General Andrew Jackson.

The Villere Plantation Home on Conseil plantation, was burnt many years ago according to a newspaper article which appeared at the time that the fire occurred. The name Conseil was given to the plantation by the owner because the old planter always counseled his sons about the management of their plantations near by, these meetings occurred regularly at Conseil. The above mentioned article which gives a vivid description of the burning of this historic homestead is in the scrap-book family file of this noted family owned by the great grand-daughter of Governor Villere, Miss Laure Beauregard Larendon formerly of New Orleans, at present residing in Atlanta, Georgia. Conseil plantation home has been replaced by a similar one to the one destroyed, and within walking distance of the crumbling ruin of the ancient de la Ronde mansion.

KENILWORTH
THE OLD BIENVENU PLANTATION

Some distance out on the road known as the St. Bernard Highway, eighteen miles from New Orleans to be exact, can be seen distinctly, as you drive from the roadway, a beautiful old plantation house sheltered by a grove of oak, cedar and pecan trees, and surrounded by a luxuriant wealth of blooming greenery and palms.

Pierre Antoine Bienvenu, who came from Quebec, Canada, in the year 1725, built the house in 1759 according to the best available record.

It is of the high basement type so prevalent at that day—the lower floor rooms having been converted into living quarters in later years. Massive wall—heavy batten shutters and an attractive outside stairway, which rises from the brick-paved lower gallery—are all typical of this type of cool and comfortable mansion. The walls of the lower floor are of brick cement-finished, while the walls of the upper floor have a weatherboard surface in lieu of the cement—a feature quite common in many Louisiana plantation houses. It is of mortised peg construction with most of the labor done by slaves.

During the period the plantation was occupied by General Albert Estopinal—who purchased it in 1887 as a home—changes in the attic were made so it could be used for bed-rooms—and the more modern window frames in the attic substituted for the original ones. Now the property of Mr. Wilson Williams, and after a considerable outlay the house has again been restored to a beautiful condition. Mr. and Mrs. Williams have restored the gardens, and planted old fashioned roses and fragrant flowers until it again appears no doubt much as it did in the original owner's day. It looks very lovely and inviting from the roadway, with its plantation and out-buildings stretching far rearward.

The room arrangement is the same upstairs and down. The kitchen as usual is an out-building connected by a covered passage way. The pigeonnaires and stables are gone as are the garconnaires, but enough remains to give a very good idea of what these old places looked like originally. Most of the slave-made heavy hardware, hand-made, on doors, windows, etc., is intact.

Filled as it is with a nice collection of antiques by the Wilson family, many of the pieces having historic association. This house has been known by numerous names—for many years as the Estopinal place, later as Kenilworth, a name by which many know it today. Another property, the Gothic place some distance away on the Mississippi River around the bend, also called Kenilworth, is of distinctly Gothic type. Both belonged to an English syndicate that at one time operated a chain of sugar plantations, most of them being purchased after the Civil War when sugar and cotton plantations could be purchased for a song.

PIERRE ANTOINE BIENVENUE.

After the transfer of Louisiana to the Spanish the French were given and accepted representation in the Cabildo according to old records of the Louisiana Historical Society. This Cabildo met in New Orleans December 1st, 1769, and besides the governor, included among others was Antonio Bienvenue (all names Latinized in this ancient record). This Mr. Antonio Bienvenue, owner of the Bienvenue Plantation on which stands the white marble marker referred to in the following article, was the father of Melicourt Bienvenue owner of Kenilworth Plantation and was the first one of the Bienvenue family to locate in Louisiana.

A bronze tablet marks the spot where the white marble marker formerly stood that is mentioned further on in this article. The father of Melicourt Bienvenue was the largest land owner in this area as the family was a wealthy one. The old plantation home was destroyed at the time of the Battle of New Orleans. Later the home was rebuilt on simpler lines.

Vincent, Chevalier de Morant, married twice. His first marriage was to Madame Constance Volant Marquise, widow of the martyred Pierre Marquise, issue one child Constance de Morant who married twice: 1st, to M. Landier, and to M. Magloire Guichard, issue one child named Josephine, who married Melicourt Bienvenue, a son of Antoine Bienvenue who was the father of twelve sons.

Antoine Bienvenue lived with his wife and large family of twelve sons on the Bienvenue plantation located in St. Bernard Parish, La.—a plantation that has gone down in history as being part of the Battle-field of the Battle of New Orleans. On the old Bienvenue Plantation one sees a marble tablet telling of the owner of the plantation, and of its being part of the battle-field. One of his sons Melicourt Bienvenue owned Kenilworth Plantation which he had acquired shortly after the beginning of the 19th century and enlarged it for his wife and family. His daughter, who had been educated in England noting a bayou in front of the plantation that reminded her of the moat around Kenilworth Castle, named the plantation Kenilworth.

From the marriage of Melicourt Bienvenue and Josephine Guichard, six children were born. 1st, Delzira who married Archibald Montgomery of Ireland, their daughter Lydia, married James Moore of Ireland; 2nd, Alcée; 3rd, Amanda; 4th, Guichard; 5th, Leontine, who married Henri Boucher, and became the parents of two children, Augustus and Charles. 6th, Louise, who married first William Crawford, and became the parents of William, who married Kathleen Owen; and Louise. Louise married secondly, Charles C. Crawford, and they became the parents of Charlotte, who married Pierre Joseph d'Heur, and became the parents of Joseph, who married Jean Martin, and became the parents of Micheline and Allard, unmarried. 2nd, John; 3rd, James;

4th, Josephine; 5th, Lewis Bienvenue, who married Louisiana Foster, daughter of the late Honorable Murphy J. Foster, Governor of Louisiana. Dr. Lewis Bienvenue Crawford, ranks high among the medical men of Louisiana and at present is located in New Iberia, La. The children of Dr. and Mrs. Crawford are Marien, Louise, and Lewis. 7th, Charles, who married Cornelia Smith.

Miss Josephine Crawford of New Orleans, La., first attended the Cenas Institute for Young Ladies; later the McDonogh High School, after which she finished at the Newcomb College of Tulane University. Studied Art at the New Orleans Art School. Also studied in Vienna and with Andre Lhote in Paris, France. Exhibited at Newcomb; the Arts and Crafts of New Orleans; at Exhibitions at Baton Rouge, La., at the Louisiana State University; also in Baltimore, New York City; and with the Central American Art Circuit.

According to family records the de Morant family came from Normandy, and were prominent Crusaders, being among the Norman gentlemen who in the year 1096 attached themselves to *Robert Courte Heuze* following his banners into Palestine. The archives of the Church of St. Laurence in Paris France, prove members of this distinguished family among these crusaders. In the year 1621 Thomas de Morant, Marquis d'Estreville, and Count de Montignac acquired the estate of du Mesnil in Normandy, which was elevated to a Marquisate, and the title of Marquis de Morant was conferred on its overlord. Alliances with such notable families of France as the Dampierres and with the princess de Beauffremont placed the already noble family high in the social calendar. One of the name founded a monastery for the use of the Dominicans; additional titles borne by members of the de Morant family were Count de Pences; and Baron de Thenon, among them were marechaux de camp of the King's army, and Gentlemen ordinary to the King.

The family of Wilson Williams of New Orleans, present owner of the beautiful ancient plantation home in St. Bernard parish, stems to the Virginia family of that name, his father being Frederick H. Williams of Richmond, Virginia, and his mother, Sarah Margaret Christian, also of that Southern city. His wife is Rebecca Wilkerson Carradine, a daughter of Leonard Wilkerson Carradine and Mary Emma Rivers, of Natchez. Mrs. Williams' parents, living in the beautiful old Natchez mansion known as "Rosalie" at the time of her birth. Leonard Wilkerson Carradine was born at Roakley Plantation, Washington, Mississippi, and Mary Rivers was born at "Rosalie" in Natchez, Mississippi. Mrs. Wilson Williams has one daughter, Miss Doris Rebecca Herbert Walker, and one son, Jeptha Freeman Walker, Jr., (by a former marriage).

Mrs. Wilson Williams nee Miss Rebecca Wilkinson, is the daughter of Leonard Wilkinson, who was born on Roakly Plantation on St. Catherine's Creek at Washington, Miss. His ancestors are numbered among that patrician group of people that we find listed as the First Families of the state of Mississippi. The family came down from Maryland and settled at Washington, Miss., where they became large planters. One of their plantations, located where we find the present "Brandon Hall", named for the famous Virginia plantation, was called "Chincapin Grove Plantation", originally laid out for William Locke Chew, a wealthy planter of that time.

Mrs. Wilson Williams' mother was Miss Mary Rivers Carradine, who was born at Wigwam, the family plantation at Natchez, Miss., the family owning several other plantations in Louisiana, among them one called "River Landing" and another named "Fish Pond Plantation". Her great grandfather, Peter Little, was the one for whom was built the beautiful Georgian mansion "Rosalie" in Natchez, Miss. The manor was named after the old Natchez fort which was located close by. It was here in early days that occurred the terrible massacre of the whites by the Indians. The lovely old home has now become the property of the Mississippi D. A. R's.

Mrs. Williams' first marriage was to Jeptha Freeman Walker of Mansfield, La., who was born on Delray plantation, near Barnville, Georgia. The two children from this marriage are Miss Doris Walker, and Jefferson Walker. Her second marriage was to Wilson Williams of Richmond, Va., now a prominent citizen and business man of New Orleans. The city home of the Wilson Williams family contains many heirlooms from these various plantation homes of their families. Many beautiful ancestral portraits by noted artists are among them, one on the stairway wall of Peter Little, painted by the naturalist Audubon. There is also much fine old mahogany and rosewood furniture, old lamps and candle-holders, ancient crystal, silver and chinaware.

CONCORDE PLANTATION

The de la Vergne Plantation was on the Lower Coast below New Orleans. It was a very successful sugar plantation with about fifty slaves including those working about the house. The plantation home was the usual 'early Louisiana type", that is, a raised basement home with an encircling wide gallery from which rose a series of collonettes supporting the wide-spreading roof. Like most of the plantation homes of its era, it had a shingled roof, brick chimneys and dormers piercing the roof. It was a fairly large home with numerous outbuildings and a spacious garden. Up until the Civil War the plantation made money, but with the freeing of the slaves, loss of the sugar mill by bombardment, and the general property destruction at that time the place was practically abandoned and gradually fell into ruin .

The home of the de la Vergne family, prominent and connected by marriage to other aristocratic families, became in olden days a rural social center. There one met the Creole families of distinction who kept up a continuous round of social activities to break up the monotony of plantation life.

CHAPTER IX.

IN NEW ORLEANS.

THE OLD De LORD SARPY PLANTATION HOME HOWARD AVENUE, NEW ORLEANS, LA.

Standing like an impoverished aristocrat among old sheds and shabby buildings, in Howard Avenue, near Camp Street, this ancient home at once impresses one as being a good example of the early plantation house of a substantial type. It is an architectural tragedy that such a fine example of our city's early history should be permitted to fall into ruin. Now that there is a wave of restoration of ancient buildings rising over the United States, it seems a pity that this relic could not be preserved for posterity.

One can visualize the old place as it must have appeared in early days, after seeing maps of the early plantations of this section of that era. At that day an avenue of trees reached from Tchoupitoulas Road, the present street by that name, to the front entrance door. This old house was a handsome place in its day, with the rows of medium-size solid brick columns heavily stuccoed, that surrounded the place originally, resting on tall heavily built brick ones. The place faced the river before the later entrance was planned, and had a beautiful garden in front. The rear gallery upstairs now enclosed, originally was closed only in the central part, the gallery on either side opening into it. Below in the rear a series of arched openings fitted with windows, but originally the plan was somewhat like the upstairs, for the lower central doorway opened on to the rear garden. This garden, according to members of the family, extended far beyond what is now Carondelet Street. The garden grounds were about an acre in width, with fruit orchards on either side, having much the

Peter Little By Audubon

Old Delor-Sarpy Plantation Home, Howard Avenue, New Orleans. Built about 1760.

Mercy Hospital—Formerly the old plantation home of the Saulet family, later Soniat du Fossat family.

same plan in front extending to the river road. A picket fence enclosed the grounds in a line with the highway. Large cement coated brick pillars supported the wide carriage gate, which was in two sections opening inward. The avenue of trees extended from the entrance to the front door of the house, a line of them on either side of the driveway. This driveway divided as a fan and encircled the house, and until the latest shed which completely covers the front yard was erected, several of the old trees and a number of the stumps were still there.

During the rat-proofing, with fire laws demands, and general remodeling that the house has undergone in past years much of both interior and exterior has been changed. The old house is a splendid example of the early home of the wealthy planter, and well merits preserving.

According to the ground plan, in the hall is located the original stairway which winds in a graceful curve to the floor above. The woodwork throughout is of good design, and the circular driveway originally was planned along the lines of the old plan of encircling the house as we learn existed at the old Chretien plantation house at Chretien Point, Sunset, La., and at Ellington on the west bank of the Mississippi River, near New Orleans. At Ellington one can still see the long avenue of trees extending far back into the plantation grounds, the large front garden and long avenue of oaks has disappeared, swallowed by the river. At the Chretien House one can trace the garden and driveway that formerly opened to the rear of the house where there is a stairway planning quite similar to that at the De Lord Sarpy plantation.

To return to this old place and its changes, one can readily detect the bricked-in alterations, that were apparently necessary when street lines were drawn and the house itself made a boundary line. The interior too, underwent some changes with the appearance of gas in New Orleans. Gas pipes were installed throughout the house, and at the time of plaster repairs, centerpieces of plaster work placed on ceilings of the center of the rooms. The wooden mantels were replaced with black marble ones of later date and chandeliers added. The house is rather a large one, conveniently arranged, firmly built of heavy brick walls heavily stuccoed and fine cypress timbers and woodwork. All of the walls are thick ones, the batten shutters and doors fitted with hand made hardware of good design. The dormer windows are especially good in design, showing them planned with double Ionic twin collonetts supporting the crown, having carefully moulded panel-caps, with expanded head moulding. Semi-circle top mullion window-pane arrangement below the gable facade completes this attractive dormer design. The whole house, even in its neglected condition, seems to indicate that the place was planned and built with the same care. A number of years ago, before it became a tenement house and part of the Sarpy family still lived there, the old house contained many beautiful pieces of old mahogany and rosewood furniture, family portraits of past generations, fine old clocks, and bric-a-brac, and was a sketching ground especially liked by the students from the Art School in Camp Street, close by.

SONIAT DUFOSSAT (OLD SAULET PLANTATION)
THE OLD SONIAT PLANTATION HOME

Opposite the Texas & Pacific Railroad Station can still be seen the splendid old mansion of the Soniat family which is now the Mercy Hospital, the immense buildings and grounds, a gift to the city to be used for hospital purposes. Originally it was a country home about which gathered much that was best in society of city and state, and the old place still presents a fairly pleasant picture with its tall trees and shrubbery.

It is of the high basement type with immense side galleries hung from the heavy two-storied Doric columns that surround it on all sides, as well as in front. A wide hallway upstairs in the center of the building separates the rooms all of which are quite large. It was one of the splendid old places that surrounded New Orleans in early days, and the city is very fortunate in being able to preserve the ancient home which again has regained a semblance to its original appearance.

A family record of this distinguished family is given in the rear of this book devoted to this purpose.

ORIGINALLY THE OVERSEER'S HOUSE ON THE
SPLENDID DE LIVAUDAIS PLANTATION

The de Livaudais plantation is another of the land grants that was not far removed from the old French city which we now know as "the Vieux Carre", originally enclosed by a moat and palisades. The ancient house, the subject of this sketch, was originally built in 1813, the newer parts of the old structure date from the days of the "Greek Revival" for the date of this architectural change is given about 1830 and James Gallier is named as the one who drew the plans and supervised the changes. The work on the house is of the same high class and the simplicity of the plan as a whole seems to point to its being the work of Gallier Pere. Originally it was the regulation overseer's home on the plantation of a wealthy planter, constructed along the lines of the earlier type plantation homes on a raised basement.

Later when the plantation manor-house was destroyed by fire this overseer's home was enlarged and remodelled on the lines of the newer dwellings being erected at that date (Greek Revival type). The de Livaudais family then occupied this home until the plantation was divided and sold this home to Mr. Toby, the grandfather of Mrs. Watts Leverich and Miss Campbell and the place became known as Toby's corner, it being in a scarcely populated area.

This section long ago became the famed Garden District of New Orleans where are still located the homes of the parents and grandparents of the first families of American New Orleans. Many families have never moved out of their beautiful old homes. The section has an aristocratic air peculiar to itself. It is distinctive and a stranger can at once see that it was and still is the center of culture and wealth.

In the Garden District are many splendid old homes mostly of brick several stories in height, the brick for most part finished in cement and tinted or painted. There is much beautiful cast iron in the form of balconies with a lace like mesh and iron columns, and tall ornamental iron fences of good design. There are flowers everywhere in the gardens beneath the great oaks and magnolias.

In this charming locality we find this unpretentious old plantation home in its own beautiful setting. It lies far back from the bricked sidewalk, great glossy magnolia and other tall trees with festoons of wisteria and jasmine and other equally beautiful and fragrant vines vainly striving to enmesh in their long curling tendrils, this architectural relic of a past era. Great clusters of butterfly lilies, cannas and crepe myrtle, all add their charm and foliage until the house is almost hidden in the blooming greenery.

The cornice of the Greek revival period and parts of the facade and side are about all that is visible from the street, their snowy whiteness contrasting strongly with the dark glossy green of the foliage. The house, which is spacious, more so than one would suppose from the outside, is of the raised cottage type, the heavy cornice surrounding the front and First Street side severely plain save for a dentil course. Square brick pillars support the wide galleries about the house from which rise medium size square posts with caps reaching to the cornice, giving an air of unpretentious dignity to the place. Matched boards of cypress ceiling face the front so beautifully done it simulates plaster. A graceful curving hand-railed stairway leads up to the main entrance gallery where an attractive doorway greets the visitor.

It was in the early fifties that Mrs. Thomas Duggan bought the place from Mr. Toby, and moved down from her earlier plantation home near Donaldsonville, La. She died in 1907 bequeathing the property to her daughter, Mrs. Gustaf Westfeldt, who lived here until 1923 at whose death the present owner, Gustaf R. Westfeldt, acquired possession. The home is a social center and the basement which is a finished one forms a meeting place for the "Garden District" Library.

The main hallway, quite wide, divides the suite of rooms. All is very comfortably arranged within and the beautiful pieces of antique furniture of Westfeldt, Monroe, Blanc, Duggan families present vistas recalling the rooms of lovely old plantation places one has visited while on the garden tours. Fine paintings, too, are found here with the numerous heirlooms of these old families.

Elaborate iron ornamental balustrade with monogram A P on
Pontalba buildings.

A corner of the porch of the Old Dugue de
Livaudais plantation home in the Garden
District of New Orleans. Now the Gustaf
Westfeldt Home. (Courtesy of Mrs. Gustaf
Westfeldt.)

The Garden of the Westfeldt Home—the Old de
Livaudais Plantation Home.

MRS. THOMAS DUGGAN.

GUSTAF WESTFELDT, SR.

MRS. GUSTAF WESTFELDT, SR.

CAPT. GUSTAF R. WESTFELDT, JR., 113th Field Artillery, U. S. A., World War.

JUDGE FRANK ADAIR MONROE—1st Louisiana Cavalry, Confederate Army of America.

MONROE.

A family of distinguished ancestry tracing to Andrew Monroe a Scotchman and member of a Highland clan, who came to America in 1650 and settled in Virginia, and became the progenitor of the distinguished Monroe family of the Old Dominion state, of which President Monroe was a member.

Thomas Bell Monroe, a direct descendant of Andrew Monroe, a native of Albemarle County, Virginia, became a lawyer of distinction in Kentucky, and recognizing his ability, was appointed by President Jackson judge of the United Stated District Court, a position which he held until the election of Abraham Lincoln as President. Near the end of the Civil War he came South and decided to locate at Pass Christian, Miss., where he remained until his death. His wife also of distinguished parentage was a daughter of John Adair, a planter of South Carolina, and a patriot of the American Revolution who after hostilities had removed to Kentucky, where his ability soon brought him into prominence, he soon becoming an early governor of the state, later becoming a United States Senator. Judge Victor Monroe, son of Thomas Bell Monroe, and Mary Townsend (Polk) Monroe. Judge Victor Monroe a native of Kentucky, born in Glasgow, Barren County, was appointed by President Pierce as the first Federal judge for the territory of Washington. In going to the territory in the early part of the Fifties, he went in company of Governor Stephens, and after a year or two reaching Olympia, Washington, his death occurred.

Honorable Frank Adair Monroe, Chief Justice of the Supreme Court of Louisiana for over twelve years, was born at Anapolis, Md., on August 30th, 1844, and was reared at the home of his parents at Frankfort, Kentucky. The mother of Judge Frank Adair Monroe was a native of Maryland and her father was Admiral Polls of the United States Navy. Judge Frank A. Monroe had one brother, William Winder Monroe, and a sister named Mary Eliza, who married George Vincent, and later became the wife of Judge Joshua G. Baker of New Orleans, La.

Judge Frank A. Monroe received his early education in private schools at Frankfort, Ky., and then entered in 1860 the Kentucky Military Institute when he had just begun his sophomore year he entered the Confederate States Army in which he served four years, first in Co. E., 4th Kentucky Infantry, then in Co. C., 1st Louisiana Cavalry. He was wounded and captured near Somerset, Kentucky, on March 1863, and was exchanged in October, 1863.

For many years following the cessation of hostilities, Judge Monroe was prominently identified with the United Confederate Veterans organization of the Army of Tennessee, Camp No. 2, U. C. V., and for many years as a member of the Board of Governors, Confederate Memorial Hall, New Orleans. After the war, Judge Monroe returned to the home of his grandfather at Pass Christian, Miss., and shortly afterwards took up the study of law, and in 1867 became a member of the Louisiana bar.

Upon being admitted to practice law, he entered on his professional career in New Orleans, and rose rapidly in his profession, and in 1872 he was elected Judge of the Third District Court, but was dispossessed of the office after a month's service by the "carpet-bag" regime. He took active part with the White League in the action of Sept. 14th, 1874, which overturned the "Packard government, and on Nov., 1876, was reappointed Judge of the Civil District Court, Parish of Orleans; was reappointed in 1884, and in 1889. In March, 1899, he was appointed an associate Justice of the Supreme Court of Luoisiana. Judge Monroe had a long and honorable career and it was his ability that won for him the appointment to the bench of the Supreme Court for the term of 1908 - 1920.

In 1914 he became Chief Justice succeeding Judge Jos. A. Breaux, retiring. Throughout his long career Judge Monroe remained a staunch Democrat, he took an active part in the anti-lottery campaign of 1892, and has always stood for those men and measures, by whom he believed the public interest would be best served.

On January 3rd, 1878, Judge Monroe married Miss Alice Blanc, a daughter of Jules Blanc, they becoming the parents of ten children, five boys and five girls. The sons being Frank Adair Monroe, Jr., J. Blanc Monroe, Winder Polk Monroe, William Blanc Monroe, and James Hill Monroe. The daughters are Alice, who became the wife of S. S. Labouisse, Kate Adair, became Mrs. Gustaf R. Westfeldt; Gertrude, the wife of T. M. Logan, Jr.; Adele, wife of Geo. E. Williams; Marion, wife of John T. Chambers.

The home of Judge and Mrs. Frank A. Monroe noted for
many years as one of the social centers of the city where a generous hospitality at all times awaited a large circle of appreciative friends and acquaintances, for the Judge and his gracious
wife and their large family had made number 847 Carondelet
Street a bright spot in the social life of New Orleans.

BEL AIR.

In a beautiful residential section of New Orleans—at number
1530 Calhoun Street we find an old plantation house that has
been transported, as it were, on a magic carpet from its original
site on the west bank of the Mississippi River near Baton Rouge
to its present location. According to family records the house
originally was built on the old plantation in the latter part of the
1700's or early 1800's. The house was said to have been erected
for Gayoso de Lemos. The land grant by Governor Unzaga and
the original survey of the plantation are framed and placed on
the wall and on the table in the hall.

The house is of a type influenced by the Greek Revival, de
void of the formal cornice and other impressive architectural
details usually found in classic structures. When it was found
that the Mississippi River threatened to swallow the house as it
had done the large garden in front of the house and the oak grove
that had added so much to the appearance of the place in olden
days, the old plantation house was dismantled. All of the important parts were salvaged and were brought to the present site
where the house was reconstructed on the original lines, making
of it again the fine old place it had been.

It is again the home of the von Phul and Cade families, filled
with the same charming furnishings that have always made the
place so attractive. The entrance hall, one of the large ones in
the vicinity, is filled with historical belongings of both families,
and arrests one's attention immediately on entering. The photo-
murals are enlargements from small negatives taken by Mr. von
Phul, except the one above the mantel-piece. This is a huge
pen-and-ink drawing with antique effect as to design, for it is a
reproduction of the frontpiece of the old family bible of the von
Phul family that was brought to America by the first von Phul
that came across seas.

A large figure of Captain von Phul who came to America in 1764, later serving as a Captain under General George Washington. Besides the figure of Captain von Phul, are several smaller figures of members of the family in the distance. Below this is a lengthy family record in German, the Gothic lettering making the ensemble unusually atractive. The wooden mantel, a handsome one, is replaced as it was in the old house plan. The andirons are attractive and originally belonged to a brother of Henry Clay who married into the family. On both sides of the central mural over the mantel hang in long narrow frames, old bonnet ribbons from a bonnet that belonged to the wistful-looking ancestress whose miniature hangs below as a pendant, a companion miniature of her husband hanging opposite. Choice pieces of mahogany furniture fill spaces in this hall on both floors. The mural on the right side is a picture of this home on its original site, the one on the left being the old Cade plantation home, Mrs. von Phul having been a Miss Cade before her marriage. The walls of the dining-room are of panelled Louisiana cypress and the soft tones of the wood form a splendid background for the fine ancestral portraits that hang in this attractive room. The large portrait on the left as you enter, is by Amans the famous Belgian portrait painter. The old French crystal oil lamps are exceptionally fine and attractive, and the old mahogany console sideboard was another antique from the Clay family. All of the fine mahogany furniture of this room harmonize and the fine Limoge fret work fruit and flower baskets are very attractive and add greatly to the atmosphere of the room. The boat S. L. Elam fills a panel and the old oak tree above stairs is a view near Versailles plantation.

Much fine furniture, rare crystal, and silver, miniatures, and a large collection of daguerreotypes add interest. Mahogany furniture of ante-bellum design—from the studios of Mallard and Signorette—fills the large bedrooms upstairs. Here, too. more ancestral portraits adorn the walls. Ancient clock sets, quaint bric-a-brac and innumerable other interesting articles make most interesting rooms. The old forty-thieve jars in the front yard, two in number, originally were buried in the ground for over a century to keep the drinking water cool. The large iron sugar kettle from Bel Air Plantation now serves as a gold fish pool. Cane juice in olden days was boiled in it and the juice was transferred

The over-mantel panel of the old plantation home of the Von Phul family.
Copied from a front page of the Family Bible brought to America by the
first Von Phul. See Vol. II, Von Phul Family.

The old plantation home of the von Phul family in its new setting
in New Orleans.

The wide hallway of the von Phul Family plantation home.

from one sugar kettle to another and the different kettles bore the following names: 1. LaGrande; 2. Propre; 3. LeFlambeau; 4. LeSirop, and 5. LaBatterie.

During the Spring Fiesta period this home which is always in the tour becomes a lovely place indeed. The garden, too, is at its best with flowers blooming below the weeping willows. Masses of spring flowers bank the mantels and tables, and lovely girls and ladies in quaint hoop-skirts and pantelets and wide spreading crinolines fill the rooms, recalling ante-bellum house parties. Hundreds of visitors gather here daily and enjoy the charm of this old home that again has taken on a new life.

Wrought-iron balcony of the
Yvonne Le Monnier family.

DE LA CHAISE

The late Charles Gayarre, Historian of Louisiana, in writing of Jacques de la Chaise who was sent by the Company of the Indies to Louisiana as Commissioner in 1722, says: "Invested with the power to obtain information on the behavior of all officers and the administration of the colony and to report to his majesty's government, reports—'He was of patrician birth, a nephew of the confessor of Louis XIV. The chateau D'Aix, the feudal castle of the family, was situated in the Province of Forez. His father was the son of George d'Aix, Seigneur de la Chaise, who married Renee de Rochefort, daughter of one of the noblest houses of France.' In the time of the Regency, one of them died a Lieu-tenant-General, leaving a reputation for uncompromising integrity and unflinching attachment to duty. Family records show that his town residence was in Chartres Street, New Orleans— a rather large and imposing place, which he occupied with his wife and two children. The de la Chaise plantation was located in the upper part of what is today known as the uptown section of New Orleans. The present Audubon Park covers part of it. The plantation itself, never a large one like most of the ones in this area, faced the river. The slaves owned by the planter were not numerous.

Dying rather suddenly in 1730, it was rumored at the time that de la Chaise was poisoned by his enemies. Through the familes of his daughters Marie Louise, Alexandrine, Felicite, Marie Marguerite, and a son Jacques who left children, many connecting links were formed with a large number of aristocratic families of Louisiana. August de la Chaise was killed in 1803 in San Domingo following his promotion to generalship. The family name has been perpetuated however by a street in the uptown section of New Orleans.

Family portraits of the de la Chaise family are in the home of their descendants, where they adorn the wall of the handsome de la Vergne, and Landry de Freneuse mansion on St. Charles Avenue, New Orleans.

THE DE BORE SUGAR PLANTATION

The de Bore plantation, according to the grandson of the old planter, Etienne de Bore, "was situated on the left bank of the Mississippi River about six miles above New Orleans", having a starting point the outer edge of the old city which is now Canal Street. The plantation above the de Bore place belonged to Paul Foucher, a son-in-law of de Bore, and the other one above that belonged to Lafrenier, who held the position of Attorney-General under the French Regime and who later became the main leader of the rebellion when Spain took over Louisiana from the French. He was shot by order of the Spanish Governor along with a number of others. The Lafrenier plantation was acquired later by the Macarty family, an ancient patrician family who became allied to the leading families of Louisiana. A daughter of de Bore's married Don Carlos Gayarre who with the Spanish Governor, Ulloa, was to have been the first Spanish governor. Don Carlos, son-in-law of Etienne de Bore, resided on his father-in-law's plantation with his family. As judge Gayarre writes "in tribe fashion all those related families were grouped about a central point, the head and patriarch of the family and the branches."

In early days indigo was the leading staple, (used as a dye for clothing, military uniforms especially.) Finally a worm that destroyed the indigo plant threatened to ruin the planters. For years the various planters had been experimenting and trying to make sugar granulate without success. When almost ruined, Etienne de Bore suggested to his wife, a daughter of Jean Baptiste d'Estrehan, that he use the last remnant of her once large fortune in a final experiment. She begged and implored him not to do so as did their relations and friends. They told him how her father and many others had lost fortunes in these sugar-making experiments. But de Bore persisted, risked all, and succeeded. His success changed conditions at once in the colony and he became the idol of the state.

BORE'S KETTLE

The original kettle in which Bore first granulated sugar—now on the L. S. U. campus.

Etienne de Bore in his younger days while in France had been a musquetaire noir, or guardsman in the household of the King Louis XV. Watching over the safety of the majesty of France, little he dreamed that the day would come when three princes of royal blood would be his guests on the banks of the Mississippi River.

In describing his grandfather's plantation the late Charles Gayarre gives a vivid pen picture of the place in detail. It had spacious garden grounds, avenue of shade trees, vineyards, orchards, large barnyards, poultry-pens, and pigeonnaires, with numerous herds of cattle, sheep, horses, mules, etc. Gayarre recalls that his grandfather made the farm both plantation and farm. In his reminiscences of olden days on the plantation, Judge Gayarre tells of the regular Sunday visits of a number of distinguished gentlemen wearing their Legion of Honor ribbands and war medals and their courteous ways reminding him of his life at the French Court. He tells of the dinners and receptions at his grandfather's home on the plantation and at their town house. Of the time after the Battle of New Orleans how he watched the army parade through the main streets of the city. Continuing he says:

One day as our family seated on the front piazza enjoying the balmy atmosphere of a bright May morning, there came on a visit from New Orleans M. de Bore's favorite nephew, Bernard de Marigny. He was one of the most brilliant, as well as one of the wealthiest young men of the epoch. He drove in a dashing way to the house in an elegant equipage drawn by two fiery horses. Full of the buoyancy of youth, he jumped out of his carriage and ran up the broad steps of the brick perron that ascended to the piazza. As he reached the top of it he said, with a sort of careless and joyous familiarity: "Bonjour, mon oncle, bonjour" and bowed slightly around to the family without removing his hat. "Chapeau bas, monsieur!" responded a calm voice of command. "Toujours chapeau bas devant un femme, et il y en a plus d'une ici". (Hat off sir! Always hat off before a woman, and there are more than one here.) A fitting apology was instantly made by the youthful delinquent.

He describes the grounds about the plantation house thusly:

From the river road an avenue of great pecan trees formed an avenue to the house enclosure (a fenced garden with a beautiful assortment of flowering plants). This enclosure was rather unusual and not noted on many plantations. The vast enclosure, with its numerous dependencies that part of the enclosure which faced the river presented a singular appearance when approached from the public road through the avenue of pecan trees. It was that of a fortified place, for there was to be seen, with a revetment of brick five feet high, a rampart of earth about fifteen feet in width and sloping down to large moats filled with frogs, fish, and eels. The rampart was clothed in clover, and at the foot, on the end of the moat, there grew a palisade of plants common in Louisiana under the name of "Spanish Dagger", through which it would not have been easy to escalade the parapet. In their season of effloresence their numreous clusters of white flowers were beautiful. They stood in bold relief from their background of green clover and towered proudly above the street and sharp-pointed leaves by which they were protected.

This picturesque and uncommon line of fortified enclosure extended a good deal more than three hundred feet on both sides of the entrance gate that opened into the courtyard at the end of the pecan avenue.

Etienne de Boré, who discovered
the process of granulating sugar.
From a drawing given to the author by his grandson the Hon.
Charles Gayarre. Drawing now in
the Cabildo collection.

White Hall Manor, built for Francois Pascalis de la Barre.

Elmwood Plantation Manor, as it appeared before the fire in 1939. (Courtesy of Bryan Black.)

NOEL D'ESTREHAN,
Son of Jean Baptiste d'Estrehan.
(From an Oil Portrait.) Courtesy
of the family.

D'Estrehan Plantation Manor, D'Estrehan, La.
Home of the D'Estrehan Des Tours family.

Ormond Plantation Home, originally built for the
de Trepagnier family, later purchased by Capt.
Richard Butler, who named it Ormond after an
ancestral castle of the Butler family in Ireland.

Old family carriage made for Captain Richard Butler in Philadelphia. It is now at the "Cottage",
the Butler family plantation, West Feliciana, La.
(Courtesy of Miss Sarah Butler.)

This may have been reminiscent of France where such chateau-like sights were frequent. While one does not meet with the moat arrangement about the mansions, it is of common occurrence to see vast hedges of this Spanish Dagger arranged as a protection against intruders on some of the plantations in Louisiana.

During the days of the Civil War Gayarre writes that at the rumored advance of the Federal Army in camps not many miles away, he thought it only an act of the commonest prudence to follow the example of his neighbors and hide, that is, bury his valuables. He therefore packed in a secure tin box all that he considered most precious to him; his wife's jewelry and diamonds and his treasured heirlooms; the shoe buckles and sword hilt studded with brilliants that belonged to his father; his grandmother's miniature in a frame surrounded with diamonds; de Bore's snuff box; in short, all the priceless, innumerable trinkets kept in his family for generations. Selecting a good spot for the purpose under a tree that he could easily identify afterwards, accompanied by his wife, he stealthily crept out to it in the dead of night, taking a lantern with them. His confidential body servant, "the most accomplished valet and rascal in the world", according to his master, easily suspecting what was in the wind, played the spy and watched the burial of the treasure. Gayarre could not sleep for thinking of his precious box under the tree. By morning he was at the spot to discover that it was gone, and with it the valet and carriage and horses as well. The plunder was sold at the Union soldier camp, and for years afterwards in New Orleans William, the confidential servant, lived on the proceeds.

It is a great pity that Judge Gayarre did not safeguard his valuable property as another Louisiana Judge did, who buried a quantity of family silver and gold coin on a spot in front of his home, on which he built a tall chicken pen which he filled with guinea hens. The latter Judge unearthed his valuables when the storm clouds of war had blown over.

CHAPTER X

ON THE EAST BANK, NEAR NEW ORLEANS.
WHITE HALL PLANTATION

THE old White Hall plantation manor still stands on the East bank of the Mississippi River a short distance from the new bridge. The old place, the ancestral home of the de la Barre family, was built, according to Dr. Frank de la Barre Chalaron, a grandson of the planter Francois Pascalis de la Barre, in the year 1850. Monsieur de la Barre, the original owner, was the first member of the family to settle in Louisiana. For years previous to the construction of the house, the usual routine of having the material prepared on the grounds by slave labor was followed. As depicted on Norman's chart of the plantations on the Mississippi River in 1858, the plantation consisted of two tracts extending from the river to the lake, the land on the New Orleans side belonging to the noted lawyer and planter Christian Roselius, while that on the upper end was the property of J. B. LeBreton. According to Dr. Frank Chalaron the de la Barre's also owned the St. Peter and the St. George Plantations beyond this site, neither of which is in existence today.

The sugar house of White Hall Plantation was operated until 1886 when it ceased to function, but the land continued to be cultivated as a sugar plantation and the cane sold until 1891, when an uncle of Dr. Chalaron's, the last of the de la Barres, sold the place at a price consistent with the depressed land values of that date. Dr. Chalaron, who was born in the old plantation manor, recalls the charm it had while he still lived there, and its present attractive appearance does not belie his praise. At that time there was an avenue of oak trees, extending from the front steps to the river road, and gone with the oak avenue is a large tract of land that fronted the house. At the corners of the garden were large Lebanon trees, orange, myrtle and date palms. Mingling with these a large assortment of fragrant blooming shrub and evergreen plants which every mistress of the plantations incorporated into her garden plan. It was a veritable fairy land to the eyes of Dr. Chalaron and today it lingers only in memory.

Some minor architectural changes have been made but fortunately these additions have not ruined the beauty of the main house. The ancient entrance steps have been somewhat altered, but can without great trouble or expense be restored to their original form. The old house, empty for a while, was later converted into a casino with gaming tables, etc. After this venture it was closed and Jesuit priests took control. Then the house was converted into a "retreat", where mentally weary business men who sought rest and freedom from everyday cares and worries might rest both mentally as well as physically. The Jesuits have since taken over the old Jefferson College at Convent, Louisiana, the de la Barre home has again changed hands. At last it has been acquired by an institution where mentally defective children can be properly treated. Here under the kind and able management of Mrs. Louise Simon Davis in a pleasant environment these unfortunates are properly cared for in a kindly manner and treated under the scientific instruction of capable medical men. The old plantation home again appears fresh and appealing in its new white paint and repairs; the flowers adding greatly to the charm of the grounds; the children are taught a little about flowers along with their other studies, including gardening and the care of plants.

During the days following the fall of New Orleans when so many magnificent plantations were destroyed and manors burned, and with few exceptions the great sugar houses and cotton gins blown to bits by the fleet of Union gun-boats going up the river, White Hall escaped all of this. General Morgan chose the de la Barre manor as his headquarters, and his Union troops were quartered on the plantation. General Morgan, a member of the House of Morgan of New York City, chose the site because it was close to New Orleans. Before the ladies of the de la Barre family left the house, they instructed their servants to look after the officers billeted in the home. So efficient did the slaves prove to be, and so greatly impressed was the Northern General by the high toned atmosphere of the de la Barre household, that instead of allowing their home to be pillaged, he placed guards about the manor and grounds to protect it until peace was declared. At that time the house and grounds, all in good condition, were returned to the de la Barre family.

ELMWOOD PLANTATION
JEFFERSON PARISH, LOUISIANA

The old Elmwood Plantation home as it was called in late years was originally built for the Lafrenier (Chauvin) family. The land grant, being an original concession, was quite large and Colonial records show that this family was one of the six early pioneer families in Louisiana to settle in the Southeastern part of the state. During the month of March in the year 1719, Joseph Chauvin (Delery) filed an application for a concession of six arpents with the Superior Council of Louisiana, the land fronting on the Mississippi River in the Tchoupitoulas section. On the same date other members of the Chauvin family also filed application for concessions, there being three other Chauvins, brothers of Joseph Chauvin (Delery), also a nephew.

This made the Chauvin family one of the earliest landed proprietors in Louisiana. Old maps show their land close (bordering) that of Bienville, at that date Governor of the Colony.

Since that date the manor and lands have passed through many hands. The old house was occupied as a residence by the Durel Blacks when a fire occurred in the early part of 1940. The house was partly destroyed, but is being restored.

d'ESTREHAN DES TOURS
d'ESTREHAN PLANTATION
LISTED IN 1858 ON NORMAN'S MAP AS d'ESTREHAN
BUT OWNED BY A RELATIVE, P. A. ROST

Now the property of an oil company, the old d'Estrehan mansion has been renovated. Without changing the building, it has been converted into a recreation place for officials and their families connected with the oil concern, many of whom live on the grounds.

GOVERNOR W. C. C. CLAIBORNE
(Courtesy of the Louisiana State Museum,
New Orleans.)

TREPAGNIER HOUSE—Spillway.

The restful, ancient, aristocratic look of the place that marked it formerly is in a great measure absent now. It is marred by a long row of small buildings in the enclosure below the line of century old oaks that fringe the large park garden along the river road.

But the new white paint of a few years ago has begun to mellow and the brickwork a little stained, adding somewhat to the charm. The garden, too, while well kept, has not the barbered look of the days when the restoration began. It is to be greatly regretted that the frames for the extensive mosquito screening could not have been planned so as not to cut up the "facade" like a checker-board, ruining the beauty of its stately architectural lines.

The d' Estrehan house is unique in that it is a development of the early Louisiana type as can be readily seen from its roof lines, which are very similar to plantation homes in San Domingo.

According to Judge Gayarre, the plan is similar in some respects to his birthplace, the old Bore plantation house, which was surrounded by a moat and which was located in a part of what is now Audubon Park in New Orleans.

Great live oak trees surround the house and tall bushes, evergreens and other plants make a charming setting to the old place. A long wide driveway between the flower beds lead to the house from the attractive gateway at the river road shaded by oaks.

The house is comparatively large with huge rooms. It appears firmly set on the ground. The brick-paved veranda fronts the lower floor on the same level, the basement rooms used as they were formerly. In the rear rooms of the left wing is a huge white marble bath tub cut from a single block of that material about one hundred years ago. The wide entrance way on the ground floor leads back to a cross hall containing a double stairway, well designed, of mahogany leading to the floor above where lies the main house.

Tall, solid-brick Doric pillars are stuccoed and finished as is the entire exterior of the house and wings. The front presents a stately appearance and the wings constructed of the same material are said to have been added twenty years later. If such be the case, the architect who made the addition did it so well that one would not know it unless told so, since the wings look as if they were a part of the original structure. The general floor plan has much in common with a place above called Ormonde, but the latter was never as attractive.

A classic transomed side-lighted doorway, upstairs and down, front and back admits and exits one to both floors. Wide galleries and the many rooms of the house are spacious and have nice plaster work. The handsome marble mantels are in beautiful condition, but must be replacements of original ones. The diminutive dormer windows cause many to wonder whether they were not used as ventilators. They seem to small for the attic to be utilized. Th woodwork of doors and window frames is of good design with fine mouldings, much of which is worked by hand.

Originally, pigeonnaires flanked either side of the house and the garden grounds were enhanced by summer houses, mazes and garden urns, but these things have disappeared with the passing years, as have so many other attractive features. Few plantation homes in Louisiana have a more colorful history than has this old place, once so beautiful.

The d'Estrehan family descends from a noble French family that came to Louisiana with Bienville, founder of the City of New Orleans. They brought wealth and position as did many of the settlers in early days.

Among the distinguished personages who visited the d'Estrehan plantation were three house guests who were entertained there in 1798 as well as by the leading patrician families of the colony. These guests were the three sons of Philip Egalete—the Duc d'Orleans, who later became King of France, the Duc de Montpensier and the Comte de Beaujolais—who were entertained everywhere in a manner which befitted their station. On their return to France when that country had begun to recover from the Napoleonic splurge, they sent valuable tokens of appreciation to those who had befriended and entertained them during their exile in Louisiana. Many an old family of this state today treasures these mementos as priceless heirlooms, and carefully preserve their letters of gratitude.

If one lends a credulous ear to the people who live near the old d'Estrehan house, you will hear the tale of the ghost of the manor. The story is about a later resident who lived there after the d' Estrehan's had moved away.

A relative of the family living in the house at the time came to pay a visit. While seated in the drawing room awaiting her hostess, she saw an old gentleman of distinguished bearing with a long white beard come, walk around the room and then leave the room by the door he had entered without saying a word. When her hostess had greeted her, the visitor told of the old gentleman's strange entrance and exit. Her hostess, after hearing a detailed description of the old man said, "There must be some mistake, as the person answering to that description lies very ill at this moment in a sanitarium in New Orleans." A few minutes later a message came telling that the old gentleman had just died. The time of his death corresponded to the time of the vision.

In the quaint old cemetery of St. Charles Parish at Red Church, near the d'Estrehan plantation can be found the tomb of the d'Estrehan family. Jean Baptist d'Estrehan gave the cemetery to the parish before his death.

The d'Estrehan High School in the parish near the old mansion is a gift of the planter's son, Noel d'Estrehan, who for many years managed the plantation. The site of the town of Gretna, opposite New Orleans, in the Parish of Jefferson was also a gift of his son, made before his death in 1848.

ORMOND PLANTATION

St. Charles Parish

This plantation derives its name from Ormond Castle in Ireland, the home of James, son of the sixth Butler of the Peerage of Ireland, created Earl of Ormond in 1321. It became the home of the McCutchon family, who were related by marriage to the Butler family through Eleanor Butler of Dangan Castle, who was descended from the Earl of Ormond. The family traces back to one Theobold Fitzwalter, who was made Chief Butler of Ireland by King Henry II whom he accompanied to Ireland.

The McCutchon family formerly owned other large plantations on the Mississippi River. They are closely related to the d'Estrehan family by marriage, as well as to many of the other leading plantation families of the state. Adel d'Estrehan des Tour (the full name of the d'Estrehan family), daughter of Nicholas d'Estrehan, a direct descendant of the Royal Treasurer of Louisiana, married Samuel B. McCutchon, and became the mother of Samuel B. McCutchon, Jr., Amelia McCutchon and Azby d'Estrehan McCutchon.

The old plantation house originally was a notable place, but in the course of time, it has been allowed to fall into ruin. It is one of the plantation houses of which scale drawings have been made showing front and rear views, also ground and second story floor plans.

Included in the sketches are detailed drawings of mantels, stairways, and architectural features generally, all of which are beautifully pictured in (Italo Williams Riccuti's) "New Orleans and Its Environs—The Domestic Architecture 1727-1870", one of the most complete books of its kind ever published in America.

The floor plans are similar in many respects to those of the old d'Estrehan plantation home. The mantels are of good design, quite similar to those of some eighteenth century ones in the "Vieux Carre". The broad acres around the Ormond house are planted in sugarcane and are now managed by a syndicate. It is doubtful if any attempt will ever be made to restore the old place because of its dilapidated state.

The early history of this old plantation house was lost in obscurity but by chance I found a member of the family from whom I obtained the following story.

The old plantation house that is now known as Ormond House was erected for Pierre Trepagnier, an army officer of the Louisiana Militia, who served under the Spanish governor Bernado de Galvez, when the Spanish forces joined with the Colonies at the time of the American Revolution against the English. As was customary in part return for his service, Pierre Trepagnier was deeded the large acreage on which he erected the plantation manor and laid out the plantation that we now know as Ormond. The plantation, under the management of a relative who lived on another smaller plantation nearby, proved a great financial success, and in a very short time Pierre Trepagnier became quite wealthy. Having "friends at court", as it were, he had means to dispose of his crops and buy slaves all with great saving to the plantation. Pierre Trepagnier, or de Trepagnier as the name occasionally appears on old records, was of distinguished appearance and of an adventurous disposition. He had no fear of danger and was somewhat of a Don Juan. He had been the instigator of a plot to get rid of individuals who were plotting against the interest of his Catholic Majesty, the King of Spain. One morning while at breakfast with his family a Spanish calash or state carriage bearing on its door panel the arms of Spain emblazoned in colors, drove up to the main entrance. An official-looking individual in uniform, with the customary long mantle, got out and requested to speak to the planter. The negro butler admitted the stranger and going to the dining-room where the family were at breakfast announced the caller. Captain Trepagnier arose and entered the room where his impressive visitor awaited him. After a few words whispered by the stranger, Captain Trepagnier re-entered the dining-room where his wife and children were still seated. He bade them a hurried good-bye, and promising to return shortly, entered the calash and drove off with the mysterious stranger never to be seen or heard of again.

The afternoon of Captain Trepagnier's disappearance the negro gardener in cleaning the grounds about the front of the house discovered a letter addressed to Madame Trepagnier containing the one word "Adios", and signed in an unknown hand writing: "Pierre". Investigation proved that the calash did not belong to the Spanish authorities in Louisiana. After waiting for months without any word from her husband, Madame Trepagnier, heart-broken, discouraged and disconsolate, disposed of her plantation home and moved to New Orleans.

At that time the renowned army officer, Richard Butler, had just recently married the beautiful and wealthy ward of the Spanish Governor, Dona Margareta Fara. The bridegroom was the son of Colonel William Butler who with his five sons had gained for the family the title of "The Fighting Butlers", all of whom held high rank under Washington in the War of Independence, and were later to be extolled as shining examples of bravery and gallantry. At a banquet which Washington gave to his officers the great Chieftain, happy to show his appreciation of their valor, with upheld glass toasted "The Fighting Butlers". Later according to the Butler genealogy Lafayette following Washington stated, "Whenever on the field I wanted a thing well done, I had a Butler do it."

Later on Richard Butler resigned his captaincy in the army and decided to become a planter, naming his home after the ancestral castle of the Duke of Ormond in Ireland. The born soldier surprised many of his friends and relatives who scoffed at his becoming a planter. However, he made a large fortune and later invested large sums of money in plantation lands in Pointe Coupee Parish, Louisiana. Besides the plantations in Louisiana, he owned jointly with his wife a plantation near Pinkney, Mississippi, called the Woodstock Plantation, also another called the Clarksville Plantation. Together these were valued at about one hundred and thirty thousand dollars.

In the year 1805 during a yellow fever epidemic, Colonel Thomas Butler, an uncle of the Fighting Butlers, died at Ormond House. Later the same dreaded terror, now eradicated entirely in this section of the country, again swept through the state and the gallant Captain Richard Butler and his beautiful wife died of the yellow fever, Captain Butler at the time being only forty-three years of age. His wife's brother, Captain George Farra, while visiting them was also stricken with the fever and a few days later died.

Having no children the large property holdings were divided between members of Captain Butler's family, his mother and his two sisters, Rebecca and Harriet. Rebecca Butler who married Captain Samuel McCutchon, a naval officer, became the owners of Ormond Plantation and manor. Their son, Samuel McCutcheon, Jr., married the daughter of their planter neighbor, d'Estrehan, thus uniting two prominent aristocratic families. Adel d'Estrehan, Captain McCutchon's bride, possessed all of the charm and beauty of Etienne de Bore's wife, who also was a d'Estrehan and a noted belle of her day. The plantation was operated successfully until the middle of the 1870's. As a result of all the horror, suffering, robbery, and every villainy one can imagine that flourished during Reconstruction Days in the South, the McCutchon's feeling that it was useless to try and retain the plantation any longer, disposed of it.

Evidently nothing has been done to the old manor house since the family moved away, for it has gradually disintegrated for want of needed repairs during all of these years. From its general appearance it is apparently in the last stages of decay. In type it has the architectural features of a blending of French and Spanish, neither of which is distinctive. Comfort and roominess are the two main features, although an attempt was made to simulate stone construction, and a few extraneous details on the exterior give it a certain distinction. Interiorly the finish originally was typical Spanish, the mantels, the chimneys, wood trim and mode of openings all possessed merit. When we remember the Spanish influence, devoid of arcades, fan windows, etc., one might readily class it an unpretentious plantation house. The d'Estrehan house on the plantation close by, of earlier construction served in a way as a model, as the houses have a number of parts in common. The main house or central building was planned as a two-storied structure originally, the same can be stated for the two buildings on the sides joined by galleries which are covered. Across the front of the main building the arrangement is quite similar to the raised-basement type homes. The upstairs gallery extending across the front has the regulation small collonettes, the upper surface being chamfered with flattened surfaces. Below, rising from the bricked loggia and supporting the gallery on low square bases of brick, rise seven Doric columns. These columns are constructed of brick and are heavily stuccoed. Within the last two years the well designed wooden mantels have been removed. The main building with its four large rooms connect at the rear on either side with the corridors which are arched passage ways. Each of the wings or garconniers contain two rooms on each floor. The entire building at present sags, and the stucco has fallen in many places. The old house because of its strange history and tragic story has been sought out by artists, writers and camera men, and many are the questions that are asked about it.

Some have thought that this house is the second built on the site. After much investigation I have come to the conclusion that the present house known as the Ormond Plantation home, is the original and first plantation home to be erected on this site. According to a member of the de Trepagnier family, the original plantation home consisted of the center building, with square pigeonnaires to either side. Later after it had passed into the hands of the McCutchon family the two wings were constructed, at which time the two pigeonnaires were demolished. Those that state that the old Mizaine plantation home occupied this site evidently have confused this place with another close by of which nothing remains, and which was called by old residents the Mizaine place until its disappearance a number of years ago.

THE MIZAINE PLANTATION.

Near Ormond Plantation, St. Charles Parish.

An old plantation mansion that went into the Mississippi River a number of years ago forms the subject of a tale of "Old Louisiana". It is based on the gruesome find of the owner's skeleton in his New Orleans mansion in the French Quarter.

It is the story of Major Hamicar Mizaine, who had lost an arm in the Mexican war. In his salad days, a friend had married the young lady to whom he had been engaged, and at once he swore that he would be avenged—no matter what the cost. As time passed he married a young lady, who also had had a disappointment in love, and who married him to avoid being a spinster. The young woman who had jilted Major Mizaine became the mother of a fine boy, and in due time, his wife presented him with a daughter. At once in his evil mind he planned that when the girl grew up she should break the heart of his rival's son as his former friend had broken his.

As time passed all turned out as he desired. Both families being in the same circles socially and the city comparatively small they were thrown in close contact. But when the time came for her to jilt the young man with whom she was very much in love, she would not do so. She married him despite her father's threats. A widow with a small babe, she returned after the Civil War to her father's home in the hope of a reconciliation, as she and her child were sick and starving. It was midwinter and pushing her out into the cold, Major Mizaine slammed the door. He evidently killed himself shortly afterwards for he was not seen again. The mother and child died the next day according to the neighbors who found her huddled in a doorway near her former home. Both mother and child were buried by the city.

Mademoiselle Livie D'Arensbourg, daughter of Gustave D'Arensbourg and Mathilde Perret. Reproduced from the life-sized portrait by Amans in the
home of her granddaughter, Mrs. W. A. Kernaghan.
See page 102. (Courtesy of Miss Edith Kernaghan.)

The old plantation home of the Welham family.

The Mount Airy Plantation House—home of the Joseph
Louis Le Bourgeois family.

For many years the house remained empty after the disappearance of Major Mizaine, for his wife had died during the Civil War days. A later owner of the property, decided to build a business place on the site. When the house was demolished to make room for the drygoods store, it was discovered that a secret cabinet had been built into the wall and hidden in the concave section to which the winding stairway clung in its sweep to the floor above. When the panelling was ripped out in this secret place was found a sofa on which lay the skeleton of a man fully clothed, all heavily covered with dust. On the floor lay a rusty pistol with one chamber empty.

The newspapers of that date paid little attention to the matter, simply mentioning the discovery of the suicide, as the papers were filled with accounts of the bitter political fight then on. The body was ordered buried in the potters field. Later when old residents of the locality began to discuss the strange find, some of them recalled the family feud and the disappearance of Major Mizaine and his bizarre story. Putting together the facts, they concluded that in a fit of remorse after ejecting his sick daughter and child, he had gone to the cabinet and killed himself. Later on when the French Quarter was ratproofed a number of secret cabinets were discovered in the old buildings which were demolished. One was found on Royal Street in a building that for years stood in ruins, located a few doors from the ancient Le Monnier home, corner of St. Peter Street, now occupied by an antique shop in the one-storied building built on its site.

The original house is illustrated in Miss Grace King's "New Orleans The Place and The People" as the home of the first Mayor of New Orleans. The iron work of the hand-wrought balcony is now to be seen in the collection of Newcomb College, having been rescued by the late Dr. Ellsworth Woodward of New Orleans. Many contend that these cabinets were constructed to hide valuables from slaves, as were the secret drawers in old furniture.

All of the families connected with this article are extinct.

TREPAGNIER

Alone and forlorn, in the last stages of decay, and cut off from a passable road, this old house now lies in the area given over to the spillway. Lying a short distance beyond Ormond the place was built during the Spanish occupation of Louisiana. The de Trepagnier house, now known as Ormond, was built for Pierre de Trepagnier, while the house described here was built by a relative of Pierre de Trepagnier, who had his own plantation, but who also was manager of the Pierre de Trepagnier place.

Up until about ten years ago the old place presented a fairly attractive picture, but it was found that the river was rapidly cutting into the land so all attempts to save the place were abandoned. It is of the smaller type of early Louisiana plantation home, of which in olden days hundreds could be seen along the Mississippi River and bayous of Louisiana. Many of them were replaced by finer homes when the "Golden Era" of Louisiana dawned. Many of these houses are still to be found in wandering through the plantation country.

This particular place now so dilapidated-looking, originally was quite an attractive and simple home. The woodwork of the doors and window frames was carefully made by hand, with neat hand—made mouldings. The glazed doors were attractively designed, and the mantels had shelves extending around three sides of the small chimneys, as we find in so many of the fine earlier homes of the French Quarter in New Orleans.

The de Trepagnier family in Louisiana stems to one Romaine de Trepignier, or Trepagay, as it is written in old records in Canada, was born in France in the year 1627. His Canadian record shows that he migrated to Canada in early times, became attached to Chateau Richer where he died on the 20th of March, 1702. The church records show that he married in Quebec, Genevieve Drouin, a native of Canada, on the 24th of April, 1656, who died there on October 4th, 1710. From this branch of the de Trepagnier family numerous members of the family descend. From Pierre de Trepagnier, who married Elisabeth Reynaud, and for whom the old plantation house we now know as Ormond was built, a numerous progeny descends, their seven children marrying into numerous prominent old Louisiana families.

D'ARENSBOURG

Johan Leonard von Arensbourg was master of the Royal Mint at Settin, as well as a director of minting concerns in Pommerania.

He had married Elisabeth Eleonora Formant - Manderstrom, who was born July 17th, 1678, and who died on October 10th, 1710. According to family records her father, Wrik Forsmander, was chief inspector of customs at Wismar, in the department of Mecklenburg, and had been ennobled in 1703 with the name of Manderstrom, which at present is that of a baronial family.

The subject of this article Karl Frederik von Arensbourg (Charles Frederic d'Arensbourg) was one of seven children, among whom are mentioned Charlotta or Carlotta as she was called, Lovisa and Christian Ludwig, both born in a German parish in Stockholm—the first in 1699 and the second in 1706. Charles Frederic d'Arensbourg, who was born in Stockholm in 1693, received a military education, later becoming a lieutenant in the Sodermandland Battalion of Boarders (naval) and was granted a captaincy, the promotion being granted per his request of May, 1719. He then served in the army of his Majesty, Charles XII, during which time he had been made a prisoner of on two occasions, and had been wounded several times. Following the Battle of Pultava, he was granted leave to visit Germany, but being without the necessary funds, and the opportunity presenting itself, he obtained service with the West Indies Company, coming to Louisiana at the age of 28 years. He landed in Biloxi in 1721, according to Hanno Deiler in his article on "The German Coast Settlement" in Louisiana.

As Russia in 1721 had gained the Cession of Livonia (which territory had belonged to Sweden), meaning that the Swedes that remained in this area would come under the domination of Russia, Swedish officers, some twenty in number, accompanied von Arensbourg to America, preferring exile to the Russian yoke. On reaching Paris they learned of the settlements being made in Louisiana by the Company of the Indies, organized following the collapse of John Law's "Mississippi Bubble". D'Arensbourg obtained a commission in Paris from the new company. They placed him in command of a large number of German settlers in readiness to be sent to the French Concessions of Law on the Arkansas river: by way of Havre from whence they were to embark.

The Portefaix on which they sailed arrived finally at Biloxi in the month of October, bringing with them a detailed account of Law's failure and flight from France. The news threw the colony into great confusion, finally reaching the small colony of Germans who had already settled on the Arkansas River and started planting vegetables and so on, preparatory to laying out plantations. Terror-stricken with the news they at once abandoned their farms, and taking their families they hurried back to Biloxi, the capital of the settlement. Intending to demand passage back to their fatherland, they stopped at New Orleans where the new city that was to succeed Biloxi as Capital of the settlement was in the process of being laid out by engineers under Bienville. At once these distraught Germans were told of the newly arrived band of their countrymen, and the plans Bienville had for them. They were finally induced to join the new arrivals under the charge of d'Arensbourg. Bienville then decided to change the original location of their settlement to that of the much preferred area on the banks of the alluvial Mississippi river, the site to be about twenty miles above his new town of New Orleans. It was here amongst these settlers that Charles Frederick d'Arensbourg planned his own plantation on the concession that he had obtained from the French government.

Tales of the suffering of others that had been shipped by Law to the Louisiana colonies brought back to them memories of their sorrows and trouble. They recalled how they had been herded like cattle after almost fighting to get places on the ship bound for America, the filth and stench of their quarters on shipboard, the sick and dying, and how disillusioned were those who had believed Law's enticing pamphlets. They had belonged to the throng of starving German peasants that daily left for French ports in the hope of bettering their condition. The Rhineland, wrecked and impoverished by the wars of Louis XIV, was better than this awful suffering. So it is little wonder that these unfortunate people were terror-stricken when they heard of Law's flight and what it might mean. Hanno Deiler, historian, writing of the early colonization by Law states:

> No pen can describe, nor human fancy imagine the hardships which the German pioneers of Louisiana suffered even after they had survived the perils of the sea and epidemics and starvation on the sands of Biloxi. No wonder that so many perished. Had they been of a less hardy race, not one of these families would have survived. It should be remembered that the land assigned to them was virgin forest in heavy alluvial bottoms of the Mississippi, with tremendous germinating powers awakened by a semi-tropical sun. Giant oaks,

with wide spreading arms and gray mossy beards stood there as if
from eternity, and defied the axe of man. Between them arose tower-
ing pines with thick undergrowth, bushes and shrub and an impene-
trable twist of running, spinning and clinging vines under whose protection lurk a hell of hostile animals and savage men. Leopards,
panthers, wild cats, snakes and alligators and their terrible allies,
a scorching sun, the miasma rising from the disturbed virgin soil and
floods of a mighty river—all these combined to destroy the work of
man and man himself. There were no levees then, no protecting
dams, and only too often when the spring floods came, caused by
the upper flooded areas by the melting of snow in the vast regions
of the Mississippi, and its tributaries, that the colonists were driven
to climb upon the roofs of their houses and up into trees, as hundreds
of miles of fertile land was inundated.

Karl Frederick d'Arensbourg proved a mighty father to these
helpless people, most of them peasants, who asked but little, and
the opportunity to earn that. They proved to be mighty workers,
the men seemingly never tiring, while the women, equally as
hardy, often in earliest days, allowing themselves to be hitched
to improvised plows as did the peasants of old Russia. All of
them would work in the fields, and in the evenings cook and prepare the meals, also attend to what mending had to be done.
d'Arensbourg spent much time amongst his people, encouraging
them in their work and in the building of their simple homes, in
organizing classes for the children old enough to go to school,
aiding parents in their purchases, etc., so that they would not be
swindled.

When Chevalier d'Arensbourg planned his own residence he
had one built larger but on the lines of the simple plantation
houses that were being erected at that date. It was a simple unpainted cottage, with a front porch and overhanging roof, supported by small posts. His home finished and his official duties
moving smoothly, he married in the year 1722 Margaret Metzer
of German birth. However, the lady frequently signed her name
Metzerine, according to some of her descendants. They became
the parents of two sons and four daughters, and left numerous
descendants who married into many prominent old Louisiana
families. One can best describe this intermarriage by stating
that their names are interwoven into the social fabric of city
and state like the threads of an ancient tapestry.

Along with ruling his colony (the German Coast), for over
fifty years again and again d'Arensbourg took part in wars

against the Indians. He also took part in the rebellion of the colonists against being transferred to Spain, and was fortunate enough to escape punishment. On August 31st, 1765 he was made a Chevalier of the French Military Order, St. Louis. For half a century he acted as judge for his little settlement, straightening out their differences when they arose, and acting as their leader when their interest was at stake. Chevalier Charles Frederic d'Arensbourg died in 1779 at the ripe old age of eighty-four. He was loved and honored by all the people, and was buried with pomp and ceremony in the cemetery at Red Church, near his plantation. The larger plantation that he occupied later, and the house he had built for his family were still standing until the Civil War. It was bombarded along with the others near by They have never been rebuilt, and their sites are marked by avenues of oak trees leading from the river road far inland to where the plantation houses stood. At present there is nothing left of the old place, but another plantation home belonging to the d'Arensbourg family, located on the West bank of the Mississippi River is still standing and the plantation is still conducted in that name.

Charles Frederick D'Arensbourg married Marguerite Metzer. Their son Charles Frederick D'Arensbourg married Marguerite de la Vergne; their son, Gustave D'Arensbourg, married Mathilde Perret. Their daughter, Livie D'Arensbourg, married James F. Freret; their daughter Mathilde Freret, married Joseph Mitchel, and their daughter, Georgine Mitchel (who owns the picture) original of this mother and daughter, married W. A. Kernaghan.

CHAPTER XI.

OTHER PLANTATIONS IN ST. CHARLES PARISH.

RED CHURCH

The tract of land on the northern extremity of d'Estrehan is called Red Church. A building of that character indicated on the map of the year 1858 with plantation in the rear and side. On the map of the year 1858 the large plantation acreage of the Ormond plantation was listed as the property of J. W. and C. McCutchon. This tract, with a smaller one separated by another small tract belonging to Widow D. La Branche, extends from the river to Lake Pontchartrain.

WELHAM

This name appears a number of times in connection with large plantation holdings indicated on Norman's map of the Ante-bellum plantations on the Mississippi River. However, this particular Welham plantation home has been the one that has managed to retain its original name while so many of the others were being changed.

It is a fairly large house and a comfortable one apparently. Of solid brick construction at present in a freshened condition after having been thoroughly restored a short time ago, fortunately nothing of its attractive architectural planning has been changed. Its front still has the white plaster-finish and its sides are of red as always, while the back of brick with the white trim completes the attractive unpretentious old manor. The garden once so beautiful which added so much to the place is no longer here, as the hungry river has eaten into the grounds the last few years. The house now stands close to the river road. The white columns, wide fan-transomed and side-lighted entrance, and the balustraded observatory are features that add dignity to the place and class it as one of the outstanding old plantation houses of the vicinity. There still seems to be a great deal of life about the place for a number of neatly dressed white children were playing within the fenced enclosure while the distant plantation grounds are alive at present with cane cutters singing as they work.

ANGELINA

Angelina Plantation is the home of the Trosclair family who own other plantations on the Mississippi River. Up until a few years ago it was a good example of its kind, but left on the outer side of the new levee, it was finally demolished when condemned.

Built in 1852, it was solidly constructed of brick with a heavy plaster finish. It was of two stories and an attic in height, with a large central hall upstairs and downstairs and wide verandas on both floors. It had many rooms, all spacious and well finished. Altogether it made an attractive comfortable mansion for a large family.

The house had many interesting detailed features, the lower columns being of the Ionic order, while those on the floor above of the Corinthian order. The Troxler family long ago knew that the old place would have to be torn down—so had not made any attempt to keep it in repair.

Shortly before the land finally caved into the river, the place was demolished so as to salvage as much material as possible. The picturesque pointed hexagonal pigeonnaire, one on either side of the house, with their ornamental weather vanes attracted passing motorists long after the house was gone, but both of them have now disappeared, only a little garconnier remaining to recall the passing of an ancient landmark of the German coast. A later visit to the old place revealed that the old garconniers, the attractive pigeonnaires, and their attractive weather vanes had disappeared, the latter at least reaching the hands of one I am told who appreciates their historical and artistic value. Also gone were the gilded race-horse and the crowing cock, nothing remaining but the little playhouse where in years gone by, have played so many generations of the Trosclair children that lived in the old mansion.

Bocage Plantation Manor.

Sugar Mill.

Union Plantation House.

Ellington Plantation House—ancestral home of
Cora Witherspoon of motion pictures. See page 166.

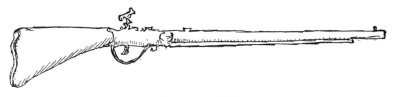

CHAPTE XII.

IN ST. JOHN PARISH.
MOUNT AIRY

Plantation Home of the LeBourgeois Family.

Located in the Parish of St. John the Baptist, the LeBourgeois plantation lands originally formed the northern boundary line. This old plantation home was originally built for a Mr. Fortin, also a planter, who occupied the place with his family previous to its becoming the home of the Joseph LeBourgeois family; and later, the home of the Joseph Louis LeBourgeois family who occupied it for many years.

The old place is still in beautiful condition, freshly painted white and in good repair, and from all appearances carefully tended. In days gone by it was surrounded by a heavy growth of oak trees, some of them of great age and spread. At that time, the place was enclosed in a beautiful wicker fence made of intricate mesh which terminated in pointed finals giving the entrance an elegant appearance. An imposing gateway opened on to a walkway some distance to the stairway placed between flower beds filled with fragrant blooming plants. The stairway is especially beautiful, being in part hand-made fret work, fashioned by slaves on the plantation.

The fence rested on a cemented brick coping and extended several acres across the front of the grounds on the river road line. The fret work iron stairway is quite attractive, a similar one of cast iron can be seen at the entrance of the old plantation home of Batchellor Plantation above Baton Rouge, on the west bank of the Mississippi River.

During the Civil War, like most plantation houses, Mount Airy was swept clean by the Union troops—stray soldiers, men from the string of barges and gunboats—who took everything they could lay their hands on, even refusing to leave a single cow on the place to furnish milk for a large family of children. Not being able to make the cow follow, one of the Union soldiers shot the animal and had the men cart it away. Bayonets were driven into every wall in search of treasure or even hidden persons and things were mutilated generally.

During this ransacking of the house, Madame LeBourgeois, who had been surprised by the visit of the Union soldiers, at a moment when the troops were in the front of the house, handed a faithful slave a large package of silver and told her to hide it at once.

Seeing a large hay stack in the back of the yard—the silver was thrown beneath the newly cut hay. Later, when the soldiers wrecking the house had grown tired, they spied the hay stack and piled on to it, joking and romping like children. They little suspected that the hidden silver was so near. Today this silver is in possession of the family of Mrs. Joseph Louis LeBourgeois, who laughingly tells how her husband's mother had saved it by her presence of mind and the help of her faithful slaves.

The family home of the LeBourgeois in New Orleans has many interesting and beautiful souvenirs of the old plantation.

Louis Sosten LeBourgeois married Erasie Becnel. They were the father and mother of Joseph Louis LeBourgeois who married Noemie Arceneau, daughter of Felix Arceneau and Domitile Arceneau.

The children of Joseph Louis LeBourgeois and Noemie Arceneau are as follows: Louisa LeBourgeois, who married Vincent Green of Mobile, Ala; Noemie LeBourgeois, who married F. W. Quackenboss; Georgine LeBourgeois, who married Joseph Walthew, an Englishman; Joseph Louis LeBourgeois, Jr., who married Mademoiselle May LeSassier; Felix Albert LeBourgeois, who married Mademoiselle Lise Hewett; Lucile LeBourgeois—single.

LE SASSIER

Henry LeSassier was the son of Louis LeSassier and Carmilite Behn. He marrid Emma Prichard. Their children are: Georgine, unmarried; Anglice, unmarried; Emma LeSassier, married W. B. McCaw, from Yorkville, South Carolina; Richard Prichard LeSassier married Ada Dangean; Louis LeSassier married Louise Dwyer; May LeSassier married Joseph Louis LeBourgeois, of Belmont and Mount Airy Plantations; Margaret LeSassier died at the age of 16; Henry LeSassier, who married Emma Prichard, owned Trinity Plantation, located in St. Charles Parish on the Mississippi River, and at one time was president of the Citizen's Bank, New Orleans. He was a member of the Stock Broker firm of Henry LeSassier and Geo. Bender, with offices at 30 Carondelet Stret, New Orleans.

During the Civil War, after the fall of New Orleans, the handsome family home at the corner of Ninth and Prytania streets in New Orleans, was seized by the Federal Troops, and the furnishings were confiscated, and sold at auction, being bought back by Miss Georgia Prichard for the family. Much of it is in the home of Mrs. Joseph Louis LeBourgeois nee May LeSassier.

After confiscating the furnishings of the home, the house was converted into a smallpox hospital for Union Soldiers. While used as a hospital, in the spacious parlors, before each of the handsome white marble mantels, the handsome floors were used to test the searing irons, for the doctors attending the men used the searing method with red hot irons to destroy the poison, as they called it, at that date—burning each pustule. The burnt stripes caused by the searing irons were never removed, as Mr. LeSassier wanted his friends to know how his home had been abused.

THE WAGUESPACK PLANTATION HOME
St. John the Baptist Parish.

The site of this stately mansion, erected in 1907 for the Waguespack family, was occupied formerly by the old Servell Plantation home—the plantation known as Sport Plantation. Much of the material used in the construction of this handsome place came from the old plantation mansion of the C. M. Shepherd family, relatives of the Minor family, known as the Golden Grove Plantation. On the site is a comfortable-looking house which serves as a country tavern for the area.

de MONTEGUT
St. John the Baptist Parish, La.

The de Montegut Plantation home is listed on Norman's Chart of Plantations on the Mississippi River in 1858 as belonging to L. Montegut.

Today the quaint old plantation home of the de Montegut

family, even in its ruined condition, is very attractive and un-usual in its planning. Like many of this type of ancient home found scattered about rural France, it too has fallen from its high estate, becoming the home of a simple farming people. Even in its dilapidated condition, one can see that it was once a charm-ing roomy livable place until allowed to fall into ruin.

The first of the de Montegut's to come to Louisiana in 1760, was Raymond de Montegut, a native of Rocas in the Department of Armagnac, France, as shown in the records of the Charity Hospital of St. Charles, as the early hospital of New Orleans was termed then.

Count Louis Philippe de Roffignac, born in Perigod, France, having served as a lieutenant of the French artillery one day while on the street in Paris during the days of the "Reign of Terror" with his friend, Jacques Pitot de Beaujardiére, another young nobleman, approached the Tower, the prison where Marie Antoinette, the unfortunate queen of France was confined await-ing death. As they drew nearer, the noisy shouting and swear-ing of the rabble increased. Louder and louder grew the noise, and soon the two young men were engulfed by the mob. Unable to move they were forced to witness a horrible sight—the beauti-ful head of the Princess de Lamballe, with hair dressed high, carried by the mob on the point of a long pole. After the Prin-cess had been guillotined, the crowd had put the blood-dripping head on this pole and had thrust it in front of the window of the room where the former queen was imprisoned, so that she might know what they had done to her friend, and realize that her turn soon would come. Losing control of himself young Pitot gave vent to his feelings loud enough to be overheard. A moment later a stranger touched his arm and whispered to him that he should leave at once—"flee from France as he had compromised himself". As he turned he saw his informant in laborer's clothing, no doubt another nobleman in disguise. Both young men heeded the warn-ing and sailed the next day for Louisiana. Reaching New Or-leans they joined other emigres and their experiences added to the list of numerous tales of horror that came to Louisiana during those terrible years.

The ancient plantation home of the de Montegut family shows from the type of its construction that it is of great age. It is said to have been erected between 1770 and 1775. Its lines are

much like those of the rural homes of French aristocrats as opposed
to the more pompous chateau type, with the difference that stone
is generally used in France instead of brick as is the case here.
It is quite a large, roomy structure, as like a French country
home, with wide chimneys, deep embrasured window casements,
a wide hall-like room and ample apartments on either side. The
deep brickwork is heavily built along European lines coated with
a thick stucco. Like typical ancient Latin houses, the main rooms
are all on the second floor, while the rooms generally found in
the basement occupy the ground floor which is paved with brick.
An attractive stairway originally led up to the second story, but
all of the balustrades have disappeared. One finds traces of
former flower-beds and garden walks. Old people of the vicinity
tell of its past glory and what an attractive place it once was.

Stories are told of the Duke of Orleans and his two brothers,
exiles at the time, being entertained at this plantation home, but
I have been unable to confirm this. What is an historical fact,
however, is that they were entertained by Dr. Joseph de Montegut
in the City of New Orleans at his then new home at number 731
Royal Street, which building is still standing in good repair. In
this ancient mansion in the French Quarter these royal visitors
were entertained in a lavish manner on several occasions. The
site of this home was included in the area destroyed by the second
great fire of 1794, and shortly afterwards Dr. Montegut had the
present home built which he occupied until 1815. The court-yard
of the old home in the French Quarter is especially attractive.

Louis Philip Joseph de Roffignac, who had dropped his title
of "count" when he came to Louisiana, married a daughter of
de Montegut, who had Louis Philippe for her godfather. Later
when an aunt living in France died, de Roffignac inherited a
chateau and a large fortune, the chateau being near Prigux, and
when he visited Paris with his wife was welcomed by King Louis
Philippe, who entertained them both at luncheon at the Tuilleries.
During the luncheon the King mentioned to Madame de Roffignac
that he was her godfather, and remembered how very gracious
her father, Dr. de Montegut, had been to his two brothers and
himself during their exile in Louisiana. Later de Roffignac's
daughter married the King's sister's secretary, and both of his
sons married daughters of distinguished families. A street in
New Orleans is named for the Montegut family.

CHAPTER XIII.

IN ST. JAMES PARISH.

JEFFERSON COLLEGE

St. James Parish

Originally this magnificent group of buildings formed the Jefferson College where were educated by the Marist Fathers (Catholic) the sons of wealthy planters from Louisiana and Mississippi.

As so many of the sons of wealthy planters were being sent abroad or to the great colleges of the North to be educated, the Jefferson College was being abandoned as a place of education, previous to 1860. At that time Valcour Aimee, an immensely wealthy planter of St. James Parish, West Bank, bought the college buildings and plantation attached, had the place put in perfect condition, and gave sufficient funds to assure the Marist Fathers of the best teachers, when the college was again resumed. It remained as such until 1928 and since then has become a Catholic retreat for men. It is now called Manresa House and is conducted by the Marist Fathers at Convent, Louisiana.

SACRED HEART CONVENT

Convent, Louisiana—St James Parish

At present a lease for four years has been made between the Sacred Heart Association of Louisiana, and the N. Y. A.—State

Commissioner of Welfare, who have agreed to restore the ancient building with materials furnished by the state. "Youths between 18 and 25 receiving N. Y. A. aid, will furnish the labor for rehabilitation of the 90-year-old building."

The ancient convent was built in 1848. It is of French-Gothic design, and the school which was originally started in 1821, took possession of the building when finished, and continued until about 1928, as a Catholic Convent, where thousands of planter's daughters were educated.

Previous to the Civil War the standard of education at the old convent was very high, as the wealthy planters demanded that the instructors be highly educated women and the letters of these ladies that attended this convent gave evidence of the culture and polish of the writers.

After the convent was closed, the buildings were separated and the convent used as a refuge f or nuns and children and priests fleeing from the persecution of the Catholics by the Mexicans.

The present undertaking intends to have the 190-acres attached to the convent, farmed as an agricultural project for young men receiving N. Y. A. aid.

BELMONT

Belmont Plantation which belonged to the LeBourgeois family, located on the East Bank of the Mississippi River in St. James Parish directly opposite to the beautiful plantation home of Mr. and Mrs. Andrew Stewart, near Vacherie, Louisiana, now known as Oak Alley, is but a memory.

Belmont replaced a former plantation home of the LeBourgeois family, and was built by Madame Louis LeBourgeois (nee Erasie Becnel) whose husband had died previous to the erection of the mansion. She planned this magnificent home so that her children should have the full benefit of her great wealth during her lifetime. Belmont was undoubtedly one of the finest plantation mansions in Louisiana, being a magnificent example of a wealthy planter's home, with its group of accompanying buildings. It typifies the luxurious scale of living during the golden era of the state. This palatial mansion, for indeed it was such, was erected without regard to cost, no expense being spared to make it both beautiful, as well as comfortable.

The cypress was gotten from the plantation woods, as were the bricks that were made on the place by slave labor, from native clay. Cabinet work, hardware, etc., were bought from further north, while the white marble mantels were imported.

Outside of the above mentioned articles, a first outlay of sixty thousand dollars was made, with another payment of eight thousand four-hundred-dollars, for the fluting of the twenty-eight massive cypress columns that surrounded the building.

A great deal of slave labor was used in the building of the mansion, and a fabulous price was paid for the twenty-eight hand-carved monster Corinthian Caps that surmounted the great columns—the caps being equally as ornate and large as those that we see today on the columns of the old John Andrews mansion at Belle Grove Plantation on the West Bank of the Mississippi River.

The architect, to avoid a too severe form of classic Greek Revival cornice, took poetic license, for a cornice of the magnitude required by a mansion the size of Belmont probably would have appeared flat. The observatory, as well as dormers, are not visible in the photograph, and the architectural deviation not sufficiently marked to mar the grandeur of the appearance of the place.

The buildings that were grouped about Belmont were arranged somewhat along the lines of those of the old Constancia, or as it is called today "Uncle Sam" for short.

The ornamentations which were carved by hand, the broken classic lines and curved brackets on the dentil course, are creations of that era which was beginning to free itself from the rigid demands of the Classic Revival in its true and more formal form. This latest architectural style lent itself to the grandiose elaboration that harmonized with the Corinthian Columned "facades" of the four sides.

Magnificently constructed, with brick walls two feet in thickness—inner walls as well as the rooms were palatial in size, height and finish—all constructed like a fortress. Even a great crevass failed to undermine it, and it only fell at a later period, as had the earlier home, a victim to flames. The hallways were equally as imposing and spacious. Its furnishings were in keeping with the grandeur of the place as is attested by what has survived in the homes of descendants. Its garden, limitless in area,

The Waguespack Plantation Home.

Ancient plantation home of the de Montegut family.
East Bank of the Mississippi River.

Jefferson College, Convent, La.

Grounds and Convent of the Sacred Heart,
Convent, La.

was its crowning glory if we are to judge from the description found in the writings of a member of the family, Adele LeBourgeois Chapin in her book of memories, "Their Fruitless Ways", edited by Christine Chapin (Henry Holt & Co., New York).

But to go back to the attic (at Belmont) and grandma LeBourgeois. There was a harp that our father's sister, little Aunt Louise, who died at the Convent de Sacre Coeur, used to play, and this harp we heard at night, played by invisible hands. This belief was based on some fact, for the strings snapped in the night, and to our childish imagination, assisted by our darkey mammy, this was quite enough.

We learned from our mother the story of grandma LeBourgeois, or rather, our mother gave us a glimpse of her. She was tall, thin and stately, and wore a three-cornered shawl about her shoulders, crossed in front, on which she folded her hands. Her old slave Lucindy, in a red turban always followed her and went before her and opened the door when she entered a room, and sat on the floor at the back of her chair.

My grandmother rarely smiled, rarely spoke, grief for the daughter who died before my mother knew her, had robbed her of all earthly joy. Belmont, with all its magnificence, was a void, the memory of that youthful beloved daughter who had died, so saddened the heart of the mother for whom this great house had been built, that only in prayer did she find consolation.

She never went out again, except to church on Sundays, in the old coach, with the handsome lining of white brocade, and the coach servants in their Sunday clothes standing behind.

Hour after hour she would repeat her litany and the rosary, also spend much time reading the lives of the saints. "This, she says, was as our mother knew her". However, there were stories of a pleasanter sort when this aged heart-broken mother was a young lady, who played the violin, danced the minuet and broke hearts of the gallant young swains who crowded about her, with her radiant smiles".

In telling of her (Grandfather Charles, our mother's father) his influence was greatly felt throughout the West"—And recalling a Civil War incident states: "A gunboat stopped in front of Belmont" after the fall of New Orleans", and an officer came to the door asking to see my mother, and when she appeared, he enquired where my father was. My mother answered that she did not know, my father purposely not having told her.

The officer went back to the boat and after a while returned and said to my mother, who was standing with her children about her, the baby in her arms, (I being the baby) and grandmother Charles by her side: "Unless Mr. LeBourgeois gives himself up immediately, or you tell me where he is, we will give the women and children an hour to leave the house, after which will fire the house."

(The houses on both sides of us had been shelled). My mother answered, "I do not know where my husband is, and the women and children will not leave the house, if you fire, you fire into women and children".

The officer answered: "you lie". Whereupon, the old black nurse, shocked at such language being used to her dear mistress, turned to my grandmother, and said: Mrs. Charles, don't let that man speak like that to Miss Lizzie (all negro servants call their mistresses "miss"—a contraction of mistress) more anxious for her mistress' dignity than frightened at the threat.

Instantly, the officer turned and looked up and said, Charles—did you say Charles?" "That is my name. I am the widow of Joseph Charles, and this is our child".

"Great God!" the officer exclaimed—"I owe everything to that man—he paid for my education, and I shall never forget his kindness to me".

"Madame, this house shall be protected", and so a guard was sent.

Plantations and houses as large as Belmont required a supervision and routine that made the system much like that of the old feudal days.

Even when the horror of the Civil War had passed and the carpet bag period was drawing to a close, when many of the planters again made an attempt to save what was left of their once immense fortunes—old ways were resumed.

Edward Everett Hale, who was an acquaintance of the LeBourgeois family, and who visited Belmont, wrote:

23 April 1876

Whether the state of society and civilization which reigns at Belmont is to continue or not, is an open question. I look more favorably on the prospects than they do themselves, and they do more favorably than they did a year ago. However that may be, it is on the whole the most finished feudalism now to be seen in America. It is more like the life I saw at Lord Hatherton's than Nellie is likely to see anywhere, and in many regards it is more feudal than that was.

Mr. LeBourgeois is one of the most satisfactory men I have ever known. He is an accomplished gentleman; I think I said before that he is four days older than I.

Now, observe that this man, like all sugar planters, has to be a farmer on the largest scale, say 800 acres under cultivation, a manufacturing chemist, in the most delicate processes known to manuture, a merchant whose combinations may result in a profit annually of $75,000, or a loss of the same amount.

He is requested at the same moment by philanthropists like you and me to supervise in its detail the greatest problem of the age, which changes untaught negro slaves into voters, and to adjust the labor problem which results from this without losing one day's work on his farms, or the proper bubble of one of his great sugar kettles.

At the same moment, under our system, he is of course expected to attend to the politics of the parish, state and country, to thwart the Kellogs and Warmouths when they needed thwarting; and encourage them when they need encouraging.

For recreation, he has five sons and two daughters, much the same ages as our children.

Of course, he would not approve these duties, but that he had a cheerful active, intelligent, prudent, careful, spirited wife who is also very beautiful.

Nothing remains of this splendid mansion. It was an outstanding plantation home in a great throng of magnificent places, many of which remain, some in beautiful condition, but the great majority in various stages of decay.

UNCLE SAM'S PLANTATION— ORIGINALLY CALLED "CONSTANCIA".

In the latter part of 1940 this splendid group of plantation home buildings were demolished as the owners wished to salvage what they could of the bricks and building material before the place went into the river.

As individual architectural examples they did not perhaps compare with many other plantation places in Louisiana, but taken as a unit, they formed one of the most atractive pages from the architectural history of the domestic plantation life of the "Old South". Even in their dilapidated condition they formed the most convincing piece of evidence of the truth of the stories told of the wealth, magnificence, beauty and grandeur which went into the lavish scale of living of these, one would almost call, legendary people of that nearly forgotten day. To the present generation many of these stories of that day seem like story-book tales, but standing before this ancient mansion and its group of surrounding buildings, lonesome and forlorn looking, nothing but its magnitude left, at once we began to realize that there must be some truth in what we have heard of the vanished magnificence of the South of yesterday.

It is stated that it took eight years to complete these classic buildings, and the graceful minor ones which added a quaint charm to the ensemble. Everything outside and in was on a splendid scale, and the history of the place is one of grandeur and wealth, wiped away for most part by the Civil War. Madame Falgot, who lived through the trying days of that era, died in 1870 while the carpet baggers were still plundering the state. With both parents dead the two daughters married the Jacob boys, who later sold the place and immense land holdings to a commission merchant in New Orleans, and moved away with what was left of the handsome furnishings. With their going, life in the old mansion ceased, leaving only the shades of the past glory of the place to hold high carnival as the wintry winds rattled the windows and whistled about the columned galleries and spacious rooms and corridors. These two daughters were grandchildren of the family for whom this old mansion had been built.

CHAPTER XIV.

BURNSIDE

BURNSIDE Plantation adjoins the lands of Orange Grove plantation on the north as is shown on the Norman Map of 1858
depicting the plantations on both banks of the Mississippi River
from New Orleans to Natchez. The large tract is unnamed and
the map gives Col. J. S. Preston and Widow Wm. Hampton as
owners. The tract is made up of the Donaldson Place, the Clark
Place and the Conway Place, Bayou Conway running through the
rear part of the land. Colonel J. L. Mannering's land on the
opposite bank of the Mississippi River was called Houma Point.

At the time of its greatest glory Burnside Plantation was
considered not only the finest but the largest sugar plantation in
Louisiana, numbering some twenty thousand acres in Ascension
Parish and stretching into neighboring parishes. Colonial archives show that it was a part of a colonial grant awarded to the
Marquis d'Auconis. Other owners were John Wren Scott, who
later transferred it to William Donaldson for whom the town of
Donaldsonville is named. Daniel Clark, who owned so much valuable plantation land on the banks of the Mississippi River, was
the next owner. In 1811 he sold the place to General Wade
Hampton who had come to Louisiana from South Carolina where
he had a large plantation and a palatial home in the City of Co-
lumbia. General Wade Hampton had been placed in full command
of the United States troops in this territory by President Madison when General James Wilkinson was removed for having been
implicated in the Aaron Burr Conspiracy.

The first mansion on the place was the old plantation home
that had been occupied by M. S. Bringier and later occupied by

General Hampton. Parts of this building still remain in perfect
condition. It is of a simpler type of construction than the handsome mansion to which it was joined when the latter structure
was erected. The architectural arcade converted into a porte-
cochére is of the type of vaulted arcade found at Linwood nearer
Baton Rouge. The newer front mansion was erected in 1840 by
John Smith Preston who married Caroline, daughter of General
Wade Hampton.

It was likewise for General William Preston that the magnificent mansion (now the Baptist Center) was erected in New Orleans. This mansion originally was one story above its high
basement with its cornice similar to the one it now has. The
building was enlarged when it became the Newcomb College for
women. It was a magnificently finished mansion, the entrance
hall being frescoed in Pompeian design on a black background.
The rooms contained a valuable collection of oil paintings and much
fine furniture. With its oaks and large grounds laid out in lawns
and gardens, for over a half century, it was one of the most beautiful places in New Orleans. Much fine ironwork and imposing
gate-urns and pillars composed the impressive entrance.

The first part built of the original plantation house of General Wade Hampton is of a much earlier type of architecture, the
wide arcade below the span of the old building, being of a somewhat different period to that constructed in 1840—a heavy Spanish type. But the ensemble forms a delightful skyline. The
newer mansion was built on a magnificent scale, recalling English mansions, and the great town homes of Charleston, S. C.
Like Bell Grove the mansion was designed on grandiose lines
with wide porches on the three sides supported by massive brick
stuccoed Doric columns—producing an effect certainly very impressive. The whiteness of the glazed observatory which crowns
the massive roof contrasts sharply with the dark velvety greens
of the canopy of oaks surrounding the place. The jasmine and
other fragrant vines that drape the front perfume the grotto-like
porch closed on the side by latticed shutters forming a delightfully
cool and private outside sitting room.

In 1857 the old plantation was sold to John Burnside, who
had come from Belfast, Ireland, and accumulated a large fortune
while still comparatively a young man. Old records show that he
paid three quarters of a million dollars for the plantation which

consisted of the mansion as we see it today, ten thousand acres, four large brick sugar houses, fully equipped boiling houses, laboratories, crystallizing sheds and out-buildings—fire-proof office buildings, splendidly planned—and an avenue of well constructed cabins that housed his numerous slaves, each cabin with its own garden for vegetables and poultry. Shortly after purchasing the Houmas plantation, Burnside also bought the plantation which joined it—this added eight thousand acres more to his original holdings which eventually became the most important sugar plantation in the State of Louisiana.

Life on the Burnside Plantation, as he later called it, was lived in lordly style. For while John Burnside had been a self-made man—he had come from good stock and had availed himself of educational opportunities—he had hundreds of friends among the cultured planters and business men of the section. He entertained on a lavish scale, and his banquets, dinners, parties, balls and other entertainments were attended by the leading people of the State. The magnificence of his plantation, and the manner in which it was conducted won admiration of all his friends and acquaintances.

All Negroes go to church on Sunday.

He was a kind master to his thousands of slaves. He treated them with great humaneness—seeing to it that they were well fed and warmly clothed—had means of enjoyment, and churches to attend on Sundays. He personally visited their cabins from time to time to show them that he took an interest in their welfare. He saw that they had ample seed for their gardens, poultry and hogs for their yards, and he appointed fishermen from amongst the slaves to furnish fish and crabs so that they might have a varied diet. Possum hunts, and fish fries, etc., were permitted as they afforded amusement and were a means of keeping the negroes contented.

At Burnside's death, he leaving no relatives, Oliver Birne his closest friend and faithful business partner, fell heir to his colossal fortune. Burnside finally came into possession of the Miles family. William Porcher Miles, who had occupied the chair of professor of mathematics at the College of South Carolina, later becoming Mayor of Charleston, S. C., and a member of Congress from South Carolina, became a member of the Confederate provincial government when that State seceded. Later donning a uniform, he was a colonel on General Beauregard's Staff.

After the War Between the States, Col. Miles again taught at the College of South Carolina, remaining in that position for two years. He resigned that he might save what remained of his family's cotton plantation, ruined by the war. He moved shortly afterwards to Louisiana where he married the daughter of Oliver Birne who had inherited Burnside's fortune.

A typical "gentleman of the old school" Colonel Miles, possessing an unusual business brain, was not slow in organizing the Miles Planting and Manufacturing Co., which was shortly to prove how efficient was his management by producing twenty million pounds of sugar annually. He purchased one plantation after the other, until a dozen more had been added to his original holdings. He proved to be a wizard in the sugar industry, as one great plantation after another rivalled the older ones. His sugar domain was the greatest in the State and the pride of all Louisianians.

Of distinguished bearing—always wearing a winsome smile and as generous and kind to his free negroes as Burnside had been to his slaves—he was held in reverence both by white as well as blacks. At his death in 1899 at a ripe old age, his magnificent library was divided between the Colleges of South Carolina and Tulane University, and is said to have been at that time the largest private library in the State. At his death his son, Dr. William Porcher Miles, Jr., inherited the plantations and in order to properly attend to his large inheritance, abandoned the practice of medicine.

Like most of the plantation mansions of the period, the garconnières flanking either side provided for the older sons of the

Sacred Heart Convent, Convent, St. James Parish.

"BELMONT", magnificent plantation home of the Joseph LeBourgeois family.
(Courtesy of Mrs. Joseph Louis LeBourgeois.)

family and their college friends. At Burnside they are unusually artistic—being hexagonal in shape with cement finish—painted white with leaf-green blinds and each crowned by a hexagonal cupola cone-shaped roof. The usual ornamental "pigeonnaires" and the cisterns five in number with ornamental finials add to the charming ensemble—immaculate in the freshness of its white beauty with well-kept garden and splendidly cared-for lawns. Climbing roses, fragrant jasmine and other blooming vines form a leafy canopy about the front and sides of the porches, delightful retreats even at mid-day in hottest summer. Surrounded as it is by an ancient grove of trees a soft greenish twilight pervades the place, enchanting and mystic.

The main and newer building has on the lower floor a wide hallway which extends the entire length of the house, dividing the six spacious apartments, planned with equal grandeur as the beautiful exterior. Spacious drawing rooms, the library, dining-room and billiard room are downstairs. The sleeping rooms upstairs, six in number, are equally as beautiful and all elegantly furnished with rosewood furniture. Each room is charming—with paintings, rare artistic treasures, all in period and in perfect accord, portraying faithfully the splendid old mansion as it appeared in the hey-day of its glory.

CHAPTER XV.

THE BRINGIER DYNASTY

COLOMB PLANTATION

St. James Parish.

L ISTED by Norman on his Chart of 1858 as the property of O. Colomb, this unusual plantation house was built between 1835 and 1840. Originally about two acres of land with a grove of trees, stood in front of the place, and in the grounds was a well kept garden, with a variety of blooming plants which greatly added to the general appearance of the place. All of this land, garden and trees have since then been taken by the river.

The Colombs, a distinguished family, were related to the aristocratic, wealthy Bringier family, who owned, one may say, the greater part of Ascension Parish on the east bank of the Mississippi River. The family formed a veritable dynasty in that day. The Colomb home has never passed out of the possession of the Colomb family, or its lands transferred, and descendants of the one for whom it was built still reside in the place.

The architectural arrangement is somewhat different to the general run of plantation homes. Across the facade eight Doric columns, with bases arranged in pairs, reach to the cornice of the roof, the gable ends sloping upwards to a large enclosed observatory. The front wall is pierced by three doorways, each with side lights and transoms over all. The interior arrangement shows a wide central hallway having double connecting rooms on each side of this roomy passageway.

One is told that what now appears as a wing, was the original house, dating from the eighteenth century. This original part of the house is beyond the spacious apartment referred to as the sitting room, which extends the complete width of the place. The front is reached by a small stair leading to the main part. This front is the later remodeling which was done between 1835 - 1840. Climbing a narrow stairway one reaches a large square room now used as a bed-room, but undoubtedly used in the early days as an observatory from which to watch the plantation, the steamers on the river, or those going to and fro on the river-road. From below, its size is underestimated and it looks like a regulation "lookout" which we find on so many plantation houses.

The finish of the woodwork is simple, but substantial; the roominess of the house and its attractive facade, etc., are its chief charm, now that the garden and trees have disappeared.

"Like the nobles of old came these patricians from old France carrying with them the code that ruled the upper classes, so to speak, and up to the present has been their guide, confirmed by the high-bred standards of the present generation."

"*Early America.*"

UNION PLANTATION
St. James Parish

A romance hangs like a halo about the old Union Plantation manor house, now empty and gradually falling into ruin from neglect. Its original roof has been replaced by one of galvanized iron, which has rusted and detracts greatly from the general appearance of the place. The home is located far back in what was originally the garden grounds which are still attractive with shade trees about entrance and rear. Descendants of the original slaves still live in the little houses to either side front and back. These little houses with fronts of (brique en porteau) brick between posts were guest houses in olden days, as the slave quarters were in the rear.

It was an attractive place, originally unpretentious, but well built on artistic lines, with an enclosed balustraded observatory.

The original entrance gate for the carriage, and a smaller gate to either side create an attractive ensemble, which even in its dilapidated condition still has charm. The front fence is of latticed bands of sheet iron, carefully done and form a most attractive way of enclosing the grounds. It antedates the Civil War and is still in good condition.

This plantation and manor house, like so many others in the state, was a wedding gift from the fabulously rich planter, Marius Pons Bringier, owner of White Hall plantation and its splendid mansion, to his daughter.

The first Tureaud appearing in America, later settling in Louisiana, was Augustine Dominque Tureaud, whose Huguenot family had become Catholics. He possessed all of the qualifications of a romantic hero—good birth, education, good looks and an adventurous spirit. When he came to Louisiana he had already encountered many thrilling adventures, escaping the horrible massacre during the negro uprising in San Domingo that sent so many planter families to Louisiana.

After many other adventures, he drifted to New Orleans and met Marius Bringier, who was so impressed with his new friend (at that time thirty-seven years of age) that he insisted that Tureaud accompany him to White Hall plantation, and remain there as his guest that they might become better acquainted. The family were delighted with their new visitor and listened attentively to his narratives. Marius Bringier, who had been a planter for a short period in Martinque, realized that the gentleman told the truth as he related his adventures, and was modest when speaking of his own feats of heroism.

During the period that he remained on the plantation, M. Bringier observed his prospective son-in-law carefully, noting his habits, his choice of companions, etc., and studied his character. Trips about the plantation were made to find out whether he was interested in agriculture and other plantation matters. Evidently Tureaud gave promise of being a good son-in-law for we learn that later great pains were taken to make a successful match.

When the family had reached the conclusion that Tureaud was eligible, and the occasion presented itself, handling the matter as it had been done for centuries in aristocratic circles of Europe, an alliance was arranged. Once satisfied that the roving cavalier was ready to settle down and become a planter, agreements satisfactory to both sides were arranged. It was agreed, however, that another year should pass before the prospective bride be acquainted with her family's plan for her future.

Marius Bringier and his wife were sensible as well as wealthy. They had witnessed among their friends and acquaintances too many wrecked marriages, to allow a young girl, without any knowledge of the world, to select any Romeo that might suit her fancy. The one thing that the fond father and mother wanted was happiness for their children. When their daughter at last learned that her husband had been selected for her, she wept and complained that she wanted to marry some one nearer her own age. At last she consented, and the marriage was, of course, a prominent one socially in the colony, and was celebrated with pomp and ceremony at White Hall. The Union plantation with the manor house, was a gift of the bride's parents to the couple.

The marriage turned out to be a most happy one and their lives on the beautiful plantation one of unending pleasure, until his old age, when Monsieur Tureaud suffered pain as a result of a wound received in a duel while a young man. For many years he was Judge of St. James Parish. At his death the plantation became the property of his widow.

TEZCUCO PLANTATION*

Ascension Parish

Tezcuco Plantation was acquired by Dr. Julian Trist Bringier, son of Stella Tureaud and Colonel Louis Amadee Bringier, in 1888, from the estate of his great-uncle Benjamin Tureaud, son of Elizabeth Bringier, daughter of Marius Pons Bringier of White Hall, and Judge A. D. Tureaud of Union plantation. Benjamin Tureaud married his cousin Aglaé Bringier, daughter of Aglaé Du Bourg and Michel Douradou Bringier of the Hermitage. Mr. Tureaud built Tezcuco by slave labor with cypress from his own swamps and bricks from his own kilns. The house was completed about 1860 after five years spent in building it.

Far ahead a great mass of trees appear in the distance, beyond the great patches of corn and limitless acres of sugar cane. Approaching the spot we note what a truly charming place it is. A gateway with ornamental top posts, beside which are smaller gates and a hedge of Spanish dagger, or Yucca plants, invites us to enter.

---

* Since this article was written a great sorrow has entered this charming home, for the gracious chatelain, Mrs. Bringier, of this old house has passed away leaving a void which cannot be filled. She was so much a part of the great charm of the place.

The driveway, a circular means of entrance and exit, winds below a cathedral-like park garden to the front of the house which blends so perfectly in coloring with the densely sheltered garden that it all seems a composite picture of rare beauty.

A velvety lawn edged with a thick growth of aphrodista lilies and endlessly long vines of English ivy combine with the festoons of moss in giving a delightful effect. One notes how charmingly the century-old trees melt as it were into the twilight dimness that lingers even at mid-day. The house, quite unpretentious, has about it the homey quality and roominess that one finds in the usual plantation home. The wide stairway leads up to a spacious porch, and a central large hallway reception room, charming in its choice furnishings of delightful pieces of quaint mahogany and rosewood.

The rooms, each in turn, have an interest of their own. Fine old silver, crystal and rare porcelain—ante-bellum bric-a-brac of exceptional beauty make of it a treasure house of interest with unlimited souvenirs of the many plantation homes listed under the Bringier name. In one corner hangs a portrait of the first Bringier to come to America, while close by is another beautifully painted portrait of a distinguished looking young man. In this room too, we find the century-old water-color painting of beautiful White Hall Plantation, the work of a son-in-law of the owner, Christopher Colomb, whose many talents and romantic disposition have given him his niche in the records of the notables of St. James Parish. The bedrooms have massive four-posters with matched pieces while the dining-room is especially attractive with its quaintly beautiful service pieces, antique furniture and pictures.

The rear of the house, too, is charming where a twilight hue also reigns at mid-day. Individual stairways lead from the rooms to the yard, with fine effect, and a large variety of garden plants make of the area a delightful spot.

To return to the park-like garden of the front, one is captivated by the grotto coolness that pervades the place. In all this drapery of wisteria, moss and honeysuckle, a fragrance prevails, and the great intertwined oak branches, like the cathedral arches, are a veritable bird haven as the great leafy canopy is alive with these feathery songsters. From the garden the lacy ironwork of the side porches recalls Belle Alliance plantation manor. However, Tezcuco plantation has a charm that is lacking in the more pretentious house. The Bringier place (Tezcuco) has much the same intriguing attraction that is to be found at Rosedown plantation, on a smaller scale than at the Feliciana plantation, but the same garden magic that captivates is found at both places.

WHITE HALL PLANTATION
MAISON BLANCHE

St. James Parish, Louisiana.

The Bringier family, who have been so prominent in the State of Louisiana from the time of their coming to this state until the present, have been like a number of other families of the state's past history, great plantation makers. They were splendid plantation home builders, leaving many fine mansions behind that tell of the wealth and culture of their dynasty. The influence of the Bringier family on the culture of the people of our state is shown in many ways.

They came as wealthy aristocrats, bringing with them the ideas and ideals of the nobles of old France. Not the foppish, fawning, ingratiating noble of a decadent crown, they followed the substantial high bred code of the noble on his estate, independent of his King's favors. The family branch in Louisiana maintained in their home the same high standard as did the seigneur in his chateau.

The Louisiana Bringiers start with Ignace Bringier, a prominent Judge of the Limogne-Auvergne district, France. He was the father of Jean Bringier, who married a daughter of Baron Douradou d'Auvergne, named Marie Douradou, whose home was the Chateau Douradou d'Auvergne. Jean Bringier was related to the Counts of Rochebriant. The son by this marriage, Pierre Bringier de Lacadiere became the father of Emanuel Marius Pons Bringier and nineteen other sons, among them, one who later became the Canon of the Cathedral of Marseilles, giving rise to the pun, "that Pierre Bringier was the father of nineteen sons and a Cannon". Emanuel Marius Pons Bringier, after an adventurous early life was to become the founder of this distinguished family in Louisiana at the time of Spain's domination over the colony.

Disposing of his estate, called Lacadiere and located near Auvergne, Emanuel Marius Pons Bringier and his wife (Francoise

Durand) sailed in his own vessel with their furniture and effects for Martinique. There a brother named Vincent, had gone sometime before to work a plantation owned by them jointly. This brother Vincent, or Victor as he was sometimes called, was lost at sea a short time afterwards. Marius, as he called himself, noting the unrest among the negro slaves on the island, as it was evident that they were being stirred to rebellion, disposed of his interest in the plantation. Hardly a day passed but what some trouble occurred. Murder and bloodshed were common. Realizing that he and his family could not continue to remain in such a place, he reloaded his vessel with his furniture and other belongings, and with his family sailed for Louisiana. He purchased a plantation near the settlement of New Orleans in the Tchoupitoulas District, but as that land frequently became inundated, he again sold and moved to what is now known as St. James Parish. There he invested on a large scale because of the fine quality of the soil, and little trouble from high water.

Here he purchased in rapid succession five fairly large plantations, combining them into one which he named White Hall plantation—one of the largest and finest plantations Louisiana ever possessed.* (Maison Blanche as it was known by the French and Creoles of the state.) In construction the house differed somewhat from the earlier type plantation homes, or those being constructed by other Louisiana planters at that date.

From a painting made of it by the owner's son-in-law and descriptions left by Mrs. Louise Bringier Trudeau, a granddaughter of the builder, who lived there each summer as a child, it was a Gothic and Romanesque combination type villa. It was two-storied with an attic, the lower floor enclosed by arcades having capitals on the pillars. Its outside surface front and sides had a veneer of a light-greyish white marble slabs over-laying front and sides. A black and white marble pavement of slabs square in shape extended entirely around the house, and the ground floor which was about six inches higher than the cloister like arcade was also similarly paved. The ceilings of the three large rooms forming the ground floor space were beamed, and the ceilings of the three large rooms made of closely fitting boards so well fitted

---

* The Burnside Home in New Orleans with roof balustrade used White Hall as a model.

A Pigeonnaire at Constancia Plantation (Uncle Sam)

Manor House Constancia Plantation.

Burnside Plantation Mansion—erected 1840.

that the ceilings appeared as if plastered. The central room served as a salon and hall, having the stairway in the rear on the left side leading to the porch above, which, opened in to each of the three rooms upstairs. A stairway on this rear porch also led to the rooms in the attic. A larger salon was on the right of the central one as you entered, and the dining-room on the left. "As I remember them on each side in front of the earlier buildings were brick buildings cement-covered and in the rear of these buildings were other structures in which were kitchen pantries, wine cellars, and house-slave living quarters. The house was handsomely furnished, mostly with European furniture of rosewood and mahogany and carved dark oak which the owner brought to America with his family in his own vessel when he left France." Much of it was of rosewood with some carving, to quote Mrs. Trudeau, but not very elaborate. The bed-rooms had sets with four-posters but, the furniture was not as massive as in some of the later plantation houses of various members of the family. To continue to quote this grandaughter of the owner of White Hall, "In the dining room were a number of ancestral portraits, while in the salle and other rooms were many fine portraits of the owner and his children, also his wife painted by noted European artists and other noted portrait painters that had been brought from abroad to paint the planters' families." Many of these ancestral portraits, family miniatures, silhouettes and daguerreotypes are scattered among the various branches of this distinguished family who have homes in the various parts of this state, in Maryland, and many in New Orleans. The painting of White-Hall ("Maison Blanche") by Christophe Colomb, painted in 1790, now is the property of the family of the late Mrs. J. T. Bringier of Tezcuco plantation, where it has hung for so many years. In this dining-room at White Hall plantation, where so many notables have been entertained, was a large ancient black oak arm chair of French Gothic design, that was given to Marius Bringier by his brother who was the Canon of the Cathedral of Marseilles, France, it originally having come from the chapel of the Chateau Rochebriant. It descended to Mrs. Louise Bringier Trudeau, who gave it to the writer, who in turn has had it properly restored and presented with its history to the Delgado Art Museum of New Orleans. In the days that Emanuel Marius Pons Bringier doubled his fortune, indigo was still a great money-making staple, and with the growing of tobacco in conjunction with indigo, he soon became one of the most important planters in the South.

Even after a most diligent search, very little can be learned about the time that White Hall "Maison Blanche" was demolished. However, Mrs. Louise Trudeau stated that during the days of Reconstruction, much of the marble was stripped from the mansion and shipped North by carpet baggers who had taken possession of the place following the bombardment of the plantation, and the blowing up of the sugar-house and other buildings. Today only the site bearing the name White Hall remains. No trace of its former splendor is to be seen, or of the ancient garden visible, but the people of the vicinity remember the tales of its past glory.

In 1798 Marius Pons Bringier entertained the three brothers, Louis Philippe, Duc d'Orleans (Later King of France), the Duc de Monpensier, and the Comte de Beaujolais. Later on and subsequent to the Battle of New Orleans, Mr. Bringier was host to General Andrew Jackson. Mr. Bringier died in 1820, and in 1821 his son Michel Doradou Bringier, bought the place from the other heirs. He sold it to Wade Hampton in 1825; and Mme. Aglaé Du Bourg Bringier, widow of said Michel Doradou Bringier, bought the place back from the Hamptons in 1848. Her son Marius Ste. Colombe Bringier, next owned it. Previous to the Civil War the dwelling house was partially destroyed by fire, was restored and again damaged by a shell from a Union gun-boat, and eventually demolished after being stripped of its marble veneer by Union men (Carpetbaggers) and shipped away.

TOWN HOUSE OF THE BRINGIERS

In old plantation days all planters of wealth in Louisiana had city homes in New Orleans. Here they came each winter with their families to enjoy the French Opera and the social season, for society at that time in New Orleans, as now, held great allure.

The town house of the Bringier family was one of the three splendid old mansions on Canal Street between Dauphine and Burgundy Streets. One of these stately places, with its heavy cornices supported by great Ionic columns, later formed the entrance to the Grand Opera House. The other two eventually were also included in the site of a great commercial and office structure. I distinctly remember them, as I was born directly across

the street in a three-storied brick structure, old number 166—
new number 912. This building in the last few years has been
remodeled into a moving picture house.

The other city home of the Bringier family, named Melpomene, stood in the street by that name and in its day, was a great
social center in the uptown area.

BOCAGE PLANTATION
Ascension Parish.

Bocage Plantation was a wedding gift from Marius Pons Bringier and his wife to their daughter and son-in-law, Christophe
Colomb, a young nobleman who it is stated traced his lineage to
the great discoverer, and who after his marriage became a planter.

Ever a dreamer with the spirit of the artist in his makeup,
he somewhat neglected the duties pertaining to the management
of the plantation, caring much more for the social happenings of
the colony. In the family traditions of this romantic young man
they tell of his little painted boat or barge. This water-craft was
gaily decorated and gilded, and had a silken canopy with crimson
fringe. The barge was fitted with velvet cushions, and he with
his lute presented the appearance of a veritable noble of the Brenta
whom he had tried to emulate. His slaves rowed him from one
plantation to another and he spent much time, both day and night,
visiting his relations and friends.

Madame Colomb, however, was of a more practical turn of
mind—she employed a competent manager for the plantation and
with him supervised the management of the plantation with great
success, leaving her cavalier to his music and his pleasures.
Christophe Colomb painted a picture of White Hall manor showing
his boat in the river in front of the house. The painting is reproduced on another page.

THE HERMITAGE PLANTATION
Ascension Parish, Louisiana.
Built in 1812, James Gallier, Sr., Architect.

Michael Doradou Bringier, son of Marius and Françoise Bringier,
who was born at sea while his parents were making the voyage
to America, later was sent abroad to be educated. After graduation he came home by way of Baltimore. His father and the

Abbé Du Bourg had arranged that Doradou stop on his way to the plantation to see the Abbé's niece, the beautiful Aglaé Du Bourg. As everything had been arranged by the elders, there was little to be done by the young people but comply with the wishes of those who had made the plans. To allow them time to become properly acquainted, entertainments were given by the Abbé. A series of dinners and parties followed, and shortly to the great satisfaction of both families it was noted that they appeared much in love with one another. The news was quickly communicated to the families of all concerned. They were married in Baltimore as had been planned, and the great beauty and charming youth of the bride ,and the immense wealth of the bridegroom's father and his good looks gave society a pleasant topic to talk about.

The Hermitage was a bridal gift of the groom's parents, while a large doll presented to the young bride is said to have contained in its body a treasure—family jewelry and heirlooms. The marriage proved to be a most happy union, Madame Bringier living to a great age. She preserved her beauty and charm and vivaciousness to the very end, where in her town house, Melpomène, in New Orleans, surrounded by her large family, peacefully she died in 1878. During his lifetime with a pride in all he undertook Doradou Bringier carried on in the Bringier manner of living, both at the Hermitage and his town house. While in New Orleans, where he made lengthy stays, he became prominent in its public life. He was an aide to General Jackson at the Battle of New Orleans, and tendered the General a banquet at his home shortly afterwards. Doradou Bringier did not live to see his beautiful plantation overrun by Union troops, who seized a cargo of indigo, worth two hundred thousand dollars, and also carried away everything they could lay their hands on in the way of food stuffs, cattle, horses, bedding and clothing, etc. It was only because Madame Doradou Bringier, who at the time was at the Hermitage, demanded from the authorities (Union) in New Orleans that they remember that she was a British subject, that the house was not blown to pieces by the Union gunboats. As it was, a cannon ball tore through a window doing great damage to the house and furnishings.

After Michel Doradou Bringier died in Memphis, Tenn., in 1847; his body was brought to Ascension Parish and placed in the handsome family tomb. Louis Amédée Bringier, son of Michel Doradou Bringier and Aglaé Du Bourg, took over the management of the plantation with great success, until the Civil War, when he became a colonel with Scott's Cavalry of the Trans-Mississippi, stationed for a while in West Texas and North Louisiana. Madame Louis Amédeé Bringier and her children, terror-stricken at what was happening to the nearby plantation homes, left the plantation with its contents, taking with her what money and valuable jewelry they could secrete, and joined Colonel Bringier in the Trans-Mississippi.

Returning to the Hermitage after cessation of hostilities, Colonel Bringier and his wife, who had been Mademoiselle Stella Tureaud, whose father owned Bagatelle plantation, again took up their life at The Hermitage. The Bagatelle Plantation home up to a short time ago was a veritable shrine of the famous naturalist, James J. Audubon. Here the noted artist spent much of his time, and the walls of the various rooms of this unpretentious plantation home were beautifully decorated with scenes of bird life by the naturalist. These were in a fair state of preservation until the building was moved back to keep it from being swallowed by the Mississippi River. During the moving the ancient plaster walls cracked badly and destroyed the artist's work. An attempt was made to save the cracking plaster, or even part of it for the value of his frescoes was great, but all to no avail, as the plaster walls literally crumbled into powder. This home never generally known as a haunt of Audubon until it was about to go into the river, otherwise it would have been saved.

After an enormous amount of work and due to the loyalty of his former slaves, Colonel Bringier surprised himself with his success, as now cane had supplanted other crops, and it appeared as if once again a golden era was in store for the South. The former slaves, realizing that their new freedom in many instances was anything but a happy state, worked with renewed vigor and enthusiasm. The great sugar house was active and all was life and prosperity about the place. The great globe coated with real gold leaf that Col. Bringier had placed on the weather vane shaft as an emblem of prosperity still glistened in the sun, but an enticing offer was made by Duncan Kenner, who too had resumed the life of a sugar planter, and in 1881 the place was sold to Mr. Kenner (who was Col. Bringier's brother-in-law).

Colonel Bringier removed to Florida to start a sugar plantation and experimental station. As a result of his activity, there
are today two great sugar companies in Florida with many
thousands of acres in cultivation. It only waits the removal of
quota restrictions to increase the acreage enormously.

The family never recovered much of the treasure that was
hidden from the Union troops. That buried at the Hermitage
was not found—nor were the great quantities of crested silver
brought from France and buried along the Bayou Lafourche ever
discovered.

The ancient mansion built in 1812, still standing like a great
villa of the Brenta, glorious in its old age, is gradually falling
to pieces. Built in the costly manner that it was, today the timbers show the 130 years that have elapsed since they were installed—slowly crumbling and too costly to replace. The place
was sold to the Maginnis family of New Orleans. The present
owner is Mr. W. R. Duplesis.

The great groves of oaks are rapidly dying—a few only
remaining—the others are mostly stumps and dead trees. The
costly furnishings also have vanished, but in the charming plantation home of Mrs. J. T. Bringier at Tezcuco Plantation, are
some of the very fine rosewood pieces, and beautiful family portraits by celebrated artists. One of these famous artists was
Amans, who was brought from Europe by the planters to paint
various members of their families. Here, too, is the oil-color
painting of White Hall by Colomb.

This beautiful old home, this ancient columned mansion, the
Hermitage, will some day form a scene for an ante-bellum story—
as this whole Ascension Parish is saturated with romances and
tragedies and it would take the pen of a Fennimore Cooper to do
justice to the theme.

Madame Michel Doradou Bringier, who had been the beautiful little Aglaé, and whose future husband remarked that she
was the most beautiful child he had ever seen, lived to a great
age, spending her last years at her town home, Melpomène, where
up to the last she retained the patrician beauty that had made
her famous in her younger years. She ever remained the social
queen, and at the end was surrounded and mourned by a throng
of relatives and friends. She died in 1878, leaving a large family
of sons and daughters. The eldest daughter Rosella married

Hore Browse Trist, a relative and ward of Thomas Jefferson. He owned Bowden plantation. Octavie married General Allen Thomas, who became United States Minister to Venezuela. Louise married Martin Gordon, Jr., of New Orleans, and as a wedding present was given the beautiful Bringier residence which is still standing—number 606 Esplanade Avenue. Later on the ground on the side was purchased and an addition in the shape of a large octagon was made. Michel Doradou Bringier bought the house in 1885 from Henry R. Denis, who had it constructed in 1832.

Another daughter of M. D. Bringier, Myrthé, married a son of President Zachary Taylor, Richard Taylor who later became General "Dick" Taylor of the Confederacy, born in New Orleans in 1826. Nanine married Duncan Farrar Kenner, who presented Ashland plantation to his bride as a wedding present.

Mr. George H. Maginnis, of New Orleans, gives the following interesting account of the Hermitage:

"Our family bought the Hermitage in the early 1880's. The mansion was then in a fairly good condition, and an architect informed us that in each of its massive brick pillars which surrounded the house was contained enough material to build a moderate-sized brick residence.

The rafters, I noticed, were held together by large wooden pegs, instead of nails. Facing the house from the river, the ground plan was as follows: A hall ran through the center—on the left being the parlor and back of it, another chamber. On the right was the dining room, and back of it, the kitchen. On the upper floor, access to which was gained by a stairway leading from the hall just mentioned, were the bedrooms.

To the rear of the house, and adjoining it, was another building, containing a large room, about 60 feet in length, in which were black marble mantelpieces. We were told that the Bringiers had used this room as a ballroom.

In the parlor was a beautiful set of rosewood furniture, pieces of which are still treasured in branches of my family.

No, none of the treasure said to have been buried, or otherwise secreted, by the Bringiers at the time of the War Between the States was ever recovered by us—unfortunately.

But there was one piece of treasure throve that did come to light. To the right and left of the dwelling but some distance away, were two ponds. The one to the left was not far from the sugar house, which lay nearer to the river than the house. It was found necessary to drain this pond. Negroes were employed to do the work, and I may mention that liberal and frequent drinks of liquor were given them to prevent their contracting malaria. On the bottom of the pond was found a sword in a rusting sheath. On the blade was inscribed the name: "Zachary Taylor".

What became of the sword, I cannot say."

———————

Colomb Plantation Home.

"The Hermitage" (See page 131.)

Entrance to Tezcuco Plantation.

Plantation Home Tezcuco.   (Page 125.)

CHAPTER XVI.

DUNCAN F. KENNER.
ASHLAND PLANTATION

Ascension Parish.

Now Called Belle Helene Plantation

WHEN the late John B. Reuss, a prominent Louisiana planter, bought the Ashland plantation he combined it with the others that he owned on the West Bank of the Mississippi River under the name of "The Belle Helene Sugar Planting Company". On the 1858 plantation map of the Mississippi coast we find Ashland Plantation adjoining the land of the old Bowden Plantation—the Trist estate.

Visiting the spot one sees far in the distance the house safe from any threat of encroachment by the great river that has destroyed so many of these beautiful old places. Located half a mile or more back from the River Road, surrounded by its grove of ancient moss-hung oak trees, gleaming in the sunlight, the immense bulk of the white mass stands out like an ancient Greek temple. The huge, tall, stuccoed-brick Doric columns that surround the old mansion on all sides silhouetted against the house of deeper tones bring out the simple classic beauty of the fine old plantation home. In the bright sunshine the contrast of the classic facade against the dark green of the oak grove makes an impressive sight as one enters the immense grounds.

At the end of the wide hall one finds a splendid mahogany stairway which winds against the cove wall to the second floor, and then on to the immense attic space. The steps are of solid cypress, each step a solid block, massive in construction, showing able engineering ability in the suspending of this great weight without loss of beauty to the spiral. This splendid old home must be examined closely, for much of its beauty lies in the details of its classic plaster-work, door and window-frames, etc. One must walk about its stately rooms and immense loggias to really appreciate its architectural charm, for a casual glance from a sight-seeing bus gives no idea of its beauty. Glancing out of the great windows and doorways, one no longer sees the immense tapis vert through which the long driveway cuts a wide path. All has been a wilderness for years. Gone too, are the box hedges for which this garden was famous. Vanished also are the botanical gardens, marble statues and urns, the former dead from long neglect or parts of it carried away from time to time by tourists, while the marble statues were carted to the North along with much of the other plunder during Reconstruction days.

This dignified temple-like old mansion is a home of much history. The man for whom it was built was a peer among the peers of his era. This home with all its costly furnishings, was a gift to his bride, the beautiful, vivacious Nanine Bringier, a daughter of a wealthy plantation family that descend from one of the proudest families of old France. The wedding of this distinguished couple was one of the most notable in the state.

Ashland became a famous social center, for surrounding this vast estate up and down the Mississippi River, and along plantation-fringed bayous were the homes of distinguished families. It became a center where one met the beauty, brains and wealth of the day. Some of the mansions of the families and friends of this distinguished couple still remain, but alas! many others are but memories.

It is a great pity that homes with historical associations such as Ashland should not be preserved for posterity. The crumbling walls of old Ashland, its falling plaster, rusting iron work and decaying wood-work, the uprooted trees and overgrown garden, circular driveway and pigeonnaires falling to pieces—all seem to murmur of its past glories, as the wind whistles through the great house and the gaunt branches of dying oaks. Deserted rooms are haunted by memories of gala days, and the banquet hall is visited by the shades of the brilliant assemblages of pre-war days.

Even in its total neglect one finds odd specimens of its once botanical rarities struggling to survive, while fragrant odors of jasmine and rosemary fill the air about the overgrown flower-beds. On the day of my last visit, for the intriguing old place draws me to its site again and again, while walking about and studying its fading beauty, I met the old negro watchman. He was the son of the previous keeper, both descendants of the slaves of the original owners. He told me how his father had related to him that after the fall of New Orleans (see memoirs) Federal troops invaded Ashland and raided the house. After taking what they wanted, they tore up the floors of the out-buildings and pigeonnaires in search of buried treasure. They found some silverware and a quantity of fine wines and liquors. They drank bottle after bottle until they were unable to move from stupefaction. Then some of the faithful slaves got the silver back and buried it in a thicket behind the slave quarters where it stayed until removed to the home of a man in whom the family had confidence. (See the Memoirs of Madame Joseph Lancaster Brent, the former Miss Rosella Kenner.) The old negro grew enthusiastic while telling about the private race-track on the plantation, and the great string of fine racing animals.

The honorable Duncan F. Kenner was a connoisseur in many ways. With his background and the educational advantages he enjoyed, he was a judge of the good things of life. His library was one of the finest in the state. The books were kept in beautifully carved Gothic-design book-cases now in his grand-daughter's home. His stock of blooded horses was as fine as his library.

The architect, Jas. Gallier I, who designed this plantation home, knowing the serious-minded disposition of Hon. Kenner, did not attempt elaborate ornamentation, but used rather the simpler classic elements of interior design, such as dog-eared door and window frames, dentil cornices, etc. Elegant white marble mantels of simple design are found in all of the rooms. Duncan F. Kenner was a son of W. B. Kenner and Mary Minor, a daugher of Major Estaban Minor in charge of the Spanish forces of Louisiana and Natchez. They were the parents of seven children, six reaching maturity.

Duncan F. Kenner was one of the ablest lawyers in the America of his time. He was deeply interested in the sugar industry, spending a fortune to advance it, and was looked upon as one of the best informed men on the subject in the state. In Feb. 1861 he was elected as a delegate to the Convention of Secession held in Montgomery, Alabama. He was later named by Jefferson Davis as plenipotentiary to England. The Federal authorities confiscated all of his great land holdings and property, not excluding his large holdings in New Orleans. The family had to leave Ashland Plantation, and after peace was declared, Mr. Kenner returned to the plantation with his family and tried to resume in a modest way his manner of living. He even made an attempt to restock his famous stables, which had been completely emptied by the Federals, but he soon abandoned the idea, as his losses had been too great and the Reconstruction period made life unbearable for him.

Of the marriage of this noted Confederate patriot and Mademoiselle Nanine Bringier, three children reached maturity,—a son, named George Duncan Kenner, and two daughters. Rosella, who married General Joseph Lancaster Brent, who became master of Ashland Plantation, when Mr. Duncan Kenner retired to New Orleans to spend his last days of his life in his Carondelet St. Home, and a daughter named Blanche who married Samuel Simpson, a New Orleans cotton factor. Duncan Kenner died in 1887 at the age of seventy-four. Notwithstanding Mr. Kenner was one of the largest slave holders in Louisiana, he suggested to President Davis of the Confederacy, that he issue a proclamation, freeing all the slaves in the Confederate states as a means of ending hostilities. A splendid oil portrait of this great Confederate hangs on the wall in the home of his granddaughter, Mrs. Thomas Sloo of New Orleans. Mrs. Sloo also has lovely miniatures and many fine portraits of her distinguished family painted by noted artists, also a vast treasure of souvenirs of this old plantation mansion, and other plantations of her family.

MEMOIRS OF MADAM JOSEPH LANCASTER BRENT

(MISS ROSELLA KENNER)

RECOLLECTIONS OF A GRANDMOTHER

New Orleans fell on April 25th, 1862. However, though my mother and her children were in the city, we left before the actual surrender took place, but after the passing of the forts by the Federal gunboats made it certain that the actual surrender would only be a question of days, perhaps hours.

All those persons who could then leave New Orleans did so, not knowing what fate was in store for them, and perhaps, "as coming events cast their shadows before," a presentiment of military rule administered by Genl. Butler was urgent in sending away all who were not obliged to remain in the city.

With us, there was no doubt or question as to going, if go we could. Our home was at Ashland, a sugar plantation some 80 miles up the Mississippi River. We had been spending the greater part of the winter in New Orleans, as usual, with my grandmother, Mrs. M. D. Bringier, whose spacious mansion, surrounded by large and beautiful grounds, was the winter resort of her children and grandchildren, though their "name was legion". My grandmother, whom we called "Bonnemaman" after the good old creole fashion, was absent from the city, having gone to visit one of her sons who lived, as did several of her children, "up the coast", (on the banks of the Mississippi), their plantations being within driving distance of each other.

She had left as her representative in housekeeping, etc., my aunt, Mrs. Richard Taylor, who was living with her mother in the absence of her husband, then Brigadier General in the army of Northern Virginia, and who had been in active service for some time.

The household comprised just then, another aunt and two cousins. The aunt was Mrs. Allen Thomas, whose husband was Colonel of the 28th Louisiana Infantry. This regiment had then just been organized and was still in New Orleans, tho ready to move at the order of Governor Moore. The cousins were Trists,—Bringier Trist who belonged to the Crescent Regiment and had been brought home after the battle of Shilo, wounded in the arm. He was still confined to his room and devotedly nursed by his sister Willie. Of course he must not fall into the hands of the enemy, and my aunts were not to be cut off from their husbands, or my mother from hers, for my father was a member of the Confederate Congress then in session at Richmond. The Federal fleet had for some days been actually bombarding the forts, Jackson and St. Philip, below the city. It had been agreed by the city authorities that if the enemy's ships should pass the forts, the city bells, constituting fire alarms, etc., and to be heard all over the city, should be rung 12 times sounded three times in succession, with a short interval between each 12. This order had been published and was familiar to all.

One reason why mother spent the winters in New Orleans was that we children might have the advantage of lessons from good teachers and accordingly, on the morning of the 24th we were as usual in the school room with Professor Melhado. He was an Englishman by birth, but long residence in New Orleans had made of him a warm Southern sympathizer, and his eldest son was in the Confederate army. The lessons were often interrupted by discussions on the war and news as it came from the front. Perhaps the old gentleman was less enthusiastic than his young scholars, perhaps also he was better informed, for when, soon after we had settled to our usual routine, the City bells began to ring, it was he who counted them, and with a growing dismay, which we shared as the fatal number rang out. As soon as he was certain that the bad news had come, and come officially, Professor Melchado took up his hat, and bidding us a most informal good morning, hurried away to ascertain what was about to happen to the city and its inhabitants.

I have no clear recollection of what we did the rest of the day, but a dim picture is in my mind of a great deal of confusion and packing going on in the house, and outside groups of men standing in the streets discussing in tones "not loud but deep" the trouble that had come, and other troubles that must follow. I remember that the carriage was ordered, and that I went in it with my aunt Octavie to a fashionable boarding school kept by Mme. Dearayaux. There we had an interview with the principal of the school, and with her permission withdrew a young girl, Miss Lydia Pickett, the daughter of Col. Pickett, a friend of Col. Thomas. She had been left, in a measure, under the care of the Thomases, and they thought it best to take her with them into Confederate lines, for it had been at once determined that we should all go to the country, to our respective homes. Col. Thomas owned a large sugar plantation, on which he resided, near Opelousas, and his wife and children were going there. Miss Pickett accompanying them, as did also Mrs. Taylor and her family. Bringier and Willie Trist were going with their brother Browse and his wife and child to a plantation owned by the latter on the Atchafalaya. The youngest Trist, Nicholas, was with the Army of Tennessee. During the day, Willie remembered that one of our cousins, Valentine Tureaud, was at the Ursuline Convent. The carriage was sent for her, and she joined our party and left the city with us. Thus we formed a large family party, of about 20, not including the various servants, who in those days were considered indispensable. Uncle Allen Thomas had arranged for us to take passage on a steamboat leaving that afternoon, and taking up the river the families of various officers. Among them was Mrs. Lovell and her children. General Lovell was in command of New Orleans and the adjoining district. I forget the name of the boat, it may have been the Pargoud (the Old Pargoud). There were quite a number of people on board and the hour came for leaving, the partings were most touching, between the wives who were going up the river, and their husbands, left with the army, which was on the point of evacuating New Orleans and going into the interior, finding their way later to Port Hutson and Vicksburg, and remained there until the surrender of that city on July 4, 1863.

The rest of the family were going further up the river, but we and Valentine, were to land at the plantation of Uncle Amedee Bringier, The Hermitage, situated opposite the town Donaldsonville. We reached our destination early the next morning, so early that "the dawn was glimmering gray" as we were landed on the levee and left with our trunks besides us. We were unexpected guests, and there was no carriage nor any one to meet us, so there was nothing to do but walk to the house not a very long distance. We were about to start when we heard the sound of horses' feet, accompanied by the jingling of sabres, etc. At least we thought so, for our minds were filled with thoughts of war, and it was evident that a body of horses were approaching. It could not be Federal cavalry, for nothing had passed us on the way, and New Orleans was still in Confederate possession, when we left the previous evening. But we were only women and children with nerves on edge, and we did not wish to encounter strangers so very early in the morning, so with natural impulse we ran up the levee, intending to hide behind it until the horsemen had gone by. We had forgotten, however, that the river was at its height, and that the levee was entirely under water on the other side. Therefore, we were constrained to emulate the King of France who, in the nursery ryme, rode up the hill, only to ride down again. By this time the horsemen had come up, and we saw with relief that they were peaceful plowmen, negroes from the Hermitage, who were riding their mules over the river field, with the plough chains hanging and jingling. Reassured, and feeling that we were on "native Hearth", we walked on to the house, where we aroused Uncle Amedee and his family and had the melancholy satisfaction of being the first to announce the bad news of the fall of New Orleans.

We remained some days at the Hermitage, and then went on to Ashland. We had not been there long when we had a visit from Uncle Amadee, who came bringing a letter from one of our connections, Mr. Wilson, who lived on Bayou Boeuf in the Opelousas country. This letter was addressed to the whole Bringier and Tureaud connections with all its branches. Mr. Wilson stated that fearing that the fall of New Orleans would make it certainly unpleasant, and perhaps unsafe for them to remain in their homes on the banks of the Mississippi, he wrote to propose that they should migrate in a body, to his part of the country and locate themselves near him at the Belle Cheney Springs, a summer resort consisting of houses, rude but comfortable, built in the pine woods, round a spring of purest water, all of which could be rented at nominal price. There, with the advantage of a healthy situation in a country filled to overflowing with all of the substantial necessities of life, they could pass in peaceful seclusion, the whole period of the war, the faint echoes of which would scarcely penetrate the pine forest which surrounded the springs.

We resumed the ordinary routine of plantation life at Ashland where my father joined us after the adjournment of Congress. He ran a great risk in coming back, but did so intending to put everything in order on the plantation, and then take us away with him. At this time, the river parishes were at the mercy of the Federals whenever they chose to occupy them, but as yet, no soldiers had been seen except those we caught glimpses of on the gunboats and transports as they went up and down the river. I remember well the feelings of dread and anxiety with which we saw the first gunboat go up the river, and they also seemed apprehensive and moved cautiously. But after a time it became a common spectacle, and as they had not yet landed anywhere, we ceased to take much notice of them, and went about very much as usual, exchanging visits with our neighbors and driving up and down the public road.

The planters, and the managers (who remained in charge where the owners had joined the army) organized a patrol corps which was to be called out in case of disturbance, keep the peace generally, and have good effect in quieting the negroes, though indeed I can recall no instance where they gave us trouble. The high water gave us more concern just then than anything else. The levees had to be watched carefully, and the back water that came from the McHattan crevasse near Baton Rouge was in our back fields about ten acres from the Ashland sugar house, and only kept from advancing further by a protective levee, built and kept up with great expense.

One afternoon (July 27th) we rode up the river on the public road, returning rather early, as we had been told that summer to do always. Removing our riding habits, my sister and I went out to the front gallery upstairs where my mother was sitting, and where in summer we usually spent the evening. We sat talking to her while the short southern twilight deepened into dark, and we noticed that a steamboat, whose repeated whistles had attracted our attention, seemed to be landing at our warehouse. This was no unusual occurrence, even then, and we did not think much of it, but gave our attention to the passing of a horse that someone was riding on the road at full speed, not galloping but running, and so fast that the desperate pace attracted our attention, and we listened until the sound died

View of White Hall Manor, Cradle of the Bringier family in America. From painting by Colomb. (Courtesy of Miss Tristy Bringier. Photograph by Richard Koch.)

Detail of White Hall Plantation Manor. (Courtesy of Trist Wood.)

away, my mother remarking, "Il est bien presse celui la" (that man is in a great hurry). Little she thought who the rider was. We resumed our chat, the calm summer evening settling into peaceful darkness, sweet with perfume of flowers, and the quiet rather added to than broken by the hum of the insects. Suddenly we heard someone enter the house by the back door of the lower hall, come up the winding staircase and along the upper hall, towards us where we were sitting near the front door on the front gallery. It was a man's step but not my father's. His was light and quick, and this was slow and heavy, almost as if the man were staggering from being hurt, or carrying a burden too great for his strength. Peaceful and quiet as were our surroundings, we know that we were standing on the brink of a volcano, and my mother, quick to take alarm, sprang up and we followed her. As we reached the doorway, we saw Mr. Graves coming down the hall, looking indeed like a man stricken by a heavy blow. When he saw us, he put up his hands to his mouth so as to form a sort of speaking trumpet, and in a hoarse and scarcely audible whisper said, "Mrs. Kenner, the Yankees have come. Mr. Kenner has gone away." If a thunderbolt had fallen upon us from the clear sky, we could not have been more horrified. Mr. Graves had received the full force of the shock, and was entirely overcome. He told us as well as he could, for he was almost breathless from emotion and exertion, what we afterwards heard more fully related.

My father had been riding over the fields with Mr. Graves and a neighbor, Mr. Henry Doyal, and about dusk, when the latter was going home to his plantation a few miles up the river, the three rode towards the river gate, my father saying there was a steamboat at the landing and he would see if some freight that was expected had come. However, before the gate was reached, they met a negro, who was coming rapidly towards them, and he called out "Mars Duncan, for God's sake don't go to the river. Dat boat is full of Soldiers, and dey is all landing." No further information was needed, and my father, realizing that it was not only unsafe to proceed further, but also to remain on the place, hurriedly gave Mr. Graves a few instructions, to go to my mother and tell her he had gone to Stephen Minor's, and then he turned his horse and attempted to ride away. That evening he was riding Sid Story, a race horse of his own which had been retired from the track, but was still sound in wind and limb, and had been selected as a riding horse in case of emergency like the one at hand.

However, Sid Story refused to start, and for some incomprehensible reason would not move in spite of coaxing and urging. Then Mr. Doyal sprang to the ground saying "Mr. Kenner, take my horse, he will go and fast. I hunt deer with him." My father mounted Mr. Doyal's dun hunter, and he was the horseman whose rapid pace had attracted our attention. My father told us afterwards that he felt confident that he could not be overtaken, with a fleet and willing horse under him, and on his own plantation, the roads of which he had laid out himself, and knew better than anyone else. He therefore stopped, nearly a mile from the river, at the house of the overseer, Mr. Brag, and calling him out, told him what had happened, and that he was going away—he did not tell him where—and gave him such instructions as he thought would help to preserve order on the plantation, for he supposed that the soldiers would remain but a short time. Then my father continued on his way to Stephen Minor's, taking the shortest of the back roads, and where he passed houses, being careful not to make his passing known.

Waterloo was reached, and might have been considered a safe refuge for the night, but my father and Stephen, after some discussion, thought best to make assurance doubly sure. The carriage was ordered, and Anthony summoned to drive it, as being a trustworthy man who would give no information even under pressure. Anthony was one of Capt. William Minor's negroes and the trainer of the race horses under the captain's supervision. The carriage was driven to Indian Camp, the plantation and residence of old General Camp, who was a staunch friend. He also helped my father on his way to safety by sending him in a skiff (row-boat) across the river to the house of another friend, and the latter sent him further on and more into the interior, where gunboats could not penetrate.

In the meantime, the Federal soldiers, some 300 of the 111th Indiana regiment, commanded by Colonel Keith, had landed and marched to the house. Their orders were to raid the place and capture my father. The transport on which they came was an ordinary Mississippi river steamboat, which the United States Government had impressed into service. The Federals had then no knowledge of the plantations. And they had instructed the pilot, also impressed into service, to reach the Kenner landing after dark, in fact well into the night, and to land silently, without whistling or making any unnecessary noise. Fortunately, the pilot was friendly to my father, and disregarded the instructions. He wished my father to escape and gave him the opportunity, of which he availed himself.

When my mother had been assured that in all probability my father was safe, she began to think of the safety of her household, and had the silver consisting of forks and spoons, for all the other silver had been packed and sent away, taken upstairs. She went downstairs to make sure that all the doors had been fastened, and me followed her closely. I remember that we were in the dining room when we heard the tramp of many men crossing the yard and coming up around the house; this was followed by a knock at the front door. Leaving Mr. Graves to open the door my mother and her three children and the maids who had gathered around us, went upstairs to my mother's bed room, and there waited—waited—in great suspense—for what was to follow. My mother was sitting, outwardly calm, when Mr. Graves appeared, accompanied by several Federal officers. Indicating one of them, Mr. Graves said, "Mrs. Kenner, this is Colonel Keith, who is in command, and who wishes to speak to you."

Colonel Keith advanced and said "Mrs. Kenner, I am in command of this expedition, and have been sent here to arrest Mr. Kenner, and take such of his property as the Government requires for its use. Can you tell me where Mr. Kenner is?" "No", said my mother, "I have not seen him since he left the house after dinner." This was a fact. We dined about three o'clock and my father usually rode out in the afternoon.

"It is very strange", replied the Colonel, "that I have met no one who has seen Mr. Kenner. However, in pursuance of my orders, I must institute a search for him, and also take possession of what I think advisable". My mother answered, "I am powerless to prevent you from taking what you please. Mr. Kenner is not here", turning towards him, "Mr. Graves will you be kind enough to show these officers all over the house, through every part of it. Let the search be thorough, so they may be satisfied that Mr. Kenner is not hidden". Mr. Graves with his military escort proceeded all through the house, and the servants who went with them to carry lights, told us that some of the men looked under beds, and in all places, possible and impossible.

They found nobody, of course, and went downstairs after the Colonel had assured my mother that she and her family would be treated with all due regard. But though satisfied that Mr. Kenner was not hidden in the house, Colonel Keith kept up an energetic search on the plantation until late in the night, and resumed it as soon as daylight enabled the searching party to look into the buildings that were not much used, and even under bridges and in the fields of cane, which at that season was tall enough to conceal a man in hiding. The neighboring places were also searched, Waterloo among others, and Mr. Minor's race horses "captured" and brought to be shipped, with my father's on the transport at Ashland landing. But Anthony did not go with his horses, and proved a true and silent friend.

Col. Keith was as good as his word and we were in no way molested. The next day, one of the soldiers having made his way up stairs and walked around in an inquisitive and annoying manner, it was reported to the Colonel, who placed a guard at the front of the staircase, and no one was allowed to come up without permission, and nothing in the house was destroyed or taken away. However, he was equally exacting in carrying out his instructions concerning the property that was to be confiscated for the use of the Government. The soldiers also were permitted to go all over the grounds and take or destroy whatever they pleased. My father's wine of which, he had a good supply, had fortunately been removed from the house and put under the flooring of one of the large brick out-houses which stood at a little distance from the main house. This had been done with

the hope of preventing any depredation in the house and also in the
hope that perhaps it might escape observation altogether. It proved
to be a wise measure, for it was one of the "supplies of war" that
Col. Keith demanded. He was informed of the location of the wine
by the negroes, who were well aware that it had been moved, and who
assisted the soldiers in taking it out, and in drinking it, which they
did to some extent, when it was carted down to the transport. But
it pronounced to "be thin weak stuff". Some other things had been
removed from the house by way of putting them in greater safety, and
unfortunately, among them were the family portraits and other paintings. These h ad been stored away in the house occupied by Mr.
Graves. Somehow it had been considered that as he proposed remaining at Ashland, happen what might, he could take better care of them
if they were in his home.

But the poor man was imprisoned in the main dwelling, and his
house was broken open and everything in it was taken or destroyed.
I can remember peeping under the curtains that shaded and screened
the upper gallery, and seeing below a soldier with his penknife busy
cutting an oil painting from its frame. It was the picture of one of
my father's race horses, and a good painting. The silver, with the
exception of the forks and spoons, had also been sent away. The
trunk in which it was packed had been taken in a cart to the house
of Jerry Segoud, who lived some miles away on New River, an out
of the way place. He had lost a leg, and could ont join the army,
and therefore would remain at home during the war. He was under
obligations to my father and therefore it was thought he would prove
a good custodian. However, the negro who had driven the cart came
forward and informed the Federals that a trunk, which probably contained valuables, had been left with Mr. Segoud, and he was arrested
and I am told, actually maltreated and beaten until he told where the
trunk was hidden.

All the white men, overseers, etc., on the plantations in our
neighborhood, were arrested and brought as prisoners to the Ashland
house. They slept in the lower hall, on a double row of mattresses,
which had been brought down from the garret, and also from the
bed rooms upstairs and on each side of the wide hall. The prisoners
took their meals in the dining room, the cooking being in our kitchen,
which was in an outbuilding. Our meals were served in the hall
upstairs, for we did not leave the second floor at all. Henry Hayman,
my father's body servant, a most trustworthy faithful man, assumed
charge of the kitchen. He had followed my father in all his travels
and had been with him in Richmond, where, as Henry said, "we kept
house with Mr. Benjamin" (J. P. Benjamin, Secretary of War.)

Therefore Henry was accustomed to soldiers, and their ways, and
knew how to safeguard his provisions. He was a good caterer and
an excellent cook, and we and the other prisoners were well fed. Mr.
Henry Doyal, who had changed horses with my father, was one of the

first persons to be arrested and brought in, and he was soon followed by Stephen Minor. The latter was allowed to come upstairs occasionally and talk with us, but he was always accompanied by a guard. When Mr. Doyal and one or two of the other men were arrested they were wearing pistols, and they contrived that these should not fall into the hands of the Federals, but sent them to my mother giving them to the colored maid, Nancy, who went down every morning to make the beds and sweep the lower hall, and she wrapped the pistols in her apron and brought them upstairs.

The Federal occupation lasted four days and during that time, everything was taken that could be moved, and put on board the transport and another steamboat which had come to the Ashland landing. The plantation was well stocked, as my father had laid in large supplies previous to leaving Mr. Graves in charge, and being absent himself for an indefinite period. In the pasture there were herds of cattle and sheep, to furnish fresh meat for the hands. The storehouses were full of salt meat and the corn cribs of corn. And last but not least, there were about three hundred hogsheads of sugar in the sugar houses. All this was shipped, and some of the things that could not be taken were destroyed regardless of the fact that there were on the plantation a large number of hands, many women and children, all of whom were accustomed to be provided for, fed and clothed. Some of the negroes went with the Federals when they left, but the majority remained at home. The soldiers had, as a rule been unkind and harsh, and the negroes were not tempted to follow them and encounter the fortunes of war. What we children felt most was the taking of the horses, except a few old mares that were not in the stables, and that the race stable boys had hidden in the woods. All the carriage and riding horses, even our ponies, were led, in what seemed to us as a funeral procession, as we saw it go down the road to the river. There were probably sixty horses in all. However, there was one horse that was not taken, because no one could ride or manage him except the grooms, who were accustomed to do so, and they refused to help in getting him off.

This was Whale, a large, powerful animal, difficult to control. He had never lost a race, though he ran many, of four miles heat. My brother's pony was given back to him by Colonel Keith, who when he heard of the little boy's distress at losing his pony gave orders that the horse should be restored.

At the end of four days, the 111th Indiana received orders to move to Baton Rouge, where a battle seemed impending. Consequently, about dusk one evening, the whole expedition left Ashland. Colonel took with him many negroes and all the white men who had been arrested. This meant, that for miles around us, there remained, to our knowledge, no white men, and we were entirely in the hands of the negroes, of whom there were hundreds in our imme-

diate neighborhood. However, there were many of the colored men
who were trustworthy and devoted to our interests, and foremost
among these was Henry Hayman. With him my mother consulted,
and in consequence, the foreman of the field hands was summoned.
He engaged to select several good men, and place them as a guard
around the house, acting as their captain. My mother gave him one
of the pistols that had been sent upstairs by the prisoners. To Henry
she gave another pistol reserving one for her own use in case of
necessity. Phil, the foreman, was very confident that he and his men
would be good protectors, and assured my mother that she could go
to bed and rest quietly. But she did not even undress.

And Henry spent the night sitting at the door of the upper hall.
We children had no thought, except that the hated invaders had gone,
leaving us in possession of our own house and premises and we went
to bed and slept as soundly as usual, and the night passed without
incident.

The next morning, a little after breakfast, a carriage drove up,
and from it alighted to our surprise, my grandmother and one of our
cousins and his wife. They told us they had come to beg my mother
to pack up and go home with them, as it would be very imprudent
for her to remain longer at Ashland. Mother was easily persuaded,
and agreed to go if she could get transportation. The carriages had
not been taken, and there were still a number of mules upon the
plantation. But it was found that the harness had been destroyed.
However, by sending some miles away, other harness was borrowed,
and that evening, we started off with another train of wagons and
servants, very similar to the one which had failed to get across the
river in the spring. Our first stopping place was the Hermitage,
where my grandmother Bonnemaman, as we called her, was staying
temporarily with her daughter-in-law, Mrs. Amedee Bringier, my uncle
having rejoined the army. We remained two or three days at the
Hermitage, and during that time heard from my father, who sent us
word that he was waiting for us, some miles down Bayou Lafourche,
and to come to meet him and go with him into the Confederate lines.
My grandmother decided to go with us, and her carriage, coachman
and maid being added to our train, we crossed the river at Donaldsonville, where the ferry easily took over our wagons, etc. We continued down Bayou Lafourche, and met my father not very far from
Donaldsonville, for the Confederate lines extended as near the river
as was consistant with keeping out of range of the gunboats. Father
told us that he had been as intensely anxious on our account as we
could have been for him, and had kept as near as was safe, so as to
hear what was taking place at Ashland. Many rumors had reached
him, one of which was that the house had been burned and my mother
taken on board the transport as a prisoner. This report had been so
harrowing that he had ventured near enough, being on the opposite
bank, to look over the river with a strong field glass, and seeing the

house standing, apparently untouched, he had comforted himself with the assurance that the other statement must also be false.

He proposed to take us some distance into the interior to a plantation owned by William Minor, in Terrebonne parish, which was still held by the Confederate forces. We journeyed down Bayou Lafourche, stopping the first night at the Tournillon plantation, and going on from there to Mr. Henry Foley's. His mother, old Mrs. Foley, gave us a most interesting account of her experience at Last Island, when that place, then a summer resort, had been submerged in a terrible storm. The hotel was swept away and many persons were drowned. Mrs. Foley and her husband had been saved by clinging to a log that floated them to a place where the water was shallow, and when the storm subsided and the water receded, they were picked up by some fishermen, but not before they had suffered much from hunger and exposure. Further down, near Thibodeaux, we stopped at the Guion plantation, and when we reached the town of Houma, we were met by William Minor, Jr., who was then living at Southdown plantation. He took us into his house, which was newly built, large and comfortable, and gave us a hearty and cousinly welcome. We remained at Southdown about three months, my father leaving us there while he returned to Richmond. My grandmother remained with us only a short time. She joined another daughter, Mrs. Benj. Tureaud, who with her husband and family passed through Terrebonne on their way to Opelousas.

My father returned to us at the end of October, by way of Vicksburg. He found us in a state of great excitement, as the Federals had advanced a large body of troops into the Lafourche country, and notwithstanding that several engagements had taken place, they were still advancing. General Taylor had shortly before this taken command of the Confederate forces, opposite to this advance. We packed up and left very early one morning with our wagons following the carriage. We went on to Berwicks Bay, where we crossed over, and then travelled slowly through the beautiful Teche cuontry, and so further along until we reached Opelousas. My aunt, Mrs. Allen Thomas, had opened her home, New Dalton, on the Courtbleau Bayou, to her family, going herself to Vicksburg to be with Colonel Thomas. We found at New Dalton, my grandmother and the family of Mr. Benj. Tureaud, and we formed part of the household until we moved to Moundville. Near the town of Washington, which is also on the Courtableau, my father and Mr. Tureaud rented together, a large house with some land attached, at Moundville. There we settled, hoping that we would be able to remain in peace and quiet. My father returned to Richmond after a short stay with us.

Linwood as it was before the Civil War.

LINWOOD PLANTATION
Ascension Parish.
Built for Philip Minor.

In the life of the artist Rubens, we learn that when he visited
Genoa in 1607, the splendor of its great palaces so impressed him
that almost at once he started work on a series of detailed architectural drawings, views, and perspectives of this most magnificent Strada Nuova.   These he published in 1622 at Antwerp with
the title "Palazzo di Genova".   Would that some artist or architect of ante-bellum days, had left some such set of drawings depicting the splendor of the old plantation mansions of Louisiana
in the hey-day of their glory!   This hey-day Mr. Dorr wrote about
while reporting on the plantation country of 1860.   This was before the time when the Union forces were to wreck and impover-
ish this "land of milk and honey".   How very interesting would
be illustrations of the many unique and fine old palatial plantation homes that now are but memories,—places like Linwood that
recall the glory of that day.

The decoration of the walls of this magnificent old plantation
mansion were reproductions of the frescoed walls and ceilings of
the splendid villas of the Brenta, so famous in their day.   Today
one rarely sees these landscape wall paper panels, save in museums or in stores like Marshall Field, where a few are to be seen
costing a small fortune.   In referring to these panels, the late
Mrs. Eliza Ripley in her "Social Life in Old New Orleans" has
the following to say:

The culmination of landscape wall paper must have been reached in
the Minor plantation dwelling in Ascension Parish. Mrs. Minor had

SHOWING THE MAGNITUDE OF "THE HERMITAGE" PLANTATION MANOR.

Page 131   (Courtesy of Trist Wood.)

The Old Ashland Plantation Mansion (Belle Helene), designed and built for Duncan Kenner by James Gallier I, in 1849, as a bridal gift to the beautiful Nanine Bringier.

Linwood Mansion, built for Philip Minor. As it appeared after the destruction of one wing during the Civil War. (See page 152.) Photograph taken shortly before it was demolished in June 1939.

"The Cottage", old plantation home of the Conrad family, known as the Conrad Plantation Home.

Tomb of George and Martha Washington, Mount Vernon, Virginia. Front shaft to the right marks the graves of the New Orleans branch of the Conrad family, related to the Washingtons. (See page 157.)

Sugar-House of "The Hermitage" Plantation with Golden Ball on tower denoting prosperity. (Courtesy of Trist Wood.)

received this plantation as a legacy, and she was so loyal to the donor that the entreaties of her children to "cover that wall" did not prevail. It was after that of mural decoration was of the past, that I visited the Minors. The hall was broad and long, adorned with real jungle scenes, scenes from India. A great tiger jumped out of dense thickets towards savages who were fleeing in terror. Tall trees reached to the ceiling, with gaudy striped boa-constrictors wound around their trunks; hissing snakes peered out of the jungles; birds of gay plumage, paroquete,s parrots, peacocks, everywhere, some way, almost out of sight in the greenery; monkeys swung from limb to limb; ourang-outangs, and lots of almost naked, dark-skinned natives wandered about. To cap the climax, right close to the steps one had to mount to the story above was a lair of ferocious lions! I spent hours studying that astnishing wall-paper (hand-painted) and I applauded Mrs. Minor's decision, "The old man put it there; it shall stay; he liked it, so do I". It was in 1849 I made that never-to-be-forgotten trip to jungle land.

The decoration referred to by Mrs. Ripley, in the original frescoed form painted by the most noted fresco-painters of that date can still be found in great number throughout Italy, especially in the region of the Brenta, where on the crumbling walls of the palatial villas still can be traced many of them.

The plantation land was acquired by Philip Minor in 1816. It remained in the family for seventy-five years, and according to records was abandoned in 1900. The old plantation mansion after serving as a home for this distinguished family for three-quarters of a century remained idle and was used as a stable until it was demolished.

Linwood, almost theatrical in its magnificence and setting, originally built for Philip Minor, joins Ashland, which was erected as a bridal gift from Duncan Kenner to the beautiful Nanine Bringier. It was once surrounded by a splendid grove of oak trees, now rapidly disappearing. Like one of the great villas of the Brenta, which served as summer homes and pleasure houses of the Venetian nobility, stands this magnificent old place. Like the villas immortalized by d'Annunzio, it too, is falling into ruin so completely that in a few years more the great classic pile, as with beautiful White Hall (Maison Blanche), Valcour Aimes' "Petit Versailles", and so many others, soon will be but a memory. Magnificent in its conception, it was to have been when completed the most palatial mansion on the east bank of the Mississippi River.

Such was the dream of the owner. And it was to be made a reality by the architect, the famous Gallier, pere who designed Linwood, Ashland, Belle Grove and a score of others, as well as the beautiful City Hall in New Orleans. It was cnosidered one of Gallier's greatest triumphs in plantation domestic architecture. In it he combined the grandeur of Oaklawn on the Teche with the splendor of the Brenta Villas. Instead of having his collonaded wings as subordinate structures, he planned the extensions of either side with spectacular effect. So well has he succeeded that even in its greatly ruined state, the building is magnificent to behold, and frescoed like the Brenta Villas.

The great porte-cochere, arcaded with vaulted ceiling, rings with the echo of the glamorous days that are no more. It forms a driveway through the building which was damaged when the Civil War wrecked the fortunes of its owner. The vaulted arcade gives the stately pile quite a distinctive foreign air, and one feels sure that the Spanish influence of the early Natchez, Mississippi days of the Minor family, had a great deal to do with the design of this mansion being selected.

The great pile contains many stately rooms, which have been stripped of the marble mantels, silver-plated door knobs and other hardware. It now serves as a place to shelter cattle, unbelievable as it seems. Hogs wallow in the corridors where the pavement has been removed, and the beautiful large pediment window with fan-transom and side lights, has few panes left and the place is flooded by each rain.

The building was another that fell a victim to the raids of Union soldiers when they found that Duncan Kenner had escaped. Mr. Kenner had angered the Federal authorities by his activities in behalf of the Confederate Cause. The Union soldiers, learning that he was at his plantation, landed at the private dock of Ashland Manor. Some of his old slaves hearing that they were trying to make him a prisoner, knowing that Mr. Kenner was out in his field, sought him out and told him what they had overheard. Mr. Kenner immediately took refuge in Linwood Manor and watched from a high point of the building. He later rode to General Camp's place, some distance below, where he rowed across the river in a skiff, going to the Lafourche District, where he remained until the troops had moved further up the river and it was safe for him to leave. When the Federal troops sacked beautiful Linwood, they took with them everything of value they could find. The Union troops removed quantities of furniture that they did not want, destroying much in their search, and as at Jefferson College, piled it high and applied the torch, burning fine pianos, furniture and paintings. Much of it they burned in a room, but slaves, returning after the Union soldiers left, extinguished the flames and saved the main building. Later when Mr. J. S. Minor returned he saw that it was impossible to continue with so large a place after having lost his great fortune. He sold the entire estate.

A newspaper of June 16th, 1939 brings the news that LINWOOD is no more and that it is now but a memory. The stately old pile was demolished a few days ago when the latest owners found that their architect told them that it would cost at least $30,000.00 to restore the mansion. The new owners, Oscar Geren of New Orleans, D. A. Vann and D. A. Vann, Jr., will make an immense stock farm of the place.

CHAPTER XVII.

NEAR BATON ROUGE.

CHATSWORTH PLANTATION

(Formerly located 15 miles from Baton Rouge)

BUILT in the early part of 1858, but not quite completed when Norman made his map that year it is listed with name, owner and acreage. In spite of the constant threat of war, work went on, but the house was of such massive size and the plans called for so much detail, that war broke out, the South was defeated, slaves were freed, the owner's fortune swept away, and the old place was never completed.

Its facade presents large Corinthian columns across its central section sustaining the Greek Revival cornice. Spaced in the center the wide steps rise to the wide gallery. All is impressive, the wings of either side of the house relieved by mouldings and pilasters enhancing the effect. The Greek Revival carried throughout, for on entering we find endless rooms palatial in their size and magnificent in finish as the detail of woodwork and plaster work is very beautiful. The hardware consists of heavily silver-plated ornate hinges and doorknobs with escutcheons. In a mansion of this sort the upkeep was immense, as rooms ranging from 30x40 feet to the smaller ones 15x20, some fifty in number, could only have been maintained during the "golden days" with its numerous slaves. The Chatsworth mansion lay idle for a long time and was never completed. It typifies the grandeur of the day at its best, and was built to house immense house-parties of weeks' duration as was customary in that era.

The family, a prominent one socially at that day, has lost none of its social lustre with the passing years. The plantation at that time as befitted a mansion of such huge proportions was large and its garden grounds beautiful.

THE COTTAGE PLANTATION

(The Conrad Plantation)

The last great plantation mansion, that we pass on our way to Baton Rouge, La., and it is indeed a grand old mansion, with its wide spreading front making a magnificent showing from the river, is the Conrad place, about ten miles below the state capitol. Built along lines that typify the luxurious comfort and cultured life of the wealthy planter in the days that plantations were plantations. Yet it was planned, first of all as a home of a family accustomed to the good things of life, who felt no need to sacrifice comfort for style.

To begin with its location, is a magnificent one; the house is far back from the river road and set in a grove of magnolias and oak trees, with much in the way of blooming greenery and shrubs scattered about at random, adding great charm to the grounds. Leading from the main gateway the wide drive is edged with yucca plants, uniform in size on both sides of the driveway, giving a spectacular effect that is most pleasing. They would gladden the heart of any lover of flowers when the plants are in bloom. It has always been known as the "Bridal Walk" as the spikes of white waxen bloom appear as pyramids of silver bells, arrayed for a joyous occasion. Maintaining all the lines of the Greek Revival, the massive classic cornice which surrounds the building rests on long collonades of solid brick columns, cement-coated and, crowned with Doric caps. The greater part of the massive brick mansion is also heavily cement-coated, and the columns eight in number, ranging across the front like those of the sides and back, support what is probably the widest balcony in the state of Louisiana, almost surrounding the entire building. The wings, designed with architectural correctness, permit the central section of the back to remain open, forming a porch of the same width with spacious rooms to either side. Heavy Doric pilasters finish the corners of the enclosure, and complete the

Greek Revival design of the mansion. A spacious roof of good design, covered with slate, has two dormers (windows) projecting from each of its four sides with good effect. The gentleman for whom this mansion was erected was Mr. Abner Lawson Duncan for whom Duncan Point was named. Mr. Duncan was a distinguished Louisiana lawyer, who lived in New Orleans, and the plantation was built in 1824, when the wealth of the South was beginning to grow. Cotton and sugarcane plantations were veritable gold mines, and Mr. Duncan, a wealthy Pennsylvanian who had come to Louisiana shortly after 1803, an Aide-de-Camp to General Jackson in 1815, invested in plantation lands on a large scale. He owned the plantation on what is now known as Conrad Point, and so as not to confuse Conrad's Point and The Cottage, the home on Conrad's Point was known as The Cottage. Later by mistake, people began calling the place which is the subject of this article The Cottage. The name stuck, and the place is now, and has for many years been known by that name. It was originally built by Mr. Duncan as a bridal gift to his daughter when she married Frederick Daniel Conrad, who had read law in Mr. Duncan's office in New Orleans. Frederick Conrad was the brother of Charles M. Conrad, who was a member of the famous New Orleans law firm of Slidell, Conrad and Benjamin. Charles M. Conrad was Secretary of War, during President Buchanan's administration, and was appointed Confederate States Minister to Germany by President Jefferson Davis. Mrs. Charles M. Conrad before her marriage was Angella Lewis of Virginia, a great niece of George Washington and a great-grand-daughter of Lady Washington. The Conrads are related to the Washingtons, the Lewises and other prominent Virginia families.

Mr. Duncan not only gave the newly married couple his blessing, but the plantation, the manor and a full quota of slaves for the house and plantation. To the plantation was attached in the rear a village of brick plantation cabins for slave quarters, a large sugar house and a cotton gin.

In construction the house is massive, having brick walls two feet in thickness, the partition walls being equally as thick, reaching from the ground to the rafters in the attic. The entire outside walls of brick are thickly coated with cement, with the exception of the upstairs wings where a weatherboard surface is used. The home contains some twenty-two rooms, most of them very large, as there are eleven rooms to each floor. The wide hall extends from the front to the rear veranda. The large fan-transom lights and side lights, upstairs and down are exceptionally fine, the lower ones of the entrance having handcarved fluted Doric columns, while upstairs pilasters are used. When the mansion was finished, the Conrads furnished it in a magnificent manner. It still possesses some of the articles that were hidden by the slaves at the time the house was swept clean by the Union forces after the fall of New Orleans. At that time its valuable contents were put on flat boats and shipped beyond Union lines. The first owners, the ancestors of the present ones, occupied the mansion for nearly half a century, during which time many notables were entertained as house guests, among them General Lafayette, President Zachary Taylor, Jefferson Davis, Judah P. Benjamin, and other prominent people too numerous to mention.

Mrs. James J. Bailey, the present gracious chatelain of "The Cottage," tells of several incidents of Civil War days that have been related to her by the family. One is how the jewels of the Conrad family were saved from the Union soldiers. Mrs. Conrad had presented her husband with a daughter (Mrs. Bailey being the daughter) a short time previously, and was still in bed when raiding Union soldiers came to "The Cottage". Having put her diamonds, family heirlooms of great value, in a chamois bag she suspended it from her neck and hid it by the elaborate lace folds of her robe de nuit. When the soldiers invaded her bed room, summoning all of her strength, she let out several piercing screams that caused them to flee in confusion, telling her that they would leave at once if she would only cease screaming as if she was being murdered.

Far back in the grounds of the rear garden, on the left side as you face the house, is a small cemetery where the Union soldiers are buried. It is a small cypress grove and the graves are all unmarked. The Union soldiers spared The Cottage, because its planning and spaciousness made it possible for them to use it for a hospital. When an epidemic of yellow fever broke out among the Union troops near the plantation, the house was at once converted into a hospital. The little cemetery in the grove of cypress above mentioned is where the yellow fever victims are buried.

The Cottage was the plantation home of the Conrads, wealthy planters, whose fortune was estimated at something over three millions of dollars, not including what would now be classed as "personal property". The jewels of the Conrad family at that date represented large sums and the costly carriages and horses, a string of racing stock and other thorough breds amounted to another fortune. The family had its own splendid coach and four, and a Virginia atmosphere pervaded the place because of the great wealth of the family and the luxuriant manner of living at all times. With so many heirlooms and other souvenirs of the Washingtons, the Lewises, Duncans and Conrad families, this home became a veritable museum of priceless treasures. The family and its branches entertained continuously throughout the year, as the home was a rendezvous of the intelligencia of the state, who knew that a house party was in progress here nearly all the time. When the Union soldiers learned that the house was one containing endless treasure, they literally swept the place clean of its costly furniture, furnishing and objects of art. The Washington, Lewis and other mementos were hidden away, but most of the contents of the house were taken. What pieces of handsome furniture that were saved, were brought out later from their hiding places by the slaves that had hidden them. Comparatively little of the once magnificent furnishings remain, few of the great array of imported sets of imported palasandre rosewood and mahogany are to be seen. A few handsome pieces which show the beauty of the periods are scattered about the different rooms. A specially fine carved rosewood etagere, a museum piece, and a number of others equally as attractive are scattered about the halls and other rooms. In the dining room are some very fine old English pieces of mahogany, making this a splendid old room.

The light graceful lines of t he wood-carver and cabinet maker at their best are in evidence, while the family portraits, mantel ornaments, china, silverware, and crystal all hearken back to old plantation days. Above stairs the rooms are all large and airy, having large windows and doorways, permitting the continuous flow of river breezes through the house on the hottest days of the long summer months. Vistas of charm present themselves in every direction, especially the view up and down the river where there is an apparent continual change of scenery. The

Concession Plantation Manor. Built in 1801 for
Mr. and Mrs. Louis Edmond Fortier. Rear of
mansion showing quaint details of architecture.
(Courtesy of Miss Marie Marguerite Fortier,
Louisiana State Museum, New Orleans.)

A garconnier at "Concession", now a negro cabin.   (Courtesy of Miss Marie Marguerite Fortier, Louisiana State Museum, New Orleans,)

Old La Branche Mansion, Rue Royale, New Orleans.

plantation acres with their endless fields of cotton, make other interesting scenes reminiscent of the good old days "be fo de war".

Having heard that the kindness of the Conrad family to their slaves would naturally make the blacks loyal, the Union officers planned unusually severe tactics to intimidate the negroes. They instructed the Union soldiers to spread the report, that unless the slaves run away, or if they remained on the plantation, the Confederate soldiers would put them in the front ranks to be killed first. In this way hundreds of the Conrad slaves were scared away, who would have remained had not this report been circulated. After stripping all of the storehouses, and taking the live stock, they blew up the sugar house and cotton gin.

When the mansion was threatened with bombardment, Mr. Duncan, who had given a great sum to aid the Confederate cause, (being seventy years of age at the time and too old to enlist) with his daughter left for St. Helena parish which was considered a safer place at that time. Before leaving "The Cottage", Mr. Duncan came near being captured by Union soldiers, and was saved by the action of a faithful slave, who hid him and prevented his being caught and probably executed for his aid to the Confederates. The old gentleman's health had been undermined by trials brought on by the war, and he died shortly after hostilities ceased. The loss of his fortune and his other worries all aided to hasten his death.

In the great garden today are traceable the glorious garden of ante-bellum days. A century-old sweet olive tree perfumes the air about the house—it is one of the largest trees of its kind in the state. Many other trees bearing fragrant blossoms make of the place a beauty spot. Some of the rosebushes have stems that are two inches in thickness.

For many years following the war the place lay empty, having only a keeper on the grounds. The fact that the home had been used as a yellow fever hospital, made it a place that tramps avoided, and looters shunned it, fearing to enter, treating it as an accursed place. Thus the beautiful old mansion was saved from having its marble mantels, beautiful ornamental doorways, fine transomed entrances, costly hardware, and many other valuable parts stripped as had been done with so many other fine old places. At the death of Mr. Conrad, the property passed to his heirs, who never have permitted the house to fall into ruin.

Even now it needs only a few minor repairs. At present Mrs. James Bailey, who was the baby of this story, with the aid of her brother and his farm hands, maintains the place on a paying basis. Her brother gave me most of the data about the house and family, when I visited the place on several occasions. He told me that making the place pay is quite an achievement because of the way planters are discriminated against at present, of which fact I too am well aware, and with the competition of sugar from the tropics. Mrs. James J. Bailey, her son and her brother (with her house servants, descendants of old family slaves), live here now and the old place is gradually being carefully restored.

The usual farm noises add to the hominess of the place. A large number of fine looking cattle graze in the field, poultry and pea fowl range about the lawns, in the rear yard an old turkey cock spreading his fan shows the peacock that he too has something to be proud of, while a flock of geese and noisy ducks seem to enjoy the turkey's performance. Pigeons in great numbers, guinea hens and other denizens of the barn-yard, show that "The Cottage" table still can boast of being well supplied, as in olden days, with a great variety of choice meats, farm delicacies, pigeon pies, squab, roast duck, goose, etc.

"The Cottage" today still remains one of the homes that has held and still holds great allure for tourists, and no doubt will for another century so substantially is it built.

On the monument flanking the Washington tomb at Mount Vernon are carved the names of the members of this branch of the Conrad family who died in Louisiana but were brought to Mount Vernon to be buried—George and Martha Washington alone being buried in the large red brick tomb of the Washingtons, now covered with a heavy mantle of vines.

For many years a large part of the collection of papers, and heirlooms of the Washington and Lewis families belonging to the Conrad family reposed in a fire-proof box in the Art Store (Seebold's) 166 Canal St., New Orleans, La., until presented to the Mount Vernon Museum by the family of Mrs. Conrad, who lived in the fine three-storied brick mansion facing Lafayette Square now occupied by the new addition of the New Orleans Post Office.

CANE CUTTERS

CHAPTER XVIII.

ON THE WEST BANK—NEAR NEW ORLEANS.

BELLE CHASSE PLANTATION MANOR.

STANDING alone in but a small part of its once wide spreading acreage, Belle Chasse Manor, at one time the splendid home of Judah P. Benjamin, evokes memories of a man who became a peer among men of two countries.

Belle Chasse is a place of much history and for that reason has been rescued and restored to its present condition. It is hoped that ere long the Judah P. Benjamin Memorial Association, whose able President, General Allison Owen has accomplished so much, may be able to carry to fulfillment the finishing and appropriately refurnishing this ancient home, that it may become a shrine to the memory of this brilliant man who has done so much for Louisiana.

As stated before, it is a place of much history—history of a man of unusual ability, whose devotion to family and state is unsurpassed. A man whose intellect at once caused his rise to fame to become meteoric, and when needed, laid at once his unusual talent undivided at the altar of the "Southern Cause".

Judah P. Benjamin, distinguished statesman from Louisiana, the son of English Jewish parents, was born on the island of St. Thomas, West Indies. His parents having come to America with their family he was enrolled at Yale University, where he displayed unusual ability at the age of fourteen years. Financial difficulties of the family cut short his college course, and feeling confidence in his ability, he started Southward, landing in New Orleans, and with little but his wealth of grey matter that soon made his worth felt.

Obtaining a position in a notary's office as notarial clerk he soon was able to send himself to law school, attending night classes. Realizing that language was an essential accomplishment, he devoted all of his spare time to this field—and at the age of twenty-one was admitted to the bar.

When he reached the age of twenty-three, with John Slidell, he compiled a digest on the laws of Louisiana. Before long he became a United States Senator, and after some years of unusual success, having accumulated a fortune, decided to purchase a plantation near New Orleans, where he could rest from time to time; and later built the mansion we see today. When the thunderous war clouds threatened to break, he gave his knowledge and sympathy to the Confederate cause, and defended in able and eloquent addresses in the Senate Chamber at Washington, the Cause of the South. At last when he saw that the die was cast, in 1861 he resigned from the United States Senate, and was appointed by the President of the Confederacy, Jefferson Davis, Attorney General of the Confederacy. Later he was appointed Secretary of State.

At the collapse of the Confederacy he fled to Florida in disguise, and then to England, where in a few years his brilliancy as a lawyer was recognized by the British. He rapidly rose, later becoming counselor to Queen Victoria, and attained the highest prominence at the English bar. Continuing in active practice until the year 1883, he was made the recipient of the highest honor, a complimentary banquet given in the great hall of the Inner Temple (recently demolished by German bombs), to which some of the greatest legal lights of that date came to do honor. Sir Henry James, rising, after a few preliminary words, asked in ringing tones, "Who is the man, save this one of whom it can be said that he held conspicuous leadership at the bar of two great countries?"

He married Natalie, daughter of August St. Martin, who lived at number 327 Bourbon Street, New Orleans, later the family lived in Paris after Mr. Benjamin retired from his law practice,

Portrait of Judah P. Benjamin, by Rinck. To be
hung in the Judah P. Benjamin Plantation Home,
now a museum to the memory of the distinguished
Statesman from Louisiana.

'Belle Chasse", the Old Judah P. Benjamin Plantation Home, as it was originally, showing garden and Box Hedges.

Seven Oaks Plantation Mansion. Built in 1830 for Madame (Widow) Michael Zerinque, later owned by the LaBranch family. (Westwego, La.)

in a beautiful villa in the Avenue d'Jena. He died in 1884 and is buried in Pere la Chaise Cemetery, where so many immortals lie.

SEVEN OAKS.

Once a magnificent plantation—Seven Oaks now belongs to an oil company whose high oil tanks group themselves about the seven huge oak trees that encompass the splendid old mansion to which they give their name. Known as the old Zerinque Mansion it was built for the widow of Michael Zerinque in 1830. Later it became the home of Lucian LaBranche, a wealthy planter, one of the richest in the state, whose family have married into many local prominent families.

Monsieur LaBranche also invested heavily in the latter part of the 1830's in property in the French Quarter. An ancestor on his father's side who came from Germany in 1724 bore the name of Johan Zweig. His son, also named Johan, married a young lady, an orphan brought up by the Ursuline Nuns whose convent was then in Chartres Street. The notary, a Frenchman, drew up the customary marriage contract, and as the notary had trouble in spelling the German surname he translated it into French—the Johan for John being Jean and the Zweig for twig, translated LaBranche—leaving it Jean LaBranche, which it has remained ever afterwards. Many of the later LaBranches were unable to speak anything but French.

The house, a rather large square structure containing eighteen rooms, quite distinctive, is of the Greek Revival devoid of elaborate details. Its handsome colonnade of immense circular columns of heavy brick work, slate roof and dormers, etc., crowning observatory—all are substantial and dignified in construction. A simple balustrade and plain cornice belies any attempt at ornamentation.

It is a typical home of a wealthy planter and a type one associates with the stories of plantation life. It accords with the riches that poured into Louisiana during its golden era and the large manner of living of that day. The garden is still attractive and the immense old oak trees with their banners of moss give a distinctive, charming note to the settlement of Westwego.

The ancient property holdings of the LaBranche family in the rue Royale New Orleans close by comprise some of the most interesting as well as artistic of the more important old residences of the French Quarter. The lace-like iron of balconies and balustrades is some of the finest of its kind in America. These ancient buildings are as beautiful as they were when first completed and cost a fortune at the time they were erected.

ELLINGTON (WITHERSPOON)

THIS name does not appear on map of 1858. However, there is no question but that this interesting plantation house was erected prior to that date.

Framed in a luxuriant growth of foliage, high oak trees, evergreens, tropical greenery and hedges as a center piece it forms a vista from the river road charming indeed. In itself, this beauty spot seems all the more attractive as the surrounding landscape is somewhat neglected acreage, showing signs of long neglect. Enclosed as is the entire house and garden area by a newly painted picket fence, the landscaping of the clumps of foliage is emphasized by the different color values and contrasting greens. With great oaks forming the background and its shading greys, a delightful effect is obtained. Blending with the dark green, the well-kept lawn stands out in the sunshine like velvet carpet. The boundaries of the path leading to the house from the roadway are broken by hedges of green foliage with flowering plants.

A curving stairway leads up to the gallery from either side somewhat after the Italian manner—a type of stairway found from time to time on the fronts of plantation homes.

This graceful stairway leads to the principal rooms of the house located on the second floor, it being of the high basement type house. The facade presents a somewhat classic revival cornice, with a balustrade crowning it, adding to the Italian appearance referred to. The first story finished in a rustic block design of stucco is a little unusual but not pronounced. It all hangs well together, as there is no feature distinctive enough to mar. As a whole the house is in good taste and is a country home unpretentious but of distinct charm. The ground floor is arranged, as houses of that type generally are, with the basement rooms located there. Here is a paved lower gallery and most of the features of the early Louisiana type plantation home.

The house appears bright and clean from the road side, and in its setting is a pleasing contrast to so many fine old places in utter ruin that one passes on the way. The distant fields give promise of a bumper crop and the great seas of waving cane and the silhouette of sugar house and smoke stacks in the distance add interest to the scene.

The basement is some eighteen feet high with a pavement of twelve-inch squares. Much worn marble slabs form the flooring of the hall way leading across the entire front in the enclosure within the original rustic heavy piers, behind the double front stairway—the former grille area is now entirely closed by a cement facing. Within, a handsome Greek Revival entrance doorway leading to the lower hallway is found where originally were handsomely finished rooms. However, of late years, these rooms have been utilized as a regular basement in which to store farm implements, etc. Above, the many rooms are large and imposing with columned mantels, large sliding doors and good woodwork.

The sides of the house have balconies and the rear of the house has an attractive stairway and rear cornice giving it a handsome appearance. Leading up to this rear entrance is a wide driveway running beneath an avenue of great oak trees that originally connected with the circular driveway from the river road which rounded one side of the old place and made its exit at the other leading to the house from the rear. Beyond this rear avenue of moss-hung oak trees on either side of the road leading to the old sugar house are long rows of ancient slave cabins still in good condition.

RANSON.

On the West bank of the Mississippi River, opposite the d'Estrehan Plantation is the former plantation of the ante-bellum millionaire planter Zenon Ranson who had married Adel Labatut, daughter of General J. B. Labatut, and Marie Felicité St. Martin.

One of their daughters named Lise, married Emile Fossier, and another daughter named Clelie, married Jules Labatut. The marriages of the two heiresses at the same Mass at the St. Louis Cathedral in New Orleans and celebrated at this plantation home with all the pomp and circumstance that an occasion of this kind warranted. It was an era of doing things on a princely scale and Zenon Ranson was profuse in his hospitality.

THE KELLER PLANTATION HOME.

Originally built for the Fortier family, according to Miss Marie Marguerite Fortier of the Louisiana State Museum, who furnished photographs for this article, the Keller house, located on the West bank at Hahnville in the St. Charles Parish, La., was built in the latter part of the eighteenth century. It has been occupied by the Keller family for over half a century. Originally this old Louisiana plantation home had many architectural features in common with the Parlange house and Elmswood which burned a year ago. It too like the old Parlange place had originally the usual garconnieres, Pigeonnaires, Coach house and horse stables and other buildings found on large plantations. Here originally were located on the ground floor basement level, the dining room, and wine and service rooms. The kitchen was in a separate building to avoid the danger of fire. We find also quarters for special servants (slaves). The wine cellars were large and fitted to contain thousands of bottles of wine, and the barrels and hogsheads rested on platforms. The floor of this room is of green and white marble squares, as this was an important department in every wealthy planter's home. It opened onto the wide brick-paved gallery also into the dining-room. On this ground floor are an immense dining-room, serving room, a service hall with stairway leading to the hall upstairs. A large fireplace in dining-room with one also in each room above. Two sleeping and an auxiliary wine room.

On all sides a wide brick-paved porch surrounded by circular pillars with bases and caps. Upstairs are a large living room or parlor which opens from a small square hall with stairway, six bed chambers and the usual wide gallery surrounded by the usual collonettes. Two stairways lead to this floor from the floor below. The floors of the galleries are of wide cypress planking above exposed beams, with beams exposed also in other parts. The stairway of good design is well placed to show the charm of the fine construction and beautifully modelled handrail and balusters, all of choice wood. The interior upstairs, like the rooms below, has a simple dignified finish, all rooms leading to the gallery. Simply designed mantels, door and window frames with woodwork are of cypress sparingly used. The side walls which are plastered, still retain the original wall paper. The window

EVERGREEN PLANTATION, built about 1840 for Ralph Brou. (For details see "White Pillars" by L. Frazer Smith, A. I. A.)

Petit Versailles Plantation Manor in its gala days.
(See Mrs. Ripley's memoirs.)

St. Joseph Plantation Manor, a gift of Valcour Aime to his daughter.

draperies and furnishings are mostly the original ones which it is stated were imported from France, as were the marble floor pavement squares and slates that covered the roof.

The Keller Plantation was once called the Pelican Plantation and even before that "Concession". It was a grant from the Spanish government and it was built by Mr. and Mrs. Louis Edmond Fortier in 1801. Their ten children were born on this plantation. Louis Edmond Fortier was the first son of Colonel Michel Fortier, Sr., who was Captain in the Campaigns of Bernado de Galvez—1779-81.

Five generations of the Haydels and Brou families were born on this plantation. Last owners of the old plantation were Mr. and Mrs. Ambroise Brou, Mrs. Brou having been a Miss Seraphine Becnel of St. Charles Parish. (Information in this chapter was obtained from Miss Marie Marguerite Fortier of the Louisiana State Museum.)

CHAPTER XIX.

ON THE WEST BANK—BELOW DONALDSONVILLE.

EVERGREEN PLANTATION.

THE attractive old mansion attached to this plantation was built about 1840 for Ralph Brou. It is of the Greek Revival type of two stories, brick construction. Tall Doric columns of brick stucco support the wide galleries. An attractive dormered-hipped roof crowned by a balustrade, and the beautiful single-curved outside stairway make of the house an unusually attractive one. Before being allowed to fall into ruin it was a most attractive place having all of the out-buildings usually attached to a fine country home well designed and well built of brick. Here we find the carriage house, barns, pigeonnaires, and toilet house, planned in attractive Greek Revival design.

Without a doubt Evergreen is one of the most interesting of the old plantations on the West bank of the Mississippi River. It is located in the Parish of St. John the Baptist. While not built on the massive scale of Oak Alley, Belle Grove, or Nottaway, it was a place planned with equal elaboration of house grouping as at Constancia. Like Constancia the garden plan was most elaborate, and it must have been very beautiful in the heyday of its glory, only traces of which now remain. Driveways, walks and communicating pathways were laid out in a formal manner, as one finds frequently in Italy in the ancient gardens attached to the great villas. Instead of the great oak avenue leading to the plantation manor, a typical garden plan similar to Versailles in France fronted the manor with numerous flower beds, fountains and other garden conceits outlined by gravelled and bricked walks. The avenues of trees were on the outer edges of the garden and extended far beyond the manor in the rear where another smaller garden similarly planned was found. These avenues, three on each side of the Manor, extended back to the cane fields, enclosing the entire garden plan front and rear. Important garconniers, pigeonnaires, offices, and additional buildings set in the grounds with mathematical precision and designed along classic lines, formed an imposing whole as at Constancia. The rows of slave cabins, planned between the last two avenues of great trees faced each other. They were located convenient to the fields and far enough away to prevent any odors reaching the big house.

On close inspection one finds that the present manor house which with its attractive roof deck dating from the early part of the 19th century, is of later construction than the surrounding buildings in the plan just described. From the details it apparently belonged to a house which this present one replaced.

In the vicinity are other plantation homes built along the lines of the old Fortier house, at present called "Home Place" or the Keller place, with out-buildings showing the same details as is found in those attached to Evergreen. It is possible that the Evergreen manor was remodeled as The Hermitage in Ascension Parish had been when the great wave of wealth prompted the planters to improve their plantation homes. This had been done at Elmwood near New Orleans, destroyed by fire a year ago, but since rebuilt on a less pretentious scale last year.

Evergreen recently was used as a school building, but at present lies empty.

Among the papers of many old plantation families one often finds plans of these splendid old plantations with detailed descriptions.

VALCOUR AIME PLANTATION
"The Little Versailles".

No plantation in all Louisiana has about it as intriguing a history as has this ancient place, which today is but a memory. Whether it be in the plantation country, New Orleans, or some smaller Louisiana city, one invariably meets with some handsome piece of furniture, or other article that is associated with this famous plantation.

It seems to be not definitely known whether this handsome

old plantation mansion was built for Don Francisco Aime, and later altered, when inherited by his son the princely Valcour Aime, known far and wide for his courtly manners, great wealth, and extravagant manner of living. Don Francisco Aime was an immensely wealthy sugar planter whose fortune had been doubled in the days when indigo was the leading industry in Louisiana, and before the invasion of the indigo bug which threatened to ruin Louisiana.

Don Francisco Aime, or as the French have it, Francois Aime, married Maria Julia Fortier, only daughter of Michel Fortier and Marie Rose Durel—Michel Fortier having been a merchant who became a ship owner and amassing a fortune in this venture. Valcour Aime was born in Louisiana, but it is not positively known, whether on his father's plantation or in New Orleans where his parents had a town house. The year of his birth is given as 1798, and he was christened Gabriel, which name later was changed to Valcour. Later his own son was named Gabriel.

Valcour Aime was in many ways like the son of another immensely wealthy planter, Bernard de Marginy. Both highly educated, cultured gentlemen loving the fine things of life, lived the lives of extravagant noblemen with no thought of the cost, providing pleasure and beauty were there, be it feast or costly gift to friend or some member of the family.

But Valcour Aime created a vast fortune out of his inheritance of one hundred thousand dollars, instead of squandering it as Bernard de Marigny did his many millions left him by his father. Once having full sway over the plantation Valcour Aime managed it in a manner that made it a veritable gold mine. His father had died while he was quite young, and his mother had him educated by special tutors brought from Europe. They apparently did not neglect their duty, for Valcour Aime was a highly educated gentleman. Shortly after reaching manhood and coming into his inheritance he married Josephine Roman, a sister of a neighbor, the immensely wealthy Telesphore Roman who owned a palatial home on an adjoining plantation. It was then that the original plantation home of his father, Francois Aime, was practically rebuilt. When completed it was considered the most costly and elegant plantation home in Louisiana, a state known far and wide for the grandeur and size of its plantation homes.

Thousands of acres were added to the already large plantation until Aime's acres numbered some nine thousand, most of which were under cultivation. He also greatly increased the size of his sugar mills and the number of his house slaves, garden and yard men, and field hands so that all could be properly attended to. He provided comfortable cabins for his slaves as he was a kind and generous master.

Great rear wings were added to the mansion, forming a court in the center, where the pavement was of black and white marble. Elaborate large parterres were laid out between the marble walks, and an elaborately carved marble stairway replaced the original mahogany one. Marble hallways were on the lower floor and a large number of white marble urns and statues surrounded the several circular fountain basins placed about the grounds. There were eight immense rooms in the main building, with four more on each floor in each wing. Kitchen, service quarters and slave rooms were in separate buildings some distance from the house. Rebuilt on palatial lines, it was refurnished in a regal manner, and so beautiful and costly was its interior and furnishings, that many of his friends felt that he was ruining himself in his extravagances. The marble mantels and crystal chandeliers were magnificent, and the immense mantel and pier mirrors with real gold leaf frames were some of the finest ever imported. The mirrors in the dining room reflected the guests at table, as in the ancient chateau de Rochefocault in the Rue Varennes Old Paris of which this room was a reproduction.

Many are the stories told of the banquets given by Valcour Aime in honor of the three royal refugees. And it is true that some of the greatest banquets ever given in America up to that date were given by Valcour Aime in this dining room. But as Valcour Aime was an infant at the time the royal visitors came to America, he did not entertain them.

In this prosaic age, the stories of his endless magnificence and extravagance seem like fairy tales, but a half dozen well-known writers whose veracity we do not question, confirm them.

This plantation was a good example of the immense fortune to be made easily from a large plantation properly managed and slaves kindly treated and cared for.

It was not an unusual thing for a wealthy planter on returning from his yearly trip to Europe to bring back to family and friends magnificent gifts costing many thousands of dollars, splendid mantel sets worth thousands of dollars, beautiful jewelry, rare and costly laces, silverware, in fact anything that was fine and beautiful regardless of cost.   The libraries of Southern planters at that date equalled any of the private ones in the world, with the exception of those of the royal houses and the greatest nobles of Europe.   Millions of dollars worth of fine and rare books were shipped North when taken from the great plantations, when Sherman began his March to the Sea.   All of the fine libraries of every plantation in every Southern state was stripped of their books before the building was put to the torch. The value of rare books was well known in the North and hundreds of libraries intact were shipped there from the South.   Today comparatively few of the original great number of fine old libraries remain.

Those unfamiliar with the lavishness of ante-bellum plantation days, readily scoff at the tales that are told of the wealth of the era, just as they do at any reference to ancestry of outstanding families.   They prefer to hold up some insignificant wealthy upstart as a type of the ante-bellum planter.

Adjoining the land of splendid old "Oak Alley" plantation, or Beau Sejour as it was originally called, is "Little Versailles" in the midst of an ancient grove of old oaks dying from neglect.   In an overgrowth of underbrush is all that remains of Valcour Aime's magnificent home.   All that can be seen is the crumbling brickwork, outlines of old flowerbeds once filled with a riot of costly plants, marble statuary, fountains, winding walks, streams, and grottoes—all densely hidden in a thick growth that forms a wilderness.   Nothing remains of the mansion with marble floors where the banquets were on a par with the state banquets in the royal palace of France.   A French gardener, a landscapist, was imported to lay out the grounds, and surrounding the mansion was one of the finest botanical gardens in America of that day.   Among the trees and underbrush one still can find traces of many garden conceits, broken marble urns, stained and crumbling marble garden benches, parts of old fountains of which there were many about the grounds, and parts of an old masonry bridge of elaborate design near the ruins of an old gazebo.   The place no doubt as elaborate and beautiful as its name suggests. The stories told about the ancient mansion, are legion, for in reality it was a veritable palace within as well as without.

On Norman's map of 1858 the Valcour Aime plantation is located directly opposite to Belle Alliance Plantation, one that was equally fine as the old mansion of the same name on Bayou Lafourche, but owned by another family—G. Mather & Son and of Madame (Widow) Trudeau. On the Valcour Aime place was the St. James Sugar refinery (largest in America at that date), and the acreage of the plantation was some 9,000 acres. At that date the plantation of Fortier Brothers, and that of the William Priestly Heirs, separated the land of Valcour Aime from the estate of Jean Telesphore Roman (Oak Alley Plantation) belonging at present to the Andrew Stewart's.

In 1860 J. W. Dorr, a newspaper man, correspondent for the New Orleans Crescent, writes in reference to Jefferson College, across the river.

> This institution was not in operation for a lengthened period, but the buildings and grounds having been purchased by Mr. Valcour Aime, a wealthy and public-spirited gentleman of the parish, it was reopened later in the fall with Mr. Hugue as President. The buildings are roomy, substantial and in thorough repair, and every way calculated for the purpose of an educational institution. There are about fifty students attending this first term of the college. If there were enough such men in the South there would be no lack of educational advantages.

At that date most of the sons of the wealthy planters were educated either abroad, or at colleges further North, or in New Orleans and Baton Rouge. Many like Valcour Aime had private tutors.

CIVIL WAR DAYS WITH THEIR TERROR AT THE VALCOUR AIME PLANTATION

Alcee Fortier, son of Edwige Aime, a daughter of Valcour Aime, writes:

> How well do I remember of the flight of our whole family (while the Federal Troops during the Civil War were bombarding the plantation) to the river front to seek protection of the levee whenever a gunboat was coming

There where we stood behind the levee, my sisters and myself, our schoolmistress and our nurses, while our father stood on the levee to look at the gunboats and at the shells that generally passed over our heads, but occasionally were buried in the levee and covered us with dust. Our home was never touched by the shells, but the houses of a number of our people, our relatives, were considerably damaged.

I remember seeing cart loads of shells strewn in the yards. I remember also the holes dug in the ground covered with beams and several feet of earth, the inside arranged like a comfortable room and filled with provisions of all kinds.

Then came the Federal soldiers in garrison on the plantation spurred on by the Federals, the insolence of some of the liberated slaves, the temporary arrest of my father and grandfather, almost laughable, the serio-comic scenes at the provost marshalls court. Then the flight of the family to the Teche and the pillage by the conquering army; the return home, and then complete ruin.

From this ruin we sons of rich planters, have now partially recovered, and the men who were boys in 1862 do not keep any unkind remembrances of war times.

The Valcour Aime plantation was purchased by the Miles Planting & Manufacturing Company while the Houmas plantation was under the management of Colonel Porcher Miles, and added to the holdings of the plantation now known as the Burnside Plantation at Burnside, Louisiana.

The late Madame Andrew Fortier, mother of Andrew Fortier and Mrs. Mortimer Walton—a relative of the late Professor Alcee Fortier—gave the following vivid account of the destruction of the plantation after the fall of New Orleans which she read in her father's diary, he being an eye witness to the occurrences:

Barge after barge chained together forming a long line between the Albatross and other gun boats, drew into sight. Many of the barges were piled high already when they reached my father's plantation. Great masses of plows, cutters and agricultural implements of all kinds that had been confiscated at the different plantations and were being taken from Louisiana plantations to the farms of the North in the Union area. Other barges likewise were piled high with household furniture of every description, and one could see that it consisted of the finest kind of beautiful carved mahogany and rosewood furniture. Great elaborately carved pieces of finest workmanship that must have cost a small fortune. Sofas, arm chairs, tables and bed room pieces, all magnificent, of their kind covered in finest brocade, piled high with large gold leaf mirrors and pier glasses. Family portraits and other works of art and a large number of barrels filled with fine bric-a-brac and clocks. Also hogsheads filled with family

VALCOUR AIME.   MADAME VALCOUR AIME.

Melle. Josephine Roman who became
Madame Valcour Aime, with her
mother. (Courtesy of La. Historical
Society.) (Courtesy of B. R. Foster
Historical Museum.)

Old rustic stone bridge-garden of "Petit Versailles."

OAK ALLEY (BEAU SEJOUR), St. James Parish.

Beautiful Plantation Home of Mr. and Mrs. Andrew Stewart, St. James Parish.

Dining Room of Oak Alley where great banquets were constantly held in ante-bellum days. Much entertaining is still being done at Oak Alley. (Courtesy of Mrs. Andrew Stewart.)

silver and china, all taken from homes they had swept clean thusly before they were fired on and burned. Other lines of carts and wagons to which were joined the long strings of cattle, horses and mules on the river road were being driven northward. These carts and wagons were being filled with the contents of the smoke houses and plantation store rooms. It seems that only the pigeons escaped, they fleeing from the vicinity, when the booming started.

On the barges were large placards bearing the wording: "To the captor belongs the spoils".

With the stripping of the plantations of everything movable and destruction of the sugar mills and cotton gins, the Union forces were making sure that the South would be unable to carry on.

The loyalty of the old negro slave house servants was a thing that the Union forces could not understand, as in innumerable instances they suffered all kinds of indignities even death in striving to save the lives and property of the masters and mistresses. One old negro butler on a plantation belonging to the Forstall family, allowing a Union soldier to shoot him, rather than tell where his master was hidden, or where his mistress had secreted her money, jewels and silverware. Madame Forstall not being on the plantation, having gone to Bayou Lafourche, and Mr. Forstall being ill had come back to the plantation on a furlough. Another family slave relating the incident, the dying faithful slave telling it before breathing his last. (For further data on Valcour Aime Plantation see Mrs. Ripley's "Social Life in Old New Orleans"—Her visit to the plantation.)

OAK ALLEY
Originally BEAU SEJOUR
St. James Parish.

Once again restored to its original magnificence, Beau Sejour mansion, as it was called when first completed, stands today in all the glory of its pristine beauty, one of the most satisfying examples still remaining in Louisiana of the homes of the Golden Era.

For a number of reasons this ancient plantation and its stately manor form such a splendid page in the history of old Louisiana plantation life. First of all, because Mr. and Mrs. Andrew Stewart, who have owned the plantation for a number of years, have restored the old mansion to its original beauty and charm. Secondly, in the furnishings they have adhered closely to the style in which it was equipped originally, and the choicest furniture still fill the splendid spacious rooms throughout. Thirdly, the plantation of some two thousand acres is in many ways

typical of the great ante-bellum plantations. Its various departments furnish besides great crops of cane, corn, rice, fruit and
vegetables of all descriptions, nuts, timber, cattle, pork, poultry
in a great variety—in fact everything needed to supply the needs
of a menage such as is conducted by the Stewarts who entertain
on a lavish scale throughout the year—both host and hostess being popular members of the social sets of New Orleans and other
Southern cities. Mrs. Stewart's gardens, a paradise of beautiful
flowering plants and greenery, are famous, and pilgrimages are
made there constantly by visiting strangers as well as by members of the local garden society to view their beauty. Mrs. Stewart,
a member of the Garden Society of America, is a most gracious
hostess, and most agreeable about permitting visitors who come
introduced to view her beautiful garden grounds.

When a banquet or entertainment of any size is in progress,
in the house and grounds is recreated the atmosphere of old plantation days. In the setting that this home provides again are re-
enacted scenes of long ago when the ancient home was in the
hey-day of its glory. The spacious hallways, lofty drawing-rooms
and banquet room scintillate with the brilliancy of reflected light
and color from the thousands of crystal prisms. Again charming vistas are reflected in the great mirrors in gilt frames that
adorn mantels and walls. The rooms, planned as they were for
entertaining on a large scale, when filled with beautiful costumed
figures flitting back and forth create a picture of surpassing
charm. Outside the wonderful avenue winds through a setting
which is almost theatrical when enlivened by groups strolling
among the garden beds and pleached walks.

Oak Alley is named from the magnificent avenue of oaks that
lead up from the river-road to the mansion. The ancient avenues
of cypress and other trees found on the country estates of Italy
are the nearest in magnificence to this venerable oak avenue near
Vacherie. The only rival in Louisiana is the one of the "Packenham Oaks" at Chalmette, named for the British General who
fell mortally wounded there.

There are numerous oak avenues still standing in Louisiana,
but they are not nearly so perfect or well kept. In riding through
the plantation country of this state one is surprised at the number that are left. In many instances no plantation house at all

remains—only charred and blackened foundations and the remnants of chimneys. Invariably one is told the mansion was burned by Federal soldiers on Sherman's order—a few places accidently fired. Here and there in an old negro cabin one detects what was once a handsome piece of rosewood or mahogany furniture. When they see you admiring it they will tell you, "Grandpa sneaked these pieces when the Yankees made us give them a hand in putting the master's things on the flatboats before burning the big house."

At Oak Alley the number of old oak trees correspond to the number of great columns around the house—and the number twenty-eight is again repeated in the original number of negro cabins in the rear. The oak avenue is estimated to be 250 years old. Who was the early colonist that planted the great avenue of oaks? Historical research has failed to shed any light, and at present his name is not known. Many of the courthouse records showing the titles to great estates were destroyed during the carpet bagger's reign in the South.

The Oak Alley mansion has often been mistaken for the old plantation home of André Roman, twice Governor of Louisiana from 1831 to 1843. Norman, on his detailed map of the plantations on the Mississippi River from Natchez to New Orleans, published in 1858, shows the present Oak Alley plantation to be the J. T. Roman plantation, which was much larger and which lies some distance to the north. In this order there are Bay Tree plantation, the property of Choppin and Roman; then the large plantation of Delongny and son; next a small plantation owned by V. Choppin; another large plantation holding of Choppin and Roman; and then the plantation of the widows C. M. and L. A. Cantrell, which brings us to the very large acreage of Governor A. B. Roman.

Jacques Roman, the builder of Beau Sejour, or Oak Alley as we now know it, was the grandson of Jacques Roman a Frenchman who had come to Louisiana in 1740, locating in New Orleans where he reared a family in what is now known as the "French Quarter." A son, named after his father, having finished his education and preferring the out-of-doors life of a country gentleman to that of the city one, after visiting various sections of the state decided to locate in the Attapas country. This is the finest cattle grazing section of the state, in fact by many it is considered the best land for raising cattle in the South.

This adventurous member of Jacques Roman's family visualized the opportunities that lay ahead. With a new country opening up and thousands of people to be fed daily, he chose then, instead of being a sugar planter, to become a cattle rancher, as he felt he could always become a sugar planter as members of his family had done, if he did not succeed as a rancher. His choice proved to be wise for in a few years he had amassed a great fortune. With money at his command, a fearless spirit and a determination not to be outwitted by simple brute strength, he dealt with cattle thieves in a ruthless manner, always seeing that no injustice was done. He soon had little to fear from their depredations.

His herds soon made him cattle king of the region. He treated his numerous cattle men, cow boys as they were termed in the West, with consideration, paying them a yearly bonus which gave him protection for his property, and enabled him to amass money readily.

While his greatest interest lay in his cattle ranch, he spent a great deal of his time visiting his relatives, who like the Bringier family, were founding a dynasty on the west bank of the Mississippi River. It was among these relatives that the grandson of the Jacques Telesphore Roman the I, the third of the name, born in Opelousas was never allowed to forget that being a planter was a calling that befitted his station as long as he had not chosen a learned profession or the Army. Planting had always been considered the occupation of a gentleman when the menial work was supervised and done by others. Jacques Roman III was to become a planter as well as cattle man. Having amassed a fortune in sugar also which combined with his ranching money and a large inheritance from his father, he proposed to build a fine house, and chose a site among the plantations of his relatives for the new home. The place he selected was that built upon in 1690 by an early French settler. This pioneer, whose name is unknown, had cleared the land and had built a primitive dwelling on the spot where the present mansion stands. This early type of house eventually developed as the years passed into the one known as early Louisiana type, and of which many are still standing. In front of this primitive home he planted an avenue of trees that led down to the front entrance at the river side for as yet no river-road existed. He had seen avenues in France which he had tried to copy, but it is doubtful if he had ever seen any that was to compare with what his avenue turned out to be.

These trees had already become great oaks when the place was purchased in 1832 by Jacques Roman III, and it was their magnificence which attracted him. Throughout the entire length of the long avenue of oak trees, Jacques Roman with slave labor laid a wide brick pavement of herring-bone design, as a walkway on either side with a driveway in the center paved with clam shells. This afforded a delightful promenade in olden days but now is replaced by a velvety carpet of Bermuda grass, for the bricks were eventually carted away during the many years that the place was unoccupied. The primitive house was demolished and an architect named George Swaney was given the commission of planning and supervising the construction of the new mansion. In spite of these facts for many years guides have been calling the place the old Governor Roman home and saying that it was designed by James Gallier.

As in the case of most of the great mansions, this place was erected in part with slave labor. It had its own brick kiln and saw mills, the boards being sawn by hand, from which came the material used in the building, while the factory work all hand-made, marble mantels, etc., came from the North or were imported. When completed the mansion was practically as we see it today with the exception of service buildings that have been removed.

That no expense was spared in the construction of the home can be readily seen if the details are examined. It must have taken a number of years to build, so solidly and beautifully has everything been executed.

The mansion, surrounded by its twenty-eight massive columns, is architecturally without a peer in the state. Restored* as it has been by Armstrong and Koch, New Orleans architects, with

---

* On an inner side of a large panelled door on the right wall of the upper hall, as you face the river, carefully preserved, is a record of when the old mansion was restored on various occasions.

nothing changed, it is a magnificent example of the Classic Revival in Louisiana with great care given to the perfection of its details.

It stands four square—its wide galleries supported by the massive columns which completely surround the house. These wide galleries are as cool as a grotto even on the hottest days, as river breezes temper the atmosphere at all times. The exterior balustrades are of beautifully carved cypress and show a design of wheat sheaves. The wide side lights and fan-transomed doorways of upper and lower entrances, front and rear, have classic columns and delicately carved beading. From the brick-paved lower verandas one enters an immense hall towards the rear part of which the stairway winds from the left to the floor above, and again to the attic where one finds that another equally long and wide hallway divides the space into a number of rooms. From these attic rooms a total of twelve dormer windows jut out from the roof furnishing air, light and comfort to these various rooms. Another stairway leads to the balustraded observatory on the roof.

Throughout the house today one finds that the furnishings are of the proper period and very beautiful. Each of the rooms is fitted with attractive antiques, fine paintings, rare bric-a-brac, handsome mirrors, drapes and carpets.

While the rear buildings which contained the service quarters and garconniers no longer stand, they are not missed. Corresponding to the oak avenue in front is a long avenue in the rear edged with a wealth of tropical greenery.

Planned for entertaining on a lavish scale, this old home was for many years the scene of an almost continuous whirl of social activity. Madame Jacques Telesphore Roman, assisted by her able husband, entertained many distinguished personages then. However, the Royal Trio who came to Louisiana, and were entertained on such a regal scale by the wealthy planters did not visit Beau Sejour, for the simple reason that this house was not built until 1832. Nevertheless, it was one of the greatest social centers on the West coast of the Mississippi River, continuing as such until the outbreak of the Civil War. As a result of the Southern reverses and their determined adherence to the Southern Cause, the once great fortune of the entire Roman clan was swept away.

During the Reconstruction Period and the years following, the plantation and the fine old mansion was shifted from one owner to another until finally it was purchased by a gentleman named Sobral. This family once again gave life to the place while the new owner by his wise management caused the plantation to flourish as formerly. He refurnished the mansion, and attempted to restore the old social life but it was too soon after hostilities. The neighboring plantations were still mostly wrecks and all of the great families were impoverished, in deep mourning and took little interest in the social affairs of that era. The Sobrals, who were from the tropics, after a few years saw the uselessness of trying to bring back the old social life, again abandoned the place to a series of new owners. During all the years that the various occupants lived in the place after the Sobrals left, no attempt was made to keep the place in repair. Roofs began to leak, windows were shattered and rain wrought havoc with the splendid rooms. Bats, birds and even reptiles made it their habitat. Plaster had fallen in all of the rooms and much of the fine hardware was being stripped from the house and carried away. Moss gatherers made the empty old mansion their headquarters, and the making of fires on several occasions came near being the cause of setting the place on fire. Finally it was boarded up and the moss gatherers compelled to find other quarters. At this time neglect too began to tell on the magnificent oak avenue which gave evidences of the ravages of decay. The trees were literally covered with moss which sapped the vitality of the stately avenue. A wild tangle of weeds and underbrush was rapidly destroying every vestige of the once beautiful garden. Marble statuary, seats and ornamental urns had been carried away and it looked like the old mansion would be dismantled. Then in the nick of time, as it were, Mr. and Mrs. Andrew Stewart, the present owners, bought it. They employed a local architectural firm that specializes in restoring homes and buildings, and told them to restore the old house to its original beauty and charm. The moss was removed from the trees and tree surgeons were put to work pruning and trimming with the beautiful results we see today.

All rotted and termite eaten wood-work was removed. At all times the greatest care taken to remove only what was absolutely necessary and it was replaced exactly as it was originally. With a new roof of the same material as the originally one—work was started in earnest, and while the cost was enormous, results proved so satisfactory that little heed was given to outlay.

Today Oak Alley is a "piece of the old South" and future ages will see there how people of that day lived. As a period of American life and a culture unrivalled now so completely annihilated that only straggling fragments remain, Oak Alley is a complete museum, a historical record, a treasure house of Louisiana's Past.

HOME PLACE

The owners of Home Place on the west bank of the Mississippi River were Eugenie Forstall Choppin and her husband, Valerian Choppin, who built the magnificent mansion as a present for his wife. As was the custom when slave labor was partly used, most of the fine cypress, bricks, etc., came from the land, the beautiful white marble mantels imported from Italy and the silver-plated hardware and cabinet work bought from factories in the north.

The house was unusually handsome within, with much fine carved woodwork about the door frames and window casements. All of the rooms were of immense size and the very wide winding stairway was imported from France. When finished Mr. and Mrs. Valerian Choppin spent a year in Paris selecting magnificent furnishings for the home, most of which were of the Empire period with costly hand-chased fire-gilt mountings. Much of this was later scattered among descendants.

The family, one of the most aristocratic as well as wealthiest in the state at that time, fitted up their plantation home on the same scale of magnificence displayed in the Forstall mansion in St. Louis Street, New Orleans. The clock sets on the mantels of the various rooms were magnificent, as were the bronzes, paintings, bric-a-brac and silver. The dinner sets had the crest and coat-of-arms on each piece. Home Place was indeed a palace within.

The receptions, balls and soirees were attended by the exclusive social set of the South, and in this beautiful home there was a continual whirl of social events throughout the years.

Avenue of Oaks—Oak Alley.

An attractive Reception Salon of Oak Alley.   Portrait of Mrs. Andrew Stewart by
Edith Duggan, over mantel.

The Stately Entrance of Oak Alley Mansion.   (Courtesy of Mrs. Andrew Stewart.)

Nottaway Park.

GOVERNOR ANDRE ROMAN'S PLANTATION

Governor Roman's plantation is shown on Norman's Plantation Map of 1858 to be an immense place located directly opposite to St. Michael's town—across the river now known as Convent.

According to his grand-daughter, the late Madame Anna de Lavillebeuvre Hyman of New Orleans, the ancient home of her grandfather was constructed very much on the same lines as "Oak Alley." It was probably not so large, as the Governor also had a splendid home in the Rue Royal—number 611 which is still standing—where he did the greater part of his entertaining dur- the winter. He preferred to recuperate at his plantation home in the summer time when he did not go abroad.

Madame deL. Hyman described the place as being very beautiful with great oaks about it, but did not say it had an avenue of oaks. This was in 1915. The place had passed out of the possession of the family, but it was still standing in a very dilapidated condition at that time.

The de Lavillebeuvre Hyman's old fashioned home in Second and Prytania Streets at that date was filled with a magnificent collection of family heirlooms from the Roman and de Lavillebeuvre families. Most of these were museum pieces.

In the ancient three-storied brick structure at number 611 Rue Royal, Governor Roman gave many a grand banquet for government officials, important visitors, and the social elite of the state. Balls for the belles of the city and debutante receptions for members of his large family were numerous, and throughout the year the mansion was the scene of continuous festivity. The plantation—one of the very large ones of the state—supplied most of the game, poultry, meats, vegetables, and fruits for these occasions. But of all the great affairs that he and his gracious wife gave in this interesting home none appeared to give this distinguished host and hostess as much pleasure and satisfaction as the banquet given in honor of James J. Audubon, the great naturalist, when he again returned to New Orleans in 1837, after he had successfully published the elephant edition of his "Birds of America".

From the first, Governor Roman had been an ardent supporter of Audubon, and not only aided the struggling artist from his own purse, but made his family contribute, and was instrumental in having the state of Louisiana officially subscribe to the publication of this world famous work.

CHAPTER XX.

ON THE WEST BANK—ABOVE DONALDSONVILLE.

EVAN HALL.

ORIGINALLY a plantation belonging to Desiré Le Blanc who had received the land as a grant from the Spanish Crown, Evan Hall later was purchased by Evan Jones from the heirs of the first owner.

Evan Hall Plantation from the time it was first laid out has always been one of Louisiana's great plantation properties. About fifteen years ago it was sold by the McCall family. Until then it was a notable social center, as the McCalls are related to many of the leading families of the state.

The present plantation home built many years ago is of a modified Greek Revival type of architecture. Several feet from the ground, there are the regulation wide galleries, and the house is surrounded by an attractive garden.

BELLE GROVE PLANTATION

West Bank of the Mississippi River

Belle Grove is unquestionably the most ornate plantation mansion ever built in Louisiana. It stands today in its crumbling state as a symbol of the dilapidation and ruin that followed the Civil War.

Mansions like this were meant for days of the "ancient regime" when thousands of acres worked by hundreds of slaves produced incomes sufficient to maintain homes of this sort in the grand manner. Household slaves were numbered by the dozen and stable men, yard servants, gardeners, etc., were twice as numerous.

John Andrews, aristocratic millionaire of Virginia, following the example of so many prominent Virginians and Carolinians, came to the far South, where the rich alluvial soil produced crops that doubled a fortune in a year. He brought with him his slaves and money and in 1850 purchased a seven-thousand-acre tract on the Mississippi River in the parish of St. John the Baptist. He called in James Gallier, Sr., the noted architect of that day, and told him to build as magnificent a home as possibly could be constructed. From what we have seen of the Gallier's (father and son) architecture, we must conclude that Andrews definitely told him to make the building ornate.

In 1857 John Andrews' mansion stood complete. It is one of the most ornate of all the plantation homes in the South. Constructed at a time when wealth accumulated quickly and plantation mansions on a grander scale than ever before were being built. It would seem that each newly finished mansion was more elaborte than the one finished previously, some of them becoming "show" mansions instead of the dignified and substantial homes planned in the pure Greek revival style which had distinguished the houses in the beginning.

Belle Grove exhibits the full-blown floral exuberance of the Greek revival with all the elaborate ornamentation that the sophisticated Corinthian design has to offer. Harmonious as a whole when viewed from the lawn, its immense proportions in its original setting of oaks and splendid garden seemed magnificent.

However, after we study the overwrought grandeur of Belle Grove we feel grateful to the Galliers, father and son, as well as to the other architects, who reared so many beautiful mansions in the South that the taste for sumptuous plantation houses was tempered by designs with lines of simpler form.

An architect, viewing the place when I visited it last, stated that "he had heard" that the semi-circle addition on the left side of the building near the front was a later addition—to supply a bath room which had been omitted on the original plan. But even the Corinthian columned and pilastered entrance to it from the drawing room, failed to convince me that the unsightly protuberance was a part of the original residence. Anyone familiar with Gallier's work, knows that it was not his work. His plan of the City Hall in New Orleans precludes the possibility of Gallier being guilty of such an architectural atrocity. Gallier was too good an architect to have his memory marred by attributing such a monstrosity to him.

Considering that Mr. Andrews, like many Virginians and Carolinians—admired this ornate type of home—Gallier has come away a winner. One doubts if any architect of his time could have done nearly as well as he has under the circumstances. All the elaboration melts away in the distance owing to the huge size of the mansion.

Originally an avenue of oak trees a mile long lead up to the entrance steps, and it widened out in front to allow a full view of the mansion from the river and road. A wide space was reserved for the lawn parties and games so popular at that date.

The place, constructed with the strength of a fortress, rests on basement foundations ten feet high. In this basement as in most large plantation houses of that and earlier dates, were dungeons with barred windows to provide for unruly slaves. Other basement rooms also occupy this area. On the north side of the house is a wing with two great verandas enclosed by tall fluted columns with Corinthian caps and pilasters, which support a cornice as do the thirty-foot columns in the front.

Rotting on the ground are elaborately carved acanthus leaf brackets that once supported the gallery above, and there are remnants of what were beautiful little garden enclosures. The elaboration of the facade is repeated on the porches on the right side but it is handled in such a splendid manner that it in no way detracts from the imposing front. The great wings of the house project to the side in the rear, but the opposite one is torn down and leaves a big gap in the place. The home has all the ostentatious pomposity of a sophisticated town house. No one could feel at home in this big house so it has not appealed to a purchaser in recent years. Besides with its 75 rooms it is entirely too large to be maintained by any one in this day of high priced domestics.

Within the house a greater dissolution greets the eye than we find on the outside. Goats and chickens roam the spacious columned and pilastered rooms and hallways, and bats fly from drawing rooms and spacious banquet hall.

The banquet hall ceiling drops plaster as do most rooms of the place, an evidence of the damage wrought by the elements during the past twelve years. Decay has played havoc everywhere.

The detail of wood carving and plaster work is very fine

throughout employing Grecian motives. From the lunettes one can get detailed measurements of the monster hand-carved cypress Corinthian capitals which are six feet in height and apparently in good condition. In the attic one sees construction so massive that if it is not demolished its walls and chimneys will stand another century.

A color print of Belle Grove in 1858 shows the mansion, its great sugar house and mill, its fields of cane and the slave quarters. It is also shown on Norman's map. When completed stables were erected to house the owner's blooded stock from which came many famous winners. His private race track was one of the finest in the state.

Once finished the mansion was furnished in a luxurious manner—in keeping with its palatial rooms. The furniture was ornately carved instead of the simple designed rosewood and mahogany furniture usually found in plantation homes. There was much use of gold leaf, and there were costly brocades and paintings by noted artists.

NEGRO CABIN
BELLE GROVE

Mr. Andrews and his family enjoyed but a brief stay in their great mansion, for hardly had he gotten everything in working order when the thunderous guns of war boomed, tearing the social structure of the South asunder and impoverishing land owners far and wide. John Andrews had his fortune swept away. His plantations, his home and its contents passed to Henry Ware, a capitalist whose family had been prominent in Louisiana since the American Revolution. In 1868 Mr. Ware became the owner of Belle Grove plantation. It remained in the possession of the Ware family, James A. Ware finally becoming sole owner.

When the war clouds had cleared the mansion again became a great social center. The marriage of Colonel Ware to Miss Eliza Stone, daughter of the wealthy and socially prominent physician and planter of Iberville Parish, took place there. Now began the real social life of Belle Grove. The many beautiful wedding gifts, together with heir-looms that came from the Ware and Stone families combined with fine silver, crystal, etc., selected from original furnishings of the home made it a palace indeed. Banquet followed banquet, ball followed ball, reception followed reception— the gala days of old seemed to return again. However, such gaity existed only in spots in the plantation area, as the destruction of the South had been too complete, and too many families still in deep mourning for lost father, husband, sons and brothers to have much heart for such gaiety. Colonel Ware's stables were famous for his many thoroughbreds.

Mrs. Tilton, who gave the Tilton library as a memorial to her husband to Tulane University, also a close friend of Mrs. Ware— entertained jointly with her at magnificent banquets in later years in New Orleans after Col. Ware's death. They used their own splendid silver, crystal, china and napery. On these occasions the greatest quantity of flowers were brought from the conservatory at Belle Grove.

At Mrs. Ware's death the property became the heritage of her only son Stone Ware, who had married Miss Gourrier of Plaquemines, Louisiana. The couple kept the place until 1925, when it was sold, the furnishings being sold at auction. Since then the house has gradually been stripped of all movable parts.

Today in its decrepitude ghostly echoes reverberate through its spacious rooms and hallways where danced each season the throng of debutantes that came to Belle Grove week-end parties. Silence reigns where walls rang with merry laughter and witty repartee. In its crumbling magnificence it forms a splendid setting for a story of plantation days. In its mournful solitude and faded majesty, one cannot but recall D'Annuncio "Il Fures" and his descriptions of the Vanishing Villas of the Brenta.

"In the great banquet hall no one dines
In the ball-room only ghostly shadows dance."

A recent visit to the place found men stripping the mansion of all the metal work. It looks much more severe and less elaborate now that the heavy lace-like iron-work of balconies and lower balustrades is gone. The great scrolls of acanthus leaves on the ornate brackets are missing in many places. In the rear of the back hall was a magnificent spiral stairway, equally as beautiful as the one in the old St. Louis Hotel in New Orleans. The hall, the banquet room and the service rooms beyond have been demolished. With them too the dungeons that were in the basement have been removed. As all of the debris has been cleared away, one can walk in this lower space which is quite high and well paved.

One can hardly believe that in the space of a few years such a magnificent place could have fallen into such utter ruin. The great garden is gone leaving, however, many fine ancient oaks.

Belle Grove in the midst of its empty acres truly looks like a ruin of Ancient Rome. Its grove of ancient oaks is rapidly disappearing, for at present men are engaged in cutting down the foremost ones to make way for a new levee that will be located nearer to the old mansion.

NOTTAWAY—BY MISTAKE NOW CALLED WHITE CASTLE

This beautiful old plantation mansion is known by a number of names. It is often called Nottaway, Bayougoula, or Randolph, named for John Hampden Randolph for whom it was built by Henry Howard, architect of New Orleans, in 1857. And now it is Llanfair as as it has been rechristened by its present owners, who have restored the place to its original charm. Built one might say while the impending war clouds were gathering with a fury that threatened to wipe out the lives and fortunes of the South, this magnificent mansion was to enjoy only a brief period of the lavish hospitality for which it was so carefully planned. Its wealthy owner spared no expense in building this house. It was designed in a regal manner—as was the fashion of that day of easy fortune making. Almost all of its forty rooms open onto the magnificent park which surrounds the place and there is a charming vista at every turn.

A Randolph of Virginia came to Louisiana and brought with him all the prestige of his family name, a prestige which this family of wealth and position had been accustomed to for centuries. Along with his good name he brought fine ancestral portraits by noted English and American artists, crested silver, magnificent clothing, household furnishings and hundreds of slaves from his plantation in Virginia.

Original oil portrait of Eugéne Forstall
who married Valerien Choppin. Owned
by Mrs. J. N. Roussel, a member of the
Dugue de Livaudais family.

Home Place Plantation, old home of the Valerien Choppin family.
Courtesy of Mr. and Mrs. Robert Dugue (de Livaudais.)

"Belle Grove". Completed in 1857. Designed by James Gallier, Sr. Standing in its wide acreage like an ancient Roman Ruin.

After arriving in Louisiana and viewing the splendid places that so many of his Virginia friends had already built, he wondered why he had delayed so long. Selecting a section of the country not far from the palatial new home of his friend John Andrews, also from Virginia, he employed Henry Howard of New Orleans to plan and build for him the mansion we see today. He invested a large part of his fortune in this plantation, the house and its furnishings.

Its great size, height and whiteness are its chief characteristics which gave it the name of "White Castle" later on.

In all respects it resembled the villas found at that date on European estates more than it did a plantation home. The plan of the facade and buildings is too complicated, the architectural details too numerous and variety too great to permit of a clear description. One has to examine the house leisurely and closely to appreciate just how great has been the task of its construction. A booklet, written about the time it was finished, describes in detail the charm of the place, in the elaborate manner of that day.

Nottaway is not really a plantation house at all, as we in Louisiana understand that type of house, but a palatial country house such as is found in early days in Virginia, Carolina, Maryland and in Europe. Resting on a high basement, with a charmingly designed double entrance and a curved iron stairway, it is a stately building. The greatest quantity of beautifully designed cast-iron filagree work—similar to that found in various parts of New Orleans—appears on the veranda and balconies which surround the house. The effect is quite intriguing.

The story of Nottaway is quite similar to that of the other great houses like it. As an aftermath of the war when fortunes were swept away, the place was sold. Its distance from the river saved it from destruction by the gunboats after the fall of New Orleans. It lay idle for many years during which time it fell into partial ruin.

When Dr. W. G. Owen, a wealthy physician and planter of Iberville Parish purchased it, he at once set about having the place restored. This took a fairly-sized fortune before it looked as we see it at present. Here this cultured family continue in a less lavish manner the hospitalities of Llanfair, as the family now called the place in preference to its former pompous title.

The town of White Castle takes its name from another plantation close by owned by Thos. Vaughn. Llanfair is in a beautiful condition and it still has its old charm. Although spacious, it is delightfully livable. While its hallway is wide, it does not appall, and so it is with other parts of the house.

The plastic work is magnificent—no other adjective seems adequate. This applies also to the interior frieze and center ornaments of all the main rooms on the first floor as well as main hallway upstairs. While certainly ornate a restraining feeling is maintained throughout, and the interior, while elaborate, is in absolute good taste. The fine ornamentation is joined with an exuberance found in some Corinthian interiors. There is no overcrowding or tawdy addition to mar the composition.

The spacious drawing room, no larger than many to be found in most plantation houses, is often referred to as the White Ball Room. It has the same type of plastic work, columns and pilasters with Corinthian capitals. An archway separates the front portion of the room from the rear which is in an octagonal form. This in a way somewhat detracts from the stately dignity of the salon, as one finds that feature in so many houses of less importance.

Elaborate mantels of white marble and crystal chandeliers with many prisms, lend charm, while the nice woodwork of the room forms an appropriate setting to the handsome furnishings.

The library and dining room, like all the main rooms, have splendid marble mantels and, as on the opposite side of the hall which is in turn is separated by a side hall to the left. In this hall is the staircase, which is a fine one, with spiral turns in parts, leads to a series of six individual apartments—three to each floor, so arranged as to be absolutely private, with individual fireplaces and baths.

The service rooms to the rear, are extensive and spacious. Another room in the rear of the dining salon now used as living quarters, originally was a smaller reception room. Endless wings on all sides house endless rooms, and much fine antique furniture, good paintings and other household belongings complete a charming home, in a gorgeous setting, as one can readily see from the illustrations. The mansion, for such it really is, has much to commend it.

CHAPTER XXI.

ON BAYOU LAFOURCHE

BELLE ALLIANCE PLANTATION

Bayou Lafourche.

Built on Almost as Magnificent a Scale as Beautiful Marble House.

CHARLES KOCK, a wealthy Belgian aristocrat, came to America in 1830 and located in New Orleans. Shortly afterwards he purchased several large plantations and combined them under the name of Belle Alliance. The plantation house on the place was burned in 1849 and the fine old mansion that we see at present was erected shortly afterwards.

At that date the planters were reaping rich returns from their investments and money was plentiful in Louisiana. Charles Kock had inherited a fortune from his family which he had invested wisely, and in the building of his new home he spared no expense.

Belle Alliance has twenty-four rooms in the main house, twelve rooms on each floor, and in the wing four on each floor, making a total of thirty-two rooms, each one carefully finished in plaster. It was built regardless of cost but planned on conservative lines, having none of the flamboyant exhuberance that is to be found on some of the other great plantation mansions. Its construction is of brick throughout and the heavy walls have their outside surfaces thickly coated with a plaster finish lined off so as to simulate stone, a style in vogue at that date. Its general style is the Greek Revival and, as in so many fine old New Orleans homes, there are ornamental iron balconies and balustrades.

These have been used without creating a discordant note as such combinations were the usual architectural acceptance at that date, having been generally used in the domestic architecture of Europe as well as in America. Within the woodwork is handsome with just enough elaboration to be in perfect taste.

This also can be said of all of the plaster-work ceilings, ornamental arches, friezes and center ornaments. The mantels are all of the finest materials, those in the main rooms being extremely beautiful. A wide central hallway extends from front to rear, and insures cool rooms in warm weather as well as privacy to each apartment. It was magnificently appointed during the occupancy of the Kock family who lived there until 1915, at which time it was sold to the present owners.

In Civil War days Belle Alliance was one of the few large mansions that was not bombarded after the fall of New Orleans, although in the archives of the Louisiana Historical Society there is a record of a battle having taken place on the plantation grounds of Belle Alliance. However, no data can be found which tells of anything being stolen or destroyed on the plantation or in the Kock home.

Like other wealthy southern planters families the Kock's visited Europe yearly and maintained their box at the opera in Paris as well as at the French Opera in New Orleans. They had a home in the French capitol as well as their splendid one in New Orleans known as Marble House.

The plantation consisted of some 7,000 acres, most of which was planted in sugar cane. It continued to function after the Civil War, and in recent years under the able management of Messrs. Edward and James Kock it was operated profitably.

The grandsons of the builder of Belle Alliance own much of the splendid family silver and costly crested crystal formerly used at Belle Alliance. In the days when the family still resided in the old mansion their entertainments were known throughout America for the brilliancy and elegance of their table appointments.

The spacious gardens of this mansion, like all else in connection with it, had about them an aristocratic air, reminiscent of old world gardens on the Continent. Like the garden on his father's estate, Mr. Kock, when his plantation home stood complete, erected handsome masonry pillars at the entrance and exits of his large grounds on which were hung splendid ornamental iron gates surmounted by an iron arcade of ornate design supporting the crest of the Kock family—two rampant lions charging each other below a golden crown. While they remained in position these handsome gateways always excited the admiration of visitors. Beneath great moss-hung oaks the gates opened into a garden fragrant with jasmine and sweet olive. Dove cotes hidden by wisteria and honeysuckle, an ancient marble fountain gleaming urns and statuary of stained and chipped marble helped to make of the place a fairyland of beauty.

Today its grandeur is desolated but much garden magic lingers here. Discolored garden vases lie broken on the ground, and the fountain is now silent and dry, but the woodland orchestra that has always been a part of the place breaks the stillness. In its partly neglected condition it has a charm that fascinates. The Churchill family, who now own the entire plantation estate, have furnished the house with their own collection of antiques, family heirlooms and family portraits, and again the old mansion is quite attractive.

Marble House, the New Orleans town house of the Kock family, was erected during the golden era and was considered one of the finest private homes in America. Palatial in its appointments like Belle Alliance, it was the scene of some of the most magnificent receptions given in the South in olden days. Marble House was demolished recently, and many in New Orleans who know its history greatly regret that it could not have been preserved. So well had it been constructed that notwithstanding its abuse while serving for years as a cheap rooming house, its splendid fluted Corinthian columns, entablature and magnificent interior woodwork were all in a splendid condition the day it was turned over to the wreckers to be torn down. It only needed cleaning and repainting to restore it to its pristine splendor.

MAIDWOOD

Maidwood was the plantation home of Thomas Pugh, who came from Albermarle County, North Carolina. Thomas Pugh, visiting William, his brother, was captivated with the plantation site his brother had purchased, and on which he had built Woodlawn.

He returned to North Carolina, disposed of his plantation as his brother had done, and returning with his money, belongings and slaves purchased a plantation also on the east side of Bayou Lafourche, a short distance from where his brother William lived.

He built his house in the prevalent classic Greek Revival style—its lines presenting the more sophisticated ancient Greek Temple appearance. Its facade has massive Ionic columns and heavy lunetted pedimented cornice with beautiful moulded gable ends towards front and rear. On a more magnificent scale than his brother William's house, using his own slave labor in part, he spent nearly five years in the completion of the mansion.

Like his brother's home, the wood used in the building was mostly cypress. In construction, it is perhaps the more solid of the two mansions, as its brick plastered walls are from 18 inches to 24 inches thick and all partition walls from ground to attic are of a thickness of eighteen inches.

While Woodlawn's interior was beautiful, Maidwood's interior is on a magnificent scale; it is still one of the most beautiful of the ante-bellum plantation homes remaining in Louisiana.

The mansion was begun in 1850, but its owner who had spent so much time and care in the choice of materials for it, contracted yellow-fever during the terrible epidemic that was raging at that time and died in 1854 without seeing the mansion finished. The widowed Madame Pugh, as soon as the epidemic had subsided and conditions had returned to normal, superintended the finishing of the work.

But few changes were made in the original interior arrangement. She enlarged the north wing so as to include the large ball room and service section. When completed, the mansion numbered some twenty rooms of importance. These were eventually occupied by some of her children after they married.

Already the storm of war had shown signs of its approach, and Madame Pugh, while still a strong adherent of the Confederate cause, when hostilities eventually reached the Lafourche country, determined, if possible, to save her family and home. Now that all the able men of the family were in service, she instructed the family and servants to refrain from antagonizing the Union soldiers. So tactfully did she manage that not only was she and her family undisturbed, but the Union General placed a guard in charge of the mansion to make sure that no damage was done to the property.

The plantation continued as one of the largest of that section until it was sold by the Pugh family in 1920. The beautiful old mansion was transferred to Robert L. Baker. At present it is owned by his widow, who with great expense was able to modernize the lighting and plumbing system after great difficulty owing to the great thickness of the walls.

The entire house is very fine, and is at present kept in very good condition. The plastic work on the interior is exceptionally beautiful and in keeping with its lovely classic exterior, the detailed ornament having the chasteness of the Greek Revival. The large hallway has wide door-ways opening into the spacious rooms on either side. A beautiful mahogany semi-spiral stairway of unusually fine design, very wide below, narrows as it sweeps with a graceful curve to the floor above. A wide classic columned entrance way leads to the spacious rooms in the rear; the wide cross hallway at this point leading to the apartments of the wings, equally as handsome on the interior as the main house. The splendid mansion has at no time been permitted to fall into ruin, but has always been carefully attended to and kept in repair. This is likewise true of the beautifully planned garden. The place is almost exactly as it was when completed by the widow of Thomas Pugh.

It is an aristocratic mansion that has never housed any but aristocratic persons from its earliest days to the present, and still is considered one of the social landmarks of the Lafourche country.

The Pugh family have married into many important Southern plantation families, and for years there has been a conundrum associating the family name with Bayou Lafourche. "Why is Bayou Lafourche like a church aisle? Because there are Pugh's on both sides of the Bayou."

WOODLAWN PLANTATION

Bayou Lafourche.

Woodlawn plantation manor, now in such a dilapidated condition, a little over a decade ago was one of the charming old places of great beauty that still held allure for the passing stranger in its unpretentious splendor. It was then the property of the Munson family and like its neighbor, a great social center. It was built originally for Colonel William Pugh of a distinguished Virginia family.

In the year 1830 the opportunity offered in Southern Louisiana to the planter exceeded that which was held out by Virginia and Carolina. Colonel Pugh sold his holdings in North Carolina and came to the Bayou Lafourche country, where he purchased a large plantation and built a home.

Selecting a spot with a heavy growth of oak trees with space reserved for the garden on front and sides, he had his architect and builder erect there the handsome old mansion we see today.

Although much of the labor used on the mansion was done by his slaves, he spent over seventy thousand dollars in the building of the place, and another immense sum for the furnishings and the laying out of the garden, which when finished furnished a gorgeous setting for the home.

Even in its dilapidated condition one can still trace some of the original beauty of the old house. The facade presents at either end of the spacious porch a massive pier with pilaster to correspond at the inner house wall. Four massive columns with Ionic caps and bases fill the intervening space of the center, supporting with paneled corner square piers an immense entablature, giving it the dignity of an ancient Greek temple.

Everything was constructed on a massive scale of durable materials. The stucco of the heavy brick walls which are still intact is a discolored greyish white, while the shutters are a faded blue green. The balcony rails which have fallen and lie on the ground below are a diamond lattice form of construction. Beneath, a wide paved veranda extends to the edge of the column bases and the large entrance door is almost as wide as the hallway. Within, other large doors lead to the spacious rooms on either side, upstairs and down. They are very high, and have partition walls of brick eighteen inches in thickness. The plaster work is simple, but beautiful in detail.

The mantels of white marble have been removed, and the rear hall, which opens from the square one in front, contains a simple lined stairway, which continues to the ample attic.

Advancing to the rear of the house a wide back gallery is reached through an attractive old bluish green doorway, giving

Much of the great bulk of "Belle Grove" has been demolished.

Nottaway, built in 1857 by Henry Howard, architect for John Hamden Randolph.

"Belle Alliance", Bayou Latourche, La.

"Marble House", palatial town
house of the Kock family in New
Orleans.

Maidwood Plantation Manor, Bayou Lafourche.

Wood Lawn Plantation Home in ruins.

Rienzi Plantation Manor, built for a Spanish Queen

"Oak Lawn" Plantation home of Judge Porter.

ON BAYOU LAFOURCHE 201

a view of what was the old rose garden at the end beyond an avenue of foliage. This rear is a recessed porch enhanced by square columns, and at the end of the gallery is another stairway with a brick enclosure. The wings or garconniers are very attractive even in their dilapidated state and are rather roomy, their pedimented roofs and classic facades must have made a most attractive appearance before falling into their present condition.

A negro caretaker lives in the rooms that were formerly used as a library and dining room, while the rest of the house is used as a hay barn and a place to store farm products. Even in its desolate condition a fragrance is detected coming from the sweet olive and jasmine, mute reminders of its past glory—of the days when the aristocratic Pugh family made merry within the ancient walls now so illy used.

The old place is still visited once in a while by Dr. Thomas Pugh, son of the planter for whom the old mansion was built. The doctor now resides at Napoleonville, a short distance away, and is still hale and hearty at the ripe old age of 85. He tells many interesting stories of his earlier days on the old plantation. And also of the splendid balls and receptions, soirees, etc., held there from time to time. This was a very aristocratic community, he says, and life was very gay and beautiful before the Civil War.

How completely the sugar industry was destroyed as the result of hostilities and the reconstruction era that followed, may be understood from the following report published in the Times-Picayune of the meeting of the Southern Historical Association, held on November 4th, 1938, at New Orleans.

Describing the effect of the war between the States on the Louisiana Sugar Industry, Walter Prichard of the Louisiana State University, told how production had been cut down "from 460,000 to some 10,000 hogsheads, almost annihilating the industry." "It was not until 1893," he said, "that it regained its pre-war level and was ready for further advances."

"Scarcity of labor and capital militated against it during and after reconstruction," he added, "necessitating the introduction of labor-saving methods and the elimination of many small mills."

Until about two decades ago, Woodlawn plantation was a going concern, managed by the Munson family, and its garden was a riot of blooming plants and fragrant greenery. The depression which swept the country at that period sounded its death knell for when the plantation was visited again in 1929 the beautiful old house was empty. The ruin has been rapid since then.

The hordes of ruffians that swamped the South during the early days of the depression sought shelter in every available empty house, and it was not long before Woodlawn, somewhat remote from its neighbors, became a refuge for them. Soon the mob began destroying the house, pulling off its hardware and whatever copper work they could find and selling it. They even stripped off the gutters and plumbing fixtures. Since then a keeper has been placed there, but too late, as the damage had been done. The place leaked with every rain and the weather has played havoc with the house since then.

The planters, for most part, were ruined by the Civil War, but the family of General William Pugh managed to hold on to the mansion and plantation until 1910 when his heirs sold the place to settle the estate. General William Pugh died in 1906 at the ripe old age of 95 years. After being in the front with the boys in grey for four years during which time he again and again was cited for distinguished service, he returned to manage the plantation which he did with success.

He took part in civic affairs and aided his fellow townsmen in overthrowing the tyranny of Reconstruction Days.

His life was full of honor. He was a member of the State Legislature and speaker of the house, and for many years he was President of the Levee Board of his district. At his death he was buried with military honors and a sorrowing crowd of friends following his remains to the grave. In the history of the state, he has a niche as one of Louisiana's most distinguished citizens— a prominent planter, honored soldier and respected politician.

RIENZI PLANTATION

Rich in romance and legendary lore, this ancient Spanish-type plantation villa overlooks sleepy old Bayou Lafourche. The old house was built, according to the best available information, one hundred and forty-three years ago for the Queen of Spain by her orders. As her colonies in their restless condition were slowly slipping from the grasp of unhappy Spain, its rulers prepared this place as a retreat in the event of abdication.

The history of the early days of this old mansion is closely interwoven with Concord, the ancient plantation seat and home of the Spanish governor at Natchez, Mississippi.

Concord, when turned over to his successor, Don Esteban Minor, was refinished upstairs and down and splendidly furnished that he might live as befitted the representative of Spain. Concord was destroyed by fire some years ago (1902) and only the splendid wrought iron stair rails and stone stair foundations remain. It is still a treasured historical landmark of Natchez. It was built in 1780, a Spanish version of the Classic Revival, as it had tall columns which rose from the bases in front of the raised basement supporting a gabled pediment front resting on a cornice. For many years, it was the leading social center of the Natchez colony.

Rienzi, sometimes classed as Greek Revival, is a distinctive type of tropical architecture, very much like the Cuban and Central American type with but few traces of Greek Revival in its composition. It is stated that a Spanish architect designed the place, and no one would doubt it. Like Concord and all raised-type Spanish houses, Rienzi was a one-storied structure resting on tall pier-like foundations of brick. Enclosed at a later date and stuccoed lower rooms were finished inside making the house larger. Originally, the basement was used for basement purposes, as at Concord, where the horses and carriage were kept.

Rienzi was built for Queen Maria Louisa, consort of the irascible Charles IV, whose irrational diplomacy antagonized both France and England, bringing on a war and causing him to lose most of his colonies. Defeated by the French armies and eventually having to flee from Spain after abdicating, the queen, fearing just such an outcome had prepared a retreat. Unfortunately the Louisiana colonies had passed out of the possession of Spain and thus she was deprived of this refuge.

Many Spanish citizens had emigrated from Spain and engaged in the sugar planting industry in Louisiana through her influence. A glance at an ante-bellum map will show how strong her influence had been. John Ignatius Egana, who was the first occupant of the mansion is said to have been her Majesty's representative in America, and legend tells of tales of the great balls, banquets and festivities given to the representatives of the Spanish Crown.

The attractive stairway of double curves that leads to the second story is reminiscent of the early Spanish house plan and is an attractive feature of the facade. Egana and his family resided in the mansion for half a century. He purchased the place when Napoleon transferred Louisiana to the United States, and was a successful planter during his occupancy. The grove of oaks that he planted or added to has now become over a century old, so that now this collection of monster trees is one of the finest in this section, a number of the trees being listed by the Louisiana Live Oak Society. I was present when the President of the Society, told Mr. Laurence Levert that several of the trees are noteworthy as being among the largest in the South.

From the time it was vacated by the family of de Egana until it became the property of the Levert family, the place passed through many hands, among them Judge Richard Allen. The Levert family who owned and still own a number of plantations bought the place over a quarter of a century ago. It was badly in need of repairs, and some additions that had been made have been removed, as the owners are restoring it to its original condition, without removing the improvements made in the basement. The work that the Leverts are doing has been carried on understandingly, and a small fortune has been spent in the restoration and beautification of the place.

Rienzi is a typical plantation home, well arranged, with large rooms and hallways all of which are furnished in plantation style. Much fine antique furniture and other interesting household articles are in the house. Modernized, without lessening the charm, it is one of the places generally listed in tours of the plantation country. With spacious drawing rooms and banquet halls which lend themselves for entertaining throughout the season, Rienzi is located near enough to New Orleans for short visits. Owned by a socially prominent family, it is a favorite place for plantation parties.

Its gardens are charming and are beautiful most of the year. The whole layout of the place is typical of the plantations of olden days, and great pains are taken to retain the ancient charm of the old house and garden that was designed as a home for a Spanish Queen.

DUCROS

Near Thibodaux we find the old plantation home of the Ducros family. It is one of many fine old plantation homes that have been built for the Ducros family, one of the oldest of the aristocratic families of Louisiana. There is hardly a prominent old family in this state but what has a Ducros on its branches.

There is a tradition in the locality of this old home that its original owner used the home of Andrew Jackson "The Hermitage" at Nashville as the model for this house. The Hermitage is a brick building while this house is built of choice heart cypress. It is two-storied with eight large square columns which support the wide galleries. At a later date a wing with roofs joining the original was added to each side when the galleries were extended across the entire front. Six long French windows hung with heavy green shutters on each floor flank the massive entrances.

Old records show that the plantation site was a grant by the Spanish Government to M. Ducros, a successful planter, who, owing to reverses caused by a yellow fever epidemic, was forced to dispose of the place in 1846. Colonel Van P. Winder, who bought it, added extensively to the original acreage. Records show that the Ducros place was the first large sugar plantation in Terrebonne Parish, at Colonel Winder's death it comprised some 3,300 acres. After Colonel Winder's death his widow remodelled the house to its present appearance, it having been occupied by both Union and Confederate soldiers during the Civil War and greatly abused.

The plantation and home was sold again in 1872 to two brothers, R. S. and R. C. Woods, who were the husbands of the Misses Margaret and Frances Pugh, of the distinguished Pugh family, members of which owned large plantations and handsome homes on Bayou Lafourche. For almost thirty-five years the two families lived in the great old plantation home, rearing large families. They finally disposed of the plantation and home to its present owner Leon Polmer, a distinguished planter of that section.

CHAPTER XXII.

IN THE EVANGELINE COUNTRY.

THE TALE OF EVANGELINE

PREVIOUS to the dispersion of the Acadians in 1755 by the English from the happy land of Nova Scotia, among the peasants of Grand Pre lived an aged farmer, Benedict Bellefontaine by name and his daughter Evangeline.

This belle of the community married Gabriel Lajeunesse, a blacksmith's son, and soon afterwards Gabriel, with the others, received the notice to meet at the Church to hear the Governor's message. Benedict, too old and feeble to stand the strain of imprisonment, when told the news that all that he owned was to be confiscated and that he was to be exiled for the remainder of his life, shortly before the men were marched to the ship, dropped dead and was buried hurriedly without service of any kind.

As the exiles were being marched aboard ship, Englishmen were busily putting the torch to the homes that the Acadians had left and in the turmoil Gabriel and Evangeline were separated. From that time on the two lover exiles spent the greater part of their time searching for each other.

As year after year rolled on Evangeline finally devoted her time to nursing and doing little acts of charity, but always with the same quest in view. At last in the land of the Quakers, after years spent in her vain search, when as a Sister of Mercy grown old and grey, on her usual mission of charity, she came upon the bed where Gabriel lay dying in an almshouse hospital. Evangeline recognizing her loved one so close to death, whispered: "Gabriel, oh, my beloved one". A loving smile played on his lips as vainly he tried to utter a word, but in a moment his smile died away with his last breath.

ST. MARTINSVILLE.

During the days of the French Revolution towards the end of the eighteenth century, a great number of the wealthy French nobles fleeing from France after landing at New Orleans, learning of St. Martinsville, moved on to this section where they located, forming what they thought would be a temporary refuge. Once settled they at once proceeded to maintain their former ways of life as far as it was possible in the new country. Their elegant ways and manner of living, their costly clothing and jewels made the natives soon call their settlement "Little Paris". All went well as long as their money and jewels lasted, the titled Royalists easily marrying into wealthy aristocratic families, the others finally became tradesmen or farmers, while some, once the Revolution was settled, returned to France. Among the old records of that date is a letter from one Suzanna Bossier, who with her father and sister Francoise, in the year made a trip through the wilderness of Louisiana.

In this missive she states that she discovered "a pretty little village . . . full of barons, marquises, counts, and countesses." Also, George W. Cable's "Strange True Stories of Louisiana", published in 1889, referring to the diary of Francoise, describes this settlement at that date, giving detailed descriptions of balls where the minuet in courtly style was danced by ladies and gallants dressed in costly costumes embroidered elaborately with jewels and gold. It tells of lavish picnics given in sylvan glades on an elaborate scale, of brilliant night performances of operas by the French Opera troupe who were summering at St. Martinsville, the village theatre serving as an opera house. Specially noted was a delightful presentation of "The Barber of Seville".

THE OLD duCHAMP COLONIAL HOME

St. Martinsville, Louisiana.

The duChamp house stands as a mute reminder of the glory that was St. Martinsville's in the days that the ancient town was "une autre petit Paris" with a culture formed from what was best in Louisiana, San Domingo and Martinique.

The old duChamp plantation home was built for the wealthy French aristocrat, whose family coming from France had first settled in Martinique and leaving that place on account of negro disturbances had gone to San Domingo where they had owned immense plantations on the Island. When Mount Pelee something over seventy-five years ago became another Vesuvius, detroying much property around it, Monsieur duChamp, who had already come to Louisiana, having sold his plantations in Martinique, because of the negro rebellion, wrote his friends there telling them of the glories of St. Martinsville, his present home. He advised them to leave the Island on account of the dangers of the negro uprisings, but they paid no heed to his letters.

In the town of St. Martinsville were at that day a number of planter families who had their homes in the town and their plantations, a continuation of their back yards as it were, as we find today on the edge of the town of New Roads in Pointe Coupee Parish. Many who came to Louisiana after the eruption of Mount Pelee three quarters of a century ago settled in St. Martinsville.

The beautiful home that Mr. Eugene duChamp had built, was planned along Greek Revival lines, and the front of the garden was enclosed with a fence designed as we see it today, but according to old residents of St. Martinsville, it extended an acre on either side of the arpent of land on which the house stands. Later on when the town grew and streets were laid out, requiring a change of property lines, the fence was changed as we see it today.

Eugene duChamp was wealthy when he came to America and his mansion has always been considered one of the finest in St. Martinsville. Built by a capable architect, it is a stately mansion with central wide hall upstairs and down and contains many beautiful spacious rooms. Like numerous plantation homes it has a cupola crowning the roof, adding dignity to the mansion.

In 1885 the house was sold to Husville P. Fournet, a wealthy resident of St. Martinsville, his daughter, Miss Eliza Fournet now being the owner.

It is interesting to know that many of the families of Martinique who had been friends of the duChamp family notwithstanding repeated warnings, remained on the island and rebuilt their homes and replanted their plantations only to lose their

The Old Plantation Home of the DuChamp family,
St. Martinsville, La.

"The Shadows", Plantation home of the Artist Weeks Hall,
New Iberia, La.

Rear view and immense lawn of "Oak Lawn Plantation" on the Teche River near Franklin, La.

The "Evangeline Oak", St. Martinsville, La.

Crowds of negroes gather about their churches on Sunday afternoons and holidays.

lives, property, or both, by the eruption of Mount Pelee (naked) mountain in the year 1902.

For many years the volcano had lain dormant, a beautiful lake filling its crater. In all these years its peak had become a veritable garden spot, and all had considered it an extinct volcano. Pleasure parties of all kinds sought this spot for their outings, little dreaming that some day it would again burst into life and with its fiery fury destroy all of them.

The history of its last eruption is a tragic one indeed, because the fiery old mountain again in volcanic spirit sounded a warning in ample time to allow all to escape. However, the narrow-minded French Governor Montet, became alarmed, fearing the place would be depopulated. When he saw the natives fleeing at the first rumbling—in fear for their lives, and thinking that their absence would mean an island deserted, called out the troops to prevent the people from leaving. He remained with his own family to assure them there was no danger, telling them if there were he and his family would also flee.

Newspapers of the day inform us that a shower of sparks on the night of May 7th, 1902, which caused the greatest alarm, was followed on the morning of the 8th about 8 A. M. by an explosion that could be heard for a distance of over a hundred miles. Lava, brimstone and ashes fell on the settlement, burying it as Vesuvius had buried Pompeii and Herculeum.

Final reports place the number of dead between 35,000 and 40,000 people who might have been saved if they had been permitted to escape when they wanted to.

OAK LAWN

Near Franklin, Louisiana.

Judge Porter's Mansion.

In the latter part of 1925, I visited the Teche country and while there had the good fortune to see the original old Porter plantation mansion. It was then a venerable mansion, magnificently planned on a grand scale. Superlatives are warranted, yet the house was simple in many ways, which gave it a charm that is lacking in many more elaborate show places, where all restraint is lost in an attempt to achieve grandeur.

Oak Lawn was built without the thought of cost for comfort of the owner's family and his many friends, whom he constantly had as guests. Its magnitude, when we consider the date of its erection, far out-distanced country homes as a rule, and even today when country places cost millions, its size is striking.

To reach Oak Lawn one passes Caffery plantation, which is complete with sugar house, black-smith shop, etc., and follows a side road along the Teche with true plantation country on all sides. There are endless cane fields like vast emerald water rising and falling in waves, while snowy cotton fields near by appear as foam.

Finally the visitor sees a great grove of oaks—today all in order with a newness apparent on all sides. When visited in 1925 there was a great growth of underbrush on the grounds, and plantation darkies, the counterparts of "Lightning" of the radio lolled and enjoyed an endless siesta.

I questioned one of them, as it was not noon hour, and his reply was: "No sah we doan works here, we lives in de big house we keepen, we doan pay rent, and all we eats grows in de place".

The great house then faced the Teche river, and what I mistook at first for the front proved to be the rear portico, which was an exact duplicate of the stately columned front. What made it more impressive was the wing of the house, a smaller duplicate of the larger building, reached by a stairway leading down. It all had a pastel greyish yellow appearance from a distance, but when I came closer, its shabbiness became apparent. The window blinds, a soft tone of blue green, forming an attractive contrast. All in all, it struck me as a magnificent place, and one could readily appreciate why so massive a house had to be abandoned for the upkeep must have been collosal. Its great row of columns, soft white, against the faded pastel tan, was beautiful to behold, and the negro men and women seated and standing on the huge veranda appeared as pigmies against the great height of the building.

The entrance door which was very wide, struck me at the time as being very beautiful and well designed—no doubt imported. The side light and arch fan—ribbed window transoms, with elaborate carved rosettes, placed where the joints met, gave a specially pleasing effect—the rear duplicating the front, with a century of dust apparently settling on all this beauty of detail.

For a small fee I was gladly taken through the place, palatial in its spaciousness. An immense hallway like the nave of a cathedral, very wide and high, extended the length of the building, which was practically empty save for a few sticks of furniture placed there by the negroes. In an angle formed by a cross section of the hall under an archway filled with a fan light, a beautiful mahogany spiral staircase wound to the floor above where the rooms were arranged much as they were below. Handsome marble mantels were in every room, the front one on the left facing the Teche is a room said to have been occupied by Henry Clay while a guest of Judge Alexander Porter, who had built the place.

The entire top floor formed a ball room—in the attic space— all in carefully plastered finish. In this ball room, say the people of the nearby town of Franklin, in the days of the Porter occupation, great balls and lavish entertainments were of regular occurrence, and the elite of the plantation world, of neighboring towns, and even from Baton Rouge and New Orleans came for the affairs. A similar but smaller top floor ball room is to be found in the old Burton plantation home near Woodville, Miss.

Before entering the rear door that I had mistaken as the main entrance, I noted the ancient dairy or milk house, once a quaintly beautiful little place of brick construction, with marble slabs to hold milk products, all gradually crumbling. The slave quarters and pear orchards are beyond.

In the front of the house are traces of what had once been a beautiful old-fashioned garden, oval in shape, with part of the ancient hand-wrought fence still enclosing it, at some distance, but directly in front of the main entrance steps. In the enclosure was a tiny wilderness, where many varieties of plants crowded each other—blooming crepe myrtle, cedars, pink and white mimosa, oleanders, sweet olive, and wild heather. All about the grounds edging the old flower beds ancient box cropped up, damaged by the cattle that grazed in the yard and lawn. Festoons of wisteria, white and lavender, draped the oak branches. "Dats de grabe yard and its hanted", said a darkey, pointing to the enclosure. Another black boy contradicted him, saying—"'taint so, mister, das no goses dar".

Another day, another visit, thirteen years later—all is newness and all serene. The great columned front mansion now houses a museum—admittance to grounds 50c and another 50c to go through the house, or really to be correct, palace, for it is truly a palace in appearance in its rebirth.

A fire swept the place after it was purchased by Mr. Claude Barber, while the house was being restored. The original heavy brickwork, heavily stuccoed, and great Doric columns of stuccoed brick survived the flames. With the aid of his architect, the owner has had the place rebuilt on the original plan but thoroughly fire-proofed. Now marble floors replace the cypress ones, and an ornamental iron stairway surplants the beautiful mahogany spiral one that was there originally. So too with the furnishings all of which are too palatial for a plantation home. It is all magnificent but the place never again will look like a plantation home. However, it is well that the old mansion has been rebuilt in a fire-proof manner as it is a type well worth preserving.

The grounds are beautiful, and the little dairy beneath the trees still stands with brickwork crumbling and marble slabs time-stained—but charming as a relic of the ancient days. The rows of old slave cabins beneath the oaks give atmosphere. They are picturesque, and harbor descendants of the original slaves who lived there.

However, the charming enclosed garden in front of the mansion is gone, and with it the quaint hand-wrought iron railing, the blooming greenery, the urn and the "hants".

MARY PLANTATION

Continuing on the road to Morgan City we reach the broad Atchafalaya. Then going up a narrow bayou for a distance of two miles, brings us to the old Mary Plantation house, which lies beyond the broad fields, where a row of low cottages, placed at right angles to the road, identifies the place.

The residence or "grand maison" as the hands call it, is somewhat different from the medium type ones we have become accustomed to on the trip. Its roof line coming down as it does in a gradual sweep extends beyond the wide gallery attached to which is an individual balustrade and stairway. Continuing beyond, the roof stretches out to a line of pillars which reach upward from the ground connected by a picket fence like the one at the family plantation home at Oak Grove near St. Francisville, La. The house is an artistic old place, like the Butler Home.

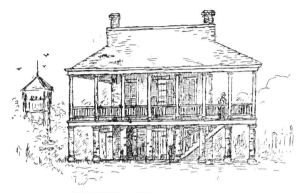

DARBY PLANTATION
On the Teche near New Iberia, La.

The Darby plantation home was a splendid example of an early Louisiana residence built before the details of the Georgian type began to influence its architecture, as we find at the old Labatut home on False River, making us conclude that Darby antedates all of these fan-window type homes.

The history of Darby is interesting, having been built by an Englishman of patrician birth for his beautiful bride, a French lady of noble ancestry, bearing the attractive name of Felicité de St. Aman.

Francois St. Mar Darby had obtained a Spanish grant on the Teche, where he had his slaves lay out his plantation and aid in the building of his home. As years passed, he became wealthy and his family increased. Like many Louisiana planters of French extraction, once having accumulated wealth, instead of lavishing it on his home as others were doing, he maintained a home in Paris and another in New Orleans, where the family visited yearly. Their children were educated in Paris, and during the social season the family spent much time in New Orleans.

What happened to the St. Mar Darby family as a result of the Civil War has been repeated in innumerable cases in the South. Proud and temperamental, the family withdrew to themselves when their former friends, unable to continue as planters, abandoned their plantations as they did not wish to make new friends with the poorer class, who in many instances replaced their former friends, dividing the plantations into smaller farms.

It is a pathetic story of the last three surviving members, growing poorer and poorer as they aged, and becoming suspicious of each other until death claimed the sister and a brother, leaving the last of the line, Francois Darby, who clung to the old house till it became a total wreck, there being no means to pay for repairs. At the time I visited Oak Lawn (before the fire) ; I also visited Darby, and the old house still contained a number of pieces of mahogany furniture and many books mostly French in fine bindings, but at my last visit most of this was gone and the old house was in a bad state of repair. The great oak trees, still very fine, heavy with banners of moss, made the place an eerie appearing spot—the ensemble a fitting setting for an interesting story with the psychological effects of the war brought to a tragic finality.

FAIRFAX PLANTATION.

Up until a few years ago, on the site of what is now a small negro settlement could be seen in a greatly ruined state the old Fairfax plantation home, the lines of which always attracted by the contour of their classic appearance. For many years it has been allowed to fall to pieces, at last being demolished and the present settlement replacing the old plantation house and garden grounds.

One could see at a glance it had been an important place in its day, for it was over a century old and had been built for the family of Dr. Thomas Bisland, a prominent ante-bellum sugar planter of the Teche area. A successful planter and doctor, when the War between the States was declared Dr. Bisland became a surgeon in the Confederate Army, and his cultured family left the plantation, going to Natchez. The plantation home at various times became the headquarters of the Confederate and Union forces and was known far and wide as "Camp Bisland." The old plantation showed evidences of the skirmishes that had taken place on the place both within as well as on the outside.

After the cessation of hostilities the family returned to their old home to find it practically in ruins. Repairs were made and an attempt was made to resume life as it had been before hostilities, but with their fortune swept away and slaves freed it became a difficult task to continue. Elisabeth Bisland, an unusually gifted young woman, born in 1861, became a notable figure after being attached to the staff of the *Picayune*. At the time that Nellie Bly made her tour Around the World, Miss Bisland was the other opponent in the contest of the newspapers.

Another sister, Miss Nan (Anne) Bisland, also became prominent in the South. Miss Elizabeth Bisland married a Mr. Wetmore, and later tells in her "A Candle of Understanding", appearing in 1902, about the return of the family to the old plantation home and the ruin encountered at the time. Mrs. Wetmore died in 1929, but the old plantation house "Fairfax" was always pointed out as one of the old houses of the locality with an interesting history.

THE SHADOWS

New Iberia, Louisiana.

After seeing so many of the fine old plantation mansions falling into ruin it is rather a treat to find the beautiful Weeks Hall place in New Iberia so well cared for.

The town of New Iberia has crept up to the very garden gate, but fortunately the house is surrounded by ample ground, and there is a screen of bamboo some twenty to thirty feet high enclosing the garden park of four acres. So secluded in this ancient manor that having entered the driveway, one readily imagines that he has left the town miles away. The birds, too, seem to feel that they are in a woodland retreat, and there is a constant twitter in the branches of the high oaks that are in fact a grove in front of the house through which a circular driveway has been planned reaching in wide expanse of the grounds from entrance to entrance. Cardinals, mocking birds and golden orioles break forth from time to time in melody, and at dusk, as the shadows lengthen and the light is softest, the trees, shrubs and walls of bamboo cane suggest an arcadian restfulness that is delightful.

On entering the grounds one catches a glimpse through the century-old oaks of the soft yellow-pink bricks and stately white columns. Between the last two columns at each end of the house upstairs and down the spaces are enclosed by movable green shutters, creating a delightful, cool shaded retreat with absolute privacy. The stairway, which is an outside one, located in the farthest enclosure, has charming lines. The details of the house are beautiful. From the dull blue slate roof to the brick pavement, all seems perfection, and the setting is ideal to display to advantage its full charm so carefully preserved in its restoration.

Within all is very chaste and beautiful. The large pair of sliding doors between the rooms have fluted pilasters supporting a simple moulding facing as a frame—the smaller doorways with fluted-moulding frames, having carved corner blocks. The ceiling frieze, too, is equally fine, and the classic-columned mantels show to advantage in these rooms that are apparently some thirty-feet square. The house is plastered throughout, with much classic detail of ornamentation. The ground floor, as in so many other important old homes, is slightly raised from the ground. In the Weeks Hall house the floor is of brick and marble.

The sitting room—or small parlor as it was called—occupies the spaces of the two front rooms. Here is found much that is quite interesting and which pertains to the house itself. There are two specially attractive colored views of the mansion as it looked in the days before the growth of the trees obscured its view from the river.

The plantation grounds up to a number of years ago encompassed much of what is now taken in by the thriving town of New Iberia. On the ground floor also are found a dining room, guest rooms, and culinary department. Changes made in the rear of the house about thirty years after it was built, which enclosed the two end rear sections, formed the present loggia or square back hall with three sets of double doors, that when thrown open, converts the space into a large room, with windows seven in number, opening onto the garden and overlooking the bayou-like river, offering enchanting vistas day and night. A stairway leads to the floor above, where another wide hallway is located, with doors opening into the bedrooms and reception room, now used as a studio by the artist owner. Three dormers of simple design break the roof line in the rear, as on the front of the roof, and the beautiful frieze of classic triglyph on cornice extends around the entire building, adding a touch of refinement not found in the usual plantation home of classic design.

The massive brick stuccoed columns are of the pure Greek Doric order, with smooth surfaces and finished bases, resting on square blocks at the edge of the brick pavement. A beautiful garden in the rear, tempts one to wander out to the edge of the Teche, but instead, we will visit the upstairs rooms.

There we find enormous wardrobes, heavy four-posters, where the beautiful Crouch mahogany reflects in its shining surface the other details of the rooms.

There are portraits of ancestors and grand aunts of a century ago, in the quaint costumes of the period, old oil lamps and ancient what-nots usually found in a century-old house that has not changed hands.

The Shadows of the Teche house was built in the year 1832, and has been in the family ever since. Unfortunately for a long period the caretaker who was placed in charge permitted the house to fall into a state of ruin. However, on the return of the present owner, a grandson of the one for whom it was built, an architect who specializes in restorations, was selected to restore it. The work he has done has again brought new life into the old home, while in no way marring its aged beauty. Nothing was changed in the building, and but few changes in the park gardens, where classic marble statues peer out from the dark greenery. The oaks in the rear garden, stretch across the narrow stream where small steamers and tug-drawn barges of cane and other produce break the stillness with their chugging.

Under the shrubbery in a corner of this park garden, sleep members of the family who have passed on, small bits of stained and crumbled marble marking their resting places.

The copper water head with leaders to the yard below, shows a motive of three stars above a spread eagle, typical of the era in which it was built. In spite of this, Riccuti in his "New Orleans and Its Environs, the Domestic Architecture 1727-1870" says in a caption below a front view of "The Shadows of the Teche": "An Eastern Georgian House, not typical of Louisiana Plantation Buildings." We Louisianians who have seen so many of these mansions, most probably not so beautiful as to details, but of the same general design, like to think that it was a type chosen by the planters who did not want wide galleries surrounding them on all sides.

The Shadows is certainly an ideal home in an ideal setting for a wealthy planter. At least it must have been in the days it was built. Its wide front porches and its latticed enclosures are certainly typical of the South. It is a home that could readily lend itself as a setting to any Southern story and achieve acclaim for its selection.

GRAY PLANTATION HOME

Lake Charles, Louisiana.

One of the leading architectural attractions of the Lake Charles area is the handsome Georgian-type home known as the Gray Mansion. It is a most distinguished appearing house built of red brick two and one half stories in height, having a gabled roof with a large central dormer and a smaller one on either side. A typical fan-transomed entrance and tall white Doric columns create a most attractive facade, all enhanced by the beautiful grounds. The whole comprises an estate of some forty acres laid out, as many of the more pretentious old plantation gardens were, into an old fashioned rose garden, a formal garden and another garden devoted to camelias, japonicas, azaleas, etc. This latter is one of the finest in the state. Splendid trees afford charming vistas at every turn, and the gardenias make it fragrant. A deer park gives this large estate a truly Virginian atmosphere, where one may roam for hours and enjoy its endless charm.

Within again one is greeted by a dining-room panelled in walnut, reminiscent of Virginia banquet halls. There is a winding stairway of delightful lines, and much in the way of interesting antiques. There are fine paintings, a large collection of beautiful miniatures, priceless fans, a great number of them inlaid pearl with elaborate attractive designs of burnished gold. A large assortment of fine silver, crystal, fine china and numerous art treasures collected in Europe complete this most attractive country home.

In New Orleans, too, Mrs. Gray owns and in winter occupies one of the most attractive of the large old mansions fringing the "French Quarter". This home, too, is a veritable museum of art treasures housed in beautiful rooms which are numbered among the handsomest in the city. This house, a very large one, was planned during the golden era of the South, and has large out-buildings that formerly housed family slaves. Mrs. Gray, prominent socially, entertains extensively and these old homes are again scenes of a brilliant hospitality.

CHAPTER XXIII.

IN TERREBONNE.

SOUTHDOWN PLANTATION

and Sugar Refinery Founded 1828

The Crest of the Minor family is as follows: A bourrelet argent and gules with a mailed forearm issuing therefrom holding a battle-ax argent. The motto is Spes et Fidelis.

The coat-of-arms: On a field of gules a bar argent with two besants argent en chef and a besant argent en pointe.

Stephen Minor (Don Estaban Minor) who had been secretary to the Spanish Governor, Gayoso de Lemos, purchased the tract on which this plantation, etc., are located in the year 1828. Here he started an indigo plantation; and not finding it profitable had his lands planted in sugar cane which has continued to be the staple crop of the plantation to the present day. The first plantation home planned along Spanish lines was a one-storied rambling Spanish plantation home erected for a son of Don Estaban Minor who had become governor of Natchez. Erected in 1858 and called Southdown because a large flock of Southdown sheep grazed on the lawns and grounds of the home which were raised by the owner who greatly admired that special breed. This first home with walls very thick—one foot in the thinnest part, remained unchanged until 1893 when a second story was added. Somewhat after the Virginia fashion collonaded walks lead to the two-storied brick building housing the kitchen, laundry, dairy and servants' quarters. While occupied by Mr. William J. Minor as a residence during the season while grinding was in progress, the manor house was a scene of constant entertainment. Southdown was a scene of constant entertainment, in fact through the entire history of this old plantation its record is one of continuous lavish hospitality—for the balls, banquets and receptions during the years that Miss Kate Minor was the chatelain of the old manor have become social history of that area. Situated in the heart of the plantation country amid endless fields of sugar cane and groves of oak trees at present is the charred ruins of the great sugar mill of Southdown Plantation.

Great oaks at intervals on each side bespeak the location of the manor. Built in 1860, the house partakes of the architectural innovations that were supplanting the strict Greek Revival style. It somewhat resembles a villa with its turret ends and spacious verandas. It is two-storied, of brick construction and finished in white. The Minor family, like the Bringiers, the Barrows, and other great ante-bellum plantation families, were great builders and have left a number of splendid mansions. Most of these houses are entirely too massive and costly to maintain in this age of small families and high-priced servants.

The Southdown garden is part of the great charm of the place. Save in mid-winter it is a vast flower-bed framed in a generous hedge not too closely trimmed. It partakes much of continental gardens, but has the vigor of a Louisiana garden with roses of every variety and size.

At different angles the house offers delightful combinations of architecture and foliage studies—collonades on side galleries where a riot of pink ramblers vie with beautiful rose of Montana draping the two-storied rear. The garden with its fragrance and beauty holds you in its spell as you pass through it to enter the house.

Within one finds a treasure store of rare portraits by noted masters, costly crystal, silver and bric-a-brac articles that have been handed down for generations—finest of antiques, rosewood and mahogany and other rare woods in beautiful and quaint design.

The great oak shaded lawn like an emerald carpet is cut by a pathway that leads to another rose enclosed garden where mock

orange and bridal wreath, oleander and althea form hedges.   In
this floral enclosure the roses bloom year in and year out.   All
the choice varieties are found here at their best.   Here it is a
continuous flower holiday.

Here we find old sugar kettles forming gold fish pools, with
waxen water lilies reflected in their depths, while the fire of a
gleaming gold fish assures one that wiggle-tails do not breed here.
Wisteria riotously climbs and twines through the crepe myrtles,
blending the lavendar and pale rose, while various shades of
oleander vie with each other in the shadow of the palms.

Southdown has always been a great social center, and until
recently was occupied by Mr. and Mrs. D. W. Pipes, Jr.   Mrs.
Pipes was Mary Minor, a direct descendant of the first owner,
and it was she that planned and grew the beautiful gardens just
described.

MAGNOLIA PLANTATION

Magnolia plantation manor, named for the grove of magnolia
trees that surround the old mansion and are scattered about the
beautiful old garden, was erected in 1858 for Richard Ellis, a
wealthy planter.   It is of the modified Greek Revival style, built
somewhat along the lines of Rosedown Plantation manor near St.
Francisville, La.

On the rear walls still can be seen the old slave bells.   Like
most old plantation homes the kitchen and service quarters are
found in a separate building.   The slave call bells, each with a
different tone, operated by special wires in working order form
an interesting relic.   These ancient slave call bells are of different sizes and tones, and are connected by a wire arrangement to
the various rooms.   Each slave (servant) was familiar with the
tone of his or her bell, and each personal maid or valet knew
exactly where to go when called.   These slave bells, which in
some of the largest of the old homes numbered at times as many
as twelve in a row, as a rule were placed in the service quarters
above the kitchen window and were sheltered by the overhanging
gallery of the upper floor.

Up until a quarter of a century ago, many rows of these old
slave bells were still to be found in most large Southern cities as
well as on the larger of the old plantation homes.   A BELL MAN,
as he was called, made a business of keeping these bells in order,

going on calls both in the country as well as in the city as do the men who attend to the gas and electric meters today. They were arranged in a row and were picturesque in appearance. A similar arrangement can be seen below stairs in the moving picture, "Wuthering Heights", so the American way of calling servants must have found its origin in Europe.

Seized by the Federal troops during the Civil War the home was converted into a Federal hospital. At that time the furnishings of the handsome mansion were badly abused and damaged. Not having a feed trough handy the grand piano was hauled to the yard, the works removed, and it was used as a feed box for the horses. Among the many attractive architectural features of this interesting old manor house is the magnificent solid rosewood winding stairway. It is always beautiful but specially so during the Fiesta when lovely Southern belles in wide spreading crinolines bank the steps.

Tradition has it that the marriage of General Braxton Bragg (whose ante-bellum plantation manor on Spring Hill Avenue, Mobile, Alabama, still stands) to Miss Ellis took place in the spacious drawing room of Magnolia Manor.

It was purchased in 1874 by William Alexander Shaffer, who restored the old house and garden to its present beautiful condition. The first floor front is of brick heavily plastered, the rest of the structure of choice heavy heart cypress lunber. Like most large plantation homes the kitchen is in a separate building. A special cooling system to keep the drinking water at a low temperature was installed in the early days. It consisted of double brick walls tightly packed between with crushed charcoal and well shaded. It is a home where much entertaining is done, the old mansion being well adapted for that purpose.

Chapter XXIV.

PLANTATIONS NEAR CLINTON.

CLINTON, LOUISIANA.

BATON ROUGE, the State Capitol, in early days was a center of a wealthy plantation country. It is a city, that unfortunately in its growth sacrificed many ancient Spanish and Greek Revival homes, plantation houses and business places that would make it a famous sight-seeing place had they not been demolished, for the background of many Baton Rouge families is equal to that of any in America. But progress had to be satisfied, and unlike New Orleans, the American invasion swept aside proud homes and other beautiful structures and replaced them with the more modern, though less attractive buildings.

From its beginning it was a wealthy community, and one that retains many of its old aristocratic families. Among the comparatively few old plantation mansions remaining is the Laycock house, about which the town has grown. Its architecture is commanding, having large Doric-capped columns reaching to the cornice of the second story. There are wide verandas on both floors, and the house contains much of its original fine furnishings. The Prescott plantation mansion, another splendid old place on North Street, dates from 1840, according to the family who still dwell there. It is a fine example of a wealthy planter's home, its heavy square brick posts supporting the roof. Here one finds a veritable museum of magnificent antiques, family portraits, and reminders of Audubon in the way of a splendid dinner set painted by the naturalist and decorated with birds.

Reading across: 1—Old Chase Mansion, Clinton, La.. 2—Row of Ante-bellum "Greek Revival" buildings, Clinton. 3—Century-old church, Jackson, La. 4—Old Bennett Mansion, Clinton. 5—Columns of the old Wyley Barrow Home, Bayou Maringouin. 6—Ante-bellum bank, Jackson. 7—Dormitory of Old Centenary College, Jackson. 8—Ancient Courthouse, Clinton. 9—The old home of the Stone family, Clinton.

Magnificent Rosewood Winding Stairway, in spacious hall—Magnolia Plantation. Shaffer Home.

Magnolia Manor, old plantation home of the Ellis family.

Innumerable other ante-bellum articles of great interest fill the various rooms. There are still a number of other interesting old houses and buildings, and one must roam around leisurely to enjoy them.

Leaving the State Capitol and travelling in a northeasterly direction for a distance of forty miles on good roads all the way, one reaches the little town of Clinton. One feels rewarded for the trip, for this place was a very wealthy community in the days before the hostilities of the 1860's, and it still retains much that is attractive. Its old buildings remind one of Williamsburg and Petersburg, Virginia. Clinton was a charming little city. Mrs. David Pipes recalls the life there over half a century ago. It suffered greatly from and as a result of the Civil War. Most of the town was burned by the Federal troops, and what survives gives one a fair idea of the type of homes and buildings that made up the lovely old town. There are still a number of fine old residences, a courthouse, and a row of old brick stuccoed buildings opposite, and a large brick warehouse which tell of the past glory of this aristocratic little community. All of these buildings are well worth preserving because of their charm and historical interest. Now that America has become conscious of the worth of these ancient structures there is a movement everywhere to protect and preserve them.

Clinton was the center of a vast cotton growing area, and money was plentiful from 1830 until 1860. The planter families had their town houses here, and for the most part they were true aristocrats and wealthy. As a result the community was a cultured one, and the social life was brilliant and gay. While these town houses were used by the planter families for a comparatively brief period, important events were planned and arranged to take place at the time that the city was filled, and when Court was in session. The social life which was gayest when the planters families were in town, and these homes became great centers of social activity, especially during the winters when life on the plantation was dull for the most part. While a few were the homes of artisans, professional men and merchants, most of them were the homes of planter families.

With the Civil War, death and destruction visited the town and impoverished the planters, for all were made to suffer greatly during and after hostilities. The surviving relics of the old town give evidence of what a charming place it must have been. The old classical courthouse in the square was carefully restored by the U. S. Government. It is beautiful in the white freshness that it originally possessed, the massive columns on its four facades strike the eye from any angle of the spacious square. Nearby is the old "Chase House", a framed two-storied structure, a typical ante-bellum manor of ordinary proportions but with beautiful and correct details of the Greek Revival. The wealth of this family was swept away and unfortunate conditions have not permitted them to preserve this architecural gem as it should be. Few houses of the period have better details. The Bennet House, built of brick stucco finish, another Greek Revival place, has fared better as it is in good condition and contains much that is interesting in the way of ancestral furnishings.

The old Stone family residence unfortunately has had its original lines so altered that its greatest beauty has been lost. More the pity, because a large sum has been spent on repairing it. Originally the Stone manor was located in beautiful grounds. It has been a great social center and has a very interesting history. One also finds in the town a number of other places of interest, old homes and public buildings of ancient construction, among them a large brick, stuccoed-finish cotton warehouse which is very tall and has a pleasing facade, a row of Doric columns making it quite distinctive. The Silliman College building is handsome and noteworthy as are many others.

Altogether the town of Clinton, La. appears a contented, serene little community where the old time courtesy noted in Southern cities uncrowded and unhurried is still quite apparent. Even the old time darkey is emulated by the younger generation of colored folks, for they bare their heads when in the presence of white people if addressed, while the colored girls and women are politeness itself in their attitude towards the whites. This region is a veritable story-book land of the "Old South", for driving out of Clinton on a straight well-paved highway a distance of five miles in a westerly direction one comes to the old town of Jackson. Here again one comes across much that is interesting in the way of old architecture with good lines and historic old buildings. Many of them have great charm and their interiors are filled with antiques of every description. In these old homes one finds fine ancestral portraits painted by noted ante-bellum art-

ists, rare pieces of richly-carved mahogany and rosewood furniture, heavy ancient silver table services, century-old dinner sets,
crystal and ornaments of rare design. The slaves as a rule were
very loyal to their masters, and when certain articles were shown
me, I was told that many beautiful articles had been saved by
being hidden in the woods or buried on the plantation by the
faithful blacks when it was learned that the Union troops were
invading homes, carrying off most of the contents and burning
many of the dwellings.

Of the once magnificent old Centenary College where Jefferson Davis attended college, only one of the wings which served as
a student dormitory remains. It is an old red brick two-storied
structure with a long row of tall Droic columns across its front.
It is at present a "Veterans Hospital", having been repaired
instead of being demolished, thereby preserving one of the town's
historical buildings. It presents a stately appearance in its new
freshness and fine setting, for the original large lawns are still
intact and well kept. A gentleman who stepped out of the old
mansion opposite that, at one time had been the home of the
Pipes family, seeing that I was taking a kodak picture of the
dormitory offered the information that the entire graduating
class of the year 1860 were among the first soldiers to enlist in
the Confederate Army from the State of Louisiana at the outbreak
of the Civil War and all were killed in action, an uncle of his being a member of that class.

ASPHODEL PLANTATION HOME BUILT IN 1835.

East Feliciana Parish.

A mile from the interesting old town of Jackson one comes to an
oil station bearing the name Fluker, located at the junction of
the road leading to the private entrance road to Asphdoel. At
the oil station turn to the right and continue until a bridge is
passed, and a short distance beyond is the entrance to the private
road to the old house. This road winds for about a mile through
a thickly wooded area, crossing Carr's Creek before reaching the
manor which sits high upon a bluff, the front of which has been
walled with brick to prevent its washing away. The house has
quite an imposing appearance from below.

The old manor, for it is rather a pretentious country house, recalls plantation homes of Virginia and Carolina, being of the Greek Revival period with details carefully planned and executed, a most agreeable find among plantation homes. The facade is imposing as well as interesting, and the rear porch, very long as well as very wide, is a most agreeable feature of the place. All of the rooms of the first floor open on to this porch, a most convenient arrangement. The house is of brick construction, having beautiful detailed woodwork within as well as without, handsome white marble mantels, nicely panelled doors and window base panels. The house plan shows a central main house with wings on either side. The rooms on the floor above are lighted by large dormer windows. As one faces the road the right wing contains the large dining-room and library combined. That this is as originally planned is shown by the built-in book cases which fill the side-spaces joining the chimney. In this room one finds much that is interesting in the way of old silver of good design, its polished beauty gleaming in the changing shadows of this splendid room. Irish and English crystal of quaint design, old china and many pieces of old mahogany, rare old volumes, a century-old mahogany writing desk and ancient pictures complete what must be very comfortable quarters.

The parlour, as they call it, has a quantity of attractive rosewood and mahogany furniture, many fine old chairs, sofas, etagerres, book-cases, desks and tables with a quantity of bric-a-brac quite similar to much that one sees in the finer old plantation homes that were not completely cleaned out by the Union troops. What collectors of beautiful things these old plantation families were! One sees at a glance that all the objects in this home are the original furnishings, in most instances occupying the same places they did a century ago. The main bed-room has a very fine Signorette bed-room set, massive in size, but very graceful in design, all beautifully carved. It is of choice rosewood, a relic of its past glory when the mansion was the pride of the vicinity. Family portraits, old pictures, and a hundred and one odds and ends in the way of mementos of past generations to which great sentiment is attached, fill cabinets and corners. The rear grounds are reached by a high step, as the house has a rather high basement. The surrounding grounds form a typical farm-yard with quantities of poultry, etc., and the accompanying noises add life to the place in its isolation.

Asphodel was erected in 1835 for Benjamin Kendrick, at a time when some of the best of the Greek Revival houses were being built. However, Mr. Kendrick did not live to enjoy the attractive home he had built, for he died about the time it was completed. The house and plantation became the property of the Fluker family and has remained in the hands of that family ever since. The present chatelains of the place, patrician ladies, gracious in manner, the Misses Katherine and Sarah Smith, have lived here all of their lives. They remind one of the ladies one meets on a tour of the old plantation homes of Virginia and the Carolinas, who for most part remain on their estates, seldom visiting places of amusement, but occupying themselves with the management of their homes.

Although no longer young, both are gracious and charming in their hospitality, love their old home and its contents, and enjoy the visits of the numerous callers who seek out this ancient home in the wilderness made bright and cheerful by a splendid array of house-plants. These ladies have always been great lovers of plants and flowers, for at every turn, on the wide porches and in the spacious rooms we find rare botanical specimens, many of them of great age and worth a great deal of money. The rooms and porches are fragrant with the perfume from these floral beauties.

Well protected both physically and financially, life to these ladies is a happy one, for they have many friends and relatives who see to it that no danger lurks in this remote locality. Asphodel is the type of house taken all in all that Myrtle Reed loved to weave a story around. One unconsciously forms mental pictures of its past glory and history. Its romantic setting, details and furnishings are all intriguing. The plantation grounds lie in the rear, and the notes of the old plantation bell wafted inward on the pine laden air, bring up visions of the high hopes of the original owner, Benjamin Kendrick, had when he planned and built this quaint architectural gem in the wilderness.

HICKORY HILL PLANTATION

East Feliciana Parish, Louisiana.

Not far from the quaint old town of Wilson, Louisiana, to be exact, some two miles further on and about three miles from the main highway on the road that leads to the private one that winds through the woods to the Shades Plantation is Hickory Hill manor. It is a solidly built structure of dignified lines constructed of red brick, and erected in the year 1810 for David McCants, who had come from Carolina seven years after the transfer of Louisiana to the United States. In type the structure is unique, as the Greek Revival was in its earliest stages of development and just beginning to replace the "Early Louisiana" type farm-houses in the plantation country.

It was erected at the time that great wealth was beginning to come to the South. Instead of hardy pioneers who were to hew logs for their log cabins, men of wealth and position were opening up great plantations, manned by hundreds of slaves.

Built above a high cellar basement on rather severe lines, relieved by a strikingly attractive classic facade, Hickory Hill Manor was elegant looking when it possessed the pair of classic urns, no longer in position, that originally occupied the caps formed at each end of the brick wall and forming as it were classic finals with dignified effect. The facade presents a classic pedimented cornice, resting on four large pillars, the two outside ones being square; the inner two circular ones, all having Doric caps. A fan window in the pediment front above the central entrance, with the high basement steps, and double balconies simply balustraded, leaves little to be desired. The ends of the porches are enclosed by the continuation of the heavy walls of the house, in which are fitted completely—glazed windows and latticed shutters with good effect, creating a distinct type. However, from the sides the house appears without porches and is quite severe looking.

According to Mrs. Mabel Richardson, daughter of the late Mrs. Blanche McCants Freeman, who owns the plantation and which she herself manages; originally the kitchen and dining-room were in an outside building some thirty feet away from the main house—a precaution used generally on plantations against fire. Later on as the family increased in number, this outside building was demolished, and four more rooms added to the main house, leaving it as we find it today with a small wooden structure on the side.

David McCants became a soldier in the war of 1812, and

years later his wife and six children, four boys and two girls, all became ardent Confederates. Mrs. McCants distinguished herself by her activities during the blockade carrying medicine and bandages to the sick and wounded soldiers. As in many another Southern household, the McCants made buttons of quinine, cloth covered, which Mrs. McCants took into the lines. During the campaign around Baton Rouge and Port Hudson, her four sons, Robert, Thomas, the youngest, and William enlisted. The plantation suffered greatly. It was raided, much property stolen, the house practically swept clean of furnishings, house greatly damaged, and plantation buildings burned. The family never relinquished their hold on the plantation. It still has much of interest in the way of antiques and other souvenirs, dating to the time the house was built. Above the mantel in the parlor hangs an oil portrait of David McCants, a gentleman in the middle period of his life, the canvas still showing traces of abuse by the Union troops when they wrecked his home.

Among special articles of interest owned by Mrs. Mabel Richardson, are several fine miniatures—one of the first Mrs. David McCants, grandmother of Mrs. Richardson, painted by this great Confederate lady, who was quite an artist, judging from the art work that she left to her descendants. The other miniatures are by other artists, one quite beautiful, of a great, great grandmother as a young lady. On the walls are several large needle-work pictures made in ante-bellum days. At that time this type of fancy work was very much in vogue, and the ladies of that period spent much of their spare time working tapestry pictures. Authentic antiques are scattered about the various rooms, where also are found many ante-bellum pieces of bric-a-brac. The garden is an attractive one, with typical old plantation garden plants, and altogether it is a noteworthy old plantation home typical of the culture of the century in which it was erected. The house has always been kept in repair.

There is an attractive painting of the old house and garden from the brush of one of the leading artists of the art colony in the French Quarter of New Orleans, Miss Alberta Kinsey, who has also a large sketch of "The Shades" hanging on the walls of that interesting old home. Both paintings are delightful examples of this artist's work. Being easy of access Hickory Hill Manor should be included in the "Old Plantation Homes Tour".

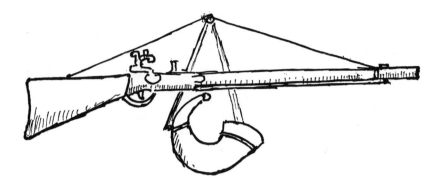

THE SHADES PLANTATION
Built for John Scott in 1808.

Truly a story-book house if ever there was one, "The Shades" has for its setting the kind of location that movie directors seek for dramatic pictures. Far away from the great highway it is reached by an overland road over a rolling wooded country.

Having visited the plantation home known as "Hickory Hill", to reach "The Shades" you continue on the highway to the private woodland road that offers wonderful opportunities to the landscape artist. The striking contrasts of the rich reds and ochers against the varied greens and yellows make it indeed an attractive country, and one can readily see why the cultured Scotch gentleman, John Scott, chose this woodland spot for his roof-tree. The present chatelain, his gracious grand-daughter Miss Eva Scott declares that John Scott chose this site having an eye for business, for it was trees he was looking for. Walnut trees at that date were numerous and large in this location. From the sale of the lumber he made a tidy fortune, which, he with Scott thrift added to his already comfortable bank account, this assuring him the comfortable life that his ancestors before him were accustomed to. For he was a true Scotch gentleman who liked to entertain as real Scotch gentlemen do—well and often.

On the way to "The Shades" riding merrily along knowing that it is the ancient abode of a distinguished family of Scotch descent you are to visit, as your car speeds onward, you seem to note the bits of heather mingling with the wild flowers of the roadside, or is it iron weed that we mistake for the Scotch blos-

"OAKLEY", festooned in wisteria—a bird haven, filled with Bird Song
and rich in memories of Audubon and his lovely pupil, Eliza Pirrie.

Truly a poem in architecture, Greenwood is magnificent to behold.

Asphodel Manor, built in 1835. Plantation home of the Misses Smith.

Hickory Hill Plantation Manor, built in 1810.

The Shades Plantation Home, built in 1808.

som. They resemble each other so botanists say. Anyway, unconsciously you find yourself humming the ancient Scottish refrain of Annie Laurie, and the words of the song form themselves in your mind. When you are thoroughly enjoying your rhapsody, the huge bulk of the old manor looms on the horizon, crowning the hill out of which it appears to have grown, so buried is its mass in the dense growth of great trees which like forest giants spread out around it. The road winding towards the hill presents the old house in all the magnificent artistry of its captivating architectural lines, a real study in graceful grouping well worth copying by architects searching for a model.

The rear building reached first from the road, contains the large dining-room and massive kitchen, its different levels outside, steps of old red brick, the warm tones of the century-old brick walls against the deep green foliage presents a true picture of parts of rural Scotland or old England. Rounding the road to the front, in its glorious setting on the hill top it looks for the world like an ancient New England manor-house that might have been immortalized by Hawthorne or Longfellow. All thoughts of the regulation Southern plantation house vanish as one sees The Shades. Instead visions of "Bonnie Scotland" are conjured up, with bag-pipe music, and kilties, Scotch plaids, banquets and feasts.

The stories and legends about this ancient home are known far and wide. In days gone by its hospitalities seemingly were never ending. At Christmas time this feast was celebrated in true Scotch manner, and as social lines were understood better in those days, the entire countryside came, each keeping nicely into his own groove, thereby assuring a good time to all. As the old-time planters as a rule "carried their liquor" like gentlemen, there was much jollification and merriment, and all knowing the strictness of this household, never infringed on the families' generosity—a fine record for so generous a hospitality during so many years.

The great charm of this house lies in its unpretentiousness, being splendidly built, and of a rambling type that permits a pleasing exterior as well as interior arrangement. Constructed mostly of brick the heavy walls reach from basement to roof in front, and to the porch line of the roof on the sides. The framework of the house is full-sap, choice cypress and much walnut is

used for the interior finish, as there was a great walnut grove
on the place when the house was built.   It is a rather long-fronted
structure with an ell in which is located the dining-room with the
kitchen adjoining, having its floor on the ground paved with
brick with steps leading up to the dining-room.   The lines of this
rear building are rather artistic, and the surrounding yard quite
attractive.   The whole design of the place seems most satisfactory, the facade presents a terrace-like arrangement, steps leading up to the front and side.   Rising from this porch are six
squatty Doric columns which support the porch roof that tapers
back to the bright red brick wall of the second story front where
three windows with latticed blinds rest, as it were, on the upper
line of the porch roof.

A central double door below a transom opens into the hall
that widens in the rear where a stairway winds to the floor above.
The living-room and library, filled with interesting articles of
every description, has an immense mirror of which the present
chatelain is justly proud.   The great book-cases are filled with
valuable volumes, and a portrait of the original owner hangs
above the mantel.   Fine old mahogany furniture fills the rooms and
beautfiul large brass fenders and andirons gleam in the fireplaces.
Outside in the rear hall suspended from the ceiling is a candle
lantern having a round globe, it is a prize relic of the old house,
and is fully one hundred and thirty years old, having hung in the
same spot since 1808.   In talking about this old lantern, the eyes
of the present owner grew misty, and she slowly said, "What happiness has not that old lantern witnessed".   And then seeing that
I was interested told me much about the lovely old house, its past
and then its later history.   And the ancient rifle of the old hunter
about whom Miss Scott talks freely—the hunting piece six feet
long if an inch is still in its usual corner—and recalls tales of the
ancestor, a pioneer from Carolina, who 130 years ago, came across
the wild country to locate a plantation site in the West Florida
section.

The dining-room of The Shades is a fitting one for such a
home, its heavy walnut-beamed ceiling of immense timbers dark-
ened with age.   Its size is impressive and recalls the dining halls
of old Scotland in the section about the moors.   Its furnishings
are fitting and in keeping.   It makes no pretense to castle grandeur, but it has the solid practical furnishings one sees in the

manors of the Lairds of the Low-lands countryside. The furniture is rather massive and one finds quantities of pewter platters, tankards, and silverware, glassware from Ireland, and crystal of rare design, and chinaware from which many a great feast was served. Here in olden days in the candle-lit room sat the Squire and his Lady doing the honors of The Shades, while the assemblage feasted on venison, partridges, quail, and other choice game brought in from hunting trips.

This grandfather of Miss Eva Scott was a typical Highland gentleman of the old school, free from the frills and pretentions of less genuine folks. He was the proud father of four sons, one Major Edward Alexander Scott, another Captain Gustave Scott. His two daughters, Mrs. Marian Scott Bradford and Mrs. Iowa Scott McKneely were representative ladies of their era. Major Edward Scott and Captain Gustave Scott served during the entire duration of the Civil War, with the First Louisiana Cavalry.

Miss Eva Scott tells of young Alexander Scott, who fired with patriotism, joined the Confederate Army, and got beyond the restraining influence of his family. At the time the plantation homes, cotton gins and sugar houses were being shelled by the gunboats in the river The Shades too had a visit from a Federal detachment bent on cleaning out the supplies of the plantation. Major Scott, at home on leave at the time came near being captured, but made his get-away by crawling through the rose garden. Spied by a raider, he received a shower of leaden bullets which did not hit him but their marks are still visible on the house.

The kitchen of The Shades is the perfect type of farm house and plantation kitchen, built with floor on the ground level, brick-paved, thus minimizing the danger of fire, a fear of which forever hovers about homes in remote places. Constructed so as to be warm in winter and cool in summer, it is artistic both within as well as without. There is an immense open fireplace at the end of the room and the entire wing upstairs and down is constructed entirely of brick and fire-proof materials. In this great open fireplace are the original andirons made by slaves when the house was finished, a fire crane and complicated pot hooks—all complete and in place. A large number of relics are found in this interesting kitchen; the old spinning wheel used by the first Mrs. Alexander Scott; much interesting slave-made kitchen ware;

ancient chairs and tables; also stools and kitchen cabinets. Friendly cats lie about in corners while a number of dogs sleep on the floor. Some cuddle up in the huge fireplace, its immense crane reminding one of fireplaces of feudal days when an ox was roasted at one time.

There is an old plant-house beneath a great tree which affords just the needed shelter and moisture to assure a tropical growth. This green house, constructed of soft brick, is filled to overflowing with wax plants, begonias with coral red and pinkish hues—attractive color tones contrasting with the varied greens of the surrounding foliage. All about is a luxuriant growth of trees and bushes. There are fig and pear trees large in size and filled with fruit. One senses at a glance that this is not a place that has been neglected at any time since it was first started. In the fields one sees a number of sheep grazing in the sweet smelling clover. The lowing cattle with the long line of cattle sheds in the distance suggests prosperity. Peacocks and turkey cocks apparently on parade vie with each other in the spread of their tail plumage, the turkey cocks' wattles bursting with indignation at being outshone by the brilliancy of the peacocks' tail-spread.

The usual plantation farm noises are heard on all sides, a plantation bell tolls in the distance, while the clarion call of a rooster starts a series of answers. A pet hobby of Miss Scott is her collection of bells, a noteworthy one of which she is justly proud. They fill two large glass cases, one on either side of the library. Many of these bells are historic as well as attractive. Many are quaint in design and beautiful in tone—Camel bells recalling desert songs, date palms of an oasis or a mirage, and one originally worn by an elephant, whether it be a circus animal, or beast of burden. They are made out of all kinds of materials—silver, copper, brass, bronze, bell metal and even glass. There are Oriental bells from Buddha temples, bells from monasteries and various cities of Europe, Asia, Africa and the South Seas. One bell is from a noted plantation no longer in existence, and another from the flag ship of Admiral Dewey, used in the waters of Manila. The garden is another hobby of this gracious lady, so capable and entertaining. Like many old plantation gardens it is filled with rare and beautiful flowers, roses, camelias, fragrant lilies—in fact all the attractive specimens found in a carefully tended century-old garden.

A visit to this quaint old house is a treat, the memory of which lingers long after. Like charming old Oakley, one must see it to appreciate its intriguing qualities, and one does not readily forget its rare charm.

The more one familiarizes oneself with the histories of these old plantation places which date back to the days that the history of this part of the South was in the making, one wonders why those in search of themes for moving pictures and books have ignored this section. A world of materials awaits the novelist who has only to delve a little into the records, or wander about the country-side while a story of great fascination and historical interest unfolds itself.

When England and Spain were making desperate efforts to hold on to their American possessions rapidly slipping from their grasp, many a thrilling episode fit for a dramatic picture fills the pages of Louisiana's history of that date. There is not a single one of these old houses but what could furnish fine material for at least one good plot. There are the tales of loyal Englishmen who after fleeing England at the time of Cromwell, and establishing their families in the English possessions in America for the second time gave up their homes when they "saw the handwriting on the wall" as the colonists rebelled and moved South. The stories of the earlier settlers of this area offered much valuble material.

The family records of these people read like romances, and are filled with thrilling incidents, such as the story of a parent who gave himself up that he might claim the reward offered for his capture, in order that he might give it to his children who were in dire need—willing to sacrifice his life to relieve their starving condition.

CHAPTER XXV.

THE AUDUBON COUNTRY.

OAKLEY PLANTATION
Built in 1808.
West Feliciana Parish, Louisiana.

WITH St. Francisville as a starting point, one drives on the main highway in the direction of Baton Rouge for about three miles when a country road on the left known as the Oakley Road is reached. Turning into this gravelled byway and driving about two miles, one notes the sign on the right bearing the word OAKLEY. Entering this woodland driveway one continues on through a thickly wooded area of virgin forest until at last Oakley is reached.

No place in the State of Louisiana is richer in memories of the naturalist John J. Audubon and his charming devoted wife than is this lovely old plantation known as Oakley or The Matthew Place. It is now the home of Miss Lucy Matthews. It is a large plantation and there are many negroes on it which provide the usual amount of amusement and activity, besides keeping the plantation and home in good condition.

Oakley plantation manor had been completed when Ruffin Gray, its owner, feeling his health failing returned with his wife to the Homochito country from whence he came in the hope of regaining his health in the hills of Mississippi. He died and later his widow, the beautiful Mrs. Lucy Alston Gray, married James Pirrie, a Scotch gentleman of means. The plantation remains in the family until the present time.

Oakley is hidden away and as secluded as it was the day

that Mrs. James Pirrie returned from New Orleans accompanied by John J. Audubon who was to be the teacher for her daughter. The beautiful vivacious Eliza would have the benefit of his instruction in drawing and painting as well as the other arts of which he was master. Mrs. Pirrie met Audubon while on a visiting and shopping tour in the Crescent City. She found the portrayer of birds in a greatly depressed state and almost penniless.

After talking with him for a few moments she discovered him to be a polished and educated gentleman, and decided that he was just the teacher she was looking for to instruct her daughter. After much persuasion Mrs. Pirrie finally induced Audubon to accompany her to the plantation on the promise that he was to devote only half of his time to teaching her daughter, and that he might have the other half of the day free to use as he wished. Mrs. Pirrie accompanied by Audubon and her retinue of servants returned by boat from New Orleans. The naturalist was overjoyed to find Oakley ideal for his purpose.

He could wander leisurely through the woodland countryside in search of birds. The naturalist at once realized that this was the opportunity that all his life he had been waiting for. Here in this spacious unpretentious plantation home, this man who was devoting his life to enlightening others, spent many months of unalloyed happiness. Here undisturbed he pursued his work uninterrupted and with a wealth of choicest materials at his very doorstep. Situated as is quaint old Oakley in the midst of a wide tangle of both white and purple wisteria whose twining vines a hundred feet long and four inches thick, hang in graceful festoons from the branches of a grove of magnolia trees, the woods of this section of Louisiana is a Paradise that one has to see to fully appreciate.

Wild honeysuckle, wild jasmine and other fragrant vines and plants that perfume the air make the woodland a truly delightful spot.

Audubon's diary of these happy days, yellow with age, is replete with charming notations and none is more pleasing than the tribute to his idolized pupil "My beautiful Miss Pirrie of Oakley".

This ancient plantation and home is now, and for many years, has been known as the "Matthew Place", so named after its present owners who are descendants of the original family.

The name OAKLEY hangs as it has always done at the entrance to the spacious grounds. The old manor is dignified and
almost stately in its unpretentiousness and the simplicity of its
planning. Nevertheless it is quite charming in its individuality
of design which blends so perfectly with its woodland setting.

On the way to the house through the woods one follows a
narrow stream with the usual growth of plants indigenous to narrow waterways. Rushes, wild iris, and pitcher-plants are noted
along the water's edge. The woodland is a veritable birds' paradise.
Feathered songsters enliven the entire area—red birds, wrens,
mocking birds, etc., all happy in their freedom. Long leaf pines
mingle with the lighter greens of the tropical plants and create
beautiful color effects. The fragrance of woodland balm pervades the place, and mocking birds mimicking the flute-like notes
of the oriole and the call of the Bobwhite makes one envision the
happiness of Audubon in this environment. At last, from behind
thick veils of greenery the house appears stately and serene. Attractive masonry pillars support the wide gateway, with smaller
gates to either side joining the fence enclosure. The entire ensemble is one of restful seclusion, charming and unique for only
in spots does color really appear, so blended together are the tones
of the place.

Oakley is without doubt, one of the most artistic plantation
houses in the entire South. With its latticed enclosed porches of
great width it possesses a charm that is lacking in many of the
great columned houses. These latticed verandas make the house
a most intriguing one. The high basement of brick construction
supports two top floors and high attic, making the house a large
one and assuredly a most comfortable country home. A wide
entrance stairway leads to the main porch and the usual exterior
plantation stairway on the left of the porch in front leads to the
floor above. Like most of the very early plantation houses Oakley has no central hall, instead a large room serves both as hall
and library with a larger one adjoining it as the drawing-room.
The house has only two rooms on each floor one room in depth,
and a large third floor or attic. The very wide latticed porches
make it quite ample. The chimneys placed on either side of the
building are heavy brick placed with good effect, and the mantels
of the house are very wide and of good design. The woodwork

Oakley Plantation Manor, built in 1799 Front view of the plantation home that Audubon loved so well, a shrine to the Naturalist.

JAMES J. AUDUBON.

MISS ISABELLE BOWMAN
Who married William Wilson Matthews

Graves of Ann and Alexander Stirling, Beechwood Cemetery.

Graves of Eliza Pirrie and Rev. William R. Bowman.

Avenue of Oak and Magnolia trees leading to Rosedown Manor.

throughout the house is well designed and carefully finished in white tones. The doorways are wide and high, and all floors are made of carefully selected wide cypress boards that now have a high polish from wear. The library hall is on the right as one enters, and throughout the house one finds the original century-old furnishings generally in beautiful condition. In this library hall we find a large mahogany book-case reaching almost to the ceiling, surmounted by a heavy cornice and occupying a rear wall panel. It is filled with old volumes, precious possessions associated with memories of Audubon, and celebrated portrait painters who were housed here while painting the ancestral portraits that now adorn the walls, and generations of the family.

The hall contains a number of antique chairs, graceful in design of carved rosewood and mahogany; swan chairs and fiddle-backs, Signorette and Mallard examples; also roomy colonial rockers; a large mahogany sofa made by Prudence Mallard's studio; a big mahogany center table with a black marble top holding antique treasures; corner cabinets and what-nots; also a large assortment of costly, unusual bric-a-brac dating to ante-bellum days when planters brought back yearly from Europe rare and beautiful ornaments and art treasures for their homes.

Throughout the house the spacious walls are hung with ancestral portraits, all of them painted by notable artists, a number of them of great value, and enumerated seperately in this article. The drawing-room is a large and rather long room, extremely attractive and interesting. It is a salon with its original furnishings all mellowed by time but still very beautiful. One can readily visualize those days that have immortalized this shrine to Audubon and his beautiful pupil, the vivacious charming Eliza Pirrie, whose portrait painted by the celebrated Amand hangs on one of the walls of this room. Above the wide mantel hangs a very large and elaborately framed mirror, the century-old real gold leaf as bright and beautiful, and the mirror as clear as when first put in place in the long ago when this home was new. One wonders how many distinguished personages have seen themselves reflected in it. Oakley was a leading social center before "Civil War Days". A gorgeous lacquer desk, a priceless heirloom, fills a corner, and a large and very handsome mahognay Empire sofa with fire gilt hand-chased mounts in flat gold occupies the rear wall panel. Above it hangs a large portrait of a beautfiul young woman. The ensemble is quite captivating, for the large mantel mirror's reflections glorify this aggregation of quaint and lovely things and their artistic arrangement. Near a front window stands an antique tea wagon on which rests the tea service waiting to dispense the hospitality for which Oakley is so famous. This splendid heavy tea-service escaped being carried away by Union soldiers at the time the house was raided after the fall of New Orleans. With other family silver and jewelry this silver service was hidden below a floor board of the attic by an ancestress, thus preserving for her descendants these priceless jewels and heir-looms. An old piano on which many distinguished people have played has beside it an old music rack holding many Civil War songs.

There are numerous souvenirs of Audubon and his wife who lived at Oakley while he taught the charming daughter of the household. Among these mementos is a study of tomatoes and cucumbers painted by Audubon, and I was told that another painting of a mocking-bird by him which formerly hung on the wall was stolen many years ago.

A hushed aristocratic air envelopes the place, and the cathedral-like silence and coolness in the dense shady places about the grounds, remind one of old English country places. The original Oakley land-grant bears the date 1770, and the large acreage is still intact.

Miss Lucy Matthews, a cultivated lady of the old school, a raconteur of tales of old plantation days handed down by older members of her family, tells many stories of Civil War days and the carpetbag period. In an interesting manner she makes them quite realistic in this setting with an ante-bellum atmosphere.

On the division wall as you enter the library from the front veranda hangs a life-sized bust portrait in oil of the Rev. William Robert Bowman of Brownsville, Penn., who became the second husband of Audubon's pupil, Eliza Pirrie. They were married in 1828 while Rev. Bowman was rector of Grace Episcopal church at St. Francisville. She became the mother of two children, one of whom, Isabelle Bowman, married William Wilson Matthews and became the parents of six children, among them the present gracious chatelain of Oakley. Mr. Bowman's portrait is a splendidly painted one in oil from the brush of a noted Boston artist. Beside it in another panel, vividly portrayed in a very life-like manner, is a portrait of Mr. James Pirrie, who became the second husband of Lucretia Alston, painted by Audubon while he lived at Oakley as the teacher of Eliza Pirrie.

In a corner panel on the same wall is a very lovely portrait, three-quarter length, of Miss Isabelle Bowman who married Mr. William Wilson Matthews. In the beautiful aristocratic face of this portrait one sees a resemblance easy to trace in the countenance of her gracious daughter Miss Lucy Matthews. This portrait is by the noted Belgian portrait painter Amand, whose work is found in so many homes of the old aristocrats. Amand was brought to America by a number of wealthy Louisiana planters who guaranteed him a certain number of commissions. It was the golden era of the South, and when Amand arrived in Louisiana he found that he had more work than he could do. He remained in the South for many years painting family portraits for the prominent families. While in Louisiana he painted several portraits for this distinguished family, among them another charming portrait of Mrs. Matthews as she appeared before her marriage when she was about eighteen years of age.

On a rear wall of this room is an attractive portrait by Amand of Eliza Pirrie, the belle of the Felicianas, who appears a few years older than in her portrait by Audubon. The Audubon portrait that now hangs on the wall in the dining-room of Rosedown Plantation manor located near St. Francisville was painted while Audubon lived at Oakley, where the portrait hung until its removal to its present location. Near by in another panel one sees a quaint and charming portrait of an ancestress of Miss Matthews beautifully painted by a Scotch or English artist. It looks like the work of the celebrated Raeburn, and pictures a dainty little old lady in an antiquated lace cap with her hands folded in her lap smiling wistfully at those who pause in admiration. This jewel is unsigned but one can see at a glance it is from a master's brush. Another corner panel contains a distinguished-looking young man, rich in coloring and graceful in his easy pose. One sees at a glance the handsome features found in so many members of the Barrow family of Louisiana. He is portrayed in a Byronesque pose and shows vividly the fine heritage of both parents, as he is distinctly patrician-looking. The portrait is that of the son of Eliza Pirrie, who eloped with the handsome and dashing young Robert H. Barrow, who was a son

of the wealthy William Ruffin Barrow for whom was built magnificent Greenwood plantation manor, the finest and most perfect example of the Greek Revival period to be found in Louisiana.
The portrait is another example of Amand's work.   A later portrait of young Robert H. Barrow was painted by Sir Thomas Sully
in Philadelphia while young Barrow and his bride were on their
honeymoon in that city.   This later portrait and its companion
of his young wife, who was his cousin Mary Barrow, a daughter
of David Barrow who built Afton Villa plantation manor near St.
Francisville, are reproduced here.   They originally hung on the
walls of beautiful Rosale Manor their plantation home which was
given to the bride as a wedding gift by her father along with an
immense plantation and a large number of house and plantation
slaves.   When Rosale Manor burned many years ago these two
portraits and some very fine family silver were saved—the only
articles rescued from the fire.   They were later inherited by a
talented grand-daughter Mrs. Mary Barrow Collins, one of Louisiana's poets.

Quaint, historic old home of interesting rooms, of lovely
memories, filled to overflowing with rare art treasures of every
description, a fitting environment for the present gracious chatelain who is the personification of all that was best of the Old
Regime!   As one rests on the wide veranda listening to the
muffled drone of plantation noises alluring as music in this sylvan retreat, and is attended by unspoiled negroes with simple
courteous ways of old, the old house with its charm recalls better
than pen can picture, the home life of a real aristocrat on a plantation of the "Old South".

Lucretia Alston, born in La Grange, Homochito, Mississippi,
in 1772, and died May 13, 1833, married Ruffin Gray of Homochito first, and after his death married James Pirrie, of a distinguished Scottish ancestry, who was born in 1769, and died March
7, 1824.   During the Spanish regime, he had been an alcalde. The
children by her first marriage were two that died in infancy,
named Edmond and Elizabeth.   Another son named Ruffin, died
October 12, 1817, at the age of twenty-two.   Another daughter,
who was named Mary Anna was born a short while previous to
her father's death.

From her marriage with James Pirrie three children were

born, two of which died in infancy, but the daughter, born October 6, 1805 and named Eliza, was to become a famous beauty and one of the most charming and sought-after belles of the Feliciana area. She was the daughter who became the pupil of Audubon and later when her father and mother had planned that she should marry Dr. Ira Smith, the vivacious Eliza and her sweetheart cousin, young Robert H. Barrow of beautiful Greenwood plantation, eloped in the month of June 1823—going to the town of Natchez to be married. Enroute they encountered the flooded Homochito Bayou, which seemed as if it wished to prevent them carrying out their plans. Young Barrow, undaunted by the high water, carried his bride-to-be in his arms, as he waded up to his chest through the stream. They were finally married but from the undue exposure in crossing the Homochito Bayou he developed pneumonia and died on July 18th, just six weeks after their wedding. A posthumous child, Robert H. Barrow, Jr., was born, who married Mary E. Barrow, a daughter of David Barrow of North Carolina. Their home was Rosale, and they had nine children.

Eliza Pirrie was married three times. Robert H. Barrow was her first husband. Her second husband was Reverend William Bowman, born December 7th, 1800, died August 30, 1835. He was a native of Brownsville, Tennessee. They were married in Grace Episcopal Church at St. Francisville. By this marriage there were two children. Isabelle Bowman, who became the wife of William Wilson Matthews, six children were the issue of this marriage. Their son, James Pirrie Bowman, married Sarah Turnbull.

Eliza Pirrie Barrow Bowman's third husband was Henry E. Lyons of Philadelphia, whom she married in 1840. She died April 20, 1851, and is buried beside her second husband in Feliciana Parish, Louisiana.

BEECHWOOD PLANTATION CEMETERY

In the little cemetery plot of this old plantation home are iron railing enclosures, three in number, creating individual burial plots. It is a calm tranquil spot in the midst of a thick growth of beautiful trees in a far corner of old Beechwood Plantation, a haven for birds apparently, for one finds the trees full of them. Somehow one feels that the spirit of the great lover of birds hovers near to the grave of his vivacious pupil of whom he wrote in his diary "My beautiful Miss Pirrie of Oakley".

In the grave nearest to the present home which replaces the original Beechwood Manor repose the mortal remains of Lucy Alston who married Ruffin Gray for whom Oakley Plantation was laid out and manor house built, and after his death married James Pirrie. The ancient cemetery shows its age by the time-stained marble slabs on the graves, the two graves besides her own in the same enclosure, are those of her two children from her first marriage to Ruffin Gray.

In the second enclosure is the grave of the daughter by her second marriage, the "beautiful vivacious Eliza", the pupil of Audubon. Beside it is the grave of her second husband, the Rev. William Robert Bowman, rector of Grace Episcopal Church at St. Francisville, La.

In another enclosure in the rear of these graves is another plot and on the marble slab is cut:

Ann Stirling
Died Jan. 2nd, 1802, Aged 35.

On another marble slab is cut:

Alexander Stirling
Died Jan. 8th, 1808, Aged 55 years.

Set into the tall marble headstone is the circular medallion emblem placed there by the Daughters of the American Revolution. Around the central portrait of Washington, on the bronze disc one reads: Alexander Stirling 2nd Lieutenant Expedition Revolutionary war, NATIONAL SOCIETY AMERICAN REVO-LUTION.

History tells us that Alexander Stirling was a second lieuten-ant in the first company, third battalion of the First Regiment of Grenadiers under the command of Henry White, that smelled powder under Governor Bernado Galvez, at the time the English under Colonel Dickson met defeat at Baton Rouge and the British colors ceased to float over Louisiana.

We return to the graves of Rev. William Robert Bowman and his wife. The marble monuments above these graves are handsome ones and designed with good taste. On Eliza Pirrie's grave is cut into the marble:

Beneath

Repose the mortal remains of Eliza B. Wife of Henry Lyons. Born October 6th, 1805. Departed April 20th, 1851.
Thou shall be recompensed at Rise of the just.
Rise He calleth thee.

On the monument adjoining in the same iron enclosure and on the surface facing Eliza's grave is carved:

William Robert Bowman of Brownsville, Pennsylvania born Dec. 7th, 1800. Died August 30th, 1835. Rect. of Grace Episcopal Church,
St. Francisville, La.
Being the second Protestant church built in Louisiana.

On the front surface of the monument is the following:

Is it nothing to you all ye who pass by to behold and see if there be any sorrow like unto me wherewith the Lord has afflicted me in his fierce anger.

According to Mr. J. Hereford Percy who resides at Beechwood Plantation, the home of his ancestors, Rosale Plantation, originally named Egypt, was the first plantation acquired by Alexander Stirling, who at his death left endless acres of valuable land to be divided between his seven children who survived him. Rosale Plantation with its beautiful manor house was later purchased by David Barrow as a bridal gift to his daughter Mary, who married Robert H. Barrow II. Accompanying the plantation was a full quota of house and plantation slaves.

Rosale manor later was destroyed by fire, the only articles saved being some family silver and the two portraits painted by Sully in Philadelphia of Robert H. Barrow and Mary Barrow while they were on their honeymoon in that city. These beautiful portraits eventually descended to Mrs. Mary Barrow Collins their grand-daughter, whose poetry has been greatly praised by prominent critics.

Mrs. Mary Barrow Collins was born and reared at Rosale, which now forms part of Beechwood Plantation.

Grave of the Union Officer who was given a Masonic Funeral by the Masons of St. Francisville, while the smoke from the bombardment of the town still filled the air. (St. Francisville Cemetery).

Architectural details of Rosedown Plantation Manor.

A beautiful old garden-house of "Rosedown", haunted by the shades of the Belles and Beaux who gathered here in ante-bellum days. (Photo by Leon Trice, N. O.)

CHAPTER XXVI.

THE ST. FRANCISVILLE AREA.

Bayou Sara and St. Francisville—-They are one in many things and two in some things. Apparently they are as much the same place as "Natchez on the hill and Natchez under the hill" are, for Bayou Sara stands at the foot of the hill and St. Francisville on the top of the hill and the two places run together and mingle on the declivity. They are one in having but one post-office, which is in Bayou Sara on the water side, and they are two in Bayou Sara being incorporated and St. Francisville not; and rather a keen operation of the St. Francisvillian is it, in keeping outside of the corporation, for being upon a lofty hill they have not the least use for the costly levees which are necessary to the existence of the settlement below the hill and which, therefore, they are not at all inclined to assist in paying for, as they would have to do, as well as be under other expenses, were they incorporated with it.

St. Francisville is the parish seat of West Feliciana, and has the fine court house and many handsome residences to adorn it, and in the central plateau of the lofty location stands the splendid new church edifice, Grace Church, of the Protestant Episcopal congregation of the place, of which Rev. Daniel Lewis is rector. It occupies the site of the old church which it replaces, and will rank among the most tasteful and substantial church buildings in the country. It would be an edifice of note in any city of the South. In this parish the Protestant Episcopal seems to be the prevailing denomination, though there are a number of other sects scattered through the country.

—J. W. Dorr.

In the days that the above was written (1860) the Mississippi River was the chief means of transportation and the Feliciana parishes rose to the height of their prosperity. St. Francisville, the parish seat, became its main commercial center and the largest river port between Memphis and the Crescent City (New Orleans). With plantations unrivalled in any part of America, and an enormous cotton crop yearly, the Feliciana parishes were assessed for more than thirty millions of dollars.

Continues J. W. Dorr:

If St. Francisville is stronger on the oranmental, Bayou Sara is out of sight ahead of her on the practical—for she does all the business and a great deal of business is done too. It is a thriving and bustling place, and contains some of the most extensive and heavily stocked stores in Louisiana, outside of New Orleans, and there are few in New Orleans even which can surpass in value of direct importance.

[Here, a long list of business firms and banks.] A prominent object in the town occupying a very handsome building is Robinson, Mumford's Bank of Exchange and Deposit, W. T. Mumford, Teller. China Grove hotel is a principle house of entertainment, there being besides smaller establishments, a very large and comfortably arranged wharf boat, which, however, is not doing a very prosperous business, the majority of citizens being opposed to the location there.

There is a Methodist Church on Bayou Sara, Rev. Thomas Donner, pastor.

Bayou Sara, located somewhat as Natchez-under-the-hill, was a much higher class place and did not have the reputation of being a nest of thieves, with dens of sporting women and gambling halls, or for being the refuge and hideout for criminals of all sorts. Like all river towns, it had "spots", but these were well policed and in no way interfered with the enormous amount of business carried on. Many fine families had homes in the section and the people of the town were law-abiding. J. W. Dorr says:

Among the prominent business interests of Bayou Sara is horse dealing, it being a great horse market for the surrounding country. Large droves of horses are brought here for sale from Kentucky and elsewhere. Messrs. Henshaw and Haile have very extensive stables and do a great deal in horse flesh. Bayou Sara is the terminus of the West Feliciana Railroad. The depot stands upon the levee in the lower part of the town, having been moved from the upper part, above Bayou Sara, a troublesome unnavigable estuary, which would not be permanently bridged, save at great cost. This railroad runs to Woodville, Mississippi, a distance of twenty-eight miles. A good steam ferry boat plies across the river to Pointe Coupee, and ought to be a paying institution, for passengers are charged fifty cents each for the luxury of riding over on it, and two dollars if they have a horse and buggy. The Bayou Sarans ought to amend this matter, for the heavy ferriage prevents much custom from reaching their market. The boat has been run a number of years and it is the property of one person. The merchants ought to form a company, buy the boat, and run it at lowest rates that will pay expenses. They might even afford to afford a little, but it would pay better at half the present rates than now.

Today nothing remains to tell of Bayou Sara's greatness and prospects at that date (1860). For years and up until recently one took his life in his hands in making an attempt to cross the river from the little flat below St. Francisville. Not long ago the flat boat that made the crossing became submerged when several automobiles were driven on it. Generally one made the crossing and returned by the Baton Rouge ferry or the one above at Natchez. But all that is changed now. Continues Dorr:

West Feliciana is one of the wealthiest parishes in the state, being considered the second rating in wealth and population next to New Orleans. The total assessed value of property is about $8,200,000.00, on which it pays a state tax of over $26,000.00, of which over $8,000.00 goes to the public school fund. There are thirteen public school districts in the parish and about five hundred educable children.

The total population of the parish is 12,000 in round numbers, of which about 2,000 are white and about ten thousand slaves, the free negroes being few.

A comparatively small portion of the land of this parish, the upper border of which is the state line, between Mississippi and Louisiana, is adapted to the growing of cane. Cotton is the principal product. Of the 227,367 acres forming the entire area, about 35,000 are in cotton, 5,000 in cane, and 19,000 in corn, leaving 165,-000 or 170,000 uncultivated.

There is much barren and sterile land in the parish, but enough that is very prolific to yield a large crop as its aggregate product. Many of the planters grow both cotton and cane, but they are generally engaged exclusively in raising one or the other rather than both.

Some of the planters of this parish rank among the largest in the state, and among the extra heavy men may be mentioned Messrs. Joseph A. S. Acklen, David Barrow (of Afton Villa), William Ruffin Barrow, Sr. (of Greenwood Plantation), William J. Fort (of "Catalpa" and "Magnolia" plantations), John Scott Smith, William Stirling, Daniel Turnbull, etc.

Hardly had our narrator concluded his trip through the State of Louisiana, when the guns of war were directed on these twin towns, so attractive and so prosperous.

St. Francisville at that day was very beautiful, with splendid homes, well laid out gardens and thriving stores.

These two places were settled for the most part by families that came from Virginia, the Carolinas, and other Northern places. not as hardy pioneers to carve their fortunes out of the wilderness, hewing the logs for their cabins with their own strength; but by a class for the most part that stemmed back to the aristocracy of England and Ireland and Scotland, who brought with them great chests of gold and silver coin, hundreds of slaves, wagon loads of fine furniture, paintings and household furnishings, and who built palatial mansions on tracts of five to ten thousand acres. Many of the mansions, still standing, bear witness of the above statements. These aristocratic families established a culture unsurpassed in America, the center of which revolved about beautiful St. Francisville.

In the little cemetery of St. Francisville, Louisiana, is a simple grave of a Union officer, on which fresh flowers are still placed. The story of this grave hearkens back to the hour that this beautiful Southern town was being torn asunder by the roaring balls from Union cannon fired from gunboats lying in the river. Year after year, it has never wanted for attention or flowers, and it is cared for far more carefully than many of its aristocratic neighboring tombs. For three quarters of a century on all occasions, Memorial Day, All Saints Day—it has had its share of floral decorations.

The story of the stranger's grave is connected with the shelling of St. Francisville in 1863 when that beautiful place of wealth and culture—defenseless save for those too old to go to the front and a few disabled soldiers home on furlough—was blown practically to bits.

In the midst of the awful carnage hysterical women and children speechless from terror vainly sought spots of safety in the midst of the falling brick walls and gutted buildings, as slate, crumbling brick and timbers crashed about them. Even after so many years some did not want to revive the memory of it. One old gentleman, a small boy then, said "Read what they are doing in Spain at present and you will get a true picture of it all."

Those awful days of 1863 followed the fall of New Orleans. The army of Butler terrified the people of New Orleans, bullying and robbing, while the fleet of Federal gunboats kept continually going up and down the river, bombarding recalcitrant Confederates. In this fleet was the U. S. S. Albatross, with Captain John E. Hart of Schenectady, New York, as Lieutenant Commander.

When in the locality of St. Francisville, after doing untold damage to numerous plantations on its way up the river the Albatross slowed her speed and like a caged lion maneuvered for ward and backwards for hours.

Among those representing St. Louis firms that had been shipping thousands of horses to this section, stationed at Bayou Sara, were many from Illinois and naturally they leaned towards the Union. These men and a few others became friendly with the Union officers and men when they came ashore to look for provisions, and horses and mules; in fact to find out where wealth of any kind could be had at the town above or on the various plantations.

The fact that there existed a rivalry between the two places, Bayou Sara and St. Francisville, furnished the reason for the destroying of St. Francisville.

In the archives at Washington, D. C. can be found the official report of the incident. It is the report of Lieutenant Commander P. Foster, U. S. Navy to Rear Admiral David D. Porter, under the date of Jan. 29, 1864, almost seven months later. The following are quotations from the report.

> Enclosed I send you a copy of a letter I was induced to write to General Wirth Adams in relation to raids made upon this place (Bayou Sara, Louisiana, close to St. Francisville) also the reply of General Adams.
>
> Before I received this reply, I was telegraphed from Baton Rouge to repair to that place immediately with two boats if possible, as it was in danger. The request was immediately complied with.
>
> On my arrival there I found the commanding officer was more frightened than hurt and accordingly, I returned next day. During my absence the reply of General Adams came to hand and was opened by my clerk.
>
> On the receipt of it my executive officer, Mr. Neeld, sent an order to St. Francisville, allowing the women and children 24-hours to leave the place. This order was subsequently prolonged and ample time given. When the allotted time* had elapsed, the shelling commenced at noon the 16th, continuing about four hours. In all 108 shells were fired slowly and with very great accuracy, each one telling.

* During this time the banks, homes, stores and warehouses of the town and the plantations nearby were being raided and robbed of all movable valuables—according to some of the descendants of the planters.

Proving the inaccuracy of this report is the experience of Mrs. Wm. Walter Leak, who is a daughter of Captain Robinson Mumford, the leading banker of Bayou Sara. She and her three children were in their home located on the bluff overlooking the river, awaiting the arrival of her husband—Captain William Walter Leak, C.S.A., who was coming home on a brief furlough— as well as innumerable others, were caught in the havoc wrought by the exploding shells. Mrs. William W. Leak (nee Miss Margaret Mumford) and her children fled to a place of safety beneath a stair leading to the cellar of their large brick mansion, which threatened to collapse every moment during the bombing, while the town was being demolished.

Continuing the report reads:

The town of St. Francisville has been a hot bed of secession ever since I have been in command of this place, and has been the constant resort of Confederates, where they were continually entertained and urged on acts of plunder and abuse upon the people of the lower town.

Union sympathizers from Missouri: Bayou Sara, for their Union proclivities. Moreover there is not one inhabitant of the place of (St. Francisville) who has ever shown himself favorable to the Union, while a majority of those in the lower town (Bayou Sara) have ever proved themselves good and loyal citizens.*

The cavalry principally concerned in these acts of abuse and plunder is largely composed of citizens of St. Francisville, who own property and have families residing there.

The shelling of the town has not injured a single Union man, while it has broken up a harbor for most violent secessionists, and driven away from there only those who are immediately concerned in the success of the Confederate cause. The result will be very beneficial, as it will show those engaged in this illegal warfare of robbery unoffending citizens and firing upon unarmed transports that they cannot do it with impunity and that they themselves will be made to suffer the penalty in their own homes and families.

In conclusion, I sincerely hope you will approve of the course I have pursued, as I think it will prove beneficial and secure quiet to the Union citizens of the lower town (Bayou Sara) who are deserving of all the protection that lies within my power.

The above is the reason given in the official Union Report in explanation for the reason that St. Francisville was annihilated

---

* The latter statement is disputed by old residents who knew the history of Bayou Sara.

and practically wiped off the map by shell fire in 1863. The reader can draw his own conclusions.

To return to Captain J. S. Hart who lies buried in the little cemetery of St. Francisville, Louisiana. From the records in the archives at Washington:

> On Board the Albatross,* June 16th, 1863, 4:15 P. M. the report of a pistol was heard in the Captain's stateroom. The steward at once ran in and found the captain lying on the floor with blood oozing from his head and a pistol near him one barrel of which was discharged. The surgeon was at once called, but life was extinct.
>
> We then got under way, and in rounding to get around the steamer Sachem, General Banks and Bee came to our assistance.

And on Captain Hart's personal official record in the Navy Department archives is the notation: "Died of wounds".

There is nothing in the record to throw light upon the burial of this Union officer by Confederate Masons, almost in the shadow of the falling shells, as there was not a piece of artillery in the town with which to answer them.

It seemed as if the end of the world had come to those who stood helpless by as the court house, Grace Church and mansion after mansion and places of business crumbled.

The handful of old men, hysterical women and children and one or two Confederate soldiers on leave could do naught but watch the scene of destruction.

After what appeared as an interminable period while desolation lay everywhere, the cannons ceased and those watching the Albatross saw a life boat leave the ship fully manned with a United States officer in the stern, with a white flag floating in the breeze.

They saw them land at Bayou Sara where they inquired if there were any Masons in the town and learned that there were two brothers, Samuel White, who owned the little ferry, and Benjamin, who owned the steamboat "Red Chief" at Red River landing. These Masons told the officer that in St. Francisville, the place they had just shelled, was a Masonic Lodge, and informed him that S. J. Powell, who was away with the Confederates, was its Master, but that Captain W. W. Leak of the Confederate Army "is home on furlough and can convoke the lodge."

---

* This was the Albatross that did the shelling of St Francisville.

The officer sent word to Captain Leak that the commanding officer of the Albatross was dead, and requested that he be given a Mason's funeral and be interred in the earth instead of being sunken in the Mississippi River. "We have Masons on board who can vouch for him and his standing. We will await your answer".

When the emissaries had imparted their information to Captain Leak, the gallant Confederate replied, all the while scanning the desolation about him: "As a Mason it is my duty to accord a Masonic burial to a brother Mason without taking into account the nature of our relations in the world outside Masonry. Go tell that Union officer to bring his Captain's body ashore. There are a few Masons left in town, most of us are at the front. I shall assemble all I can." Speaking to the White brothers he said: "You too are Masons, I shall want you at the funeral services."

Then the body of Captain J. E. Hart in his uniform was brought ashore, and in their Confederate uniforms, with their Masonic regalia worn above—was received by four members of Feliciana Lodge No. 31 of St. Francisville, and the two brothers, Samuel and Benjamin White. The Masons of the U. S. S. Albatross identified themselves to the Masons of the Confederate Army. Together they bore his body to the little Masons Lodge still standing—now the town library—and when the full Masonic funeral rites were completed, they carried the body to the newly dug grave, placed among others that were torn and broken. Here, they with "Masonic ritual consigned all that was mortal of Lieutenant-Commandant John E. Hart, United States Navy Commander of the U. S. S. Albatross gunboat to sleep his eternal sleep".

As the last clod of earth had been placed above the newly made grave, those who had come from the Albatross saluted and departed, and reaching their ship, sailed down the river.

Many have said that the suicide was the result of a fever. Some have doubted it, believing that remorse brought about such an end, especially as Captain Hart had friends in St. Francisville and had been entertained there. There are even hints that he was in love with a young lady who lived there. He was forced to bombard the city because ordered to do so. One theory is that this preyed on his mind and he took his own life.

Captain Leak, who died in 1912, after living to become worshipful Master of Feliciana Lodge No. 31, was honored on his

"THE COTTAGE" Plantation, Cradle of the Butler family in Louisiana.   Home of Miss Louise Butler, Louisiana Historian.

"THE CEDARS", Plantation home of the Misses Sarah and Mamie Butler of New .Orleans.   (See page 249, Vol. II.)

Mrs. Thomas Butler neé Mary Fort, daughter of Mr. and Mrs. Wm. Johnson Fort of Catalpa Plantation, West Feliciana, La.

Thomas Butler Plantation Home.

55th Anniversary as a Master Mason in that Lodge. His son, Hunter C. Leak, became honored in that same lodge on his 55th Anniversary as a Master Mason.

It was Captain Leak who first started putting flowers on the Union officer's grave, a practice that has been kept up ever since. Today as one motors to St. Francisville, be it from New Orleans or from Natchez, the impression is much the same.

We find St. Francisville the aristocrat still, but now grown old and helpless against the invasion of new comers. A different element entirely threatens to abolish the faint aristocratic traces of its ancient regime entirely. Could those who lie in the old cemetery by the church, who passed on just prior to the destruction of this fair town return they would not believe it to be the same place. No more stately homes shaded by ancient oaks, and no more do we find business places and banks peopled by the class of denizens of that day.

Here were the haunts of Audubon, when after a day's tramp through the forest and glen in search of new subjects for his brush he rested and refreshed himself as he was wont to do before returning to the plantation mansions where he and his wife lived. She had been Lucy Blakemore, a young English girl who became his wife in 1808. She, realizing his genius, did all that lay in human power to aid him. While he roved the woodlands, she taught the children of the different plantations, earning the family living. First, according to a copy of part of an old diary of Audubon (copied by Miss Felicie Bringier) he taught at Oakley, "the shutter house" as it is entered in his diary, forever cool and delightful. Here he taught painting to the children of the family, dancing also, while his wife taught the more essential studies. He remained here during the summer months of 1821 from June to October, as the family then went to New Orleans for the winter season. Another entry—after a lengthy description in the shadow of the giant oak trees, recalls in a quaint way, its past glory and culture.

Most of the old places have about them an individuality. One seeks out the old plantation places of the neighborhood still rich in historic interest, beauty and individual charm, rare in their glorious settings. A culture is found in the Feliciana parishes that readily recalls that found in older parts of Virginia and the Carolinas, where survivors of the Civil War, though impoverished, never have lost their family prestige—where family traditions, good birth and breeding come first—then the means to sustain these things follow as best they can. Care must always be taken not to tarnish the family escutcheon. Somehow one still senses this attitude when visiting these old homes, as the atmosphere is entirely foreign to the up-to-date ways of the city.

Here in this St. Francisville country is recalled from the faded grandeur of the days when the Barrows, Pipes, Butlers, Stewarts, Sterlings, Bowdens, Forts, Percys, Bains, McGeehees—all names with historical associations—owned these glorious old gardens and ancient homes, the brilliant history and achievements of these people.

Of Bayou Sara nothing remains. The terrible bombardment of St. Francisville also spelt its doom. Shortly after the destruction of that beautiful place great fissures appeared in the sandy soil of the lower town. These fissures gradually grew larger forming rivulet like places that were filled with the debris taken from the ruined buildings which the people of St. Francisville knew would never be rebuilt. It also meant the end of its prosperity as well as that of Bayou Sara whose existence too was to be short lived. Left like a wrecked barge to rot on the shore, the place was practically abandoned for years, and later during a very high river, all that was left of Bayou Sara was swept away, leaving the coast much as we see it today.

WAVERLEY PLANTATION

Rescuing it from ruin, the Jack Lesters have gradually restored the old Waverley place. Like most of the plantations in this area, Waverley lies in a semi-secluded spot some distance from St. Francisville—in a section where electric lights as yet have not replaced the oil lamp and candle. The lack of modern lighting lends it a charm in keeping with the history of the place.

For a few years following the Civil War Waverley was inhabited, but for over a quarter of a century the old house lay hidden and almost forgotten in the jungle that had grown up about it. In the years following the exit of the carpetbaggers, when planters tried to recoup their scattered fortunes, Waverley's acres yielded a fair return from cotton. But it became harder to contend with the difficulties that yearly arose, and finally the owner gave up its cultivation but held on to the land. He removed a few belongings to one of the little houses that formerly was one of the slave quarters, and closed the manor, abandoning both house and garden to ruin and neglect. Such its condition was when the Lesters purchased it, and they have done much restoring since owning it.

The original Spanish Land Grant of the plantation later known as Waverley was made to Patric McDermott in 1804. His daughter Emily later married a young Englishman named Dr. Bains, and Waverly was built in 1807 and named after his English residence. Soon the place became a great gathering place for the cultured colony that had come to this area. Great mansions were springing up on all sides, and the section became important socially as well as financially.

Sheltered as it is by the grove of trees, the appeal of hominess is intensified by the border of blooming plants fringing the pathway leading up to the front steps. From the traces of ancient flower-beds the former glory of its garden can be surmised. From these quaint century-old flower-beds where "flying Charlie" so often landed, today the perfume of old plantation flowers greets one on all sides, as cape jasmine and other fragrant blossoms pour their perfume into the air. Flower-beds of oval, diamond, and circular-shape tell of the old formal garden.

The house is designed with the grace and lightness of a piece of Chippendale furniture. It has simple, square collonettes and a plain balustrade. The entrance doorways are unusually beautiful and correct in detail with overhead fanlight transoms and side lights—all true to form, with carefully moulded trim finely proportioned, and planned to show to advantage the pure Georgian details beautifully executed. If one is conversant with hand-carved mouldings, he will recognize in the irregularities of the lines here and there that it is real hand-carving. The door and window trim too have the same perfection of details as we find on the mantels in the various rooms. A hallway is moderately wide, and at the rear is a graceful stairway with handrail and balustrades of mahogany. The rooms are all well proportioned and have the same careful treatment as have the mantels of Adam design, which have typical country fire-place openings built for burning logs. In the rooms above stairs the woodwork is not as fine as on the lower floor. The rooms are large, well lighted and ventilated, and like the rest of the house are furnished with appropriate mahogany plantation pieces, and many souvenirs of Audubon who here taught the children of the aristocrats of this vicinity to dance.

OAK GROVE

Oak Grove is properly named and properly placed in a country long famous for its beautiful trees. A long walk or drive brings one to the house where the road widens out as is customary in many of these old park-like gardens.

The size of the house is indicated by the careful placing of a pair of unusually attractive pigeonnaires, octagonal in shape with cone tops. These architectural bits do wonders in adding charm to the place, the gleaming whiteness of the bricks contrasting with their green trim.

Three nicely planned dormer windows crown the roof, the slope of which is quite marked—the outer slope reaches out beyond the house porch, a line of collonettes on bases support it.

Entirely of brick is the body of the house, except that part just above the porch. It is quite simple in plan, but charming and of good construction.

Oak Grove is the home of the Butler family who trace their lineage to Theobold Fitzwalter, who went to Ireland in the train of Henry II, in the capacity of Chief Butler of Ireland—hence the name. He died in 1206. Later in 1321 James, son of the Sixth Butler, was created Earl of Ormonde (Peerage of Ireland).

ROSE DOWN PLANTATION

Built in 1835.

West Feliciana Parish, Louisiana.

Not far from Afton Villa lies Rose Down, as beautiful as its name, deeply hidden away from the roadside. Its very seclusion adds a charm to the place, which it would forfeit if situated on the highway flaunting its grandeur in the face of every passing stranger. Its setting is considered one of the finest in the United States. The mansion, built in 1835 for Daniel Turnbull, has caused globe trotters to state after visiting house and garden grounds, that it is one of America's most beautiful ante-bellum homes.

James Pirrie Bowman, born in 1832, the venerable stately-looking old gentleman, who was so much a part of Rose Down, the father of the Misses Bowman, passed away several years ago, aged 94 years of age. Up until the end of his days he used to jokingly tell how it happened that Rose Down was spared by the Union soldiers when they were setting the torch to most of the fine plantation homes of the South. Always immaculately clad, and during warm days, in white linen accompanied by his golden collie, he could be seen walking about his wonderful old garden enjoying the beauty of his flowers, or sitting on his wide front gallery with some visitor, who had come from afar. On other occasions with neighbors or members of his family, he would reminisce and tell of the time when the Union scouts searching the countryside for what they could commandeer, steal, destroy or burn, on seeing the marble urns and statuary at Rose Down, fled from the place thinking that they had invaded a cemetery.

Retaining most of its original charm, Rose Down is, if anything more beautiful that it was in the days of its making. Like a beautiful old piece of furniture, the years in their passing have added a patina. The gardens of Rose Down possess all the charm of old world gardens that have been carefully but not over tended. There is an air of mysticism in its restful quiet, its great shaded places, and its soft grey green and endless pennants of moss swaying in the fragrant breezes. Azaleas and camelias ten feet high in season are converted into great masses of gorgeous bloom. Night jasmine, gardenias, magnolia fuscati and endless fragrant blooms, make of the grounds a delightful spot indeed.

For almost half a century the birds have never been disturbed, so there are thousands of feathered songsters nesting in the trees, and at times a dozen crested cardinals sway on branches about the house awaiting to be fed. The place is like an enchanted garden for nothing seems to have been disturbed for a century, except the grandeur of the grounds which have been enhanced by the passing of time. The small twigs have become great oaks, arching and entwining overhead like the groins of a vast cathedral. The stillness of the place is broken only by the song of a mocking-bird, a bob-white, or the cooing of wood doves Its great grove of oaks set back from the roadway is well spaced, and forms a continuous leafy canopy over the long avenue which widens out as the driveway reaches the house.

No longer do fete champetres and gay parties break the stillness of a cathedral-like silence that pervades the place. The Misses Bowman, grand-daughters of the original owner still dwell there. They are quiet, unassuming ladies who time and time again have refused huge sums for their lovely old home and grounds—even when the proviso was made that they be permitted to live there during their lifetime undisturbed, the land, house and garden to be relinquished only at their passing. Being financially well situated they preferred not to disturb the tranquility of their lives and as a matter of pride they wish the place to go to relatives and thus remain in the family.

Rose Down is a place to inspire a poet, a novelist, an artist— a place about which much romance and history could be written. The material is abundant, especially if the scene is laid in antebellum days. The place possesses much garden magic and allure and would make a marvelous setting for a story.

There is the story of the beautiful Eliza Turnbull (grandmother of the Misses Bowman) whose wealth and beauty and intellect made her nationally famous. The costumes she wore at balls, receptions and for street wear immediately became the vogue. The famous watering places of the East and South thrilled to learn of her arrival, for her presence insured a delightful time for all the guests—so great was her vivacity, charm and personality. She was always accompanied by members of her family and a number of colored maids—slaves from the household as well as her own personal one. In her father's coach and four, with trunks filled with finery she would saunter along leisurely, stopping to visit at the plantations of friends en route. The Misses Bowman always beam with pleasure when showing the beautiful portrait by Sully of this ante-bellum belle, which hangs in their dining-room.

The old plantation mansion was built in the mid-thirties—to be exact, in 1835. The house is still in a very good state of preservation, although here and there age has began to tell, for it is a frame structure. Of a pleasing type of the Greek Revival, with a double tier of Greek Doric columns and balustrades of the same period, the entire house is built of solid cypress with the exception of foundations and chimneys.

The main entrance door, placed in the center, has the classic sidelights and transom fitted with leaded glass. The entablature of cornice like the rest of the house is correct in every detail and shows strongly the Virginia influence where so much thought was given to these matters. The window blinds are of the movable type throughout the house except where they act as louvres in the gables at either end of the building. The cornices of the wings of the house have each a frieze of classical triglyphs—with details absolutely correct. They support a porch with balustrades similar to those on the front of the main house.

When the family traveled afar they collected for their beautiful home rare objects and works of art. While they spent lavishly they practised a cultivated discrimination and used rare judgment in their purchases. At Rose Down there are heirlooms, too, for many generations have added to this collection of rare and beautiful objects where in a subdued light in the old rooms hung with antique brocades and old lace, exquisite crystal and silver gleam. Family portraits and other paintings by noted artists grace the walls above polished mahogany and rosewood furniture. signed bronzes and rare bric-a-brac vie with each other for the attention of the connoisseur. All are mementos of the happy days in this old home now so quiet. Old carpets with velvet softness evoke the shades of the distinguished company that gathered here for generations before the recent days when the doors are now thrown open to the public so that it might too enjoy the glories of the past. Rose Down is still the home that it always has been, probably showing its age a little, but it is not a place tidied up for exhibition purposes.

There is a needle point fire-screen worked by Martha Washington, descending through a member of the Custer family. There are rare engravings galore in folios dating back to the days when Queen Victoria started the craze of collecting and showing them to visitors.

In the library is an elephant edition of "Birds of America"; also a painting by Audubon—a portrait of the vivacious Eliza Pirrie.

Having viewed the various apartments, you are treated on your return to a view of the garden. The great charm of the garden is the diamond-shaped space in front enclosed in a box a century old. Pathways lead in every direction through the trees to garden houses latticed and moss grown. Marble urns and statues are placed among the tropical greenery. Splotches of sunlight filtered through the dense foliage, create delightful effects and one is held spell bound by the rare beauty of it all. All parts of the world apparently had been combed for rare and beautiful plants to make this wonderful garden. These pathways lead one to encounter all kinds of pleasant surprises—grape arbours, orchards, lily ponds and a little villa where the Misses Bowman learned their three R's. One also finds the old plantation bell, a pleasant reminder of the days when thousands of acres were worked by hundreds of slaves.

When the avenues of camellias and azaleas are in bloom and the fragrance of jasmine and sweet olive fill the air, the fanciful tales and stories of ante-bellum days assume reality, and it is easy to believe that such a place with the wealth of those days and hundreds of slaves to do their bidding, existence was indeed far removed from this prosaic work-a-day time of ours.

These ladies will tell you, "It is a beautiful, dear old place, but it takes lots of work to supervise and keep it up, and neither of us are young any more, but we love it."

Share croppers cultivate the land now which for most part brings in the revenue.

As they retrace their steps after showing you where their father had his huge hot-houses for rare plants and roses, in the twilight caused by the overhanging oaks, you realize that old plantation days have not been exaggerated in song and story—only we have not known before how truly beautiful it all was.

Judge Peter Randolph of Virginia and Mississippi.

Miss Sallie Cocke, who married Judge Peter Randolph.

Oak Avenue—Thomas Butler home.

"GREENWOOD MANOR", Plantation home of the Edward Butler family. Built in 1820. Contains rare antiques and a splendid collection of ancestral portraits.

"WAKEFIELD", built for Lewis Stirling in 1833. Constance Rouke, novelist, has dedicated to Miss Helen Allain, a part owner of "Wakefield", his biography of "Audubon".

CHAPTER XXVII.

THE BARROW DYNASTY.

WILLIAM BARROW, of distinguished English ancestry, married on July 8th, 1760, a daughter of Robert Ruffin and Anne Bennett. He became a wealthy planter and was high sheriff of Edgecomb County, North Carolina. He was the father of eight children and died at his Tarborough homestead on January 27, 1787.

In 1798 his widow, Mrs. Olivia Ruffin Barrow, in consultation with her three sons, Bartholomew, John and William, when many of their friends were migrating to Louisiana, decided that they too, would go South. Getting their business affairs in order, and disposing of all their immovable property, converting their lands and improvements into cash, they organized a caravan. First in covered wagons and then on barges they with their chests of gold and silver, furniture and belongings, slaves, came down the Mississippi River through Tennessee to Nuevo Feliciana, then under the domination of the Spanish. On this lengthy, hazardous trip with Mrs. Barrow came three daughters and three sons. Two of her sons who remained in North Carolina later came to Louisiana. Here they took up extensive Spanish grants of land and shortly began to erect splendid plantation mansions. Purchasing other land, their tract soon amounted to seven thousand acres. Many of the splendid plantation homes built by this family still remain.

The first family home was built and named Locust Ridge—which is still standing and renamed later Highland Plantation. It is a large house, simple of line but magnificently constructed of choice cypress lumber. The floors throughout the house are very heavy, in the main rooms being two inches in thickness, and are still in a splendid state of preservation. The rooms of the house are quite large, several of them being 22x24 feet. All of the materials were made on the plantation except the windows and window frames, which were shipped from the North.

Olivia Ruffin Barrow, died April 2nd, 1803, five years after she had settled in West Feliciana, and is buried at what is now Highland Plantation, in the ancient cemetery which lies north of the old manor house. Here she rests with a number of her descendants.

These pioneers, proud descendants of noble English lineage, who settled in Nuevo Feliciana, or "Realm of Happiness" were stars in the brilliant pages of Louisiana history. Their bravery, chivalry, intellect, talent and beauty served the State in good stead.

The children of William Barrow and Olivia Ruffin Barrow, were: (a) William Barrow, born November 29, 1761, died November 27, 1762; (b) Robert Barrow, born Feb. 18th, 1763, died Nov. 9th, 1813—he married Mary Haynes, no children; (c) William Barrow, born Feb. 26th, 1765, died Nov. 9th, 1823. The second William married Pheraby Hilliard, in North Carolina, June 26th, 1792. Pheraby Hilliard was born Feb. 10th, 1775, and died Oct. 10th, 1827. (*See genealogy rear of book.*)

William Ruffin Barrow, born December 21, 1800, died March 22, 1862, was a son of William Barrow and Pheraby Hilliard of Highland Plantation (formerly Locust Grove). He married a cousin, Olivia Ruffin Barrow, who was born April, 1806, died June 1, 1857—who was a daughter of Bennett Barrow and Martha Hill. William Ruffin Barrow became the father of six children by this marriage.

Other plantations belonging to the Barrow family are Ambrosia and Independence owned by Mrs. (widow) Nicolo Hall Barrow, who also owned the old Live Oak plantation home recorded as one of the oldest in that section.

AFTON VILLA.
West Feliciana Parish, Louisiana.

Flow gently, sweet Afton, among thy green braes,
Flow gently, I'll sing thee a song in thy praise;

My Mary's asleep by thy murmuring stream,
Flow gently, sweet Afton, disturb not her dream.

Located in what is known in Louisiana as "Audubon's Land," this quaint old mansion, possesses an individual charm entirely different from that associated with the other great plantation mansions of the state. The original home named "Afton" was an old type Louisiana plantation home, which has been enclosed by this later Gothic Villa structure.

The Barrow brothers, good business men and keen planters, prospered from the first, investing the gold they had brought with them in some of the finest cotton land in Louisiana. Early in 1800 William Barrow purchased the older simple type plantation home and land of John Croker, whose large plantations were near the settlement of St. Francisville ,and in the parish of Pointe Coupee. Later on William sold his brother, Bartholomew, the St. Francisville Plantation (the present Afton Villa) on which was the old house consisting of four large rooms upstairs, and an equal number on the first floor. This first house had been built in a substantial manner by John Croker in 1700. The years passed by and the family grew richer, and in 1820 Bartholomew Barrow sold to his son, David, the plantation and house for $100,000. David Barrow married and by that marriage became the father of two children. His daughter Mary, was a beautiful sentimental young lady, who loved the tender lament of Burns for his Highland lassie, in "Flow Gently Sweet Afton", which she sang so sweetly that her friends and admirers soon began calling the place "Afton" while only the first house was here. Mary was not only very beautiful, with a lovely voice, and a wealthy father, but best of all possessed a charming disposition that made her loved by all. She was the toast of the countryside, and sought in marriage by a throng of the most desirable young men of the South.

Following the example of many of the Barrows, she married her cousin, the handsome, wealthy young Colonel Robert H. Barrow. As a wedding present her father gave her a large plantation, Rosale, well equipped with slaves. Here she reigned as queen, dispensing a lavish hospitality. The home burnt to the ground some years ago. Among a few things saved were two splendid portraits reproduced in this book, fine examples from the brush of Thomas Sully, now in the possession of their grand-daughter, Mrs. Mary Barrow Collins. With the portraits of young Colonel Robert H. Barrow and his wife Mary Barrow, a number of costly pieces of silver were also saved from the flames. From a description of Rosale, it was a splendid example of the Greek Revival type of plantation home. Part of the plantation land is now incorporated in what is known as Beechwood Plantation. After Mary's marriage David Barrow a widower at the time felt the need for companionship, and a wife to care for him and his home, and soon married the beautiful young widow, Mrs. Susan Wolfork Rowan of Kentucky. She later became the mother of two more Barrow children: 1, Florence Barrow who became Mrs. Maximillian Fisher, mother of David B. Fisher of New Orleans, La.

Now David Barrow's young bride, seeing great plantation mansions being built in all parts of the state, being wealthy in her own right, and having a wealthy husband, expressed the desire for a new home in keeping with their wealth and social position. This wish, David Barrow granted, with the proviso that the old mansion in which he and his family had been so happy would not be demolished, but should be incorporated in the new building.

It was the year 1849 and the vogue of French Gothic architecture was beginning to appear in some of the states further North as types of country homes. So instead of selecting the Greek Revival type for their new home Mrs. David Barrow II, selected a design of French Gothic villa, with all of the elaborate detail in evidence at that time. (It is stated that the model selected was a chateau villa in Tours).

A fortune was spent in the remodelling of the place, the French architect and landscape gardener spending years in the completion of the work. True to her promise, the original walls, and framework of roof of the pioneer plantation home remain, and when finished the new appearing mansion held on to the name, becoming Afton Villa, as we know it today. The home became one of the greatest social centers of the South, people coming from Kentucky to attend the great balls and endless series of entertainments.

Another fortune was spent in furnishing the place in keeping with its elaborate architecture. All were chosen with great discretion, as one finds upon seeing remnants of the original furnishings scattered among David Barrow's descendants. In St. Francisville can be seen two handsome Gothic chairs at Grace Church, that were given by Mrs. Barrow's daughter. Originally these carved Flemish oak chairs graced the spacious hallway of Afton Villa. Gorgeous mirrors in handsome real gold leaf frames, crystal chandeliers, cut velvets, brocades, real lace window curtains, in fact all of the costly articles, and art treasures that went to furnish the palatial home of a wealthy planter were to be found here. Music was dedicated to the new chatelain of Afton. The "Afton Villa Waltz", the theme of which is a sad lament, was dedicated to Mrs. Susan Barrow. The descriptions of the great balls, banquets, and soirees read like those held in old castles in Feudal Europe. Afton Villa is rather too elaborate to describe in detail, as the latterday French Gothic usually is, with much carving, etc.

After the Civil War the fortunes of the family being swept away, the place naturally suffered greatly from neglect. When the Union army, bent on burning every Southern mansion passed the place it was saved, because the immense elaborate Gothic gateway, appeared to them as the entrance to a cemetery, instead of the entrance to a plantation home.

Like most of the great plantation homes in Louisiana, Afton Villa has its own cemetery enclosed by elaborate iron work. Here lie a few members of the numerous Barrow family. Buried beside his first wife lies David Barrow, the second Mrs. Barrow being buried in Lexington, Kentucky, the place of her birth. Close by Mr. and Mrs. Barrow are two of their children. Near by lie the graves of the mother and father of Mr. David Barrow. Bartholomew Barrow, his father was born in 1766, and close by is the imposing monument erected by Congress to the memory of Senator Alexander Barrow, an early U. S. Senator who died in office in the year 1846. The senator like many of the Barrow family was noted for his culture, handsome stature and manly beauty.

The gardens of Afton, are beautiful, and the present owners Dr. and Mrs. Robert Lewis, have spent a fortune in restoring Afton Villa and its beautiful garden. They have made of it one of the leading show places of the Feliciana country, and deserve great praise for preserving this relic of the golden era of Louisiana.

ELLERSLIE

Olivia Ruffin Lane, daughter of William Lane and Mary Barrow, born May 16, 1771, married first William Ratcliff, and for her second husband chose William Wade, who with his wife's financial assistance, was able to build lovely Ellerslie, in West Feliciana Parish, Louisiana.

Beautiful and stately of line, occupying a prominent site high up on a bluff in the Tunica hills about ten miles from St. Francisville and far from the highway, it is considered a perfect example of the Classic Revival. It was erected in 1835 for Judge William C. Wade and his family.

Like many another rich planter who came south in the early thirties, Judge Wade, with a caravan, chests of money, a train of slaves and household equipment, joined the throng of Virginians and Carolinians who were settling in Louisiana. Many located in West Feliciana, others on the banks of the Mississippi and still others in the Bayou Lafourche section.

Reaching the West Feliciana area he found a large settlement of distinguished planters and their families, whose mansions bespoke wealth and culture.

Purchasing twelve thousand acres he at once laid out his plantation and built a house, the one we see today. The house cost about one hundred thousand dollars, besides the timber from his land, and a great deal of slave labor in the making and laying of bricks. The facade of the house presents eight long heavy solid brick circular Doric columns supporting a heavy cornice and nicely lined roof surmounted by a balcony enclosed observatory all cement finished.

Completed, Judge Wade furnished his home in a fitting manner, and his family joined the social colony formed by the Barrows, Ratcliffs, Scotts, Lanes, Hamiltons, Perceys, etc. Judge Wade lived only fifteen years to enjoy the beautiful home which he had built. He was buried in the family burial plot to the rear of the house. His wife, who had been Miss Olivia Lane, with his son, inherited the place. Under their skilful management the plantation was continued on a successful basis, until the Civil War broke out, when her son, who had studied medicine, became a surgeon in the Confederate army.

As usual, the house was raided by the Union soldiers and large numbers of the cattle stolen and carried off. With the freeing of the slaves and the immense losses incurred by the war, there was left neither money nor labor to run the plantation and the place began to disintegrate. Mrs. Wade dying first, and her son in 1900, the heirs moved to a smaller home that they were able to maintain. They sold the house and 2,000 acres of land to Edward M. Percy in 1915. Mr. Percy found that the place he had purchased was literally falling into ruin, and set to work at once to have the needed repairs made. He has restored the greater part of the old mansion.

As it stands now it is again quite beautiful and impressive. Ivy clings to the great Doric columns and reaches to the roof. The beautiful circular stairway of San Domingo mahogany is lovely again and the great avenue of oak trees are well cared for. The garden too, shows attention and care, blooming shrubs pour forth their fragrance in return.

The plantation, now a cattle ranch, has become a paying investment, and should be included in a tour of the plantation country.

The New Orleans home of Mrs. Robert Ruffin Barrow, who was Miss Jenny Loviski Tennent, daughter of Charles Tennent, and a great-granddaughter of Governor Gayoso de Lemos, is a veritable museum of beautiful heirlooms of the Barrow, Gayoso, DuBoise and Perez families. Among its prized possessions is the splendid carved Spanish bed used by her noted grandparents, the Gayosos. Beautiful ancestral portraits of this family adorn the walls of the many spacious rooms filled to overflowing with the many choice articles that furnish and adorn this most interesting home. Much of Mrs. Barrow's collection has come from the first Afton Villa, which was originally owned by the father of Robert Ruffin Barrow, Sr., and which later became the home of David Barrow who rebuilt it in its present form when he married a second time.

The following genealogy is found among the family records of Mrs. Robert Ruffin Barrow of New Orleans:

1. Thomas Barrow, a native of Lancaster, England, came to Virginia in 1680. Settled in Southampton County, Virginia, on the Nottaway River where he died when over 90 years of age.

2. A son of the above Thomas Barrow, also named Thomas

Barrow, married Elizabeth Atkinson, and moved to North Carolina.

3. William Barrow, a respected farmer of Brunswick County, Virginia, late in life moved to North Carolina, being a great-great grandfather when he died at the age of 91 years.

4. David Barrow, (great grandfather) born in Brunswick County, Virginia, in 1753.

5. William Barrow, born in Montgomery County, Kentucky, April 17th, 1835, died January 3rd, 1916. Married Elizabeth Floyd Curry, and Adeline Bush, of Clark County, Kentucky.

(From family record of Mrs. Robert Ruffin Barrow, Jr., of New Orleans.)

GREENWOOD PLANTATION MANOR

Built 1830.

Greenwood, the most magnificent example of the Classic Revival architecture in Louisiana, is a poem in architecture. Nowhere in the entire South is there to be found a place so restful and so beautiful. William Ruffin Barrow, cultured gentleman planter, a member of that distinguished family who were to build so many fine homes in Louisiana, came from the Northern part of Carolina to this state and located in West Feliciana Parish shortly after 1803. Selecting a tract of 12,000 acres in the most beautiful section of the Feliciana country, he at once set his slaves to work building brick kilns, cutting lumber and getting ready for the mansion he planned to build.

When completed Greenwood with its twenty-eight massive columns, its wide surrounding porches, its splendid cornice, surmounted by a great observatory, was fine indeed. From this observation post he could readily survey his estate of twelve thousand acres at will, and know what was going on in the various parts of the plantation.

In the center of this great mansion from front to rear extends a very wide hall seventy feet long at the rear of which a splendid mahogany stairway winds to the floor above. A beautiful black marble mantel having Ionic columns, above which was a large mirror in ornate gold leaf frame. This mantel is one of the many lovely ones each of which originally was surmounted by mirrors equally as handsome.

Mrs. Jack Lester in period costume in front of "Waverly", her beautiful plantation home near St. Francisville.

"WAVERLY" Plantation home where Audubon taught dancing to the children of the patrician families of the area.

Greenwood was about four years in building, and quantities of costly wood-work and other materials were brought from the North for the interior finish.

The mansion stood complete according in the year 1831, when attention was given to the additional buildings attached to the plantation. The immediate grounds about the mansion were planned as a deer park with an artificial lake in which the mansion might be reflected. Here grew a variety of water plants among which swans and other aquatic birds sported. Some distance in front of this deer park a private race-track was laid out, and here a great many races with the aristocracy as spectators took place with fortunes changing hands.

Far to the right was laid out the slave village, remote enough from the house to avoid odors being carried from the quarters to the mansion by the wind. Here a hundred brick cabins, a church, a hospital, a place for amusements, baths, etc., needed by such a colony were found. Large sunken brick-lined cisterns dotted the grounds in goodly number to furnish good water at all times. A great coach house, stables, kitchens and smoke house—in fact some forty extra buildings are recorded as being completed according to the original plans. Most of these buildings were constructed of brick, some of Greek Revival design. Like a great English palace in all its glory each formed a part of the original ensemble when Greenwood Plantation stood complete. When the Union soldiers blew up the sugar houses and cotton gins, most of these buildings were destroyed after their contents had been carried away.

When the plantation buildings were all finished, Mr. Barrow and his family gave a series of entertainments that recalled the ones given in the palatial homes of the old Cavalier Families of Carolina and Virginia.

Wealth poured into the coffers of the planters, cotton and sugar bringing fabulous prices, with England clamoring for more cotton for her mills. The great estates of England were being divided making room for the cotton mills that were springing up on all sides. New Orleans, Bayou Sara, Natchez and Vicksburg— all were busy with shipping plantation products and every one apparently making money.

Gradually the war clouds gathered, and Judah P. Benjamin, the able United States Senator from Louisiana also a planter and close friend of the owner of Greenwood Plantation advised Mr. Barrow to dispose of his large holdings even if he had to do it at a great sacrifice. Noting that matters were getting worse, after a consultation with the different members of his family Mr. Barrow decided to follow his friend's advice. Finding Major Reed anxious to possess Greenwood, reserving a few articles, he sold the place intact to Major Reed who with his son, an able planter, was able to hold on to Greenwood Plantation until the latter part of the war. Learning that plantations were being swept clean of their contents and the mansions burned by the advancing Union Army, and realizing that Greenwood's turn would soon come, Major Reed sold what cattle and other products that he could. But to protect his beautiful home and its contents seemed an impossible task. Finally he had all of his valuable possessions boxed and crated and shipped to New Orleans where they were put in storage. After the fall of New Orleans Ben Butler seized all the movable property he desired, shipping immense quantities of solid silver table services, barrels of silver spoons (gaining for him the name of "Silver Spoon" Butler) and other valuables to the North. Confiscating the contents of banks, he proceeded to claim bank funds out in the state.

As the Federal troops advanced upon Greenwood, the owner having learned that his belongings stored in the city had been confiscated by General Butler, felt sure that Greenwood would be burned, and he fled to a thicket to watch the destruction of his beautiful home. But after viewing the mansion the Union Officers decided that it would make a good hospital, so spared the building. But everything that could be carried away from the plantation was taken. With the freeing of the slaves, it was impossible to maintain such an enormous place. The Reeds finally seeing no possibility of holding on to it, disposed of the mansion and estate to the present owners Mr. and Mrs. Frank Percy. They have restored the place to its present beautiful condition, and furnished it splendidly with appropriate belongings and many fine antiques, many of them heirlooms from both sides of their families.

The Percy family, another distinguished plantation family of the Feliciana area, is related to many noted families in the state. They are a cultured people, descending from Robert Percy of Shenandoah Valley, who built Beechwood Manor which he had laid out in 1804 on Little Bayou Sara, then a thriving place. Beechwood Manor has been replaced with a simpler country home and is at the present the country residence of Mr. and Mrs. J. Hereford Percy who live in Baton Rouge, Louisiana. In olden days Beechwood Plantation was a rallying ground for the patrician families of the vicinity. Its history is closely interwoven with that of Audubon, and with the romance of beautiful, vivacious Eliza Pirrie, who eloped with her cousin, the handsome young Robert Hilliard Barrow, son of the man for whom magnificent Greenwood manor was built. After the elopement Audubon who had been teaching Miss Pirrie, left Oakley, Miss Pirrie's plantation home, and became the tutor of the Percy children. Mrs. Audubon later enjoyed the hospitality of the Percy family while the naturalist sought a publisher in London.

Greenwood manor has been restored beautifully, and it has again become one of the most charming plantation homes in Louisiana.

CHAPTER XXVIII.

PLANTATIONS OF THE BUTLER FAMILY.

THE COTTAGE PLANTATION.

BUTLER HOME.

West Feliciana Parish, Louisiana.

HIDDEN away deep in the woods some seven miles from St. Francisville and far away from the main highway, The Cottage is built upon a great burnt sienna colored bluff—the trail's end of a long sandy road leading to the house.

At Catalpa P. O. the distance from the highway is about a mile. On the way one crosses Alexander Creek, which like the Homochito Bayou, following prolonged rains assumes the size of an angry stream of sufficient height to isolate this charming old domicile.

The road from the highway is through a woodland country somewhat like that around lovely Old Oakley Plantation Manor, but at times the road to The Cottage becomes a trail. One is well rewarded for the journey, for at the Cottage as at Oakley, one finds the unpretentious old home filled to overflowing with a rare collection of historical and artistic treasures.

In 1811 Judge Thomas Butler, from whom this prominent branch of the "Fighting Butlers" stem, located in this parish and purchased the plantation. He obtained two tracts of land, which the Spanish Crown according to the aged yellowed paper worded in Spanish and bearing the signature of Governor Hector de Carondelet, granted to John Allen and to Patrick Holland in the year 1785.

True to the blood, many of these Butlers have been prominent personages. In this home still live Mr. Robert Butler and his sister Miss Louise Butler, the prominent Louisiana Historian, who with their old negro servants, continue to maintain a gay and interesting life in this old Spanish plantation home deep in the woods. Miss Butler's writings are highly prized by the Louisiana Historical Society, for at no time does she permit the romantic to cloud the varacity of her statements. What she writes is authentic, and recognized historians hold her articles in high esteem for that reason.

The Cottage is undoubtedly one of the most charming old plantation houses in the entire Southland. Its history is also interesting. Constructed originally along the substantial, unpretentious lines of provincial Spanish plantation homes in 1811, and added to from time to time by competent builders who retained the original lines in their additions, it is harmonious and pleasing in its simplicity. The woodwork within, as is generally the case in Spanish houses, is simple in design for most part, and shows the handiwork of finished craftsmen. Throughout the house the mullioned transomed windows, hand-carved doors, built-in cabinets, panelling, and unusually handsome wooden mantels are all the work of experienced cabinet makers and wood carvers.

Especially is this the case in the original house where an air of elegance marks the finish of the rooms. The salle or parlour is a rather large room of great distinction. It is a period-room of about 1811, being in great part as it was originally, its draperies having much in common with the beautiful ones in the drawing room at Greenwood Manor the charming home of Mrs. Edward Butler. The handsome furnishings are original, and like those of the Edward Butler home, one is impressed at once by their quaint beauty. The rooms possess the restfulness not obtained where the reproduction of an old room has been attempted. A color scheme of old ashy reds predominate, forming a splendid setting for the pieces of fine old carved rosewood and mahogany furniture, and the paintings of old masters in their handsome real gold leaf frames of a century ago, the freshness not dimmed by the passing years. There are splendid chairs and sofas in their original French and English brocades—individual chairs of beautiful design. There are cabinets and whatnots, all filled with exceptionally rare pieces of bric-a-brac—Dresden, Sevres Doulton, Limoge and endless other pieces equally as fine that were collected in olden days, when European tours were made yearly. The brocatelle designed Brussels carpet matching in tones the voluminous handsome window drapes is as beautiful as when placed in this room a century ago and one marvels at its splendid condition.

In the rear of this attractive drawing-room is the library and music room combined. Here originally was one of the choicest collection of rare books to be found in a section noted for its fine libraries. A large size organ handsomely designed with gilded pipes forms a center of attraction in another room, and opening as it does into the salle, contrasts pleasingly, the immense panelled doors giving a typically Spanish appearance to the room. Among the innumerable articles in this home are dozens that are museum pieces. Of marked interest are the immense Audubon prints (First Editions), an old curio console, and an immense mahogany couch of colonial design nine feet long that would make the heart of a collector glad—it is massive in construction and long enough to seat the entire squad of "Fighting Butlers", at a time and still have ample room for Andrew Jackson.

A number of old mahogany bookcases of good design are filled with rare volumes, most of them having costly bindings, a number of them first editions. Among these volumes is an elephant edition of "The Costumes of Ancient England and Ireland", a magnificent book of its kind. It is profusely illustrated, each of the steel engraved plates colored by hand with the exquisite illumination and perfection of detail found in old missals. These books were retained by the family from the priceless library of several thousand volumes that were collected by the great soldier-statesman, owner of this home. At present it is a part of the fine collection of the Louisiana State University Library and is kept together under the name of the Thomas Butler Collection.

In the dining-room the Hero of Chalmette and his staff of officers, with eight "Fighting Butlers" amongst them, dined and wined during their stay at "The Cottage" enroute to Natchez, after the Battle of New Orleans. In this stately room are magnificent pieces of ancient dark oak furniture elegantly carved, the massive buffet of attractive design with an upper glazed section containing rare pieces of Wedgewood, Spode, Chelseaware, and much fine old Irish and English crystal ware. The matched pieces of the dining-room set and large table are all splendid antiques of great beauty, and complete a most attractive room. The andirons are all solid brass, slave-made and somewhat unusual.

The bed-rooms all have high ceilings, and some of the mahogany four-posters are ten feet high with heavy cornices. The rest of the furniture of the rooms is equally as attractive forming stately chambers wherein have slept distinguished visitors.

The treasures of this interesting home go back to Europe of past centuries, some coming through marriage into other prominent families, brought from abroad by members of the family and admiring friends. All are in harmony with the restful unpretentious surroundings. Above the stairs by way of the hallway what appears to be the attic is in reality a series of rooms ample in size, used in olden days when the family was larger. They are equally as well finished as those on the first floor. All have fine antique furniture, elaborately carved four-post beds, etc.

The estate is almost a village in itself, with its many and varied buildings which always have been kept in good repair and well painted. In the old carriage house, along with two antiquated buggies, is the ancient state carriage built in Philadelphia specially for Captain Richard Butler at a cost of one thousand dollars. This was in the year 1808, when he bought the plantation home in St. Charles Parish which he named Ormonde, purchasing it from the widow of Captain de Trapagnier who was kidnapped some time before. Madame de Trapagnier later married a Monsieur de Macarty, member of the prominent New Orleans family.

In the house are vast quantities of tokens, mementos, old letters—affectionate and dramatic—ancient documents of every description. There are nine trunks full of them, containing a world of data about the Butler family and dozens of other prominent families of the State. All this material was collected for most part by Miss Louise Butler, the gracious chatelain of The Cottage.

In the rear of The Cottage Plantation garden grounds is found a brick enclosure with an attractive iron gate, and here lie many members of the Butler family. White marble headstones mark their resting places, all neatly cared for. It is fittingly located among the trees, and the birds with their cheery song somehow make of it a place devoid of gloom.

THE EDWARD BUTLER PLANTATION HOME,
GREENWOOD PLANTATION AND MANOR,
FIRST REBUILT 1820.

In a group of historic old plantation homes we find an unpretentious one, which replaces the beautiful Manor house built for Dr. Samuel Flower and his family. Dr. Flower came to Feliciana in 1778, when the country was in the making. The second house was further added to in 1850, when a number of white marble mantels were substituted for the wooden ones then in use, leaving the house as we see it today—a comfortable, rambling, interesting home.

A long and pleasing driveway leads from the Woodville Road to the gateway which opens onto a splendid wooded park with sunken garden and other attractive features that are generally found on a large estate. An odor of pines mingles with the fragrance of cape jasmine and sweet olive, for this is an old fashioned garden retaining all of its ante-bellum charm. Great trees are everywhere, which at midday create strong contrasts with their varied hues in the bright sunshine. On moon-light nights while the leaves are still on the trees, if one is in the right mood, in the imagination, one can see the great park peopled with shades of the many distinguished men and lovely ladies that in days long past made merry here, when life appeared like a long holiday, leaving capable overseers to attend to the plantation details.

It is true if you investigate too closely these shades of the ancient gentry may turn out to be only flitting shadows. But watch some night when fragrant breezes stir the air and set the leaves to dancing, and you will see willowy ladies in wide spreading crinolines treading the step of a dance with gallant swains, perhaps in the whirl of a dreamy waltz. Then the great lawn becomes a gala ball-room floor and the park a plantation drawing-room. Of course to visualize these things, one must know the history of this old home, or be told about its olden days in the time when those whose beautiful portraits now adorn its walls walked and roamed about these grounds, gathering flowers or enjoying themselves in various ways.

This is "The land of Audubon" and one can readily understand why, for the air is filled with bird song, and the feathery songsters nest above the wide stairway leading up to the roomy

Volumnia Huntley, who married Robert Ruffin
Barrow, Sr., and her daughter, Roberta Barrow,
who married 1st, W. J. Slatter of Winchseter, Tenn.,
and secondly Albert Woods. (From an oil portrait
painted by Amans, and owned by Mrs. W. J. Gui-
dery. Courtesy of Mrs. Robert R. Barrow, Jr., of
New Orleans.)

Mrs. Jeanne Catherine DuBoise, who married Don Manuel Perez.

Don Manuel Perez. Courtesy of Mrs. Robert R. Barrow, Jr.

THE MYRTLES, built for the Stirling family. Located near the "Greenwood Manor", home of the Edward Butler family. (See Vol. II.)

porch which stretches across the front of the house. The main
entrance hall with an attractive winding stair in the rear leading
to the apartments above, is a large hallway in keeping with the
rooms of the house. Family portraits of past generations painted
by distinguished artists of a century ago adorn the walls. Above
a handsome large antique claw foot mahogany sofa, hangs a life-
size portrait of Mrs. Harriet Flower, portraying this lady as she
appeared later in life, while on the opposite wall is a three-quarter
size portrait of Judge George Mathews, a replica of which hangs
in the portrait gallery of the Louisiana Historical Society. This
fine unsigned portrait is attributed to Jarvis, a distinguished
portrait painter of ante-bellum days.

Distinctive pieces of furniture, all genuine antiques owned
by generations past, are placed about the hall. The drawing-
room to the right as you face the garden is English in style. In
the rear of the English drawing-room we find a remarkably fine
old concert grand Pleyel piano, of a very graceful design with
brass inlays. No doubt it was made for display, for it is one of
the finest ever made by that celebrated French piano factory.

In this room we find more fine old family portraits by
Armand, Sully and others equally as famous, in fact this lovely
old home, like charming Oakley manor, has a fine collection of
ancestral portraits all of them painted by distinguished artists.
Here again is much quaint rosewood and mahogany furniture,
Sevres vases, century-old ornaments of unusually beautiful shape
and coloring, along with other articles such as lap desks inlaid,
fanciful curio boxes, gaming tables, etc. In the rear of this room
is the library, a room that a lover of Audubon would revel in, for
on the walls are many fine old Audubon prints, all first editions—
those that were first printed and sold to subscribers to enable him
to publish his elephant edition of the "Birds of America". A
large case of stuffed birds of various kinds mounted by a man
who was taxidermist for the naturalist, hangs above a large antique desk, and all about this interesting room are mementos of
the great lover of birds.

The dining-room is large as most plantation dining-rooms
are, and is a treasure house of beautiful and interesting things
each one a relic of old plantation days, when this community
could boast of being one of the most cultured as well as aristocratic in America. The furniture of this room is mostly ma-

hogany of the early Victorian period before it fell under the influence of the East-Lake style, which became popular during the latter part of her Majesty's reign. It is distinctly European, a style that was reproduced by Signorette and Prudence Mallard in their studios in New Orleans. The dining-room chairs have spindle or balustraded backs and are unusually attractive in design, while the sideboard and buffets are handsome with their crouch panelling. Both are laden with rare china, fine Irish and English crystal, and pieces of extremely fine silver with full molded grape design beautifully finished by hand after removal from the molds. In reality many of the articles in this home are museum pieces. Attractive mantel sets, other ancestral portraits add to the interest of this room, while large fruit baskets filled with luscious-looking peaches, grapes and other tempting fruit give a practical touch to a room that is put to daily use.

The drawing-room like the one at "The Cottage" (Butler Home) could be used as a model of the best period of Louis Philippe, devoid of the Empire "mixture" we so often find. The drawing-rooms in the Butler homes are somewhat distinctive, and different from the drawing-rooms one usually sees in the finer old plantation homes of Louisiana and Mississippi. Not that they are more elaborate, but they have a European touch in their decoration while others have less of that European distinction. Especially are their window draperies captivating and they create an individual atmosphere. To the admirer of olden periods they are the appropriate hangings to bring out the beauty of the various articles in these handsome drawing-rooms. The unusually attractive carpet with center medallion is much like some that we see in fine old Virginia homes. In this room again we find ancestral portraits of beautiful women and handsome men, a distinct one is the life-sized three-quarter length portrait of Mrs. Penelope Stewart Mathews, daughter of Colonel Tignal Jones Stewart, and wife of Charles Lewis Mathews. This portrait was painted by Amand, who also painted another one of this lady's sister in a slightly different pose, but in the same size as that which now hangs in the attractive nearby plantation home of her daughter's family, the Thomas Butlers. The portrait of Charles Lewis Mathews, son of Judge George Mathews which hangs in the hall, was also painted by Thomas Sully, while on the mantel of the drawing-room is a portrait of the son of Charles Lewis

Mathews by Amand. There is also a portrait of Charles Stewart by Amand, and another fine portrait of Mrs. Harriet Flower, as a very beautiful young lady (wife of Judge Mathews). It too, was painted by Amand.

In 1850 when other changes were made in the house, the fine white marble mantels were put in, replacing the original wooden ones. A tall pier mirror of the Louis Philippe period overlaid with gold leaf—the handsome frame is as beautiful as it was the day it was placed in this home nearly a century ago—adds great dignity to the room and reflects the many attractive articles in it. Filling an opposite wall panel is a fine large rosewood etagerre on which are many pieces of bric-a-brac, the most attractive piece being a large Limoge china fruit basket of gold open work, supported by two kneeling angels on a base finished in Roman gold—a most rare and attractive piece. It is an heirloom, as are the figurines, antique lamps and hurricane shades. Each helps to make a satisfactory picture of a drawing-room of a wealthy and cultured family of a century ago.

The original brick outside kitchen of the first Greenwood manor stands some distance from the house. It is an attractive building of simple lines, much in use when the banquets for which this old plantation was famous were prepared.

CATALPA PLANTATION
(No longer standing)

Catalpa, a rambling, roomy, comfortable old house in the midst of its fascinating garden, a house in which the old families of the vicinity loved to gather—"there is always such a good time to be had at the Fort's," was the saying by both young and old who enjoyed its hospitalities.

Built in the days when the Felicianas were one and the best blood of the country seemingly sent representatives to perpetuate names with valor, honor and distinction behind them. Such were the builders of Catalpa and this old plantation that holds such pleasant memories for the surviving members of the family and their friends.

The Forts came from Carolina and as was customary once having finished their manor, filled it first of all with treasured heirlooms, old family portraits, family silver, crystal and china, along with fine miniatures, painted by noted artists.

This home, the center of life on the old plantation, was a scene of endless gaiety. Vivacious daughters, equally as beautiful and charming as their lovely mother, whose own youth had been a constant series of social triumphs, presided at balls, receptions, banquets, hunting parties, etc. In this prosaic age for those unfamiliar with life as led on an ante-bellum plantation, it is hard to visualize the gay and joyous life led by these favored people.

Charming ladies and gentlemen still in our midst living in homes filled with much of the artistic treasures remaining from the days of which I write, confirmed in their own reminiscences the glories of the era before the Civil War, which wrecked this land once so prosperous. We know that what they tell us of this past era is true.

Mrs. Thomas Butler, a grande dame of the old regime, who passed away a short time ago at the age of eighty-three, in her reminiscences writes of her parents' plantation and their lovely old home:

CATALPA.

Catalpa, one of the most beautiful places in West Feliciana parish, was owned by Mr. and Mrs. W. J. Fort, who were married in the early forties and being artisitic in their natures and lovers of the beautiful, made it their life work and pleasure to create this lovely and most attractive home, all accomplished with their own slaves under their direction and guidance.*

The gardens and grounds comprised about 38 acres (without plantation lands) of level and rolling land, the house, a large old fashioned Southern home situated in the center of the grounds.

The front entrances through two gateways, about 300 yards apart, opening into two most picturesque winding live oak avenues leading up to the house. These wide gravelled avenues were bordered with large pink lined conch shells, producing a lovely and unusual effect.

It is interesting to note that these shells were washed from time to time by the slaves.

North and South of the house, as far as the eye could reach, was a perfect landscape of flowers, shrubs of every variety, grass plots and white gravelled walks, intervening, leading through the lawns.

----

* Among the Fort slaves were expert carpenters, brick masons, and skilled mechanics generally costing as much as $5,000.00 each.

"LOCUST RIDGE", later called "Highland" Plantation, was erected about 1800, the first home built by the Barrow family in Louisiana.

"ROSEDOWN" Manor with a garden-party in full swing.

"AFTON VILLA", West Feiiciana Parish, built in 1849 for the second Mrs. David Barrow.

Old Elleslie Plantation Mansion. Containing much that is interesting in the way of antiques and family portraits.

"Greenwood Plantation Mansion", built in 1830 for William Ruffin Barrow, I. In its setting it is the most magnfiicent example of the Greek Revival in the South.

Bennett Barrow. (From a picture at the Highlands Plantation.)

Capt. John Barrow, son of Bennett Barrow of Highland.

Robert Ruffin Barrow I. (Courtesy of Mrs. Robert Ruffin Barrow II.)

Robert Ruffin Barrow II. (Courtesy of Mrs. Robert R. Barrow, Jr.)

Lodiska Perez.

Volumnia Huntley as a young girl. (Courtesy of Mrs. R. R. Barrow, Jr.)

A large fish pond attracted the eye on the North, with a fountain in the center, and swans swimming around an island, with small trees and grass was most alluring for picnics and fish-frys, skiffs and boats a means of conveyance. A smaller island, covered with reeds, was the home and nesting place for ducks. Two large pigeon houses, (typical pigeonnaires as was customary flanking either side of the mansion) overlooking the pond.

North and South, supplying a plentiful lot of squabs, and on the level side a long line of Lombardy poplars added to this beautiful view.

Fondly recalling the memory of those happy years spent on this lovely old plantation, so rich in pleasant memories to all of this charming family who survive, she continues:

I miss those old days—I have heard many a friend say, some of the happiest days of their lives were spent on that old pond.

Near by was a fair sized deer park, most interesting to the young people; this park was also frequented by gorgeous colored peafowl.*

It is needless to say this was the most attractive part of the grounds. Now we will turn to the South of the house, through rose bordered creeks we come to the green house, a magnificent structure of glass and of unusual dimensions. At one end grew a large orange tree, bearing fruit; and at the other end a clump of banana trees bearing delicious bananas. In the center was a large stage with lovely flowering pot-plants of great variety, and through the entire length of the green-house overhead clustering vines with gorgeous blooms, a feast for humming-birds. A latticed walk extended around the stage, the warm air from the furnace coming up through the openings and permeating the atmosphere with warmth and fragrance. Tropical plants, tea, coffee, cinnamon, guava, mandarins and many other kinds grew around the borders; it was indeed a fascinating bit of fairy-land. Mr. Fort bening well versed in floriculture as well as in architecture; this green-house was the wonder and admiration of all who saw it. The genii who presided over all this beauty was an intelligent negro slave. He had charge of all the flowers and decorations when entertainments were given and his artistic arrangements elicited admiration and surprise.

The writer remembers him so vividly, a pompous old negro with a bald head and roll of white hair surrounding it, standing at the green-house door, ushering in "Company" with great ceremony, show-them around and giving as he thought the botanical names of the

---

* On almost all of the more important plantations peafowl were to be found and still are to be seen on many of them.

plants. This had a comic side, of course, but his dignity was such that no sign of amusement was shown. But we cannot tarry too long in this fascinating bit of tropical land, for outside new vistas of beauty await the eye. Far down the lawn spreads a green carpet, I visiualize a picture of old Father Time his scythe (The old gardener) an old bent slave mowing the grass with ceaseless and perfect rhythm, having a beautiful sward, with blooming flower-beds and foliage of diferent hues. Here and there are cosy nooks with iron chairs and sofas, and in sunny spaces an old fashioned sun-dial. We pause to listen to the singing of birds, riotously happy for they feared neither traps or guns; and the swarms of bees, flying hither and thither, laden with sweets for the bee-hive—an humble tenant of every old time garden. Here is the "Old South", too beautiful to last. But we cannot dream too long, there is the beautious little summer house, just below festooned with the purple drapery of wisteria vine, a large cistern underneath, supplying water for the flowers. This was a most attractive place, as there were seats around, and ice-cream and fruits were often served there in summer. What added immensely to the view was a patch-work garden of animals extending from the side, and truly the flower catalogue must have been rifled to supply this beauty and color. Just above this garden was a long line of brick cement pits for growing pineapples and 'forcing vegetables. It was said that there were deciduous fruits, one can hardly realize it now, pears, peaches, plums, and nectarines with a variety of figs and luscious melons. The writer remembers seeing luscious pears gathered by the cotton baskets.

The poultry yards invite our interest, here was variety, the flocks of turkeys, tended by "Espy" a little negro girl and herded to pastures ever new. The great delight of visiting old Aunt Winnie and Uncle Derry (the old slaves) who raised the ducks and who lived in the little hut just down the slope, where a stream of water ran, ideal for ducks and for children too (so thought these youngsters in those days).

The old couple always had something for the children from the "big house" strings of chinquapins, tiny ears of red pop-corn (which seems to have lost out since the Civil War) and bitter fancy gourds, all bringing thrills of delight to the young folks.

Again this grand dame of ante-bellum days, who was a little girl when the storm of war broke, recalling her happy childhood and the loyalty of the old-time darkie who realized what their master's protection meant said:

Those were happy days, showing the pliability and adaptability of the old-time slave, whose great incentive was to please the appreciative Master and Mistress.

So true the saying—"A good master made good slaves". The owners of this lovely home lived many years to enjoy their beautiful creations, but alas! the cruel war came on and ruin and wreckage followed in its wake. Mr. Fort died about that time: most of the slaves grew panic-stricken and fled; (When they saw how plantation mansion after plantation mansion were burned, and how the slaves were being put into corrals and kept there like cattle by the Union soldiers when they would not turn against their masters. How they were dying of Typhoid fever and other diseases, uncared for after the Union troops had driven them off of the various plantations.)

Gateways and fences were torn down by bands of soldiers, letting in cattle, for horses and all destructive elements, trampling and destroying. The green-house was shattered: neglect and ruin everywhere met the eye, where a few months before such beauty and symmetry reigned.

Mrs. Fort with her family of young children passed through the trying vicissitudes of this fearful war, with the courage and bravery displayed by many Southern women, never deserting her home, rearing and educating her children under great difficulties, and living to a good old age, surrounded by her children and grand-children, who now own Catalpa, and served by a few of the faithful servants who never deserted the family and their old Missus.

It is interesting to add that Mrs. Fort, though blind the last years of her life, never lost her artistic tastes and magic touch with flowers as well as music.

As the gracious lady who has penned these memories of her childhood sat reading the original manuscript surrounded by so much that recalled the past, one could perceive a slight tremor in her soft modulated voice and see her gentle eyes grow misty. For again she was transported as in a dream to those glorious days of old, and again for a moment became a little girl with sisters and playmates on the old plantation feeding the peacocks and swans of dear old Catalpa. Across the hall opposite the room in which Mrs. Butler sat while reading, above the mantel hangs a life-size portrait of a lovely young woman painted by the celebrated Belgian portrait painter, Amans. It is the portrait of Mrs. Fort in all her youth and beauty. Continuing her memoirs we read:

Now a lingering good-bye to Catalpa of the olden days, it is past and gone like its creators and lives only in the memory of a few who were fortunate enough to enjoy its rare beauty and gracious hospitality. Time brings us to the Catalpa of today, still beautious with its fine old park of forest trees. Time and seasons multiplying new growths. The pond is still there like an old landmark, shrunken with age, only a few scattered shrubs of camelias, japonicas, that queen of flowers, once firmly rooted in the soil, defies even the elements of war. A modern house stands where the old one was burned years ago, and I must add, traces of the old home hospitality and good cheer linger around still.

> A last farewell to those old days—
> Far down the flight of time
> In some dim halls of memory
> Those bright visions shine
> And flit like phantom shadows
> Through dreams of happy mind.

Four Generations. Mr. Jules Labatut, who married Miss Clelie Ranson. Mrs.
Olivier O. Provosty (neé Euphemie Labatut), daughter of Jules Labatut and Clelie
Ranson.

In White.—Mrs. John F. Tobin, (neé Eliska Paule Provosty), daughter of Mr. Olivier
O. Provosty and Euphemie Labatut.

Baby.—John William Tobin II, son of John F. Tobin and Eliska Provosty.

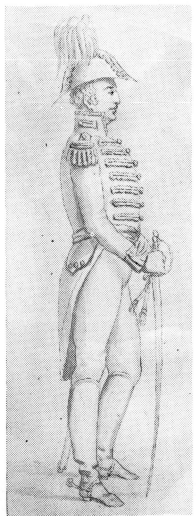

General Jean Baptiste Labatut

Old Labatut Plantation Home.

old Plantation
Kitchen

CHAPTER XXIX.

IN THE FALSE RIVER SECTION.

THE OLD LABATUT PLANTATION HOME

Built for Evarist de Barra.

AT first glance the ancient plantation home on the west bank of the Mississippi River above New Roads, La., built for Don Evarist de Barra, a Spanish nobleman who came to Louisiana during the Spanish regime, appears to be just another of the many old plantation homes still to be found in Louisiana. However, the student of architecture sees that it is an old plantation home built on charming lines. It is very much larger than one would judge it to be from a casual glance, and its details are many and beautiful and well worth preserving.

The fan-transomed sidelighted doors front and rear are of a very attractive design, and are placed in the center upstairs and downstairs in the front and rear with good effect. Smaller fan lights again above the French windows with blinds, attractive dormers, balustrades and a dozen other architectural features form a notable ensemble, and in earlier days the house must have been quite beautiful. The lower floor is built of brick with a heavy cement coating while the second story is of frame construction. In the rear instead of the porch extending across the entire length from side to side, rooms occupy part of the space on both sides, and a balcony occupies the central area with charming effect. Below a stairway leads to the second floor and a court encloses a part of the large rear area.

The ancient home was erected over one hundred and fifty years ago, and at present is seen at a somewhat disadvantage, for the hungry river has gradually eaten away the front land and the River Road is now quite close to the house, separated only by a neat picket fence. An old photograph belonging to a member of the family shows the house while it still retained much of its land frontage with a grove of huge oak trees, and it was a charming place indeed. The grove of great oaks that originally fronted the place is gone, and the levee now in front reaches nearly as high as the porch of the second story.

A series of well designed Doric-capped circular columns are to be found front and rear, above which graceful collonettes reach to the eaves. The old place was built for most part by the slaves belonging to the old Spanish nobleman with cypress lumber and bricks prepared on his land. The doors, windows, window-blinds, transoms (fanlights) and other special woodwork, with the mantels and glazed doors and windows, were brought from the north on flat-boats.

There is a wide central hallway, quite wide upstairs and down, and on the upper floor four large bed-rooms and cabinets, while on the ground floor are parlor, dining room, and two pantries. The kitchen laundry and what were originally quarters for house slaves are in a separate building as was the plantation custom.

Jean Baptiste Labatut, of patrician birth, came to Louisiana in 1781, and married Marie Felecite Saint-Martin. He became attorney-general of the Cabildo under the Spanish regime, and was made treasurer of the city of New Orleans when Louisiana was transferred back from Spain to France.

When the colony became part of the United States and the English invaded Louisiana, Labatut was appointed an aid to General Andrew Jackson with the rank of general and was given charge of the defense of New Orleans, acquitting himself with honor. His son Jean Pierre Labatut married Euphemie Barra, a sister of Don Evariste Barra, the Spanish nobleman for whom the old plantation house described here was built.

In the St. Louis Cathedral in New Orleans before the Civil War a marriage ceremony was performed which united at the same mass Lise Ranson and Clelie Ranson, both daughters of Zenon Ranson who had married Adele Labatut, a daughter of

General Jean Baptiste Labatut—Lise marrying Emile Fossier and Clelie marrying Jules Labatut. Zenon Ranson was an immensely wealthy Louisiana planter, and as a wedding gift in keeping with his wealth, as was the custom among opulent planter families— each of his daughters received a dot of one hundred thousand dollars. The wedding reception was one of the most important social events of that year in the plantation country, and terminated with a ten-day house party on the Ranson plantation, given by the parents of the bride to the wedding party.

A daughter of Clelie (Mrs. Jules Labatut) became the wife of Justice O. O. Provosty of the Supreme Court of Louisiana; their children were: (1) Olive Provosty, wife of Edward Carrere; (2) Adina Albertina, wife of Ulysse Marinoni; (3) Eliska Paule, who married John F. Tobin; (4) Andre Provosty, who married Clifton P. Walker; (5) Michel Provosty, City Attorney of New Orleans.

Lise Ranson and Emile Fossier became the parents of Stanislaus Fossier who married Albertine d'Hemecourt J. Fossier, their children are: (1) Walter S. Fossier; (2) D'Hemecourt J. Fossier; (3) Albert Fossier, M. D.

To the ancient plantation home of the old Don Evariste Barra came shortly after the Civil War, Jules Labatut with his wife who had been Miss Clelie Ranson, and their four oldest children Clelie Labatut, Euphemie Labatut, (Mrs. O. O. Provosty), Emanuel Labatut and Albert Labatut, all born in New Orleans, their youngest children were born in this old plantation house. To the union of Albert Labatut and Valentine Dayries, who were married in 1900, were born ten children, their first two in this plantation home; (1) Jules Labatut; (2) Celuta Labatut; (3) Emanuel Labatut; Anita Labatut (deceased); Eugene Labatut, Francis Labatut, Cidalise Labatut (who became Sister Marie Adele of St. Joseph's Academy); Laurence Labatut; Eliska Labatut, (Mrs. J. E. Gondeau of Baton Rouge, La.), and Virginia Labatut.

False River in the Parish of Pointe Coupee, Louisiana, was originally an auxiliary channel of the Mississippi River which was cut off in 1722. The country along the isolated river, now in reality a lake, and the section of land in its embrace is called the Island. It is delightfully picturesque. The scenery on all sides is charming. There are moss-hung oaks in groves, singly and forming archways. Water hyacinths and willows edge the river, above whose bank a fine highway winds on past one of the oldest plantation settlements of the state. Many of the homes were erected for families bearing aristocratic names, and are still the roof-tree of their descendants. The town of New Roads, a rather busy place for its size, lies on the road to Morganza and the settlements further along the highway.

LAKESIDE PLANTATION

Above West Baton Rouge, La.

This old plantation takes its name from the lake-like section of the river in front of the plantation. It is an imposing brick structure of two stories with an attic—the massive house raised high on a well finished basement. Unlike the plantation mansions one usually finds in Louisiana, Lakeside, or the Bachelor Place as it is sometimes called, is built in the sophisticated style of urban homes, instead of that of the usual plantation house. The bricks used in its construction, and the elaborate cast-iron work, of which there is the greatest quantity, came from Pennsylvania, for the place was erected shortly before the Civil War.

Lakeside is constructed in a splendid manner and cost a large sum. It is beautifully finished within, having fine marble mantels in all of the principle rooms. The house has many elaborate balconies of cast iron, with heavy iron columns, recalling many of the similar ones in the Garden District of New Orleans. The high basement is as well finished as the upper part of the house, and serves as living quarters, for this is a plantation where weekend parties form a part of the social season. The oaks are numerous and beautiful, and are a splendid setting for the old mansion, over which a riot of climbing vines twine with abandon.

THE LEJEUNE PLANTATION HOME

New Roads, Louisiana.

As one drives through the town of New Roads in Pointe Coupee Parish, a little beyond the Court House far back in large grounds, now a part of the town, can be seen an ancient plantation house. At present in its new coat of white paint, it appears quite attractive, as its garden with large lawn and great trees is well kept.

Unfortunately the original dormers facing the road have been replaced by the more modern method of affording space in the attic. This change gives the house a modern appearance, and detracts somewhat from the quaintness of the old mansion.

The history of the place goes back to the early part of the eighteen hundreds. At that time the plantation was bought by Francois Samson and on the site of this house he built a two-storied plantation home for himself and his family. This house remained until 1856, when as many of the planters who had made money were doing, Mr. Samson decided to build a finer home.

At that time a newly-arrived builder, Francois Avernant, from Bordeaux, anxious to show his ability, told Mr. Samson that he would build his new house at a very reasonable cost. Mr. Samson agreed to the proposition, and the first house was at once demolished, and work soon started on the new. Avernant took a year to complete the house, as everything about the building was of the best.

The elaborate transom frames of the various doorways, the ornate mouldings, and other carved woodwork was all done by hand, nothing but the finest cypress lumber being used. The result was an unusually attractive house within as well as without. During construction Avernant was often criticized because of the time that was being spent on this elaborate carving, but the builder only replied that the house would be there in generations to come. Today with but few small changes, the old plantation house is exactly as it was when completed.

It is a spacious home of the modified early Louisiana type with large rooms and high ceilings, and wide porches front and rear, having stairways to both porches. The rear porch closed forms a large summer living-room. The dining-room which is quite large, the pantry and kitchen, besides wine cellar and other store-rooms occupy the basement floor with exposed beam ceilings. The parlour, as the French called their living room, is a large rectangular room with an attractive hand-carved mantel of good design. A number of roomy bedrooms on either side are equally as well finished, all with fine hand-carved mantels. A large quantity of well-designed antiques of rosewood and mahogany, are scattered about the various rooms—roomy sofas, arm chairs, cabinets, quaint tables, mantel mirrors and a quantity of

ancient bric-a-brac. Great four-posters with dressers and com-
modes to match, also immense wardrobes are in each room.

The Lejeune house has changed little in a century. When
the builder, Mr. Francois Avernant, an extremely religious man
completed the house, he presented Mr. Samson with a framed
carved statute of St. Francis of Assisi, both frame as well as
statue carved by himself, requesting that the statue always be left
in the house, and so it has remained until the present day. Shortly after the house was completed the builder from Bordeaux died
and was buried in the New Roads cemetery.

Mr. Francois Samson died in 1850 and is buried in the
family plot of the same cemetery. His grand daughters, Mrs. A.
Bernier, Mrs. J. B. Lejeune, and Miss Louise Chenevert inherited
the plantation. Mr. J. B. Lejeune managed it for the owners for
a number of years. Later several crevasses occurred, and with
the depressed conditions that followed, when many large land
holders had to sacrifice their property, the plantation became
heavily mortgaged, and was later sold to Mr. James Richy, except
the home and the large plot surrounding it. This was inherited
by Mrs. Francois Lejeune, and when she died in 1909, her husband and children inherited it. At his death the children became
the owners, and still retain it as the old family home. By a
strange coincidence both Mr. and Mrs. Francois Lejeune were
born in this old plantation home.

THE MARYLAND OAK TABLET

Placed by the ladies of New Roads to the memory of
James Ryder Randall.

The Poet James Ryder Randall, an English teacher, who also
taught Latin in the Old Poydras College lived near the site of the
ancient tree we now know as the Maryland Oak. Old residents
of Pointe Coupee recall the poet and the tales they heard about
him in those seemingly far off days.

He was born in Baltimore, Maryland, but always claimed a
close kinship to the people of the Acadian Lands of Louisiana,
whom he frequently visited during his outings, remaining at their
simple homes over the week-ends.

He never lost an opportunity to let them know that his family
stemmed back to the Canadians who had come as settlers from

France. Always a great reader, the poet saw in the tale of Evangeline the story of his own ancestors, and read everything he could find pertaining to the expulsion of the Acadians of Nova Scotia by the English. He verified what Longfellow had put in beautiful meter by reference to Halburton's history—learning that his great-great grandfather, Rene Leblanc, was one and the same person, who drawing himself up and assuming all the dignity he could command, spoke thusly to the English authorities in Nova Scotia: "We hope that you will not plunge both ourselves and our families into a state of total loss; and that this consideration will cause you to withdraw your savages and troops from our district".

Rene Leblanc, at the time of the English Invasion 1713, was a notary and one of the five most important personages in Grand Pre (Great Meadow) in Acadia, as it had been formerly called by the French. It had been up to 1713 ruled successfully by the French, when as a result of the Treaty of Utrecht, it was given to the English ever to remain a province of the British Empire.

At the date of the expulsion of the Acadians the greater part of the population of Nova Scotia were farmers and fishermen, descendants for most part, of the peasantry of France. They led simple lives, raised large families and dwelt together in peace and contentment.

One will find much the same kind of existence, and simple homes in the Acadia of Louisiana today. They bore no grudge against the domineering English, and only wanted to be let alone. In 1749 began the immigration of the English into this area and the beginning of the settlement of Halifax.

The Latin temperament in the Acadians, began to show itself in some of the younger and stronger men who showed their antipathy towards the English. Finally, in the year 1755, and without taking into consideration that these simple people could not readily understand why they had been handed over to the English to control, the Crown authorities in Nova Scotia, without official permission, "planned the Acadians one and all should go."

They decided that these Acadians should be exiled to the French lands of America. The one who directed the expulsion was William Shirley, a New Englander, the Colonial Governor of Massachusetts, who felt that their presence in Nova Scotia was a menace to the security of the English colonies.

This decision was one that demanded rapid action, so on the second day of September 1755 John Winslow, Lieutenant-Colonel of Massachusetts, under orders of Governor William Shirley— proclaimed in the province that "all the men and boys over ten years of age are to meet in the Church of Grand Pre to learn the message which had been sent them from the Governor of Massachusetts."

Here they were kept prisoners by the soldiers who surrounded the building once that place had been filled. Here, on September 8th, 1755, they were to hear the tragic orders which he read to the Acadians. "Your lands and tenements and cattle and livestock are forfeited to the Crown. You yourselves are to be removed from the province". According to Parkman, no attention was paid to their pleas or lamentations. The men were held prisoners, and at last when the boats had arrived from Boston, the unfortunates were made to line up and march from the Church where they had been improsoned to the ships. The cries and lamentations were heart rending, according to a witness, as many families were separated, never to see each other again.

Thus by September the 10th, 1755, seven thousand Acadians were sent into exile, eventually landing in various parts of the now United States. Most of them drifted to Louisiana, known now as the Evangeline country. The family of Rene consisted of twenty children, and some one hundred and fifty grandchildren scattered to the different parishes. Some of his descendants settled in Pointe Coupee parish, and judging by the numerous LeBlancs in the State, the strain is as vigorous as ever.

RAMSEY- PLANTATION HOME

False River, Pointe Coupee Parish, La.

The present owner of Ramsey Plantation is Mr. Allen Wurtele, a graduate of the United States Naval Academy. This 5000-acre tract is one of the finest in the state, and the soil is unusually rich. With the limited cane quota allowed planters, Mr. Wurtele like many others has been forced to diversify his crops, and raise cattle to make his plantation pay. Being of an inventive turn of mind, and an able engineer, his latest achievement is a mechanical sugar harvester, which may not only save his own sugar crop, but that of the other planters of the state. Early freezing weath-

Miss Euphemie Tobin, as a Carnival Queen; daughter of Mr. and Mrs. John Tobin
(Miss Eliska Provosty).

The old Plantation Home of the LeJeune family, New Roads, La.

Maryland Oak and Tablet to the memory of James Ryder Randall, New Roads, La.

Driveway to the Plantation Home of Allan Wurtele, Ramsey Plantation, False River, Pointe Coupee Parish, La.

er often means the loss of millions of tons of sugar cane, and Mr. Wurtele's invention will help save crops and place him in the same class with Etienne de Bore.

The Ramsey plantation home, quite unpretentious looking from the highway is indeed a charming place within. The house is of the early type Louisiana raised basement plantation home. A spiral stairway forms an attractive feature of the hallway, and with its tasteful furnishings it is one of the most charming plantation homes in the False River section. The large garden has an assortment of blooming plants which make of it a beauty spot indeed.

According to Rev. Father Ecke, S. J., "It was in September of 1938 that I visited Mr. Allen Wurtele to ask permission to offer the Holy Sacrifice of the Mass in one of his tenant houses. Since this section of the congregation of the Colored was the second most heavily populated, and because the people of this section were fairly far removed from the New Roads Church, I thought it might be well to establish a place for divine worship in the (old Mix plantation section) Louisiana section. No sooner did I propose this enterprise to Mr. Wurtele, the present owner of the Ramsey plantation, than he eagerly endorsed the plan. He granted permission to use a house for the exclusive purpose of religious services. Since then Mr. Wurtele has presented the building and land adjoining as a Parish Church which is known as *St. Catherine's Chapel, Mix Post Office, Louisiana.*"

ST. CATHERINE'S CHAPEL.

For many years the chapel was known as the Old Oliver plantation house, located on the bank of False River. The name Oliver unquestionably is a corruption of the name of one of the plantation's early owners whose surname was Olivette, according to old maps and records of the plantations of this area, a monsieur Olivette having purchased the plantation and home from a Spanish official named Trudeau or Trudo, obtaining a clear title in the year 1791.

The structure, undoubtedly the oldest plantation house in the vicinity, dates from the period that another ancient plantation on the Island owned by the Lebeau family, it being the ancestral home of that plantation family. Both old places being over a century and a half old. It was until recently, when given as a chapel for the Catholic colored people of the vicinity, a part of the holdings of the Ramsey Plantation. According to the best available data, this ancient plantation home was built about 1740, and Don Trudeau having been its original owner.

The family of Trudeau in America traces to Canada where a number of the members of the family signed themselves Trudeau de Longeuil, designating their alliance to the noble French house of that name, the crest and coat-of-arms of the family showing in the quarterings the great houses of the French nobility to which it was allied. Other branches of the family spelled the name Trudo on the Spanish documents. It is a family connected by marriage to the most aristocratic families of Louisiana, and are prominent in the various professions as planters, and as residents of Canada, the State of New York as well as of Louisiana.

The old plantation house of the very early Louisiana type, in structure like many small buildings of its type found in the state, instead of being built of wood, brick or plaster, here we find a doby mixture used, and filled in the framed work as bricque en porte. The interior planned with five medium-sized rooms and two chimneys for heating. It fills the needs of a chapel in order that the colored population of the area might attend Divine Service.

POYDRAS PLANTATION

The Poydras Plantation, on False River, Pointe Coupee Parish, was bounded on the North by the plantation of Arthemize Chutz and on the South by the plantation of Dr. A. Ferrier, the lands of the Poydras Plantation about three times the size of both these plantations combined, according to Norman's map of 1858.

Julian Poydras de Lalande was born in France, and as a youth enlisted in the Navy of that country, later being captured by an English vessel and made a prisoner. Managing to escape, he fled to San Domingo, where he became interested in plantation life. Learning that money was to be made by bringing ribbons, laces and other necessary articles to the different remote areas, he came to Louisiana in 1786 and started as a traveling merchant, with a peddler's pack on his back, visiting the plantations. His personality and clean method of dealing with the families he supplied soon gained him the respect of communities he visited. His thrift soon permitted him to purchase piecemeal the plantation and home in which later on he was to entertain the Duke of Orleans, who later became King of France.

On the plantation of Julian Poydras, where Randall lived for a while, an uprising occurred in 1795 and it was only through the loyalty of a house slave on the Denis plantation that a general massacre was averted.

ALMA PLANTATION.

Pointe Coupee Parish, Louisiana.

Another plantation belonging to the POET PLANTER and philanthropist who has done much for Louisiana.

This old plantation has a background of historic interest. Julian Poydras, going from place to place, selling ribbons and laces, etc., to the ladies of the various plantations, and saved enough to leave a number of large bequests to New Orleans, and the town of New Roads, La.

This ancient early type plantation home belonging to Julien Poydras had fallen into a ruined condition, but two of the rooms have been incorporated into the plan of the later home now on the site occupied by the family of Mr. Harry C. Pitcher, who lives there at present.

This original old plantation house was built in the year 1789, and the family of the present owners and operators of Alma Plantation for the past seventy-five years have been actively engaged in the planting and sugar manufacturing business, their plantation and sugar mill being one of the largest in this section of Louisiana.

Learning of the massacre of the whites by the negro slaves, and the success of the "Slave Rebellion" in San Domingo a few years earlier, in the month of April 1793 occurred the "Black Rebellion" planned to follow the example of the slaves of San Domingo and exterminate the whites of the area, excluding the adult white women who were to be left to the mercy of the blacks.

The plot had been carefully planned, but the time at which the slaves should strike became the bone of contention, and quarrels soon started among the ring-leaders of the plot, when one of the slaves, dissatisfied at the way he had been treated by one of the black leaders after having been promised absolute pardon and a reward of freedom and transportation out of the slave area, obtained an interview with the Commandant (Spanish) of the area and related in detail the plot of slaughter that awaited all of the adult males. After obtaining full details and names of the ring-leaders notices were sent to the planters of the area to fully arm and details of the plot, and precautions to meet the situation were discussed.

Then began a large number of arrests, the ring-leaders being taken first; but learning that their leaders had been taken—the slaves rose up in mass to save their chiefs, causing a great riot at which time a large number of whites and negroes were injured and twenty-five persons killed. The rest of the rebellious slaves were imprisoned and tried, ring-leaders executed, and many of the others severely punished, sold to other plantations where the negroes would be less liable to give trouble, and scattered generally. A driveway through the Alma Plantation known as the haunted road or "Sycamore Cut" is cautiously avoided at night-time even to this day by the negroes of the plantation, and the stories of the ghost of the white over-seer who was slain by the slaves forms part of local legends as told in the various negro cabins of the area. The negroes will swear by all that is holy that they have seen this ghost again and again, and many of the ignorant whites also believe the tale. The Pitcher and Churchill, both old plantation families of note are related, the latter having a branch of the family now living in the fine old plantation home of the Kock family "Belle Alliance" on Bayou Lafourche owning also the plantation.

The plantation home of the Pitcher family, while not a typical old plantation home has an interior plan quite similar to many of the larger ones. Within one finds many choice old mahogany and rosewood pieces, among them old four-posters, one having the little mahogany ladder step to reach the comfort of its billowy bed. Good paintings, fine crystal and silver and the endless accessories that lend charm to old houses of cultivated people such as we find on Alma Plantation.

"Ramsey" Plantation, home of Allan Wurtele, False River.

REV. A. J. ECK, S.S.J.
Founder of St. Catherine's Chapel

St. Catherine's Chapel, donated by Allan Wurtele.

The young Marquis de Ternant (with small cravat).
A spoiled son of a wealthy mother. (Reproduced from
an early daguerreotype——Courtesy of the family.)

A Garden Party beneath the oaks of Parlange park.

The Parlange Family Plantation Home, False River, Built in 1780.

One of a pair of pigeonnaires that flank the old plantation home of the Parlange family, False River, Pointe Coupee, La.

Imposing old Mausoleum of the de Ternant and Parlange families, removed from the east bank of the Mississippi River to the cemetery of the town of New Roads, La.

Chapter XXX.

THE PARLANGE PLANTATION HOME.

On False River, Pointe Coupee Parish, Louisiana.
Nearly One Hundred and Seventy-five Years Old.

"THIS is to certify that the historic building known as Parlange Plantation, in the county of Pointe Coupee, and state of Louisiana, has been selected by the advisory committee of the Historic American Building Survey as possessing exceptional historic and architectural interest, and as being worthy of most careful preservation for the benefit of future generations; and to this end, a record of its present appearance and condition has been made, and deposited for permanent reference in the Library of Congress.

Attest: Signed,
  Richard Koch,   HAROLD L. ICKES,
    Dist. officer.   Sect. of the Interior."

The above certificate hangs at present on the wall of the dining-room of the old Parlange plantation home.

Proud indeed must feel the owners of this charming old plantation home which has woven about it the romance and historic lore of over a century and a half.

The house is of a type that was built by the aristocrats of France who had settled on their plantations in the West Indies; combining the comfort, roominess and coolness of a tropical home, with the elegance of the smaller chateaux of France. It is the type of architecture that became the vogue in early Louisiana days, replacing the first simple type of planters home without a basement floor. It was copied on a smaller scale later on in great numbers owing to the inundations of the river, so frequent at that time.

When built in the early decades of the Eighteenth Century, the present city of Baton Rouge, Louisiana, was but a small village where there was a military post. The Marquis de Ternant who had come from Dansviller sur Mars, France, to Louisiana, obtained on account of his prestige, an immense land grant from the King of France, in one of the most desirable areas in Louisiana, on beautiful lake-like False River in Pointe Coupee Parish. There was at that time quite an aristocratic settlement in that locality.

On this land de Ternant erected the charming old home that we see today.   Much of the lumber, all choice cypress, was obtained from his own land.   Here he lived with his bride the life of a wealthy aristocrat in the midst of his great land holdings, as his family before him had lived in their chateau domain of Darnsville sur Mars, France.   The Marquis died on his plantation on False River in January 1757.

His son, Claude Vincent de Ternant, who inherited his father's title of Marquis, continued to operate the plantation, and like his father and mother before him, also maintained a home in the city of Paris, France, which he and his wife visited yearly where they entertained on a lavish scale.   During these visits to the French Capital many of the choice articles which helped to fill this spacious home were purchased.   It was in Paris that the immense oil portrait of Madame, which originally hung in the old mansion, but, now hangs in the Delgado Art Museum at New Orleans was painted.

In later years when during the social unrest in France Marquis de Ternant following the example of the French aristocrats dropped his title, for the patricians realized that changes were taking place, occasioned by the reckless extravagances of the French Court.   However, in Louisiana until their deaths, the Marquis and his beautiful wife continued to be addressed by their titles.   Here he lived until his death in 1818, his wife remaining at the plantation a prominent figure in the social life of the state until her death.

Coming to Louisiana with great wealth as did the first Marquis de Ternant, one would expect an unusual home, and we find that this one lives up to our expectations.

While in Spartan simplicity the finish of the interior is all hand work, beautifully done.   Devoid of pretentiousness, it has the exquisite grace and charm of a jewel in the pureness of its design which lends it great dignity.   The coves and frieze of the various rooms; also the hand-made mouldings about the walls in the main house have this same simplicity. The ceilings are of choice cypress and the boards are fitted so perfectly, one is led to believe that they are plaster. This is true of the carved central ceiling ornaments.

A high basement on the first floor has heavy brick walls with thick battern doors barred and bolted with heavy slave-made hardware. The openings upstairs correspond to those below, also with heavy fittings which remind us that in old slavery days houses were partly fortresses. The main floor above, also with white walls, has long French-door-like windows with fan transoms in rectangle frames. The heavy shutters open outward against the house, while the French glazed doors open inward. All is as French and charming as a manor in Touraine. Doric columns of brick, stucco finished, form a collonade about the outer gallery line of the entire house with fine effect, the bricks having been made in triangular moulds by hand. The old moulds still can be seen among other slave-made articles on a shelf in the rear. These columns support the wide gallery which extends around the house, a little narrower on either side, and here one notes that the windows are barred with iron grilles, dating back to an era when in sparsely settled communities extra precaution was necessary. In the rear the dining-room occupies a part of the rear gallery where we find a double row of collonettes similar to the ones that rise from the balcony edge.

The lines of the house are charmingly restful. The slant of the roof is pierced by two typical French dormers which is repeated in the rear. The setting is a park of century-old oaks heavily bannered with moss, and an avenue of cedars leads to the house which is flanked by a pair of octagonal pigeonnaires. The ensemble appears as if it might have been transported from rural France, and forms a grouping that has no rival in the South. There is an aloofness about the house and its setting reminiscent of the old regime that is broken by the cordial greeting of the owners when one enters.

Within one finds all harmony. There are many beautful mantels all of good design and hand carved. The one in the Salle or parlour with double Ionic columns supporting an arch on which the shelf rests, reaches around to each side of the chimney. This quaint type of mantel arrangement, found also in the "French Quarter" of New Orleans, lends a distinct antiquated air to a room, and permits of a charming mantel setting. In this room of the Parlange place, the central ceiling ornament above the ancient crystal chandelier of attractive design is of carved wood beautifully executed. There are two sofas that have been in this home over a century. The deep fireplace has slave-made andirons. There are also a quaint spinet on which the first Marquise played, and a very early designed Playel piano, brass mounted, having candle-brackets of ornate fire-gilt in sweeping scrolls. A tapestry frame used by an ancestress in the days that this art was as fashionable as bridge is at present is seen. Adding an aristocratic air is an attractive large, century-old mantel mirror with an elaborate Louis XV filagree scroll and floral design ornament over the entire top, all heavily overlaid with real gold leaf, the most important ornaments burnished. It is a most alluring over-mantel decoration.

In this salon also are other long, but simpler framed mirrors in gilt enclosures. Here are many carved chairs in which notable people have often sat, for the house is one where much entertaining took place. There are Fiddleback chairs, Signorette's, Mallard's, as well as sleepy hollow ones. There is Empire furniture and several Directory tables—one, an ancient piece of four sections, which when fitted together makes a comfortable-sized center table; the sections now filling corners of the various rooms. On the walls one finds ancient wood-block, imported wall-paper of a soft grey tan against which old family portraits, miniatures, and daguerreotypes hang with good effect. One of the daguerreotypes is that of a spoiled son of Madame la Marquise whose history is at the end of this chapter. The house is equipped with electricity, but so skillfully is the lighting done that a candle-light effect is obtained. The draperies harmonize with the general effect of the room, where Louis XIV brass cornices, figurines, and ante-bellum bric-a-brac, bronze whale oil lamps, all original pieces, create a room of great interest. A large spining-wheel that has been in use many years on the plantation, now peeps from behind a roomy mahogany lounge near the mantel.

The large dining-room looks much as it did in the long ago. The mahogany furniture is of the Louis XIV and Empire period. Much fine old French and English china, hand-engraved crystal, large tureens, and immense platters recall the splendid banquets for which this home was famous. The immense brass mounted mahogany china-cabinets, hold a wealth of fine crystal, silver, and many-piece dinner sets of rare hand-painted porcelain dating back a century ago. In this dim-lighted room with hand-carved freize and early block wall-paper of pastel tones, a number of rare old decanters of ruby and emerald toned Venetian glass send forth jewel lights from the deep shadows. Dainty cordial and liquor glasses and containers of graceful shapes shed prismatic hues that sparkle like rare jewels and blend with gleaming lights from old silver goblets, recalling pages in Myrtle Reed's stories, "Old Rose and Silver" and "Lavender and Old Lace". A restfulness pervades every room of this old house, and the scenes from her books are readily visualized. On the walls are old duelling pistols, a rapier, old slave manacles, and a number of old iron keys large enough to fit a bastile. The crossed swords on the wall were left by Confederate soldiers who found them on the place when the Federals hurriedly left at their coming. There is a sword cane dating to the days of the Code-duello.

To the right of the salon is the bed-room and bed where in turn slept Generals Bank of the Union Army, and Fighting Dick Taylor of Confederate fame, who occupied the room shortly after the former had departed. The room is now a guest room containing two large old mahogany four-posters with heavy canopies having lace valances. Beside each of the beds are spiral-leg tables, holding fine crystal toilet outfits. The master bed-room has a most magnificent carved four-post bed with heavy tester, the carving known as pineapple design. The other furniture of the large room is equally as handsome, and as finely carved. Another room is the son's room when home from college. Here the furnishings are equally and attractive, as massive and of the same fine quality. Beautifully matched pieces complete both of these sets, and a lit d'nuit is placed at the foot of one of the beds. Pieces of choice bric-a-brac are found in both of these bedrooms, along with the numerous interesting articles found in century-old homes. A fragrant odor of cedar and pine fill the house, wafted in from the great park and garden. One is told that the house originally contained much more but that it has been divided among the different members of this family. It is so well filled, now one wonders where they could have fitted in any more, as most of the contents of the various rooms are original furnishings.

Yearly visits to Paris by Madame la Marquise de Ternant

would mean a yearly addition of costly treasures for her plantation home, for she had exquisite as well as extravagant taste, and was never happier than when purchasing rare and costly art objects for her various homes.

Like many of the wives of wealthy planters, she maintained her box at the Opera both in New Orleans and in Paris, where she retained a residence, repairing each season during the social whirl. She entertained on a lavish scale during her stay in Europe. Among the very interesting relics of olden days on this plantation, is an unusually elaborate harness equipment, magnificent in design and trimming. It recalls the gala days of coach and four, when the family with negro postillions in uniform in attendance rode about the countryside from plantation to plantation like princes of the realm. All these and many other souvenirs of long ago bespeak the cultured lives of generations. This plantation was well managed but was conducted in much the same manner as were the old seigneural estates of Europe. Old diaries in minute detail, books of accounts and directions, inventories, etc., all attest to the careful way it all was managed.

One prized possession of the family is an old inventory filling the pages of a large ledger, listing all the things on the plantation in the year 1842. In the steel-engraving-like spidery script of that day everything is enumerated in detail. Made at the time of the owner's death, everything from attic to cellar is listed, from bedsteads and fine linens to the quantities of rare and aged vintages in the cellar storerooms.

There are detailed descriptions of all the fine laces and linens used in the wardrobe of a gentleman of those days as well as costly silks, brocades and jewels of a belle and grand dame of the time. The names given livestock were, mules—Sasparilla, Bonapart, Papillion, Jupiter, while horses were called Fly, Priscilla, and Fairenough. And the slaves each had a fitting designation.

Here, too, is listed the amount of iron money used by the slaves as well as the gold and silver when the inventory was made, which amounted to $3,000,000.00. Later follow page after page of equipment of every description found on a plantation of this size at that date.

All who visit this home enjoy the rare charm of the environment where everything has been so perfectly preserved, and fortunate are those who share the hospitality of this genial host and hostess, and are given the treat of viewing their interesting collection.

Mrs. Walter Charles Parlange, who was Miss Paule Brierre, a member of an old and distinguished aristocratic Creole family of New Orleans makes a most charming chatelaine to this very lovely old plantation home. She shares with Mr. Parlange the wish to preserve the ancient atmosphere of the place. That they have succeeded cannot be doubted, for the home has the charm that most places strive for. Mrs. Parlange, a great garden lover, has gradually restored much of the beauty of the rear garden, which was totally ruined. Following the Civil War when the place was empty for many years, the garden was a cattle grazing ground. When General Banks was sent South to replace General Butler (silver spoon Butler) whose stealing proved too much for Washington, he and his aide were later quartered on the Parlange Plantation in this old home. The troops were tented in the park as were the very welcomed Confederate troops later on.

Madame Virginie Parlange, ever the French woman and Grand Dame, greeted the Union officers with great tact and diplomacy, well knowing that her famed cuisine would cause even the Federals to forget whatever plans they may have had to destroy the house. The Union troops, however, soon left when the Confederate Army under General Dick Taylor advanced into that section. With the exception of the destruction of the formal French garden by the Union cavalry, and the theft of a shetland pony belonging to Judge Charles Parlange, then a boy of ten, later returned to him by General Banks, no other damage was done to the plantation. When Madame Parlange learned that the Union troops were on their way to False River, she collected all of her fine silverware, and hid it in the wide embrasures above the window casements. Putting all of her gold coin amounting to nearly half a million dollars in a strong box, she buried it beneath one of the great oaks near the house.

Gradually, as the storm blew over, articles of value hidden in the attic, basement and other secret spots, were returned to their places in the house. The silver was brought out and none found missing, but the iron strong box with its precious contents of nearly half a million dollars was never recovered, although much digging and hunting has been done in the hopes of recovering it. At that date a large quantity of rare wine was stocked in the basement, part of which so warmed the hearts of these Union officers, that for years afterwards Madame Parlange used to say that the wine and her chef had saved the heritage of her children.

Chief Justice Edward Douglas White of the United States Supreme Court learned his early lessons in law on the wide gallery of this old home. Later on he became the law partner of the Honorable Charles Parlange, Judge of the United States District Court, the father of Mr. Walter Charles Parlange.

In the earliest days indigo was the staple crop of this plantation, as with most of the others in the state. It was sold in great quantities to Prussia for the coloring of the army uniforms. When the indigo bug threatened to ruin the planters of Louisiana and de Boré discovered how to granulate sugar, the Marquis de Ternant, who was a very progressive man, ordered two immense sugar houses built on his plantation, and put all of his field hands to planting sugarcane. The result was that his plantation up until the ruination of the entire state by the Civil War and the Reconstruction Days that followed was the largest and finest sugar plantation in Pointe Coupee Parish, La.

You will have been fortunate to have found Mr. Parlange in a communicative mood during your visit, for he is a great raconteur and can tell most interesting stories. Having viewed their large and interesting collection of ante-bellum articles, shared their generous hospitality, and then bidden your charming host and hostess adieu, as you leave, the mystic spell of the great park affects you as do ancient historic places of Europe. Your last memories are of the two quaintly beautiful dove cotes in their immaculate whiteness—aristocratic emblems, which recall old feudal days so fittingly—reminders of this ancient home with the air of an antiquated chateau of rural France, beautiful in its unpretentiousness.

In the cemetery of the town of New Roads not far from the old Parlange family plantation home, located near the gateway of this sacred spot, enclosed by a handsome hand-wrought iron railing of unique design, is the imposing family tomb of the de Ternant and Parlange families. Years ago it stood on the opposite bank of the Mississippi River, in a cemetery that has since then been swallowed by the ever hungry river. When the

Parlange family learned that there was danger of this happening, they had the beautiful and costly mausoleum taken down and removed to its present location.

There is a most interesting story about this tomb before its removal. Undoubtedly it is one of the most attractive tombs in this part of the state, and its time stained marble slab bears the date 1757, the first tomb to be erected in the cemetery of New Roads.

Madame la Marquise Claude Vincent de Ternant who had spent so much of her life on the old plantation, had died, and had been buried with many of her costly jewels, a custom that had been adhered to occasionally in wealthy families at that date. Among the jewels placed in the tomb was a magnificent pearl necklace costing many thousands of dollars. Grave robbers, learning of this, broke open the tomb and stole the pearls, but they left traces behind. The robbery was discovered, and detectives put on the case, which resulted in the robbers being trapped, convicted and imprisoned. The recovered jewels with the pearl necklace, were found in New Orleans, and placed in the Court Registry until it could be determined what disposition the rightful heirs of the family wished to be made of them.

It seems that Madame la Marquise de Ternant had reared her son like a prince, and having great wealth, she granted him his every wish. Like many another spoiled son of wealthy parents, he had grown so accustomed to being supplied with unlimited ready cash from the family coffers for his extravagant expenditures, that when he had recklessly gotten head over heels in debt, he became panic stricken. No longer could he go to the fond mother who was always ready to help him. His creditors knowing the wealth of the family, and their horror of notoriety, taking advantage of his position, threatened him with imprisonment. Being a true de Ternant, terrified at the thought of disgracing the family name, in a moment of desperation, he sold to one John Boudreau all his interest in the entire estate left him by his mother.

At last the time came for the disposition of the jewels held by the Court, and all the heirs presented themselves to claim their share. With the other members of the family came the young man who had been so extravagant and gay; somewhat tamed by now for he now had to live within the sums allowed him by his relatives. Like a bird of ill omen also appeared John Boudreau to snatch away what one would almost believe was a last legacy from the grave—a donation that this fond mother, this grand dame of the old regime, had made for the last time so that she could again come to the aid of her errant and idolized son. Young de Ternant's hopes had risen when he had learned that the jewels had been recovered. He disputed Boudreau's claim, stating that he did not include in the sale his interest in the jewels buried with his mother, any more than he had his interest in the family tomb, as these things, as the French have it, were "hors du commerce" out of the transaction. The Court nevertheless finally decided that when young de Ternant was reckless enough to sign away all his interests with full inclusion of everything that would come to him through his mother's succession, he left the Court powerless to help him, much as it would like to. To John Boudreau was given young de Ternant's share of the jewels.

On the slab of the tomb of the de Ternant - Parlange family, which stands in the shelter of great magnolia trees, below the name of the mother who idolized him, one reads his name. Many in the vicinity of New Roads know the strange pathetic story of this young man spoiled by his fond mother, humoring his every whim, as so many parents do in their blind love for their children. Visitors who have heard the story come great distances to see the tomb, and get a glimpse of the beautiful old manor hidden by the grove of great trees.

CARVED ON THE SLABS OF THE DE TERNANT TOMB IS THE FOLLOWING:

ICI REPOSENT SAINVILLE TERNANT

fils de
Claude Vincent Ternant
et
Constance Lacour
decede le 24. Decembre 1820.
et
Dorothee Legros
epouse de
Claude Vincent Ternant fils.

ne le Novembre 1791
decede le 16. Mai 1835.
Ici Reposent
Claude Vincent Ternant
ne a Damvillers sur Meuse France.
le 22 Janvier 1757.
Decede le 3. Janvier 1818
et
Constance Lacour
son epouse
nee le 20 Aout 1766
decedee le 12 Novembre 1837.
et
Marius Claude Vincent Ternant
ne le 14 Mai. 1836
decede le 14 Janvier 1861.

CHAPTER XXXI.

SEEBOLD PLANTATION.

Country Home of the Seebold Family

Oscar, Louisiana.

REPLACING the old Bigman plantation home which was destroyed a number of years ago, the present Seebold country home is a charming place, located far back from the road, hidden by great oak and pecan trees a century old.

Its massive columns and classic facade of gleaming white contrast strongly with the deep green of the surrounding trees. It is a spaciously planned country home with immense hallway having an unusually attractive stair. There are fan windows front and rear, upstairs and down. The very large rooms on both floors with long windows and glazed doors, have old columned mantels, all with interesting histories, having been collected many years ago when these old historic places were demolished. Much that has gone into this later house has associations that hark back to homes that were social centers of the plantation country of Louisiana. There are mantels from the old de Marigny home in the faubourg de Marigny, that had lain in storage from the time the old place was demolished, after a fire had damaged parts of it.

A view of the house is to be seen in Cable's "Creoles of Louisiana" There are glazed doors from the old de la Chaise plantation mansion, that lay empty for many years and had become known as a haunted house. Other equally interesting and historical parts of famous old plantation homes helped in making this home the beautiful place it is. The garden about the house is an unusually attractive one, a mass of bloom most of the year, and planned as one usually finds them in plantation places. The rose garden enclosed by hedges of althea contains a great many

Entrance Gateway to Seebold Plantation, False River, Pointe Coupee Parish, La.

Plantation Home of the Seebold family, False River.

Old negro cabin, Seebold Plantation.

Rear of Seebold Plantation home, showing the ten-foot wide fan-transoms.

Oak and pecan trees in garden grounds.

A pigeonnaire in the garden-grounds of Seebold Plantation.

Mrs. W. E. Seebold, neé Lisette Boehm. (From photograph taken in 1870.)

Mrs. Andres Molinary, neé Marie Madeleine Seebold, among the roses in the garden of the old family home, 2322 Canal Street, New Orleans.

Mrs. George Ossian MacPherson, neé Stella
Lisette Seebold. Educated at the Cenas Institute and Newcomb College of Tulane University, New Orleans.

THE OLD FAMILY HOME OF THE SEEBOLDS, 2322 CANAL ST., NEW ORLEANS. "It was long the residence of the late W. E. Seebold and family, and a mecca to which many artists turned their footsteps." John F. Coleman—Fine old New Orleans Homes series. New Orleans States, May 2nd, 1924.

varieties of choicest specimens whcih show to advantage against a background of attractive weeping willow trees. The climbers cover the rustic arbors and archways, summer houses and fences. A pigeonnaire, rustic gazebos and trellises are bright with wisteria, rose of Montana, and honeysuckle. Cape jasmine, gardenias, magnolia fuscata and Confederate jasmine add their fragrance making a delightful spot of the wide porches. Immense beds of zinnias, fleur de lys, hollyhocks and china-blue morning glories as large as saucers form spots of color about the grounds most of the year.

The rooms are spacious and contain family portraits of the Seebolds and Kinneys of past generations, quaint old fashioned prints, silhouettes, daguerreotypes and miniatures of both families. Here, too, are heirlooms from both families in the way of articles of furniture—old mahogany and rosewood. In the cabinets are numerous mementos of celebrated personages, in most instances gifts from the distinguished individuals themselves.

The rear enclosed porch, fifty feet long by fourteen feet wide, connects with the service department in an adjoining building—an old one planned in the usual old plantation style, and not altered. This porch makes an ideal place to show moving pictures, for animated scenes on the plantation tours, New Orleans Fiesta, or Garden pilgrimages, showing Southern society in hoop skirts, pantelettes, and the ante-bellum finery. The service bell is one from a set of ante-bellum bells that hung above the kitchen window of the old Seebold residence on Canal Street in New Orleans. At present this bell is managed by a needle-point pull-cord.

The bed rooms upstairs contain four-posters of old mahogany with the rest of the set to match. Opposite are the guest room and a spare room in the wing. The large dining-room is twenty feet by thirty-six feet, having a fourteen-foot ceiling, with long French windows overlooking the garden. On the walls of this room are ancestral portraits and two large murals from the brush of the celebrated French artist Raphael Collin which originally came from the collection of Senator William A. Clark of Montana. These murals along with others now in the New Orleans home of the Seebolds having been removed from their former New York home, Chateau Fleur de-Lys overlooking the Hudson. In the dining-room is the old dining table from the Seebold family home in Canal Street, New Orleans, which can seat thirty persons at a time as was often done in the old Canal Street home.

From 1879 until 1916 nearly every painter of note that visited New Orleans has dined at this table. The dinners, suppers and banquets for artists, who met here regularly in this old home during all these years, were frequent and the guests of honor helped to make the evenings of special brilliancy, for those talented in other directions besides painting did their bit to make the evenings successful. The first artist dinners given by Mr. and Mrs. Seebold in their first Canal Street home before 1879 were attended by Richard Clague, Julio and Roudolph. These three artists like Taffy, the Laird and Little Billee, made the Seebold art gallery their headquarters. This gathering ante-dated any formal association of artists, and these dinners followed later in the second Canal Street house, Number 2322 Canal Street, when a larger number of artists joined the colony that met in this larger home. Each Sunday throughout the year as a rule brought a gathering of artists. In this group there were a number of stags, so it was an easy matter to assemble a congenial company. Those too, were the days when the servant question was not the problem it is today, and Mr. and Mrs. Seebold never happier than when surrounded by this artistic crowd, always found some artist who was having a birthday, or contrived some equally good reason for a gathering. The circle gradually widened, and writers, musicians, and poets began to attend regularly.

At the approach of the 1880's New Orleans began to plan for the Cotton Centenial Exposition that was to bloom forth a few years later, drawing notables to the city from all parts of the United States, Canada, Central America, and South America as well as Mexico. Mr. Seebold at once took an active part in the organization of the Exposition Art Gallery, and with men like Major B. M. Harrod, the Westfeldt brothers, Thomas Sully, and other representative citizens and leading artists formed committees for the collecting of objects of Art to be placed on exhibition along with the paintings from Europe and America. From that time on the old Canal Street Home became an art center, where for over a half century, this artistic group met not only for companionship, but in all seriousness to encourage art in its various branches.

Mr. Seebold became a charter member of the New Orleans

Art Union, the first group of artists and those interested in art to form an association of this kind in Louisiana. Although the city of New Orleans had a well established reputation as an art center with many fine private art collections in wealthy homes, there was no organized interest in art before this.

Even when the Art Union disbanded for lack of interest, these gatherings at the Seebold's home continued regularly, and finally the artists and those interested got together again and formed the Art Association which has continued as we know it today.

This later Association, which was an organization with an Art School attached, had its headquarters in Camp Street. The regular monthly meetings were followed by exhibitions of the artists and students work, and a formal reception to which the public was invited. Many of the leading merchants of the city contributed articles to help furnish the rooms of the Association. So that the various studios and class rooms might have the appearance of the regulation studios, Mr. Seebold, who had a large assortment of plaster casts of classic subjects, donated a large number of them to the Association, along with easels, palettes, etc. Many of the ladies, prominent socially, donated prizes for the best work shown at these monthly exhibitions. B. A. Wikstrom, artist and musician, for many years selected the musical programme for the evenings, being conversant with good music and in touch with the musical members of the coterie, as well as the members of the Art Association.

Among the many who attended these gatherings during the years were President and Mrs. Jefferson Davis; Miss Varina Davis; Lafcadio Hearn; George W. Cable; Professor Alcee Fortier; Samuel Clements, (Mark Twain) ; George Clements, Artist and writer; Mr. Lamar Quintero, American Consul to the Argentine; Mrs. Quintero, Sr.; Charles H. Chapin, Artist, member of the Lotus Club of New York City, who at the time was painting the portrait of the celebrated Polish actress Mojeska, both accompanied by William Tracey, noted animal painter; General de Trobriant; Archille Perelli, noted Sculptor; Mr. and Mrs. Joseph Jefferson, the former an artist of ability as well as noted actor; George Innes, celebrated impressionist artist who gave an exhibition of his work at the Seebold Art Gallery, and a talk on impressionistic Art on this occasion of his visit to this home.

(A souvenir of this visit is a little sketch of his boat used while he sketched in the bayous of Florida, now hanging in the studio of Mrs. Marie Seebold Molinary) ; McKnight of the same school also lectured in this home on the occasion of his visit when he also gave an exhibition in New Orleans; Major and Mrs. B. M. Harrod, the Major an engineer of Panama fame; Major and Mrs. Davis of the New Orleans Picayune; Judge and Mrs. Gayarre; Eugene and Frank Cox, scenic artists; Palmer Cox, of Brownie fame; Professors Ellsworth and William Woodward and their wives; Charles Boyle, artist; Andres Molinary, portrait painter; B. A. Wikstrom; Mr. and Mrs. Graner, the former a noted Spanish artist; Mr. and Mrs. Gustaf Westfeldt, Sr.; Mr. Patrick Westfeldt, artist; Eugene Field, poet; James Whitcombe Riley, poet; Mrs. M. R. Field, Southern writer; Mrs. Mary Ashley Townsend; Mrs. Flo Field, Southern writer; Charles Dudley Warner, journalist; Dr. Standford Chaille, Dean of the Medical Department of Tulane University; Mrs. Henri Wehrmann; Mr. Henri Wehrmann, violinist; Mrs. J. G. R. Pitkin, vocalist; the Misses Boisseneau, musicians; Edith Sansum, Cora Loyd, both artists; A. J. Drysdale, artist; Theodore Behr, noted mural painter; Miss Amy Bemis; Mr. and Mrs. Emile Dantonet; Mr. and Mrs. W. L. Saxon, the latter an artist; Mr. Lyle Saxon, Sr.; Mr. and Mrs. Zamora, Mexican Consul and his wife; August Norerie, musician and artist; Mr. and Mrs. John Vegas; Dr. and Mrs. I. M. Cline; Judge and Mrs. Frank D. Chretien, and many others too numerous to mention.

Art to an extent at last has gotten a fairly strong foothold in New Orleans. The French Quarter is an ideal setting for the numerous studios where many serious artists and art students now work. In the days of which I write, the quarter had not revived as yet from the depressing effects of the Civil War, for as yet no attempt had been made to take advantage of its artistic possibilities, and Art struggled on. But the people were not allowed to feel that it was dead or about to become a thing of the past, but rather held only in abeyance until conditions could shape themselves, so that artists could command a fair price for their work. The notable artists from other cities whom Mr. Seebold met while he took his yearly business trips North, or who came as visitors to New Orleans, all of them close friends, realized the true conditions of art in this city. So by their presence, with talks and exhibitions at the Seebold Art Gallery, they became a great help in stimulating the younger artists and art students, when the art outlook was darkest. Even artist materials, canvasses were furnished or long credits were extended to encourage those who did not have the money with which to develop their talents. Strange as it may seem, I never heard my father mention the name of a single artist or art student that abused his kindness. A favorite Christmas card on many an occasion was a receipted bill to deserving ones.

John F. Coleman, journalist and historian, in his series of articles written for the New Orleans States on notable old New Orleans residences on May 2nd, 1924, had the following to say of the Seebold home.

The house was, until three years ago, the home of an old Confederate soldier who, in the emergency of the situation, could have exploited his alien birth and national predelections had he so chosen, and thus escaped the exactions of the draft, but like Mr. I. E. Glenny, and other distinguished resident foreigners of that day in New Orleans, Mr. W. E. Seebold, when the storm of war broke upon the South forthwith rallied to the defense of its flag and most gallantly fought its battles until the cause went down in unshadowed glory.

The old house has seen many happy days, and has been the witness of many happy incidents, of happy re-unions, of feasts and festivals and over and all about it there is a lingering of happy memories.

The Seebold home was a place filled with art treasures, Sevres, ornaments of gilded Limoges enamels, silken materials of the finest textures, pictures, statuary, souvenirs and great quantities of bric-a-brac. The furnishings, too,, were costly, and in design and finish of the most exquisite handiwork.

Mr. Seebold was, perhaps, the most prominent art dealer and connoisseur of art in the South. No one knew better than he how to create an art atmosphere and in the conduct of his business everything was subordinate to that end. Mention has been made of the distinguished art gatherings a coterie comprised of such men as Joseph Jefferson, Chapin, Geo. Clemence, Geo. Inness, Tracey, Wikstrom, Boyle, Graner, Molinary and the others. These meetings were always exceptionally bright and enjoyable affairs in which the good things contributed by the gastronomical department of the Seebold home, and the good things said at its table, gave assurance of a delightful evening. Mr. Seebold was a gourmet, and the members of his family no less so. The menu embracing as it did the luxuries and delicacies of the four quarters of the globe, was of course an unfailing feature of the occasion, which, with the scintillating beverages of sunny France threw a gleam of geniality and good fellowship over the assemblage,

at the same time preservin'g the flavor of art as well as the spice of
mirthful enthusiasm.

It was always with regret that these occasions, so replete with
the elements that take the sting from the briars of this work-a-day
world, had to have an ending; and today they live only in the memory
of the survivors as among the pleasantest of life's unforgettable
episodes.

Around the hospitable table of the Seebolds, were to be found
the wichery of the poet, the reasonings of the philosopher, the culture
of the scholar, the tones of the musician, the creators of art in all
its varied and enchanting forms, and withal the wit that gave piquancy
and spirit to the feast.—John F. Coleman, New Orleans States, May
2nd, 1924.

After the cessation of hostilities and peace had been declared,
New Orleans was flooded with plantation families of good birth
who had been immensely wealthy, but had lost their entire fortune
as a result of the war and the thieving manipulations of the carpet
baggers during Reconstruction Days. With most of the men of
their families either killed or wounded, any number of aristocratic
ladies, in fact hundreds of them, came from their plantations to
the Southern cities vainly striving to earn a livelihood. For without money or slaves and mules and the other requirements to run
a plantation, it was impossible to continue. It was at this time
that so many formerly immensely wealthy ladies, who had had
their own private maids, and every luxury that money could purchase, found that the talents that they had cultivated stood them
in good stead. They found that they could put into use this
knowledge in helping to support themselves and their families.

In that era New Orleans, like the rest of the country had a
goodly number of widows and orphans, as well as a large number
of maimed and crippled men. Ladies who were musicians taught
music. Those who could draw and paint taught those arts, while
others adept with the needle taught sewing and fancy needlework.
Others opened private schools, or taught in the other local schools.

These were the terrible Reconstruction Days, when the pov-
erty and hardships came as an aftermath of the long and bitter
struggle of war. It was the era, when those who had poured into
the South to prey on the wrecked country, reaped great harvests,
and bought at trivial prices articles salvaged from the wreckage
of splendid homes. Comparatively few families in New Orleans
and the South in general, but what had lost heavily by the War.
However, those who had not lost their fortunes were most gener-

ous in helping the impoverished ones. Among New Orleans merchants who did a great deal to ease the plight of many families was the firm of D. H. Holmes, then as now an important business firm. The firm made it a point to give positions to as many impoverished ladies as it could afford to do. This gave tone to this establishment which has continued to the present.

W. E. Seebold, who had been honorably discharged at the end of hostilties, had been a member of Scott's Louisiana Cavalry Company I. Having a knowledge of art and art objects, shortly after his marriage, he opened an art store on Canal Street on the site where Loew's Theatre now stands. At that date many artists were struggling to carry on, and Mr. Seebold sensed the need of assistance by men who were talented but needed an outlet for their work. Into the Seebold art store came many of the artists of the city. Also there came many members of once wealthy families, bringing their work to be placed on sale. Others came bringing cherished articles they had saved from the wreckage of their plantations to be left on sale, for so many of the dealers who had come from other parts offered so little for them.

Being aware of the value of art articles generally, and with the true understanding of one who had fought shoulder to shoulder with their fathers, sons, husbands or sweethearts, my father took care of their belongings and saw to it that when the objects were sold that those who had left them on sale got a fair price.

New Orleans previous to the Civil War was noted as an art center, for a number of wealthy families living in the city had fine art collections. Many of the plantations also had many valuable paintings, besides the fine family portraits and miniatures. Many of these works of art found their way to the Seebold establishment, and in this way from the very first the place became an art center. Many valuable works of art were placed on sale there. An artistic and cultured element became patrons at once, first because of the attracive goods on display, and secondly, the families and friends of those who were being aided did all they could to help. Here one found besides the regular stock, fine signed bronzes and bric-a-brac and all kinds of ornaments—many with interesting histories attached to them.

Being an art connoisseur he became not only their friend, but adviser and sought as purchasers for many of the objects those whom he felt would appreciate their real artistic value. When some special painting needed appraisal to set its value, he sought the advice of his artist friends, for Richard Clague, Julio, Roudolph and other artists of note came regularly to the establishment all willing to help.

The patronage of the Seebold establishment increased rapidly, and the art store soon found that it needed larger quarters. The business was moved to (old number) 166 Canal Street, now 912 Canal Street, at present occupied by a moving picture theatre. At that date it was a large three-storied structure, the building of brick, and designed along the lines of the large places in the French Quarter. That is, there was a residence above with an entrance vestibule and stairway to the west side, the other space being occupied by a large store extending half of the block back where a wide alleyway afforded light and ventilation to the rear rooms. All of the hardware on doors and windows was like that still to be found in the French Quarter—great bolts and hinges, and immense heavy locks with brass keys almost a foot long.

Among the young ladies that placed their work on sale was Miss Winnie (Varina) Davis, beautiful daughter of President Davis of the Confederacy. A gentleman from the North, learning that the work was that of the daughter of the Great Confederate, wished to purchase it on condition that he might have the letter which she wrote when sending in her painting to be sold. Miss Davis' permission was obtained, the painting was purchased, and a neat sum turned over to the delighted young lady.

Few commissions were being given for portraits at that date and capable artists found it a difficult matter to make ends meet, so Mr. Seebold had fitted up a large studio on the second floor which he let the artists have free of rent. It was in this atelier started by Richard Clague, Julio, Roudolph, and Moise that the beginning of the art colony that was to develop into the present Artist Association began. From that beginning it was to continue with added members for over half a century. First they gathered here for their art discussions and little reunions, and later at the newer home of the Seebold family, where the family moved in 1879. This later home with its spacious rooms gave better opportunity for their monthly gatherings. Soon the musicians, writers, and poets found this coterie, and regularly made

Mrs. H. deC. Seebold below a portrait of her father painted by
J. Raeburn Middleton, a nephew of the noted Scotch artist.

ACHILLE PERELLI,
Sculptor and Painter. (Portrait by A.
Molinary.)

BROR ANDERS WIKSTROM,
Marine and Landscape Painter.

MAJOR B. M. HARROD

MRS. GEROMINA MOLINARY,
mother of the artist.

this hospitable home a rendezvous. Here for over half a century came every distinguished artist (painter) who visited New Orleans during all these years.

In the meantime in the immense front room on the second floor of 912 Canal Street—the Art Gallery of the establishment—monthly auctions were held for the benefit of the local artists, following their exhibitions. Mr. Ed. Curtis and Mr. Ben Onorato acted as auctioneers, and often the sales reached large amounts. The auctions gave local and visiting artists an opportunity to dispose of their work. So popular did these sales become that many of the prominent artists from other parts of the country came to New Orleans with large exhibitions of their work which they displayed at the Seebold Gallery later auctioning their paintings. In this way many of the fine art collections of Louisiana were formed. Art was stimulated and numerous art collections started, for at these gatherings the intelligencia of the city were to be found. Until the interior decorators persuaded the public that bare walls were much more desirable, in almost every important home good paintings by prominent artists were to be found. However, many families paid little attention to the decorators and still retain their paintings along with their art objects. Often these auction sales were for the benefit of Confederate veterans and their widows as well as for other charitable objects.

Realizing how much help those in need were getting by being able to dispose of their belongings, many years ago a number of prominent New Orleans ladies under the leadership of Mrs. George Q. Whitney held a meeting in the art gallery of the Art Store, Number 166 Canal Street, when the idea of the Christian Women's Exchange was born.

Later another meeting of the same ladies was held at the home of Mrs. Spofford, and it was arranged to purchase or rent a home for the purpose. Then the organization moved to the first home of the Christian Women's Exchange which was a one-storied structure in Bourbon Street, where lunches also were served. Later the Exchange moved to larger quarters corner in South Street, where they remained until their removal to their present site with headquarters in the fine old home of the Grima family in St. Louis Street—one of the finest of the aristocratic old homes in the French Quarter with a charming spacious court-yard in the rear of the roomy building.   Only those who knew the history of this noble organization, are aware of the wonderful amount of good this crowd of ladies have done, and still are doing. I am proud that my mother was a member for many years, until her death.

CHAPTER XXXII.

OTHER FALSE RIVER PLANTATIONS.

THE LOCKE BREAUX PLANTATION HOME

False River, Pointe Coupee, La.

WHILE the newness of its restored condition leads one to believe it to be recently built, this old home of the Locke Breaux family antedates the Civil War.

It is a large and well designed country home of the "Old Louisiana Type", of West Indian inspiration. Its lines are beautiful, having all of the charming architectural details that gives distinction to the ensemble. In the restoration the present owners have preserved the original charm of its architectural lines. The general layout of the garden grounds also seem to have been preserved.

The tan color which the house is now painted does not show it to advantage, causing it to lose much of the charm that it would have, had the standard colors of these old places been followed. However, this is a small matter and can always be easily rectified. Its entrance garden, well kept and usually bright with flowering plants, has an enclosing paling we usually find attached to these old places. A wide stairway easy of ascent leads to the wide gallery surrounding the house. An extremely attractive entrance doorway with side lights and fan light overhead transom—opens into a wide hallway with spacious rooms on each side.

The Breaux family was both distinguished and wealthy, Mr.

Locke Breaux, being a brother of Chief Justice Breaux of the Louisiana Supreme Court. Quite naturally this beautiful plantation home, like the equally important neighboring ones, in days gone by, was a social center where legal lights, as well as social butterflies gathered to enjoy themselves. Tales are told of the great banquets given here in olden days, when the planters representatives were entertained by the brother of Chief Justice Breaux—when hours were spent at the banquet board enlivened by brilliant repartee.

Turkey, squab, and a whole teal duck to a portion were served along with rare wines. Sometimes one wonders how they reached the ripe old ages they did, eating as heartily as was the custom of those days, when the banquet board literally groaned beneath the weight of delicacies placed before the diners, and wines of rare vintages flowed freely.

The plantation, always an immense one, still yields heavy harvests of cotton, cane and other crops—while a large stock farm has been added by the present owner Colonel Henry Rougon, who, with his family, occupy the place. The garden is specially attractive throughout the year as it always is a mass of blooming plants, which display to advantage the spacious grounds. The plantation became the property of the father of Colonel Rougon in 1886. Mr. Joseph Aubin Rougon lived until his death on Austerlitz plantation (as it had been named when the house was completed in 1832 by its original owner). He was a great admirer of Napoleon Bonaparte, and the house in early days of its history had many souvenirs of the exiled emperor.

Since the Rougon family have owned Austerlitz plantation, much time and money have been spent on both house and garden. Great masses of azaleas, of many varieties make of the place a beauty spot. The azalea collection numbers some 200 large bushes and trees, many of them very fine. In this beautiful garden are some very large and rare camellia trees, besides a large collection of other attractive garden plants.

Austerlitz plantation, containing some 3000 acres, is one of the large land holdings of this section. Colonel Rougon has some 42 tenant families on his land, all of whom appear to be contented and happy.

Madame Mojeska, celebrated Polish Actress.

Joseph Jefferson, Actor and Artist.

The Lock Breaux Plantation Home,
False River, Pointe Coupee Parish,
Austerlitz, built in 1832.

Interior of upper hall, Austerlitz Plantation, False River.

Col. Henry Rougon at his Austerlitz Plantation Home.

River Lake, old plantation home of the Arthur Denis
family, False River, Pointe Coupee Parish, La.

"Pleasant View Plantation", home of the Thos. H.
Hewes family.

Pigeonnaires at River Lake.

PLEASANT VIEW

False River, Pointe Coupee Parish—The Old Plantation

Home of the Hews Family.

Pleasant View Plantation is literally named. It affords one of the most beautiful outlooks of the entire False River section. Located on a point of land this pretty old plantation home has about it a rural charm that is quite inviting. Perched high on a heavy brick basement its square brick pillars fore and aft, support the very wide galleries, where typical old plantation stairways lead from the brick paved lower verandas to the floor above.

It is a roomy house, and much larger than these early plantation houses usually were. Also typically French in its Spartan simplicity the real beauty of the columned mantels stand out in their purity of line in the large rooms. Heavy shutters open outward with French glazed and panelled doors folding inward as in most early plantation houses. The central rooms are the living room and dining-room—with bed rooms and bath to either side. Ancestral portraits by noted artists adorn the walls, and ancient bric-a-brac, solid, large brass whale oil lamps, and other ornaments fill mantel shelves and cabinets. An immense mahogany four-poster and matched pieces of crouch mahogany are found in the master bedroom with other mahognay sets in the other bedrooms. Quaint needle point chairs, mahogany and rosewood arm-chairs, tables, couches, and lounges fill the living room.

The garden, always bright with flowers, has many special features, among them the immense sweet olive tree, one of the largest in the state. A magnificent double crimson camellia, bearing thousands of blooms at a time yearly, and other attractive white, shell pink and other camellias vie with azaleas in beautifying the grounds.

The family burial plot, like those of many of the old plantation places is beautiful most of the year, sheltered as it is by luxuriant blooming bushes. Great moss-hung oaks and pecan trees make of it an attractive place indeed, and its extensive plantation acres are fully cultivated. The garden widening around the sides and rear unfolds itself in a series of flower beds each striving to outdo the other apparently, as the masses of color enthrall the eye and spill their perfume into the air. Every flower

one can think of seems a part of this garden.   Vine clad barns
and poultry pens, from which issue the droning noises, and cock
crows add their own note.   A picture of rural content and plantation charm is completed when the old mammy in turban and
starched apron feeds the flock of turkeys that assure good dinners from this well stocked poultry yard.

RIVER LAKE

False River — Pointe Coupee

Built for Isaac Gaillard.

The ancient plantation home of the Arthur Denis family with its
pair of time stained pigeonnaires flanking its front garden attracts by the harmony of its setting.   The great century-old oaks,
both in the ample front grounds and rear yard, with their heavy
banners of moss complete a pleasing picture.   It is one of the
few of the remaining old places in the False River area that retain so completely the air of its earlier days.

Probably not as prim as many of the others, still in its apparently neglected state, it possesses a charm such as one finds
in ancient houses of old France in rural sections.

In its unpretentiousness lies its chief beauty for it remains
almost entirely the same fine old plantation manor that it was
when bought by the Arthur Denis family in ante-bellum days.
Fortunately it has not been changed by alterations or improvements that would mar its aged beauty.   However, the ancient
pigeonnaires housing many pigeons, are beginning to show the
need of repairs.

The house is of the typical old Louisiana type, adopted from
tropical lands, with wide galleries, overhanging eaves and rows
of graceful collonettes.   Its history up until the Civil War is that
of the home of a successful aristocratic planter, with all the life
and gayety that was associated with a home having two attractive
daughters who made of such an ideal setting a center about which
revolved the social life of the distinguished families on the various large plantations in this section.

The second owner was Mr. Arthur Denis, a wealthy planter
and large slave holder, with extensive acreage under cultivation.
Patrician born, he was the son of Henry Denis, in turn a member

of a distinguished family, who had married Mademoiselle Aimee Derbigny, a daughter of Governor Pierre Auguste Charles Bourguignon d'Herbigny, who was born in Laon, near Lille, in the Department du Nord, France, in the year 1767. Pierre was the son of Augustin Bourguignon d'Herbigny, being the oldest of five sons, his brothers were Alphonse d'Herbigny, aide-de-camp of General Jean Marie Philippe, comte de Seurrier, a Marechal de France, who lost his life during de Serrurier's glorious campaign while in Italy fighting under Napoleon. Francois Xavier d'Herbigny, became general secretary de Prefecture du Nord, Casimir d'Herbigny, officer de la marine. Antoine Valery d'Herbigny, directeur de l'enregistrement a Bordeau en Arras (Man of letters and a poet of distinction).

In 1792 to escape the guillotine, as the heads of aristocrats were falling fast, Pierre d'Herbigny fled to San Domingo. At the time of the slave uprising he left the Island, going to Pittsburgh, Pennsylvania, where he was married to Mademoiselle Felicie Odile de Hault de Lassus whose father was a knight of the grand cross of the Royal order of Saint Michael. His daughter, Mademoiselle Aimee d'Herbigny, became the wife of Henry Denis, and their son Arthur, who later became a wealthy planter in Pointe Coupee, dwelt in the old plantation house with the attractive pigeonnaires flanking the entrance gateway, which is the subject of this article.

The ancient home during the occupation of the Denis family contained much fine furniture, family portraits and the general furnishings one usually found in the homes of wealthy, cultured plantation families. Much was moved to the old Parlange plantation home later, for Mademoiselle Louise Denis, a daughter of Mr. Arthur Denis and Mademoiselle Antoinette de Beauvais de Cuir, was born in this old plantation home, and married the Honorable Charles Parlange, U. S. District Judge. She became the mother of Mr. Walter Charles Parlange, who with his charming wife and son, Walter Charles Parlange, Jr., now occupy the beautiful Parlange plantation home near by.

The old Denis plantation home, now the residence of the Major family, is extremely attractive in its fine setting. It is well kept and greatly admired by the many tourists that pass this way.

CHAPTER XXXIII.

IN THE GROSSE TETE SECTION.

LIVE OAK PLANTATION

Rosedale, Louisiana

On Bayou Maringuoin.

IN no section of Louisiana are the oaks grander and more stately than they are along Bayou Maringuoin. If one judges from the old groves still standing, those of ante-bellum times must have been more numerous and even more magnificent. The bayou in olden days was the means of transportation. For a quarter of a century, it has been choked with a wild growth of aquatic plants, but is now again navigable for the cane barges that haul the sugarcane to the sugar-mills. Most of the other products of the farmers is transported by motor trucks. The beauty of the scenery reminds one of the Teche country and its lovely river immortalized by Longfellow. There is an almost continuous fringe of ancient bearded oak trees on both sides of the bayou, and on every plantation there is a grove of oak trees around or leading to the "big house" or to where the manor house formerly stood.

This was once strictly a plantation country, a community of aristocrats, and one can readily see why Bayou Maringuoin was so desirable. The soil was rich and fertile, the climate temperate and the country beautiful. The descendants of these old Bayou Grosse Tete and Bayou Maringuoin planters look back with pride on their ancestral roof-trees. A few of the charming old houses, relics of ante-bellum days, stand forth in their ancient glory, as vivid reminders of the old regime. Alas! They are too few.

Here in this once sylvan community, stands a large old mansion, about which much history hangs. This is the Live Oak Plantation at Rosedale. The house was built for comfort and liv-

Live Oak Plantation Home, Rosedale, La., home of Mr. and Mrs. J. R. Mays.

Stairway in Plantation home of the J. R. Mays family, Rosedale, Louisiana.

Shady Grove Manor, built in 1858 for Isaac Erwin, Bayou Grosse Tete.

The Wyley Barrow Plantation Home, Bayou Marin-gouin, Louisiana.

ing on a fine scale, and is devoid of the ostentatious display that we find in some of the other places. It is a home delightfully situated, with wide verandas, upstairs and down, having many spacious rooms, well lighted and ventilated. Its two and half stories are lighted with French windows which make the rooms cool in summer. Each floor has a twenty-foot hall which widens out in the rear, where an unusually bautifully curved stairway winds to the floor above. The stair lines are graceful, and it is unique in the manner in which it is suspended from the inner wall. Two large connecting rooms on either side upstairs and down assure roominess and comfort as well as privacy.

Here have been housed on many occasions, distinguished guests for this home has always been known for its gracious hospitality. Columned mantels of good design, nicely finished woodwork, and silver plated hardware, are all attractive features of the place. Much beautiful old rosewood and mahogany furniture, fine old family portraits, crystal, old silver, and fine china indicate a cultured people, who come of a long line of distinguished ancestors stemming back on both sides of the family to historic names. The house in its rustic setting is the kind of a home that attracts by the dignity of line, and home life environment. Those who live here are calm and unhurried, much as their ancestors lived in the long ago. Colored mammies, turbaned and wearing large starched white aprons, come and go noiselessly in smaller numbers than in old plantation days, but they still maintain deference of manner to their superiors, an attitude that is pleasing to old-time Southerners in this streamlined age of colored college graduates.

Live Oak Manor is delightfully planned for entertaining. It has large drawing rooms, as well as a spacious dining-room. In olden times on gala days the master of Live Oak Manor entertained on a lavish scale, and then the great hall was converted into a banquet hall where many were served at a sitting. A large finished attic gives additional house room when needed for week-end parties. Of the original out-buildings containing kitchen service quarters, laundry, etc., two remain, the kitchen connected by a lattice enclosure which eliminates food odors and kitchen noises. Other buildings that stood opposite have been demolished, and remnants of the old slave quarters are found in the rear by the ancient chapel where each Sunday the slaves worshipped. A travelling minister preached each Sunday to the dark assemblage and the slave burial ground was an enclosure in the rear of the little brick chapel.

In 1828 Charles Dickinson and his bride came to the Gross Tete country from Nashville to start a plantation as his grandfather guardian had done years before. He found that a crevasse had just occurred, flooding the entire area. He did not become discouraged knowing that his grandfather lived in this section, and had made a great fortune from his crops. Looking the surrounding country over as it were, young Dickinson noted several spots that were not under water, and he selected the largest of them as a site for his future home. He also noted too that the oaks there were unusually large. There he built a house and his young wife remained at his grandfather's home until it was completed.

A number of fine plantation houses were scattered about the section—all the homes of wealthy planters. Game was plentiful and the woods were filled with beautiful birds of every description. At that date tribes of Indians occupied places along this bayou, and they became so friendly with the Master of Live Oak that they frequently came to the house. Mrs. Dickinson, always afraid of the Red Skins, surprised one day while her husband was away in the woods, at seeing the head of one of the Indians against the window, rushed out the back door into the thicket. The Indians who were very friendly with Mr. Dickinson, fearing she would get lost induced her to return. When Dickinson heard about it, he forbade them ever to come near the house when he was not there.

Charles Dickinson, the owner of Live Oak, was the son of the Charles Dickinson who became entangled in a quarrel with Andrew Jackson. Joseph Erwin had a stable of blooded stock on his plantation, Clover Blossom, not far from the Hermitage, Andrew Jackson's plantation home. "Plow boy" was the pride of Erwin's stable, while Old Hickory's favorite horse was the famous Truxton. The two horses were matched in a race which resulted in a misunderstanding between Erwin and Jackson. The son-in-law of Erwin, Charles H. Dickinson, espoused his father-in-law's cause, later resulted in a duel in which Dickinson was killed, the owner of Live Oak, being an infant at the time. Previous to the duel

Dickinson made his boy a ward of his grandfather in the event he was killed, and Captain Erwin saw to it that his ward and grandson was reared and educated as a gentleman should be. When the young man had reached manhood, and married, bringing his bride with him to the Grosse Tete country, his grandfather who had charge of the fortune that his father had left him, on the arrival of young Charles deeded to him a large tract on which this plantation was later laid out. Capt. Erwin, himself, owned immense areas in the Grosse Tete section.

The Live Oak plantation house is almost one hundred and ten years old, and since 1915 has been the home of the charming family living here at present, Mr. and Mrs. J. R. Mays of Rosedale, as the village that has grown up about the old plantation is called. The Mays came from Baton Rouge, where the family were prominent. They came into the property through Mrs. Lavinia Davis, an aunt of Mrs. Mays, who had purchased it at the time it was sold by members of the Dickinson family. Mrs. Mays, a most charming woman, well versed in the legends and history of the plantation country of Louisiana, was Miss Lula Barrow of the notable patrician family of that name, who have left so many magnificent homes in the state of Louisiana.

The beautiful collection of historical treasures in this home, for the most part are heirlooms of the Mays and Barrow familes. Ancestral portraits, silverware, crystal and costly china, with rare pieces of carved rosewood and mahogany furniture give the old plantation home the air of olden days. In the rear of Live Oak, or Oak Grove as it is sometimes called, we find the old slave burial ground, in a section far to the rear of the row of old slave cabins. Charles Dickinson has left a record as a successful planter. He was a kind master to his slaves, attending to their wants and spiritual needs. His death occurred in 1848; he left a widow and three children. Mrs. Dickinson proved herself capable of managing the large estate. She was also a prominent leader in social and community affairs, and the principal stockholder of the Louisiana Central Railroad. At Mrs. Dickinson's death the plantation and property was sold in 1885 to Mrs. Lavinia Davis, later passing to the family of Mr. and Mrs. J. R. Mays. The Mays live oak is a member of the "Live Oak Society", being the largest oak tree in the vicinity.

SHADY GROVE PLANTATION MANOR

On Bayou Grosse Tete.

Facing Bayou Grosse Tete about mid distance between the villages of Maringuoin and Rosedale stands what was once the home of Isaac Erwin, an immensely wealthy planter and great sportsman with a string of famous race horses, and a private race track to which the blue-bloods of the Southern States travelled from afar to witness the famous meets. The old mansion, erected in 1858, was an immense one with many rooms to house the distinguished personages that were Col. Erwin's guests weeks at a time. The race horses of Lexington and LeCompte were tried out on this track. Monsieur LeCompte being a close friend of the owner of Shady Grove. Like Live Oak near by, Shady Grove has been the scene of innumerable hospitalities for entertaining was lavish in these Bayou mansions. Dr. Campbell, who often attended these feasts, is quoted as saying, "the people of these bayous dig their graves with their teeth." He tried to introduce the custom of simpler dinners, but without success. The Shady Grove house, constructed of the finest material, a pleasing type of modified Greek Revival architecture, was originally set in magnificent grounds, which unfortunately have been so mutilated that most of the grandeur of the old place has vanished. The building has become a school, and modern-looking buildings have crowded the fine old house so as to make one wonder why steps were not taken in time to preserve the beauty of the mansion's setting by leaving more ground space between it and the new building.

BELMONT

The Wiley Barrow Plantation Home.

In the Bayou Maringouin (mosquito) country near the bayou, standing like old Roman ruins, one sees a group of crumbling brick-stuccoed columns surrounded by a group of fine old moss-hung trees. This is all that remains of the old home built for Wiley Barrow as the war clouds of the 60's were gathering, but it survived the wreckage of the Union soldiers, their pillage and destruction. For many years it was the home of the Barrow and Sparks families whose members, still residing in Baton Rouge, recall the happy childhood days spent on that old plantation.

While built on a less expensive scale than many of the other Barrow homes, it was a large and very comfortable home. Some years ago the plantation passed out of the family's hands and the house lay empty for a long time. When the purchaser had the place inspected with the idea of restoring it, he found that the termites had so riddled the woodwork that the house would have to be rebuilt. It was then dismantled and the doors, windows, etc., used for repairing old buildings and cabins on the plantation. The wife of the present owner states that some day she hopes to have the old place rebuilt as a summer home, as there is a fine grove of live oaks on the grounds.

Members of the Sparks and Daspit family, descendants of the builder of Belmont, living at present in Baton Rouge, possess many articles that came from this old plantation home, among which is a quantity of fine mahogany and rosewood furniture, and a splendid life-size bust portrait of Senator Alexander Barrow, who is buried at Afton Villa where a handsome marble monument was erected to his memory by the United States Government. There is also a very beautiful ivory miniature of Senator Alexander Barrow which looks like the work of Rembrant Peale.

In this section of the state there are many other old plantation homes of more or less interest, but those described here are the more important. Many that were important in the long ago are falling into ruins, while others have been restored. A grove of magnificent oak trees, almost as fine as that of Oak Alley and the old de la Ronde place can be seen here, the mansion having been burnt during the Civil War. A trip made slowly about this section well repays the visitor and sight-seer.

TRINITY PLANTATION

Bayou Grosse Tete, Louisiana.

Trinity House was originally the plantation residence of the late Dr. George Campbell and his artistic family, a daughter later became a prominent portrait painter. Located in the best part of the Grosse Tete country of Louisiana, it has always been one of the show places of that section.

Dr. Campbell, a member of an aristocratic Kentucky family, came to Louisiana and settled in New Orleans as a young man. Good looking, cultured, wealthy, a physician of more than ordinary ability, he became at once prominent as a medical man as well as a great social favorite. With wealth pouring into the city at that date, it was not long before he had doubled his fortune, already a large one. Plantations were the gold mines of that era, so it was but natural that Dr. Campbell, a Kentucky man of a plantation family, should become interested in a Louisiana plantation. He purchased a place which he named Trinity, and built the charming plantaiton home that still stands and which at present is in beautiful condition.

This home, like his palatial city home in New Orleans, became a great social center. For in the city his drawing-rooms were filled with noted artists, actors, and musicians as well as the elite, for the great mansion corner of St. Charles and Julia Streets at that date was one of the finest private homes in America. It was the rival of Marble House, the handsome home of the Kock family which stood, until a year or so ago, on Rampart Street near Tulane Avenue. Its interior too, was exceptionally fine and beautiful as well as spacious. During the Civil War the Campbell mansion was seized after the fall of New Orleans by "Silver Spoon" General Butler.* Mrs. Campbell was rudely evicted from her city home after she had retired. She was forced to leave the house at once, and allowed to take only the dress that she had donned after getting out of bed and changing from her robe de nuit.

Dr. Campbell's mansion was a treasure house of valuable art objects, many which disappeared with Butler when he was recalled by Washington, when his stealing became so great that the Union authorities themselves had to replace him with General Banks.

* Mrs. Warren Stone, wife of the celebrated New Orleans surgeon, having heard how Butler was taking all of the silverware from every home he searched, to save her beautiful family silver, made a large package of it and gave it to her faithful negro butler saying, "I want to be able to tell the truth if questioned about where the silver is hidden. If I do not know, I can truthfully say I do not know where it is, and can swear to it if they make me. So take this bundle of silver and put it in some safe place, but under no circumstances tell me where it is or what you have done with it." Dr. Stone operated at the "Hotel Dieu", a hospital on what then was Common Street. Taking the bundle to the Catholic Sister in charge, the faithful slave told the Sister that Mrs. Stone wanted the bundle put in a safe place.

When peace reigned again in New Orleans, the faithful black one day brought back the bundle just as Mrs. Stone had given it to him. "Where did you hide it?" she questioned. "The Sisters hid it under the altar of the Sacred Heart," the old fellow replied, grinning broadly.

Miss Frances Campbell, a daughter of Dr. Campbell's, was a pupil of Healy who painted so many fine portraits of Louisiana people—among them, the magnificent life-size portrait of Mrs. Thomas J. Semmes, which at present hangs in the home of her daughter, Mrs. Sylvester P. Walmsley. In the same room over a mantel is a beautiful portrait of Mrs. Walmsley as a young lady painted by Miss Frances Campbell after she had risen to fame. Other noteworthy portraits by Miss Campbell are those of President Theodore Roosevelt, and one of Mrs. Tilton—the Tilton portrait hangs at the entrance of the Tilton Library of Tulane University in New Orleans, which she gave this institution as a memorial to her husband.

Trinity Plantation a few years ago became the property of Mr. T. G. Markley, who had it carefully restored, and furnished in period; and again it ranks with the fine old plantation homes of Grosse Tete of olden days. Mr. Markley who has oil interests in the Lake Charles area, no doubt will spend much time at the Old Trinity Plantation.

CHAPTER XXXIV.

IN PLAQUEMINE PARISH.

SAINT LOUIS PLANTATION

Originally called *HOME PLANTATION*

West Bank of the Mississippi River.

CAPTAIN Joseph Erwin, born 1750, according to authentic family
records, comes of patrician ancestry, stemming to Scotch-Irish
parentage that had settled in North Carolina. This line continues
unbroken to the family of Erwin of the County of Orange in
the district of Salisbury whose residence in America antedates the
Revolutionary War. Members of this family became prominent
citizens occupying distinctive positions in the communities where
they resided. Among them were Colonel Robert Erwin, Lieutenant Colonel John Erwin, and Captain Erwin, who later crossed
the mountainous country and settled in Tennessee. Captain
Joseph Erwin, with his family consisting of father, mother, and
six children accompanied by a few slaves in the year 1800, settled
in Davidson County, Tenn. His wife was Lavinia Thompson, and
these were their children: Isaac Erwin who later built "Shady
Grove Manor" on Bayou Grosse Tete; Leodocia Erwin, who married William Blount Robertson; Eliza Erwin, who married Nicholas Wilson; Joseph Erwin, Jr.; Nancy Ann Erwin, who married
Andrew Hynes; Jane Erwin, who married Charles Henry Dickinson killed by Andrew Jackson in a duel and whose son, Charles
Dickinson II, later built "Live Oak Plantation Manor", located in
the village of Rosedale, La.

Trinity Plantation Manor, built for Dr. George Campbell, Bayou Grosse Tete, La.

Magnificent solid rosewood stairway in the old mansion of the Campbell family, New Orleans, still standing.

Fiesta Party—Magnolia Plantation, Shaffer Home.

GENERAL BRAXTON BRAGG.

Reaching their destination eventually Captain Erwin became the owner of a splendid cotton plantation consisting of about one thousand acres in 1806. As the Mississippi River was a means of transporting his cotton to New Orleans where Captain Erwin's agents were located, his future son-in-law Charles Henry Dickinson accompanied the shipments of cotton to New Orleans, where he represented Captain Erwin in the disposition of his crops. It may have been the glowing tales of the splendid plantations with their magnificent mansions that were being erected on them, and the apparent wealth of the state whose soil at that date was rated as being the finest in America, or maybe for other reasons, but it was not many years before Captain Erwin while retaining his Tennessee cotton plantation, removed to Louisiana where he continued in the plantation business. Leaving his married children in Tennessee, Captain Erwin moved by flat-boat taking some of his belongings with him, and after a trip filled with thrilling escapades finally chose a suitable location on the west bank of the Mississippi River about ninety miles above New Orleans which at that date had become a part of the United States and was bustling with evidences of prosperity.

With the same business ability which had distinguished his past career Captain Erwin soon was prospering and became an important figure in the plantation world of Louisiana. His first purchase of plantation land in Louisiana on the Mississippi River amounted to $10,000.00 for which he paid cash. From this start he continued to increase his land holdings until he was reported to be the largest land owner in the state at the time of his death, which occurred April 14th, 1829. He was buried on his plantation.

In Iberville Parish, he resided with his wife and unmarried children on his plantation known as "Home Plantation", which was located two and one-half miles nearer New Orleans than the entrance to Bayou Plaquemines. The plantation house, like its owner was a substantial unpretentious one. It was well-designed along the lines now known as the "Early Louisiana Type" with a wide hall in the center upstairs and down and four rooms on each floor surrounded by wide galleries, collonettes above square brick pillars. The kitchen was in a detached building to lessen the hazards of fire. His wealth became great, his slaves many, but the ever hungry river finally took the old home, as it had so many others.

Mrs. Joseph Erwin, nee Lavinia Thompson, died in 1836 and was buried beside her husband on the plantation. Andrew Hynes married Nancy Ann Erwin, daughter of Captain Joseph Erwin, on the 2nd of March 1817, Rev. Gidio Blackburn performing the ceremony at the old home of Captain Joseph Erwin in Tennessee.

Andrew Hynes, had been Adjutant General of the State of Tennessee, and a colonel at the Battle of New Orleans, and had brought General Andrew Jackson's troops from Tennessee to New Orleans, succeeded Captain Joseph Erwin at his death in the management of the Tennessee plantation.

Edward J. Gay, I, married Lavinia Hynes October, 1840, at the home of Colonel Andrew Hynes located near the state capitol of Tennessee, the same home in which her mother was married. After his marriage Mr. Edward J. Gay, I, bought out the interest of the other heirs in the "Home Plantation" in Louisiana and in 1858 built the plantation house which still stands. He renamed the place the "Saint Louis Plantation".

Mr. Gay was a very successful planter, and built the first sugar refinery in New Orleans approximately seventy years ago.

GAY FAMILY.

Edward J. Gay, I, son of John Henderson Gay, was born near the town of Liberty in Bedford County, Va., on February 3rd, 1816. The family moved to the state of Illinois in 1820, and later to St. Louis, Mo., in 1824. Edward J. Gay was placed under the instruction of Mr. J. H. Denis, an accomplished teacher residing in Belleville, Ill., and later attended Augusta College, Kentucky, graduating in the class of 1833-34. Young Gay was unusually bright and he was graduated with honor from Augusta College.

From early manhood he manifested a strong inclination towards business, and did not study for a profession. Even while at college his character was marked by great boldness in all that he undertook, and his parents had firm confidence in their son feeling that in whatever life work he chose—he would succeed. Edward J. Gay ,I, liked solitude, for he was a deep thinker, and when after calm deliberation, he came to a conclusion that was satisfactory to himself, he upheld and defended it without change. So it was no surprise then when he embarked in business, his father and friends noted that he conducted affairs in a bold and daring manner. With good judgment and ability he soon amassed a fairly good-sized fortune. In 1840 he married Miss Lavinia Hynes, a daughter of Andrew Hynes of Nashville, Tenn., whose mother was Nancy Ann Erwin, a daughter of Captain Joseph Erwin, who had built "Home Plantation Manor" on the Mississippi River near Plaquemines, La.

Ever with the thought of some day becoming a planter, Edward J. Gay, I, moved South to Louisiana where he was to spend most of the remainder of his life. He added to his holdings some of the best sugar land in the state. From early manhood he had been a deep student of industial and political economy knowing its bearing on every type of business. His plantation home, pictured among the illustrations, shows a manor house of the modified Greek-Revival type much in vogue at the date of its erection, a splendid one of its type and typical of the wealthy planter. Located in a grove of moss-hung oaks, amidst a large garden with spacious lawns and with the innumerable accessories of a country home, it is a delightful spot indeed. Among its many interesting mementos were some connected with the early days of the City of St. Louis, Mo., and others dating to Revolutionary times, for a grandfather of Edward J. Gay, I, had been a soldier in the War of Independence.

Always interested but never active in politics, his knowing friends realizing his deep sense of justice and high principles soon sought to have him represent them in Congress. At the time he was advanced in years and was enjoying the seclusion and pleasures afforded by his wise early planning. In the year 1884, having lived through all of the trials and tribulations of the aftermath of the Civil War, he yielded to the solicitations of his friends and became the Nominee of the Democratic Party of the Third District of Louisiana for Congress. As his state needed his services at this time, under the circumstances he felt that he could not decline, and he defeated William Pitt Kellogg, the last survivor of carpetbagism in Louisiana for the office. As a Legislator, his record is a vindication of the judgment of his friends, for he did fine work as a representative of the State of Louisiana; his years seemingly not having dulled his keen vision and ability to master difficult situations. As one scans the record of his legislative career, one notes that he was ever vigilant in the interests of the state. He studied deeply the questions most vital to the state. His ability was recognized and he was placed on the Committee of Appropriations, which important Committee passed economic questions involving the appropriation of hundreds of millions of dollars for governing the country's sixty million people.

His career as a statesman, like his entire life, was one of eminent success. He died at his beautiful plantation home, the "St. Louis Plantation", and the papers of that date said, "One of the chief pillars supporting the social, industrial, and political institutions of Louisiana gave way, his life and character afford a most instructive lesson to the youth and manhood of this country."

ANDREW HYNES GAY

Andrew Hynes Gay, son of Edward J. Gay and Lavinia Hynes, was born in St. Louis, Mo., September 25th, 1841. He attended schools of St. Louis, Mo., and left the one at Webster Grove, to volunteer in the Confederate army at the outbreak of the Civil War, entering 1st Louisiana Cavalry Co. A, under Colonel Scott, serving the entire duration of hostilities. After the war he acquired what is now known as Union Plantation, located two miles above the town of Plaquemines. When his father, Edward J. Gay, I, went to Congress in 1884, Andrew Hynes Gay managed all of the plantation properties belonging to his father as well as his own. He never cared for public office, and declined to become a candidate although solicited to run for Congress, and at one time urged to be a candidate for governor of Louisiana. He married Lodoiska Clement, daughter of Dr. Charles Clement, the first physician to practice in Iberville Parish. At the death of his father, he became the first president of the Edward J. Gay Planting and Manufacturing Co., which comprises all of the properties now known as the St. Louis Plantation. He was an authority on Flood Control—and served as president of the Atchafalaya Levee Board, and later he was president of the Police Jury in Iberville Parish. He died November 29th, 1914.

EDWARD J. GAY, II.

Edward J. Gay, II, son of Andrew H. Gay and Lodoiska Clement, who was a daughter of Dr. Charles Clement, the first doctor of medicine in Iberville Parish, Louisiana. Young Gay attended the

ANDREW HYNES

Manor House, St. Louis Plantation.

EDWARD J. GAY.

ANDREW HYNES GAY.

Old Plantation Home built for Hypolite Chretien in
1835 at Chretien Point. Still standing.

Showing grove of oak trees and spacious lawn.

Oil portrait by A. L. Boisseau dated 1865 of the wife of Hypolite Chretien, who was Mademoiselle Celestine Cantrell, a member of the prominent plantation family of that name. (Photo by Richard Koch.)

Drawing room of the Chretien Plantation home.

schools of Iberville Parish, and then a preparatory one of Charlottesville, Virginia, from which he went to Princeton University. At that time President Wilson, whom Mr. Gay knew, occupied the chair of jurisprudence at Princeton. As a planter Mr. Gay occupies a prominent place in Louisiana, diversifying with cotton and corn, not confining himself to the growing of sugar-cane and manufacturing of sugar alone. He is the head of the St. Louis Plantation Co., and has been president of the Louisiana Sugar Planters Association, and later the American Sugar Cane League.

He was elected to the Louisiana Legislature from Iberville Parish in 1904 and was returned each succeeding term, serving under the administrations of Governors Blanchard, Sanders, Hall, and Pleasant. He served for four years as chairman of the Committee of Public Works, Lands and Levees; eight years as chairman of the Committee on Ways and Means, considered the most important committee in the House of Representatives, and as a ranking member of other important committees. He was a delegate to the National Democratic Convention held in the city of St. Louis in 1908, and chairman of the Louisiana delegation at the San Francisco Democratic Convention in 1920.

Honorable Robert F. Broussard having died in 1918, Mr. Gay announced his candidacy to fill the vacancy to a seat in the United States Senate by the death of Senator Broussard, and was elected, defeating Gov. L. E. Hall and John H. Overton.

Edward J. Gay, II, was married to Gladys Fenner, daughter of Honorable Charles E. Fenner of New Orleans and Carrie Payne, daughter of Mr. J. U. Payne, a prominent and wealthy planter and cotton factor also of this city. The children of Senator and Mrs. Edward J. Gay, II, are two boys and two girls—Edward J. Gay, III, Charles Fenner Gay, Mrs. Carolyn Gay Labouisse, and Gladys Gay.

The children of Honorable Charles E. Fenner are: Charles Payne Fenner, Dr. E. D. Fenner, Guy C. Fenner, Gladys Fenner (Mrs. Edward J. Gay, II).

CHAPTER XXXV.

CHRETIEN POINT PLANTATIONS.

CHRETIEN PLANTATION

Chretien Point, Louisiana.

STANDING alone in the midst of a wide acreage that dips down to a small bayou running through the grounds some distance in the rear of the old house is the original abode of Chretien family. Surrounded by its grove of ancient oak trees, it appears indeed a restful place that has changed but little since the days that the fortune of the family was swept away as a result of the Civil War. The original land grant dates from 1776,* but the house was not erected until the year 1835, according to descendants of the old planter for whom the place was built. Started in 1835 it was not completed until 1839, the owner Hypolite Chretien died a short time afterwards. Madame Felicité Chretien neé Felicité Neda, now a widow and a very capable one, with the aid of an able manager conducted the plantation as a profitable concern until her death.

A splendid old plantation it was in its day when five hundred slaves worked its fertile fields, one of the greatest plantations in this section. After the death of her husband, following that of her son, she continued to reside on the plantation with her family, until the Civil War freed her five hundred slaves and swept away the greater part of her remaining fortune, all enjoyed to its fullness the great wealth that Hypolite Chretien had left them.

---

* The original land grant, given to one, Pierre de Clouet in 1776, in Spanish accompanied by an English translation is in the possession of one of Hypolite Chretien's descendants, the present owner, Mrs. C. A. Gardiner.

During the Red River Campaign at the time of the Civil War when the plantation houses, gins and sugar mills of the area from Opelousas to the town of Natchitoches were burned to the ground, Madame Chretien's relatives, the Arnoulds, the immensely wealthy Fusiliers, the Dazincourts and others had their handsome homes burned to the ground following the Yankee General's orders "to torch the mansions." Of fifty handsome houses only one was spared. The reason for this, so Madame learned, was because the Mistress of this home had spread beneath the trees in front of the mansion on long tables a great feast, and had emptied her wine cellars to supply the Union officers with choice vintages. This lady, it seems, had heard that during Napoleon's invasion of Germany, a German Countess spread a feast for the French soldiers and officers and Napoleon spared her castle.

From a slave returning from Opelousas, Madame Chretien learned that the soldiers were on their way to burn the Chretien mansion. She decided that if food and drink could save her property, she would give the best she had. She ordered the kitchen force to kill all the poultry they could find on the place, a number of hogs, several sheep and a cow, and barbecue the meats. Then she ordered them to empty the wine cellars and bring out the finest vintages. Knowing that the invaders would soon come, she prepared a great meal for the expected enemy. Never in the history of Chretien Point had such a feast been spread.

As General Banks entered the main gateway, Madame Chretien who appeared to be cutting flowers greeted the General in her most gracious manner in French. The General dismounted as he saw a lady approaching and returned her greetings in English. Reaching in her pocket she took out a bunch of keys and smilingly extended them to him, saying in French (as Madame spoke no English), "I extend to you and your men the hospitality of our plantation, my servants have prepared food and drink and refreshments for you and your detachment, I hope that all of you will accept. My home is also at your service, on this bunch are the keys for everything, I have disturbed nothing whatever not knowing where to put it. I learn that you have your orders to burn every home, so I am not blaming you, only please let me and my family remain here until we can find somewhere to go."

"Madame", replied General Banks, "We must search the

house for Confederate soldiers, but I assure you that you will not be disturbed otherwise". A search was made and only a very old man, a distant relative, too old to be in the service, was found hiding in the attic. However, after the Union Officers and men had wined and dined, one of them who had imbibed too freely fired at the old man as he appeared at a doorway on the second floor, but he was not injured seriously.

Even though General Banks had promised that the contents of the house would not be disturbed, the soldiers took with them every movable thing they could carry away, including a large quantity of furniture and household articles which they loaded on army wagons.

The mansion was spared, but the sugar house was set on fire as were the negro cabins after the slaves had scattered and warned not to return or they would be shot. The large store-house, smokehouse, and cotton-gin were blown to bits, thousands of pounds of cotton hauled away, and all the horses, mules and livestock confiscated.

With the freeing of the five hundred slaves, the death knell of the splendid Chretien Plantation was sounded, for there was no one to work the twelve thousand acres. It was not many years before the place began to show the ravages of time. Gradually the long rows of brick slave cabins, fifty to a row, the slave church, the slave hospital and the many farm buildings were demolished and the bricks sold. Members of the family died, others married and moved away, and a few years ago the last of the family to live on the plantation abandoned the old house. Until they moved away the walls of the ancient home were adorned with old family portraits of the Chretien ladies of olden days and other members of the family of the same era.

The property still belongs to a descendant of old Hypolite Chretien who built the house and who provided so bountifully until the family were despoiled of their fortune as a result of the Civil War. Planned somewhat in the manner of "The Shadows", belonging to Mr. Weeks Hall, the Chretien place lacks the glorious setting of Mr. Hall's home. However, it is larger and was very handsome until allowed to fall into ruin, as is evidenced by the fine plastic work and magnificent black Italian marble mantels, On the upper floor the mantels were marble while replicas of them in wood are to be found in the ground apartments. The

MRS. F. D. CHRETIEN,
(neé Blanche Williams.)

MRS. GARDNER T. VOORHEES,
(neé Ninette Chretien.)

MRS. GINDER ABBOTT,
(neé Stella Chretien.)

MRS. WARREN STONE PATRICK,
(neé Bertha Chretien.)

The late Honorable Frank Dazincourt Chretion, Judge of the Supreme
Court of Louisiana.

house plan is distinctly French, having the salon (parlour) on the second floor and the large bed-rooms having ante-rooms attached serving as bath and dressing rooms.

On the ground floor are the central sitting-room and entrance hall combined, with dining-room and pantry to the left, and library on the right. What is still a very attractive stairway winding to the floor above is located to the right in the rear, and a doorway formally opening on to the garden. Very fine is the original woodwork, beautifully carved mouldings, panelling, arched mullioned transoms and a dozen different architectural features were all finished in a manner regardless of trouble or cost. There is a large wine cellar, and until a few years ago, a number of outbuildings containing quarters for the numerous house servants, kitchen, laundry store-room and endless other rooms were also part of the place.

Its exterior was imposing-looking with its thick solid brick circular columns heavily stuccoed, and numerous tall arched windows and doors, wide porches and heavy cornice. The great high ceilinged rooms are empty now, the splendid furnishings imported from France that were left behind by the Union soldiers have been divided among members of the family. In the former Canal Street home in New Orleans belonging to the Honorable Frank D. Chretien, Judge of the Supreme Court of Louisiana, were a number of antiques that came from his grandfather's plantation home at Chretien Point. Among them were several family portraits; a very fine French Clock; a set of Sevres china; a number of fiddleback mahogany chairs; a dining-room set of mahogany of unusually fine design, all of the pieces being very large with chairs to match; some solid mahogany four-poster beds; and a handsome ruby-glass punch bowl, barrel-shaped with cover and glasses to match. A number of these things now belong to Mrs. Gardner Voorhees of Winnetka, Ill., who is Ninette, the youngest daughter of the late Hon. Frank D. Chretien, and great-great-granddaughter of the planter Hypolite Chretien who owned the home at Chretien Point.

In the ancient cemetery of Grand Coteau not very far away, are a number of tombs with hand-wrought filagree iron crosses above the graves. In what was originally one of the most imposing burial plots in this cemetery, surrounded by a handsome iron railing, an enclosure some twenty feet square contains four low but large tombs, each with a thick marble slab darkly stained with age. On the first one—cut deeply into the slab is the following in French:

> Hypolite Chretien Born May 30th, 1781.
> Died September 29th, 1839.

This is the tomb of the planter who originally owned the plantation at Chretien Point. On top of the tomb is laid a large cross of white marble many shades lighter than the slab which covers the tomb. On its surface is carved *Hypolite Chretien*.

On another quite similar tomb beside it is one containing according to the inscription in French, the body of a son of the planter who built the plantation home. On this slab not quite so dark as the first one, deeply cut into the marble is:

> Hypolite Chretien Born April 23, 1827
> Died May 21st, 1870.

Above this tomb is a handsome white marble urn out of which issues a "flame of life". Beside this is another in which is buried the brother. Deeply carved like the others in French is the following:

> Jules Chretien son of Hypolite Chretien and
> Felicite Neda.
> Born May 13th, 1838. Died October 20th, 1838.

Below the inscription on the tomb of Jules Chretien is the following:

> Nous l'avons aimé, ne le delaisons pas parce que nous ne l'ayons pas introduit par nos larmes et nos prieres dans la maison du Seigneur.
> S'Ambre.

When translated means literally—

> We have loved him, let us not forget him, because we would not have introduced him by our tears and our prayers in the home of the Lord.

Placed lengthwise in this iron-railed enclosure across the bases of the first two tombs, having the same height and general construction, is another tomb. However, there is no indication of any one being buried in it, as a large marble slab which is placed on its top is free from any inscription whatever. Jules Chretien died on October 20th, 1838, and the affectionate father following him to the grave the following year. Those were the years of the terrible epidemics of yellow fever, and it is stated by some who profess to know the history of the ancient Chretien Manor that this was the cause of both of their deaths.

CHRETIEN.

Frank Dazincourt Chretien, I, married Eleonore Virginie Briant—their son Frank Dazincourt Chretien, II, who became Judge of the Supreme Court of Louisiana, married Blanche Williams, daughter of Maria Bushnell and Josiah Pitts Williams; their children are as follows:

Francis Dazincourt Chretien, who died in infancy.
Bertha Chretien, who married Warren Stone Patrick.
Stella Chretien, who married Ginder Abbott.
Ninette Chretien, who married Gardner T. Voorhees.

WILLIAMS.

Miss Blanche Williams, who married Honorable Frank Dazincourt Chretien, had three brothers and two sisters. Archie Williams, Austin Williams, Pintard Williams, and Josephine Williams, and another sister whose name is not recalled.

Austin Williams married Margaret Porter, and they became the parents of two children—Lester Williams, who has become a prominent surgeon in Baton Rouge, La.

Laura Williams———

Archie Williams married ————————, and they became the parents of (Minnie) Maria Bushnel Williams, Josephine Williams, LeBlanc Williams, and Rita Williams.

Josephine Williams married Thomas Lewis, and they became the parents of James Lewis, John Lewis, Thomas Lewis, Maria Lewis and Bessie Lewis.

GRAND COTEAU

On the main highway as you leave the False River country headed towards the town of Opelousas, La., on the right hand side, one passes a side road which leads to the section known as Grand

Coteau, which lies inland about three miles from the main high-way. As you reach your destination, the charm of the place is at once apparent for an old world atmosphere pervades, and the section is one of great interest.

The present St. Charles College, a century-old Catholic insti-tution, that is now a Jesuit Seminary for the priesthood, was erected in 1909 replacing the ancient one which was burnt in 1900. The history of the settlement dates back, so it is stated by some of the oldest residents of Grand Coteau, to a very early period almost to the days that Natchitoches was founded. One of its first settlers was an immensely wealthy Frenchman who became a planter—Fusilier de la Clair. He had been a prominent judge in France ,and the name symbolized wealth in this community until his fortune was swept away by the Civil War. It is to planter Fusilier that the honor of first settling the place is given. Among ancient documents in the Cabildo in New Orleans, the name appears from time to time, and one gathers that he was one of the most prominent as well as wealthy men in the section of Grand Coteau. The plantation was an immense one and one con-cludes that the plantation home was in keeping with his promin-ence and great wealth. No doubt it was of the "Early Louisiana" type, but we can feel sure it was a fine one of its kind. All that remains of the plantation is one of the very large avenues of oak trees at the end of which originally stood the old house.

The history of the destruction of the old manor is as follows:

In 1864 a number of Confederate soldiers were home "on leave" at the time that the Union troops invaded this area while General Banks' Red River campaign was in full force. They surprised a dinner party, a rather large one which the grandson of the planter was giving to his friends. Some of the faithful house slaves learned that the Union soldiers were surrounding the house and feared that the young Master and his comrades would be shot. Having heard that some Confederate soldiers had gotten through the lines by disguising themselves as run-away slaves, they blackened the faces of the Confederate soldiers, dressed them in slave working-clothing and as they ran out they appeared to be running away from their owner. The slaves who arranged the escape waited in the dining-room with candles lit and shades pulled down. The Confederates made good their escape to the

Lafourche country where they joined their company. When the Union soldiers found out that they had been outwitted, their commander ordered the ladies of the household to get out immediately, as the place was to be burned at once. Thus was the home with its entire contents destroyed. It is stated that a great sum of money hidden in the house was never found.

On all sides are magnificent avenues of oak and other century-old trees and a woodland grove of fragrant pines. A large Catholic church built in 1819 in beautiful condition is a prominent feature of the place. At the time it was built the old planter donated to it much land. A little further on in the rear is the ancient cemetery with a large number of interesting old tombs and graves, many distinctly quaint and individual, recalling century-old cemeteries of Europe. The wrought-iron work of the railings and enclosures and the crosses are of exquisite designs. The epitaphs are most interesting and touching, many of them like those of old England and France with distinguished family names amongst them. On a later grave placed there by a heart-broken son in memory of his mother are the simple words, "Your boy." One can almost see the tear stains on the marble slab where the pathetic tribute to the mother he loved so well is carved into the marble slab above her grave.

Many prominent old French family tombs are found here with unique given names, some of the graves being close to two centuries old.

RETRIBUTION.

This ancient cemetery is a sacred spot surrounded by a group of buildings devoted to educational and religious purposes. Amongst the dead in this beautiful antiquated cemetery sleeps a son, a good man, far different from his vindictive father, the mad Union General, who when power was placed in his hands, crucified the South in a manner that appalled the civilized world at that date. This son devoted his life to the service of God. One hears from those who knew him that time and time again he was horrified upon learning from the families who had been made to suffer the destruction his father had wrought. This man of God seemed distracted on learning these things, and spent much time in prayer, until the other priests associated with him, began noticing evidences of the hereditary curse of a twisted brain. At first his condition was mild, but as time passed, he lost his mind completely, was forced to resign his post and became invalided in an institute for the feeble-minded. He remained there until his death, when he was buried in this little cemetery of Grand Coteau—his grave shoulder to shoulder, as it were, to those of the families whose homes were burned to the ground by his father's orders that "no aristocratic's mansion be spared."

Thus in the very heart of the region he laid waste—and his soldiers noted his sardonic glee at the burning of towns and mansions—lies buried his poor insane son. So the scales of Divine Justice are balanced.

CHAPTER XXXVI.

PAYNE - FENNER PLANTATION

*THE OLD PLANTATION HOME OF THE PAYNE FAMILY
NEAR WASHINGTON, LA.*

THIS house was originally built for Dr. Archibald Webb about the year 1850. Dr. Webb did not live to enjoy his plantation home, for he died shortly after it was completed. His widow re-married several years later and afterwards sold the place to Mr. Jacob Upsher Payne, a prominent cotton broker located in New Orleans. Mr. Payne, who owned many slaves, built a brick kiln on the plantation and the slaves made the thousands of bricks that went into the construction of the splendid Southern home that he erected in New Orleans at the corner of First and Camp Streets. The bricks were hauled to the city in a plantation wagon drawn by plantation mules and driven by capable slaves.

During the Civil War Mr. Payne converted his plantation home into a hospital for Confederate soldiers and others needing medical or surgical attention. After the fall of New Orleans, the home was filled with sick and wounded, and the Federals, fully aware that the home was being used as a hospital, bombarded it a number of times notwithstanding that pleas were made that the bombing be stopped. A large number of those in the building were killed and wounded and the house badly damaged.

At the time the plantation home was converted into a hospital a number of interior changes were made, and the house never was restored to its original condition. The family of Jefferson Davis, along with many others were house guests on various occasions, and people of the vicinity recall the gala days in this quaint old place—intriguing now in its newly freshened condition, for again it appears inviting in its gleaming whiteness which contrasts with the rich green of surrounding trees.

After the place was sold by the Payne family, the house remained empty for many years, during which time, as with old houses that are empty, strange stories began to be circulated about it. Somewhat isolated, the old dames and wags of the vicinity made it the topic of conversation, and the weird tales grew with each telling, until the children and ignorant people of the locality considered it a haunted place. It had become the kind of spot that Geo. W. Cable loved to find and weave a strange story around. Several persons have owned the place since it was sold by the Payne family, among them a plantation family by the name of Thistlewait.

A short time ago the place underwent repairs, and at present is attractive and inviting again, and quite an addition to the plantation area, so depleted of fine old places by the Civil War.

Returning again to the city home known as the Payne-Fenner house, we find it to be one of the most attractive of the fine old residences in the beautiful "Garden District" that never has been allowed to fall into ruin. This is an outstanding one in a section of aristocratic homes and it has been a social center almost continuously from the time it was built to the present. It is one of the most interesting homes in the city. While occupied by the Payne-Fenner family during the lifetime of Jefferson Davis, first and only president of the Confederate States of America, the owner always insisted that his close friends make his home their headquarters while staying in New Orleans. Mr. Robert Blakely, who at the time was manager of the St. Charles Hotel in New Orleans, likewise a close friend of the Davis family, also wished the Davis family to make his hotel their stopping place while in the city as his guests. President Davis, a close friend of my father's, on one occasion jokingly told him that the Davis family often had to slip into New Orleans and drive directly to the Payne-Fenner home, where they would remain a while before letting Mr. Blakely know the family were in town, so as not to offend Mr. Blakely who out of admiration for the family was continually planning delightful dinners in honor of them. It was in this fine old First Street home that the "Great Leader" wrote the "Rise and Fall of the Confederacy."

Jesuit Seminary of St. Charles, at Grand Coteau, La.

Somes graves in the cemetery at
Grand Coteau are nearly 200 years
old.

The Old Plantation Home of the Payne - Fenner family.
Near Washington, Louisiana.

The Payne - Fenner home, New Orleans, La., First
and Camp Streets. Where Jefferson Davis wrote
"The Rise and Fall of the Confederacy". This
home has become a shrine to the memory of the
great Confederate.

JEFFERSON DAVIS

SARAH KNOX TAYLOR
First wife of Jefferson Davis.

MISS WINNIE DAVIS

(From an early daguerreotype)

CARVES A CAREER WITH HIS SWORD

A young man named Jefferson Davis (shown with his wife, Varina Howell, above), thin-faced, burning-eyed, his forehead arching beneath a tumble of hair, was carving a career with his sword while, far away, another named Abraham Lincoln was raising his high-pitched voice in Illinois courtrooms. Of these two was the tragedy of a nation spun and they were fated to blow black death across state lines in one of the bitterest struggles in history.

Jefferson Davis and his second wife, Miss Varina Howell who became the mother of Winnie (Varina) Davis—Daughter of the Confederacy.

This immense brick stuccoed mansion is quite similar exteriorly to the famous old Rosedown plantation home in West Feliciana, with tall wide windows and doorways, with other attractive features found at that inviting old place. But in this house the hall is much larger and wider. The interior is well arranged and with wide galleries and a spacious garden in which the family entertained. From its earliest days this home has been the scene of many splendid entertainments. But none was more beautiful relates a lady who was present, than the reception given there to introduce the lovely daughter of President and Mrs. Jefferson Davis to New Orleans society. It will ever stand out as an event in the social life of our city.

President Davis died here. The Payne-Fenner family, learning that the "Great Chieftain" was ill on his plantation, had him brought to their house in New Orleans so that the best medical attention that the city offered might be obtained. As he had pneumonia, he was placed in the room that had been occupied by young E. D. Fenner, now a prominent physician, instead of taking him upstairs to the "Davis room", the front corner room overlooking First and and Camp Streets. In this ground-floor hall room, a large lovely room located on the left side of the wide hallway as you enter, directly opposite the spacious dining-room overlooking the beautiful garden surrounded by his family and devoted friends, he breathed his last. This stately old house of so many memories, both joyous and sad, has again become the home of a prominent Louisiana family, the Forsythe family.

The "Spring Fiesta" brings hundreds of sightseers, when it is thrown open to the public, to view the various rooms containing a priceless collection of antiques and heirlooms. On other days many visit the spot where they carefully read the marble marker, admire the exterior of the house and lovely garden, and perchance pinch a twig of some shrub as a relic of the house where the "Great Confederate" died.

The Daughters of the Confederacy have placed on the outer side of the lawn, edging the sidewalk, a white marble marker which states that President Jefferson Davis died here. This home is a shrine to the memory of the "Great Confederate Leader". The garden grounds about the mansion are beautiful most of the year with a variety of blooming plants and vines that fill the air

with fragrance, and the perfume of the Confederate Jasmine
wafted towards one seemingly recalls the memory of the "Lost
Cause".

JACOB UPSHER PAYNE

Jacob Upsher Payne, a member of a patrician family of Kentucky
was born in that state, and at an early date evidenced marked
ability to deal with matters usually alloted to men of mature years.
At the date of which I write the position of High Sheriff was
more of an honorary one than a moneyed one, and was purchasa-
ble, provided the applicant possessed a good reputation, had physical strength and a pleasing appearance. Evidently young Payne
possessed these attributes, for we learn that this attractive, ath-
letic-looking young gentleman was appointed to the position of
High Sheriff shortly after he had passed his sixteenth year, a
position he held with credit for some time. He later went to
Vicksburg, Mississippi, where Mr. Payne engaged in the business
of supplying the planters of this section with implements and general plantation necessities. His ability as an executive soon
marked him as an outstanding man in this community. It was
not long before he had associated himself with such men as Sear-
gent Prentiss of Natchez and public-spirited citizens of Vicksburg
as a vigilence committee to exterminate the gamblers that had
almost taken over the town of Vicksburg. They were driving
away the decent element, so rough had the place become. Vicksburg, the center of a wealthy cotton-plantation country, was
naturally a magnet which drew the sporting crowd by the thousands. The relentless manner in which Mr. Payne and his associates got behind them soon freed the city of these undesirables,
and restored its good name. A bachelor, and living above his
place of business, much the same way as families in the French
Quarter in New Orleans have always done, Mr. Payne's apartments became the meeting place for the members of this vigilence
committee during their campaign of cleaning out the gambling
element.

Later Mr. Payne became a cotton factor and removed to New
Orleans, where his firm was known as *Payne, Harrison & Co.*,
later to become *Payne, Hunter & Co.*, and still later *J. U. Payne
Co.* Mr. Payne remained a bachelor until he was about forty
years of age, when meeting the charming Mrs. Caroline Downs

Haynes, a widow of grace and distinction, he lost his heart completely to her. Their daughter became the wife of the distinguished Confederate soldier, judge, and associate justice of the Supreme Court, the Honorable Charles E. Fenner of New Orleans.

CAPTAIN CHARLES E. FENNER

Captain Charles E. Fenner, distinguished in the annals of the Confederacy as commander of a famous Louisiana battery, and since the war eminent as a jurist, was born in Jackson, Tennessee, in 1834. His family moved to New Orleans in 1840. He was given a thorough education at the Western Military institute in Kentucky, and at the University of Virginia, and in 1855 was graduated in law at New Orleans, where he started practicing law. On April 15th, 1861 he entered the Confederate service as first lieutenant of the Louisiana Guards, which became a company of Dreux's battalion, and soon afterwards he was made captain. In this capacity he served at Pensacola and in the Virginia Peninsula until April, 1862, when the battalion was disbanded at the expiration of his twelve months' enlistment. He then organized a company of light artillery from members of the battalion, completing the organization at Jackson, Miss., when he was elected captain.

This battery with the Fourth Regiment and Thirtieth Battalion, Louisiana troops was attached to the brigade of General S. B. Maxey, first stationed at Baton Rouge, and afterwards a part of Gen. W. W. Loring's division of Gen. Joseph E. Johnston's army in Mississippi. Capt. Fenner took part in the campaign for the relief of Vicksburg and the fighting between Johnston's army and Sherman at Jackson, Miss. In the fall of 1863 the battery joined the Army of Tennessee at Dalton, Ga. Capt. Fenner and his men distinguished themselves in the campaigns which followed, including the siege of Atlanta, and in the Tennessee campaign, winning special renown by their gallant fighting in the rear-guard actions covering the retreat from Nashville. In this campaign Captain Fenner commanded the artillery battalion with which the battery had been associated since joining the Army of Tennessee. The last service of the gallant captain and his men was the defense of Mobile in the spring of 1865, and after the evacuation of that last seaport of the Confederacy, they surrendered with the troops of Gen. Richard Taylor at Meridian, Miss.

Captain Fenner returned to New Orleans and resumed the practice of law, to which he gave his attention until his death. He was a member of the first legislature after the war. In 1880 he was appointed an associate justice of the Supreme Court of Louisiana from which he resigned in 1894, after a continuous service of fourteen years. During the era following the Civil War when the negro element became so abusive to the whites and the Crescent regiment of volunteers in old state militia was organized by the White League, Judge Fenner was made Colonel. Judge Fenner was the organ of the Supreme Court of Louisiana which rendered the decision against the Louisiana State Lottery.

FENNER FAMILY

Charles E. Fenner was descended from distinguished Revolutionary ancestry, three of whom were officers in War of Independence. Dr. Richard Fenner, one of these officers, and grandfather of Charles E. Fenner of New Orleans, left a brilliant record as soldier and jurist. After the cessation of hostilities Dr. Richard Fenner was one of the founders of the Society of Cincinatti, George Washington being its first president, the society composed of officers who served in that war. Dr. Richard Fenner, who was born in North Carolina, was the father of six sons, five of whom following in their father's footsteps became physicians, one of them Erasmus D. Fenner, became the father of Judge Charles E. Fenner, who was born in Wake County, North Carolina. Dr. Erasmus D. Fenner was graduated from the Medical Department of the Kentucky University, and located in Clinton, Mississippi, at that time the center of a rich cotton country, where lived many wealthy planters. Here he practiced medicine for a number of years removing to New Orleans in the year 1840. Unusually brilliant, it was not long before he became one of the leading medical men of this state. In conjunction with Dr. H. Hester of New Orleans he founded the New Orleans Medical Journal, both being pioneers in medical journalism. Dr. Fenner was ceaseless in his efforts to aid this community with his medical knowledge and that of the other medical men of the state and was one of the leading organizers of the New Orleans School of Medicine of which he occupied the chair as dean for many years. Active in civic and social affairs of the city of his adoption. He married

Anne America Callier of patrician lineage. Their son, Charles E., becoming in after-years a distinguished soldier and jurist, was born at Jackson, Tenn., on February 14th, 1834, and came with his parents to New Orleans in 1840.

CHAPTER XXXVII.

CANE RIVER SECTION.

MARCO PLANTATION HOME.

THE old plantation house that was known as Marco and which was located in the vicinity of the old John Abrahams Plantation home on Cane river, was one of the most artistic of all the "Early Louisiana type" plantation houses in the entire state. It was originally built for Nicola Gracia, a Spaniard of wealth and culture, which accounted for the beautiful architectural lines and the elegant style and finish of its wood-work and masonry. It is an architectural tragedy that the old mansion was not restored, for it had many beautiful architectural features not to be found in any of the old plantation homes of its type.

Nicolas Gracia and his family had called the place "Home Place", and its name was changed to "Marco" when it was purchased by his nephew Marco Givanovich in 1863 for the sum of $325,000.00. In this sale was included everything on the plantation—lands on both sides of Cane River, the house and other improvements, all of the slaves on the plantation, livestock, etc., including the furnishings which were very fine.

Marco Givanovich, a bachelor not nearly the cultivated gentleman that his uncle had been, led a free rollicking life, with the result that many in the vicinity, claimed to be his descendants. However, he conducted his plantation as a going concern until his death which occurred in 1896, his will showing that Marco Givanovich had left his entire estate to a nephew in Austria. This nephew dying in 1926 left the estate to seven children living in

Austria who sold it in 1929 (with complications) which prevented a complete sale. Finally the matter was settled, and the old house demolished by the new purchaser who did not care to spend the required amount to restore the old place.

The estate was managed by the law firm of B. B. Breazeale, for the last twenty years, and had been under the supervision of the Breazeale firm all told for nearly forty years. Mr. Phanor Breazeale having much to do with its management.

The will of Marco Givanovich was probated Feb. 24th, 1896. W. Hyams, clerk (at Natchitoches, La.), No. 22918. Book 94, Page 52. Dated Feb. 24th, 1896. Last Will and Testament. The statements of those who claimed descent from old Marco, seemed to have fallen on barren soil, for nothing definite has materialized to have confirmed the truth to any of the claims. The records of the courthouse being a confirmation of the true history of the interesting old house.

The Marco house was of the high-basement type plantation home, with very wide central hallways on both floors, the one on the ground floor being paved with brick, making a porte-cochere, similar to the ones in the French Quarter of New Orleans.

It was a splendidly constructed old house, with large rooms and French windows with transoms and shutters, with a typical outside stairway on the right as one faced the building. Doorways opened on to the wide gallery in front, and both sides of the wide central hallways, upstairs and down. Unusually large fan windows fitted both of these central arcades. Below the transom bar of the second story in the door frame were fitted very wide glazed doors, which opened into the rooms. Latticed blinds opened against the outside walls.

On the ground floor the glazed doors were replaced by a pair of heavy panelled doors which closed the space, and folded inward against the hall walls. In the rear the customary pigeonnaires of the square type flanked either end of the massive old brick house, from either side of which extended outward picket pailings. The house although in a neglected state, was extremely attractive and held great allure for those interested in good architecture of an earlier date.

To reach the old place when it was still standing, was a rather difficult task, and only a light car could have ventured in safety, as it was located far down Cane River at a distance from the highway, and in rainy weather the trip was not without danger.

Fortunately much of the woodwork has been saved, preserved and placed where the memory of its pleasing old lines can be recalled. Unfortunately the South has made no attempt to retain in public parks such architectural examples, as Philadelphia has been doing for years, making Fairmont Park of that city a rival to Williamsburg, Virginia. Hardly a month passes but some of these relics of our state's early plantation history is demolished.

MAGNOLIA PLANTATION (HERZOG)

Cane River.

Leaving Melrose Plantation and following the gravel road South, we soon pass an old plantation now occupied by colored folks. Its present condition is deplorable, and soon will, like the artistic old Marco plantation, with the architecture of which it has much in common, it will be but a memory. Restored, it would make quite an attractive plantation home.

A little further on we come to the plantation home of the Herzog family, MAGNOLIA, so named for the magnificent grove of magnolia trees, which with century-old oaks form one of the finest plantation-home settings in the entire South. The fine old mansion, so attractive and comfortable looking, typical of a wealthy planter's home of an earlier date, was rebuilt along simpler lines.

Sharing the fate of fifty other plantation homes, all the great houses with one exception between Opelousas and Natchitoches, Magnolia plantation manor was burned to the ground during the Civil War. The Herzogs, a plantation family of prominence from early days, own the old plantation now in ruins and at present occupied by negro field hands. In ante-bellum days the family was an immensely wealthy one. It is still among the largest land owners in the state.

The Magnolia plantation home that replaced the one burned by the Union soldiers is a splendidly built structure of brick, which, painted grey, appears serene in its gorgeous setting. The approach to the house through the avenue of splendid old trees is impressive and terminates at the stairs which climb above the high basement to the deep gallery, a most inviting spot for lounging. A wide central hall with large rooms on either side allows

Old Plantation Home of G. L. Fuselier de la Clair, Baldwin, La.

Old Overseers House on the Frotscher Plantation, near New Iberia, Louisiana.

MARCO PLANTATION HOME.

Yucca Plantation Home, now known as Melrose.

The Good Darkie—Bronze Statue, Natchitoches, La.

Old iron stairway of Prudhomme home, 600 Front Street, Natchitoches, La.

fresh air to sweep through the house and affords privacy to the rooms. High ceilings and large windows add to the general comfort. Appropriately furnished to harmonize with its beautiful setting it suggests in a vivid manner country life on an old plantation as it was in the long ago.

Near by is the Chopin Place, in ante-bellum days the McAlpin plantation about which hot and heavy discussion has taken place, many contending that it was McAlpin that served as model for the despicable character of Simon Legree in the story of "Uncle Tom's Cabin." However, the Louisiana Historical Society has destroyed that myth. The plantation in the story is differently located, and as for McAlpin's being Simon Legree, it is a case of mistaken identity. Those who knew McAlpin state that he was an inoffensive old man, who would be horrified now to learn that he is said to be the prototype of such a character as some of the people in the vicinity of his old home would have one believe.

YUCCA PLANTATION

Cane River.

Now Known as Melrose Plantation.

As we continue northward towards Natchitoches, we reach Yucca Plantation. The old plantation store and post office face the highway. Adjoining is a very attractive country garden of no distinctive plan, but with many blooming plants, shrubs and trees. There are splotches of color in all rainbow hues everywhere, for the garden is permitted to grow in riotous freedom with resultant bounteous bloom throughout the year. This old garden is quite large, covering several acres. Winding pathways thread themselves in and out among the various masses of blooming plants, reaching a brick walk that leads to the old plantation house.

The facade is quite attractive, and before the cone-shaped roof-octagons were added, which somehow do not blend with the architecture of the place, it must indeed have presented a pleasing picture, framed as it was by this old garden. Mrs. Cammie Henry states that they were added many years ago when more room was needed.

Of the "Early Louisiana Type" with high basement, the ground floor is now used as living quarters, and contains a num-

ber of attractive as well as serviceable rooms. Brick floors and
seven-foot wooden mantels of good design are in the study or
library which is fitted with built-in book-cases and shelves. The
other rooms are equally well modelled in woodwork of the proper
period. Mahogany furniture of correct date, bric-a-brac and pictures all go to make harmonious rooms. The quite spacious dining-room with sideboard, serving table, center table and chairs—
all of mahogany and simply designed—make a most inviting
room. It is well ventilated and lighted, having doors opening on
to wide verandas front and rear. An ell, joining the house on
the rear on the right as you enter, contains store-room, pantry
and kitchen, with other rooms above.

In the rear grounds are a number of interesting old buildings.
In one a Southern writer of note has his workshop where he is
free from noises and distractions. A cow-bell hung into the
framework of the gate warns the writer of the arrival of some
one. His den is pleasing, with reference books on tiers of shelves
and a few paintings on the walls, having historical as well as
artistic value. An attractive French gilt clock and other ornaments, and appropriate furniture complete this most attractive
retreat. The building is partly brick and partly timber to rein-
force the brick wall, all originally coated with stucco. Its generally antiquated appearance and the fact that it was a slave
hospital in ante-bellum days makes it quite intriguing.

There is another quite different building, its real history
still an unsettled question. In its architectural make-up it is
similar to the huts of San Domingo negroes, only on the Island
the roofs are constructed of palm leaves instead of shingles as we
find here. Another old building Mrs. Henry moved to the plantation, and she used it as her weaving room. Still another building serves as a retreat for another writer who lives here the
greater part of his time.

Yucca, or Melrose as it is now called, was built originally for
Louis Metoyer who had come from San Domingo to open up a
large plantation in the Natchitoches section on Cane River. As
a planter he succeeded beyond his greatest hopes, but old residents of the vicinity will tell you that his first home was an adobe,
hut, a small house with but one room, built for most part by his
own hands. Others will tell you he was rich when he came to
the Natchitoches Country, and had many slaves. Anyway, as

historians contend that Natchitoches is the earliest settlement in the state, it is a locality full of contradictions, so we will not pry too deeply into planter Metoyer's private financial affairs. We do know, however, from authentic hearsay that he built this first little house previous to the year 1820, and at that time laid out the plantation today owned by Mrs. Cammie Henry.

Later after prospering, he employed a builder to erect for him the house we see today, without the additions. In its construction it is like the houses of the "Early Louisiana Type". The basement floor is of brick with walls two feet in thickness, while the second floor is brick entre poteaux covered with weather boards to protect the soft brick. The house is a pioneer-type home, with numerous heavy hand-hewn timbers of choice cypress, hand-made hardware, and slave-made bricks. It is anything but a pretentious house, yet it is quite charming, both without and within. It has the usual row of brick pillars, square in shape, below the wide gallery which rests on them and which support the collonettes with square bases, which in turn support the roof. Plain balustrades enclose the gallery. The roof is high pitched and is pierced by dormers, two in front and two in the rear. The details of these dormers are quite similar to the ones on the old Delord Sarpy Plantation House in New Orleans. Architecturally correct and very attractive, these dormers have carefully planned pilasters and arched windows without shutters, while those of the old Sarpy house have columns. The open space below the wide spreading porch, and the simple-line stairway reaching upward to the porch above forms a charming picture, framed as it is by luxuriant greenery.

Louis Metoyer lived royally in this house with all the elegant equipment that he and his wife deemed becoming to their means. He had hundreds of field hands, and a dozen house servants. Like the country gentlemen of San Domingo from whence Metoyer had come, the Curé dined at his home each Sunday and on holidays. He was generous to a fault, and aided all who flocked to the locality attracted by the stories of his prosperity. He gave to the Isle of Breville on the opposite side of the river the Church that we find there today, and his wife donated the vestments. He was also very kind to his own family. Each had a personal slave-servant as well as generous allowances. The families that lived on "The joyous Coast" as they called this area, enjoyed life thoroughly and the Metoyer family were leaders. With few exceptions, the people of the locality looked upon him as an adviser and a friend.

Metoyer's fortune at one time was estimated at between one-half and three-quarters of a million dollars, a great fortune at that time. A number of reasons are given as the cause for the loss of his fortune, one is that he stood responsible for a friend's debt. But that seems hardly possible. What seems more plausible is the reason advanced for his failure by a distant relative: Some years previous to the Civil War when there was so much talk of freeing the slaves, Louis Metoyer realized that such a step would mean ruination to the South. He also figured that should there be war, the South would be impoverished for a long time. So for years he converted his securities into gold coins, that he carefully secreted, as he did not put much faith in banks. Someone—just who it was has never been determined—learned where he had hidden his strong box with his wealth of gold coin, and when the chance came stole the strong box with all Metoyer's money. Always in the hope that he would be able to get back at least a part of his fortune, he did not report the theft to the authorities. "Misfortune never travels alone" and when a supposed friend failed to repay the money loaned him, Louis Metoyer was forced to sell his home and broad acres at public auction.

The plantation was purchased by the wealthy planter, Hippolite Herzog, already the owner of many plantations in Louisiana. Mr. Herzog managed the plantation successfully until the Civil War wiped away a great part of his large fortune, compelling him to dispose of this as well as other plantations he had owned in Louisiana. However, during all these years of ups and downs of the various owners, the land was not allowed to lie fallow or the plantation house to fall into ruin.

Mrs. Cammie Henry is a serious student on all subjects pertaining to the history of Louisiana, Old Louisiana and especially its plantations and plantation life. She has one of the finest collections of material on this subject to be found anywhere. Her library is also one of the best in the State.

Her son, Mr. Henry, an able planter, manages the plantation which is a thriving concern. Another son, Stephen, has just been made a Brigadier General.

BERMUDA

Ancient Plantation Home of the Prudhomme Family
On the Banks of Cane River—"La Coté Joyeuse".

Bermuda, unpretentious and lovely in its old age, is a splendid example of a plantation house of a wealthy planter of early Louisiana. It is a house that was not changed when the wealth that poured into the state after 1830 tempting many to alter or rebuild on a grander scale. Favorably located, high and over-looking Cane River, this old plantation home is the abode of an ancient line, for the Prudhommes have been prominent in this part of the state from the time of their coming. Related to many families in the vicinity and other Creole families directly or indirectly, many bearing the name live in New Orleans as well as in the Natchitoches area.

This old plantation home was built in 1821 for an ancestor of those who dwell here now. The plantation land grant dates from 1787, and since occupied by the Prudhommes, has never changed hands or ceased to operate as a plantation. It has the appearance of having been prosperous for a long time and this tallies with the history of the place. The Prudhommes and other prominent Creole families living in this section named the banks of the then Red River, "La Coté Joyeuse" (The Joyous Coast). It was a happy community living in contentment and luxury, all greatly interested in each other and their doings, giving out-siders little thought.

Bermuda is of the early Louisiana high-basement type of plantation home and covers a large area. Wide galleries encircle the house and furnish entrances to the many rooms. The house is planned for convenience and comfort and protection. The wide spreading roof, which reaches beyond the narrow facing, is supported by the many graceful swelling collonettes which surround the building. The usual simple, square brick pillars and balustrade and a number of attractive dormers make the facade charming, and the wide massively-constructed brick steps reach upward to the wide galleries within the picket enclosure and com-pletes the alluring picture. Placed as it is in the protection of a monster oak that seems to mother the house, it forms a charm-ing scene.

The rooms with high ceilings, most of them quite large, with their old mahogany furniture unfold a century of good living, substantial and sane. On the walls hang ancestral portraits painted in Europe in 1821, while the family was sojourning there, waiting for the house to be completed. At that time, as was the usual procedure, clothing, furniture, jewelry, etc., were purchased along with the wines of ancient vintages. Miniatures, daguerreotypes and silhouettes of the family and quaint bits of bric-a-brac, fill the numerous rooms.

A fragrant breath of sweet olive and Confederate jasmine float in as one listens to stories of pre-Civil-War days, told by older members of the family. One is told how the Yankees— some of Gen. Banks' men—tried to decoy Mr. Prudhomme away from the house so that they could burn the place after having ransacked it for gold and valuables. Having heard that an immense chest of gold had been hidden in the old Metoyer plantation home, they got the houses confused and searched instead the Prudhomme house. Suddenly Mr. Prudhomme, realizing that they were planning to burn his house, grabbed his shot gun and defied any of them to enter the place. Seeing that Mr. Prudhomme meant business, they left for the next plantation.

The real charm of Bermuda is that its original architecture has not been disturbed, or changed with one exception. With no more slaves to do the work, Mr. Prudhomme had the building that joins the original house on the left in the rear erected. So carefully was this addition made, following the declaration of peace, that unless one were told, one would suppose it to be a part of the original building. It is a large kitchen, a typical plantation kitchen, built on the ante-bellum plan and equipped according to the standards of 1865.

Joining the wide rear porch, there is a large pantry and store-room, built at the time the kitchen was. Near by is a large outside chimney and fireplace, that in earlier days heated the office of Madame Prudhomme, to which, as was customary on well-regulated plantations, each morning the house-slaves reported to receive their orders for the day. A wall of the office was lined with book-cases and cabinets, in which were kept the household files and recipe books for the many varieties of preserves, condiments, wines and cordials made on the plantation. Judging from the quantities of aged and yellowed formulas, the women of each generation of the Prudhommes faithfully kept for their daughters all the recipes that had been carefully saved for the mothers, adding others from time to time. The banquet room (dining-room) is one of the largest and finest in this area of the "Joyous Coast", where life appears in ante-bellum days to have been one of continuous social activity. The room is attractively designed for the purpose it was to be put to, with an immense fan transom above an arrangement of French glazed doors, which separated it from the salle or parlor—almost continuously open for the feasts prepared for the throng of guests that ceaselessly visited here. In the rear wall of this banquet chamber other large glazed doors folded back into the room. With the wide covered gallery beyond and the garden in view, it made a most attractive place to dine. A very large mahogany dining-room table fills the center of the room, and originally a set of twenty-four fiddle-back chairs stood about. The number of chairs have dwindled, with the passing years, as members of the family have married, and have taken their quota of family belongings to their own newly made homes. The large sideboard is also of mahogany with its array of goblets, glasses and decanters, carafes and other belongings, all bright and gleaming in the strong sunlight as of yore. In one corner once stood a magnificent grandfathers clock, with its massive case, bright and beautiful, by whose splendid dial the old gentleman of the painting with the cotton boll set his watch. Never in all these years has this masterpiece of the clock makers' art been allowed to run down. It is now a treasured heirloom belonging to a descendant of the owner of the "House of Prudhomme", now living not far away, only the old plantation store separating them. This home, too, has its quota of antique treasures, originally from the old manor house.

Against another wall of the dining-room is a fine old mahogany secretary with desk combined, cupboard and bookcase above. Here we find rare editions of French books, all having bindings of tooled leather. Below in the cupboard section are record books, folios, receipts, and old pre-war account books. There are old diaries, books and pamphlets and slips with various notations pertaining to matters of the plantation, all time stained and yellow, many fragrant with bits of rose-mary crumbling with age, placed there by some sentimental ancestress of a century ago. Among the articles the writer noted was a copy of the Prudhomme coat-of-arms.

The century-old punka-fan, swaying from the ceiling in the dining-room, which Nino (the little black slave) pulled back and forth with a cord while the quality folks dined. These little black dining-room attendants were the precursor of our present day electric fans and cooling systems. The "Salle" or parlor, another large room equally as spacious as the dining-room, opened on the wide front gallery. In this room above the wide mantel of good design, hangs a large French mirror in a wide gold leaf frame as bright and as fresh as it appeared when placed there a century ago. What joy and sorrow has it not reflected? Six generations of Prudhommes have been born in this old home, and it looks like it could easily weather another century. A tall mahogany book-case occupies the right wall panel as you face the great fan-transomed doorway. Above the book-case hangs an oil portrait of Emmanuel Prudhomme, painted in Paris, France, in the year 1821, picturing him with a cotton boll in his hand. Mr. Prudhomme was very proud of the fact that he was the first one to successfully grow cotton in the Natchitoches area. In the book-cases are a number of fine books. On another shelf is a collection of bric-a-brac, amongst the things some quite attractive French figurines. A black marble clock with antique bronze ornament and companion pieces adorn the mantel shelf. Opposite Emmanuel Prudhomme's portrait is one of his wife painted in Paris at the same time. Both are interesting as French primitives. Quaint mahogany chairs are scattered about the room, and the arm chairs seem to invite one to a comfortable seat. An old-fashioned upright piano is below the fine oil portrait of Mr. Ambrose Lacompte, owner of the celebrated race horse, and for whom the town of Lacompte was named. Mr. Lacompte had initiative as well as wealth for it was he that built the Lacompte Hotel now the Nakatosh Hotel. Attractive old mahogany tables, what-nots, and other cabinets holding interesting odds and ends.

An immense portable lap-desk is filled with ancient family papers and documents, many fragrant old letters on which the faded writing stands forth like ancient engraving. About the room in various places are numerous old and interesting objects that accumulate in an old home during a century. Another life-size oil portrait of Mademoiselle Lise Metoyer hangs in the center wall panel. During the Civil War the Union soldiers drove their bayonets through the canvas, the rents still showing. In an in-

Bermuda, old plantation home of the Prudhomme family, Cane River.

MRS. EMANUEL PRUDHOMME.
Painted in Paris, 1821.

MR. EMANUEL PRUDHOMME.
Painted in Paris, 1821.

MRS. PHANOR PRUDHOMME
As she appeared on her Golden Wedding Anniversary.

PHANOR PRUDHOMME
As he appeared on his Golden Wedding Anniversary.

laid box are kept a number of treasured family papers, among them a bundle of old letters written by Lestant Prudhomme (a young man of fashion in 1850), which form chapters of Mr. Saxon's "Old Louisiana".

The bedrooms of the house are many and large, and have the appropriate massive handsome furniture of the period. The bedsteads are of beautiful design, mostly four-posters ten feet in height, the posts ten inches in thickness, and the grain of the mahogany very beautiful. The bedroom sets are completed with handsome dressers, washstands and immense wardrobes. The wardrobe in the second bedroom, massive in proportion with heavy cornice and arcaded facade supported by heavy octagonal columns, forms an unusually beautiful piece of antique furniture. Each of these rooms in this interesting home has its quota of attractive pieces and representative of the Golden Era of plantation days at its best. These antiques appear as beautiful as they must have appeared when new.

The out-buildings are many in number. Among the most interesting is the old carpenter shop, where in slavery days a skilled slave mechanic (sometimes costing as much as three thousand dollars) spent many hours a day making by hand the fine woodwork used in the house, as well as linen presses and wardrobes used in the less important rooms. The brass knobs were purchased in Paris, but all of the iron-work, latches, bolts and hinges were made in the machine shop.

In the smoke house were prepared the hams that would make the mouth of a true Virginian water. Bacon was smoked with wood from chestnut trees to give it the proper flavor. Venison and other meats were as carefully prepared to make them fit for the banquets, dinners, etc. The many pigeonnaires furnished an ample supply of pigeons for pigeon pie, squab on toast, broiled and roasted squab formed part of the regular menu in olden days.

In the basement today we find a museum containing articles made by the slaves. It is a most interesting collection. Most of these articles were made a century ago in the old blacksmith shop which is still standing. Every household article that one can think of appears in this collection, from a primitive coffee pot to an iron horse-collar.

The cattle and poultry pens, horse stables were all well ventilated, and well planned for this plantation prided itself on its fine stock of all kinds. The quaint old flower beds are outlined with old bottles laid bottom side up, a design greatly used in rural France in the wine sections. These old bottles, in a way, are a record of the vintages used by this hospitable family, who entertained elaborately and frequently. All of the fine old vintages are represented. Cognac, rum, benedictine, the herbs and fruits for making cordials, cherry-bounce and peach brandy, fine dried fruits, and the various confections and delicacies for which plantations in olden days were famous were bought in France. They imported great quantities of fine clarets, sherry, sauterne, the sweet and dry wines, also quantities of sparkling wines, for the community of the "Joyous Coast" was forever celebrating some event, be it birth, christening, first communion, graduation, engagement or marriage. All that was needed for a banquet, party or dance was the excuse of the occasion.

Some day the history of this plantation and the many interesting personages of its gala days will be written by someone capable and with the time to go into full details. There is a world of valuable material awaiting the opportunity to be properly used. Bundles of old letters tied carefully with faded ribbons, old documents, old scrapbooks, faded photographs, daguerreotypes and miniatures, silhouettes, old sheet music and music books used by the "Belles of Joyous Coast" in the long ago, are there. Such a story will unquestionably become a best seller. These old inlaid treasure-boxes wherein have reposed these faded documents are veritable literary gold mines awaiting the miner who can dig out the ore and refine it into gold.

The stables of the plantation were once filled with blooded stock, horses for hunting, and horses for the carriages of which there were a large number. The harness and trappings were elaborate as well as practical, the special harness for state occasions, having costly mountings with initials and monograms. These outfits were a necessity in a household continuously on the go, for the period was one of endless entertainment. The carriages became a necessity as well as a luxury.

As this book goes to press, an invitation has come telling us of the reception of the Golden Wedding Anniversary to be held on Feb. 3, 1941 when Mr. and Mrs. P. Phanor Prudhomme will again, as in olden days, gather about them in the ancient plantation home where he was born, their many relatives and friends. It will be a happy gathering for the entertainments at this home have helped make local history.

TOWN OF NATCHITOCHES, LA.

When Anthony Crozat leased the Territory of Louisiana in the year 1712, he appointed Cadillac to take charge of the colony. In 1715 St. Denis was sent to the Natchitoches country by Governor Cadillac to establish a post to act as a barrier to the aggression of Spain, as well as to establish trade with the people of Mexico.

In the early part of 1715 St. Denis reached Natchitoches. Leaving shortly afterwards, he left a few of his men to establish a trading post there. This was the beginning of the town and it still retains the name of the original settlement "Natchitoches", which proves it to be the oldest city in the state. This early settlement never became much more than a post until some families of French origin settled there.

The life of St. Denis is a rather romantic one. St. Denis was quite fastidious about his personal appearance and had an extensive wardrobe. He eventually married Donna Manuela de Sanchez, a grand daughter of Don Diego Ramon, commander of the presidio. The old records of the Court House of Natchitoches and of the Church of the Immaculate Conception help unravel the interesting events which occurred at this time. At the Courthouse is found an itemized statement of St. Denis' account with the Company of the Indies, and his last will and testament dictated during his last illness and signed simply St. Denis. The yellow crumbly pages of the church French records list births, marriages and deaths of members of this family. They also testify to the popularity of St. Denis as a godfather for his name appears frequently, sometimes acting in that capacity for some friend's child, sometimes for one of his slaves. He died at the age of sixty-eight in the year 1744, as expressed in the old writings "fortified by all the sacraments of the church". He was buried by Father Barnabe near the old church on the site now occupied by McClung Drug Company in Natchitoches. He lives through tradition in the hearts of all who have heard his colorful story. At number

400 Front St. in the town of Natchitoches is a tablet placed there by the Daughters of the American Revolution.

Soon after the settlement of Natchitoches in 1714, a small log church was built by the Catholics on this corner, on the very bank of the then Red River, just back of it was the little grave-yard. In this spot the body of the illustrious founder of Natchitoches, Louis Juchereau de St. Denis, wis laid to rest in 1744.

In 1823 the little cemetery, the old log church burned down, and started a conflagration that consumed sixty-five houses. A semicircle was laid waste, with the grave-yard as a center. A second church was built nearly a block further back (Church of the Immaculate Conception) from the river. In time business interests encroached upon the site of both log church and cemetery, and the exact location of St. Denis' grave was forgotten. In 1839 (95 years after the burial of St. Denis), a two-storied building was erected on the corner, but was destroyed by a second fire in 1881, the present building is the second on the site.

Natchitoches is without doubt the prettiest small town in the state of Louisiana. It is also one of the most interesting because of its history. It contained the town homes of prominent planter families and other notable characters of the day when the history of the town was in the making, the homes of those who created the "Joyous Coast".

In the town of Natchitoches among the many places of interest is the Tauzin House with its sunken garden, built in 1776. Another is the Prudhomme building, 600 Front Street, built in 1853, which has much elaborate cast iron work on its ornamental balconies, and a splendid spiral stairway of cast iron in the rear. It rises from the court-yard for the old place is patterned after the Spanish houses of that day. The statue of The Good Darkie is a monument to the faithful slaves of pre-war times placed there by a citizen of Natchitoches. Sibley House boulder marks the site of the plantation home of St. Denis. At 319 Jefferson Street one finds the summer home, or old town house of the Serdot Prudhomme family. Nearby is the St. Amant home, residence of the aristocratic wealthy family of that name. Mr. Grimmer, who dedicated his waltzes to the "Belles of the Joyous Coast", later lived in this house as well as did other important personages. A dozen or more historic old homes are to be found in the town, all containing interesting antiques and heirlooms of the families of that section. Many of these places are still in the hands of descendants of the original owners who proudly preserve them and keep up the ancient gardens.

Nearby the town is the site of the beautiful and romantic old town of "Grand Encore". On the high bluffs are located the earth works used by the opposing Confederate and Federal forces that faced each other during General Banks' Red River Campaign in 1864. They are still in a wonderful state of preservation, but now goats peacefully graze where men fought and died. This town is in that section reaching to Opelousas where under the Union General's orders every plantation mansion of any size was put to the torch, leaving nothing but the tall brick chimneys to tell of their former grandeur.

CHAPTER XXXVIII.

IN RAPIDES PARISH.

EVERGREEN PLANTATION

(Clara Compton Raymond)

Mrs. T. L. Raymond, in her recollections of Evergreen Plantation where she spent much of her early life has the following to say of Evergreen Plantation, and her family and friends:

Shortly after the Louisiana Purchase a new world was building in the newly acquired territory. From the original thirteen states Americans crowded into the new lands and hopes were high.

Family tradition says Horatio Sprigg had run away from his father's home in Wheeling, W. Va., to join the navy. That he fought with Stephen Decatur and served on board the Constitution (Old Ironsides). In about 1812 he was commissioned to bring three gun-boats from Joliet, Ill., down the Mississippi River to New Orleans and was made Commander.

Louisiana must have seemed beautiful and alluring to him for he obtained permission to retire from the Navy, and went to Rapides. There he bought land and slaves and built a home, married and sent to West Virginia for his belongings, furniture, etc. It is unlikely that he had had experience in planting cotton, or marketing it. He could not have known but of the climate and yet in general he prospered; Horatio Sprigg died in 1847, leaving his widow to manage the plantation:—She is the grand-muzzie of the Recollections I am now to read to you.

THE OLD PLANTATION HOME

My earliest recollections are of sitting in a small chair on the side gallery at Evergreen, having my nurse Nummie brush my hair in rings, round and round a long curling stick. She would dampen the brush and smooth and smooth the hair around, then slipping out the stick, leave a stiff curl, like a sausage—a row all around my head; golden in color at that time, brown later in life, and now hard to believe, white, but still rebelliously curly.

In "Pierre Noziere," Anatole France, tells of a boy that was himself, a shadow playing and walking before him, but of whom he knew all of his thoughts and feelings. So one may write of that little shade without conceit since it is just a far-away shadow—no more of the present than a figure of the imagination.

I recall one morning Nummie's snatching me out of the chair, clasping me in her arms, and having been joined by some of the darkies, who were crying out excitedly, "De yankees is comin' ", she ran to the far corner of the yard, where we could see way over the broad cotton fields, the "Big" road, and the Fork, with its sign-post, pointing to the main highway. Breathless we climbed the fence to see a cloud of dust and many soldiers galloping on horseback, blue coats and shining guns glistening in the sunlight. Trembling, we watched.

They reached the Fork, halted. Would they come on towards us, or would they turn at the Fork? We could hear our hearts thumping with fear, and I clung to Nummie only half understanding what it all meant.

"Dere, dy done turned," and away they thundered down the highway leaving a cloud of dust behind them—on to "Inglewood" where "Mama" lived, six miles away, and where "Doc" and his three brothers were. Would they stop at Inglewood? Would my cousin Doc see them?

Another vision——I was playing on the floor at the long French window in Grandmuzzie's room. It was raining. I saw soldiers outside, sentinels, stalking in rain coats, thumping the ground here and there with the butt of their muskets. Searching for buried treasure? (Ed Hobbe, Grand muzzie's most trusted servant had buried the family silver, except what we used at table, some place only known to himself, back of the garden, where he dug the hole in the dark of the moon, and dug it up again after the war, none the worst for its long interment).

A step—a soldier walked into the room. I hid under the bed. From this point of vantage I saw him look all round the room, and examine a little silver clock that was ticking away on the mantelpiece. He put it in his pocket and walked away.

Life at "Flowerton" in 1868-70.

The Reconstruction Period.

This period was a time of walking on red hot stones for those who had been through the War: But was hardly felt by the young ones whose joys in plantation life were thrilling and adventurous. The tragedy was for those brave men returning to devastated homes. War worn, lame and weary; shorn of all they had held dear. Disfranchised: Having to bear the insults of carpet baggers and politicians, we seemed to be out of it. The women, the courageous women, everywhere, were busy reorganizing lives, building up new homes out of the wrecks. As time rolled on the fields of Flowerton began to blossom in acres and acres of sugar cane.

I remember once going with Mamma to pay a call on Gov. and Mrs. Moore, in a rather shabby carriage with mismated horses, along the road where she once drove in her Victoria behind spanking bays, holding her tiny little black lace parrasol, with the folding handle. We drove by the beautiful old avenue of oak trees, where three tall chimneys stood up stark and bare, all that was left of the Governor's once lovely home; burned down during the war (by the Union soldiers). We found the Governor and his wife living in a negro cabin at the head of the quarters. I have never forgotten the stately old gentleman with snow white hair and beard, who welcomed us as if we were entering a palace instead of an unpainted negro cabin. Not a word of apology: (He had been Governor of Louisiana during the Civil War). The dogs hanging around the gallery were ordered off. There was something pathetic in his way of offering Mamma the common rocking chair, and in seating himself in a stiff raw-hide bottom chair. His eyes under the heavy projecting eyebrows looked strickened, his features carved into nobility by the tragic expression. Through the open door I could see his portrait, so out of place hanging on the whitewashed wall, and glimpses of lovely old cups and saucers shining on a home-made shelf: It all made an impression on me I've never forgotten. It is good to know that he lived to see better times and his grand children restored to comfort, in possession of their broad acres of land.

The writer of these memoirs of her youthful days on Evergreen Plantation is a daughter of a prominent Surgeon of Ante-Bellum days who was House-Surgeon of the Charity Hospital of New Orleans, La., in 1856, for Dr. T. W. Compton was a noted physician as well as prominent surgeon.

He served during the Mexican War, also as Major in the Civil War with the Confederate forces, his services on both occasions being distinguished. Dr. Compton was born in Baltimore, Maryland, and came to New Orleans as a youth, found a position and financed his own medical and surgical education, graduating 1847, became a successful practitioner, and became house surgeon of Charity Hospital in 1856. He retired from practice after the Civil War and became a planter, but resumed practice in Alexandria, La., in later years, and died in New Orleans in 1889.

It was very interesting to watch aunt Liddy make candles for home use in tin moulds, six to a side. With the cotton wicks threaded in and tied at each end on a cross bar or stick. She would pour the hot melted wax in each mould, and when cool enough she would cut out the lower wick end and very slowly draw on the cross stick, and out would come six shining candles (yellow) which were then hung up to harden. I recall the dining-room wall-paper at Evergreen; so unique, four large design medallions encircling views of Rome, picturing scenes of Roman ruins. The house was square, surrounded by galleries up and down stairs, twenty feet wide, seventy-five feet long in front. White fluted columns, six rooms down stairs and six rooms up stairs, besides dressing-rooms and library, with books from floor to ceiling, with a ladder to reach the upper shelves and cases of magazines. No public libraries in those days. Every planter had his own complete library. Books, silver, fine linens—were hobbies then. Upstairs my uncle Horatio had his billiard room, with walls hung with racing horse scenes.

You know of course that Grandmuzzie had two daughters, Frances and Clara. Frances (My mother) married Dr. T. W. Compton, a native of Baltimore, but then a young surgeon living in New Orleans. My old nurse took me on her lap once and said "Chile, you know why everybody loves you so much? It's on account of your mother—everybody, white and black loves Miss Frances." She married and went to New Orleans to live, they had a house on Royal Street. The following summer she came to Evergreen to be confined, and I was born in her beloved room with sweet jassemine bush near the window. She had puerpural fever and died when I was nine days old. This was a frightful blow to Grandmuzzie and Mamma (her mother's sister), who adored her sister. Her dying words were: "Mother and Sister, I leave my little girl to both of you." And so, out of the anguish of their sorrow, they lavished on me the love of two mothers.

The most beautiful tribute to the women of the South, which I think has ever been written, is that appearing on the monument erected:

TO THE SOUTH CAROLINA WOMEN OF THE CONFEDERACY.

Erected by the Men of the State.

The Women were Steadfast and Unafraid.
They were:

Unchanged in their Devotion
Unshaken in their Patriotism
Unwearied in their Ministrations
Uncomplaining in Sacrifices
Splendid in Fortitude;
They Strove While they Wept.

In the Rebuilding after the Desolation:
Their Virtues stood as the Supreme Citadel,
With Strong Towers of Faith and Hope
Around which Civilization Rallied and Triumphed.

Clara Compton Vance Raymond, born at Evergreen Plantation, Rapides Parish, La., July 26th, 1857. Married to Dr. W. D. Vance in 1880; he died in 1881. Later married to Thomas L. Raymond (Civil Engineer) in 1889, and he died in 1901.

Children*—Frances Sprigg Raymond, married to W. Lyall Howell—two sons, W. Lyall, Jr., 19 years; Thomas Raymond Howell, 17 years; Mary Clara Raymond, at present executive of Social Agencies in New Orleans; a son, on staff of Los Angeles Eve Express, California, married to Elizabeth Douglas of West Feliciana—one child, Clara E. Raymond, 13 years.

---

* Mrs. P. L. Girault, sister of Mrs. C. V. Raymond, resides in Boston with her daughter, Mrs. R. W. Stratton. Her oldest daughter, also her only son and Mr. P. L. Girault died in Chicago.

CHAPTER XXXIX.
IN MADISON PARISH.
POINT CLEAR PLANTATION,
Madison Parish, Louisiana.

THOMAS PHARES KELL, son of a Mississippi plantation family, came from his parents' plantation, Solitude, Miss., twenty five miles from Natchez, Miss., in the early 80's as a young man, and settled in this part of the Louisiana country and bought Point Clear Plantation.

He married Miss Bessie Evans, daughter of David Mandeville Evans a member of a prominent South Carolinian family, who was a planter and merchant of Bastrop, La., whom he met when she came to visit her uncle, Dr. William D. Kelley, in Madison Parish, La.

He became a member of the State Legislature where he served for many years and later was president of the Fifth Louisiana District Levee Board. In this position he fought the flood fights of 1912 and 1917, a tragic, losing battle, for a crevasse each time left the rich cotton lands of this section ravaged by overflow.

Mr. Kell cleared more land of its virgin timber and put more and more land into cotton. Point Clear was rather isolated from white neighbors and became a center of hospitality for travelers through that part of the country. No one ever arriving there at time for dinner or at night time was turned aside without food and lodging. The life there was feudal in its adherence to the old pattern of slave days on a cotton plantation.

During influenza epidemics the plantation owner visited his

sick negro tenants, administering medicine and nourishment because a doctor could not be had. His chief interest, aside from
cotton, was in horses and he raised and kept fine saddle horses.

The old house in which all of his children were born was
built in the '40's on a bluff overlooking Bayou Vidal and the inter-
section of another small bayou within three miles then of the
Mississippi River. It sat back in a grove of live oaks and pin
oaks with a side garden of such old-fashioned flowers as sweet-
olives, crepe myrtle and quantities of violets, roses and bulbs.
Marechal Niel and pink Killarney roses covered the side galleries
to the roof.

The house was big and rambling, comfortable rather than
elegant, with galleries supported by square wooden pillars around
three sides, wide hall through the center and high-ceilinged white
plastered rooms. It was two-storied with an attic in which
Grant's soldiers had scribbled their names on the walls.

Chief historic interest in the house was that Grant had
camped there or used it for his headquarters on his march through
East Carroll, Madison and Tensas parishes. He crossed the
river in Tensas Parish to attack Vicksburg from the rear. He
burnt almost every house in his path, leaving this and a few
others as quarters for his men.

The old house burned and was replaced by a large two-story
white columned house with galleries around the side. When the
Mississippi River Commission engineers decided that a levee
should be built through the site of the plantation house in the
middle 1920's the house was moved into a vacant pasture, the
grove of oaks was cut down as were the fruit trees that filled a
large orchard, and the flower garden was destroyed.

Point Clear is still owned and operated as a cotton producing
plantation by the Kell family as is "Hermione", a plantation inherited by the four Kell children from their uncle, Elett Kell,
which is located in Madison Parish, also, three miles from Tallulah.

Mrs. Kell and her son, Mandeville Kell, live in Tallulah, La.,
the other members of the family consisting of Elizabeth Kell
Perkins (Mrs. Logan Perkins), Society Editor of the New Orleans

General Horatio Stephenton Sprigg.

Mrs. Horatio Stephenton Sprigg.

MRS. T. L. RAYMOND,
(neé Miss Clara Compton.)

MRS. P. L. GIRAULT,
(neé Miss May Eliza Compton.)

An oil painting of Mrs. Logan Perkins, who as the society editor of
the New Orleans States writes under her maiden name of Elizabeth
Kell. This painting by the New Orleans artist, Nell Pomeroy
O'Brien, was exhibited in art shows over Texas and Louisiana.

A view from the side of the old Point Clear house which was General Grant's headquarters during the War Between the States.

Mr. and Mrs. Thomas Phares Kell on horseback, across Bayou Vidal, with the house in the background. The type of private levee used in the early '90's when this picture was taken is shown. It was later cleared away when the great levee fortresses were built by the Federal government.

States, her sister, Miss Cornelia Kell, reside in New Orleans, while another brother, Lancaster Kell, makes his home in Baton Rouge, La.

All of the above mentioned children of the Kell family were born and reared on Point Clear Plantation, Madison Parish, La., a plantation which they still own.

Mr. Logan Perkins, descends from the McCutchon, Butler, and d'Estrehan families, all notable plantation families of Louisiana, as well as from the Logan family of Virginia. His mother was Mary Logan, of New Orleans.

END OF VOLUME I

INDEX

INDEX TO VOLUME I

FIRST TOUR, EAST BANK OF THE MISSISSIPPI

NOTE

A tour of the old plantations in and around New Orleans will prove most interesting. Only the sites remain of some of the plantations but their histories are important and this warrants their being included. Even the spot on which a famous old house once stood is hallowed ground.

(Obtain State Road Map)

Leaving New Orleans and taking the River Road leading North one continues for a short distance — the first old plantation you come to is that of the de la Barré family now given over as a school for mentally weak children.

The second plantation home we come to a short distance further North is the Elmwood plantation; the house recently rebuilt as a home for the Durel Black family. If one desires to visit the house they should phone the family first.

The next old plantation Home is that of the Soniat du Fossat family, now remodelled into the Colonial Country Club.

The next Plantation of note is D'Estrehan, which at present belongs to an oil company. It is an old plantation home well worth visiting and is listed among the places that one can obtain permission to visit.

A short distance north is the location of "Red Church" no longer standing.

Ormond is the next plantation house along the route now in a partly ruined condition.

The area that is given over to the Spillway makes the road that passes the old Trepagnier plantation house in ruins impassable, so one turns to the right on the connecting road leading to the Highway known as the new Baton Rouge Highway, to again turn on the connecting road to the left leading to the River Road, at the end of the Spillway. Reaching the river road and turning North—shortly we note the old plantation home of the de Montegut family now the home of a number of tenant families.

Reserve plantation, then looms into sight, a busy place most of the year. Welham plantation house, close to the river road is a pleasing relic of Old Plantation Days in good repair, but all of the front land has gone into the river.

Mount Airy Manor, the old home of the Joseph Louis Le-Bourgeois family is in good repair — and as much of its garden ground is still intact — is well worth the trip to see.

Belmont — a magnificent plantation home of the "Golden Era," no longer standing, was located a short distance further North.

We are now approaching the College of St. Michael in what is known as St. Michaelstown. No longer an educational institution it has become an institution connected with U. S. Government work, the College Buildings and chapel a retreat for business men who desire a mental rest.

Further on we come to the Convent of the Sacred Heart, now an institution connected with U. S. Project Work.

The next place of interest is the old site of the Constancia Plantation group of buildings demolished last year when it was found that the levee line had to be changed.

The attractive old plantation home of the Colombe family greets us next. — It too stands close to the roadside.

Further on is the site of White Hall Plantation Manor, old home built for Marius Pons Bringier.

Further on we come to the settlement of Union, named for Union Plantation, the Home of a member of the Bringier Family, and a wedding gift of Marius Pons Bringier.

Ahead we come to a great grove of oaks in which is located the lovely old home "Tezcuco" seat of the Bringier Family who still occupy the home and conduct the plantation.

Further on lies Burnside Plantation and its beautiful plantation home one of the finest in the state, open only on special occasions.

Another Colomb plantation Home lies a little further North in its garden grounds.

Beyond — located far back in the grounds among oak trees we find the Hermitage Plantation Manor, the old home of Michael Doradou Bringier and his beautiful wife who was the lovely Aglaé DuBourg de Ste. Colombe. It is open to visitors if contact can be made before hand.

Close by is Bowden, the old plantation of the Trist Family. And then Bocage — a large two storied plantation home in a neglected state located far back from the River Road.

Ashland, or Belle Helene as it now known, stands like an ancient Greek temple in the midst of an oak grove — far back from the River Road, magnificently constructed and well worth visiting.

Linwood, recently demolished, joins the plantation grounds of Ashland.

Further on the site of Chatsworth — a magnificent old plantation home that never was completed owing to the Civil War.

Beyond and about fifteen miles from the city of Baton Rouge lies "The Cottage," the F. D. Conrad Plantation Mansion in good condition and open to the public—a magnificent type of the home of a wealthy ante-bellum Louisiana planter.

Next is the old Laurel plantation of the Ramsay family; and then we reach the old "Hope Estate," the plantation of Colonel Philip Hickey, whose beautiful old plantation mansion forms the frontispiece of Vol. II. The ancient plantation home no longer standing, was considered one of the finest of the early Louisiana type plantation homes erected in this state.

A guide book of the town of Baton Rouge will give all the important sights to be seen in this city, among which are several interesting old plantation homes.

Having visited the important points of Baton Rouge we now proceed to visit the plantations in the Feliciana area.

Leaving Baton Rouge on Highway 65 to within three miles of St. Francisville we find the gravel road on the right which leads to Oakley Plantation. Turning into this road we continue for about another three miles when we see the sign OAKLEY on the right. Here we turn into the narrow country road leading to Oakley Manor.

Returning on this road to the highway we continue on to St. Francisville, having seen the points of interest of this place we visit the plantation garden and home of the Thomas Butler family, then Rosedown garden and plantation home which are open to the public for a small fee, then continue on to Afton Villa, another plantation home and garden open to the public for a small fee. Waverley and its garden too are open to the public for the usual fee.

Near by are Greenwood, the Myrtles, the Cottage, and Beechwood cemetery where are found the graves of Eliza Pirrie and other notables.

In East Feliciana we find Locust Grove, Greenwood Manor, the old plantation home of the Percy family, also Ellerslie another Percy home. Wakefield plantation lies on the Woodville road beyond Afton Villa, and one can visit Jackson and Clinton, both interesting old-fashioned towns well worth seeing, having attractive ante-bellum houses.

Returning to St. Francisville by the way of Wilson, one can visit Asphodel plantation home, Hickory Hill plantation home, and the Shades plantation home of the Scott family, all interesting.

Returning to St. Francisville by way of Jackson one has the choice to cross the river to New Roads on a small ferry or to cross the New Mississippi River bridge which lies on a road midway between St. Francisville and Baton Rouge.

In the town of New Roads can be found the old Lejeune plantation home on the outskirts of the town. Returning and driving in the opposite direction a little beyond the edge of town one finds the marble tablet to James Ryder Randall and the Maryland Oak a short distance back from the road. Next point of interest is the plantation home of Allan Wurtele, its garden and the little chapel that he donated so that there may be divine services for the colored people of the section. Parlange Plantation and its beautiful park and garden, one of the most interesting old plantation homes in Louisiana, is open to the public for an admission fee, having a large collection of ante-bellum articles in its many rooms.

The Seebold plantation home is open to public on special occasions.

Austerlitz Plantation Manor, private; Pleasant View Plantation Home open to the public for an entrance fee; River Lake plantation Home, private, and Alma Plantation Home some distance away also private. All along False River are many early type plantation homes and beautiful oak trees.

The plantation homes in New Orleans can be visited with a local guide book to best advantage.

———————

SECOND TOUR, WEST OF THE MISSISSIPPI

Leaving New Orleans on Highway 90 and crossing the Mississippi River Bridge you proceed to Allemans, continuing past Houma and Morgan City encountering small plantations en route —continue on to the town of Franklin near which is to be found the rebuilt old plantation home of Judge Alexander Porter, now a museum well worth visiting. "Oak Lawn", rebuilt in a fire-proof manner preserves the original lines of the original splendid mansion. Then on to Baldwin where we find the old Fusilier plantation home—and further on we reach New Iberia where in the center of the town enclosed in its own spacious acreage surrounded by a high cane hedge is found "The Shadows", one of the best preserved and most pleasing of the old Louisiana plantation houses.

If one wishes to visit the beatiful estate of Mrs. Matilda Gray at Lake Charles (write for permission first) continue west at this point to Lake Charles; otherwise continue to Lafayette and then north on Highway 5 to Sunset and the Old Chretien plantation home at Chretien Point near Shuston will be found.

Retracing to the Highway, the old cemetery and other interesting points of Grand Coteau will be found to the right as one proceeds in the direction of the town of Opelousas, near which are located interesting plantation houses, among which is the plantation home of the Payne family located near the town of Washington.

At Lebeau, which joins Highway 71, continue on 71 to the town of Alexandria where you proceed on Highway 20 to Natchitoches. Visit the main points of the town then take a trip to the ante-bellum settlement of Grand Encore, returning to Natchitoches and cross Cane River and visit Bermuda Plantation, Magnolia Plantation (Herzog), Melrose Plantation, home of the Henry family.

Returning on Highway 20 at Alexandria change to Highway 71 and continue to Lebeau on to Kroth Springs, then going East to Livonia, where you change to Highway 65 on black top road to visit plantation homes of Bayou Maringouin, Rosedale, and Grosse Tete all well worth visiting—the homes in good condition and interesting. The oak trees along the edges of the Bayou are quite attractive.

Continuing on to Plaquemines—then on to Highway 34 where we pass Nottaway on Highway 168, also McCall plantation on our way southeast to Donaldsonville. He we cross Bayou Lafourche and continue down the Bayou a short distance when Belle Alliance is reached.

Further on down the Bayou we come to Maidwood and Woodlawn plantations, further on opposite the town of Thibodaux is "Rienzi" plantation home, far beyond and still further on Ducros and Southdown plantations all well worth the trip.

Otherwise one can continue on to the West bank of the Mississippi River and visit the old Fortier plantation home near Hahnville, Evergreen plantation and home, St. Joseph plantation home, Oak Alley Plantation near Vacherie.

Returning from Vacherie (Oak Alley) on Highway 30 to Luling and continuing on this road to Westwego we find Seven Oaks Plantation, and further on Highway 31 is located Belle Chasse, Plantation home of Judah P. Benjamin.

Here we may drive to Algiers and cross by ferry to New Orleans and continue on to the plantation country of St. Bernard Parish visiting the ruin of the Old de la Ronde mansion, the Battlefield of Chalmette, the Renee Beauregard Plantation home, the Three Oaks plantation, and Kenilworth Plantation Home.
